"Anyone who believes that images of war and mayhem were invented by Hollywood or Atari should read this impressively erudite and thoughtfully argued book. From cave paintings viewed by flickering torchlight to virtual battles followed on computer screens, humans have been fascinated by depictions of organized violence. But this is far more than a history of war pictures. Perlmutter's analysis ranges across centuries and continents, combining cultural and technological history into a narrative that illuminates our past, our present, and our future."
— Larry Gross, The Annenberg School for Communication,
University of Pennsylvania

"Thoughtful, provocative, beautifully written, Perlmutter's *Visions of War* should give us all pause! We have landed on the moon, but have we really come as far from the cave as we think we have?"
— William M. Hammond, author of *Reporting Vietnam:*
*Media and Military at War*

"A well-written authoritative account of war in historical context from prehistoric times up to the Persian Gulf. Perlmutter shows how the ethos of war varies with time, place, and standpoint, and how war will always be with us, despite universal condemnation as a social pathology."
— Geoffrey A. Clark, Professor of Anthropology,
Arizona State University

# VISIONS OF WAR

## PICTURING WARFARE FROM THE STONE AGE TO THE CYBER AGE

DAVID D. PERLMUTTER

ST. MARTIN'S GRIFFIN
NEW YORK

www.stmartins.com

Design by Maureen Troy

Grateful acknowledgment is made for permission to reprint the following: lines from Homer's *The Iliad* on page 105, Richard Lattimore, translator, © 1951 by the University of Chicago; lines from the television lyric on page 89, © 1999 United States government as represented by the Secretary of the Army.

ISBN 0-312-20045-5 (hc)
ISBN 0-312-27332-0 (pbk)

First St. Martin's Griffin Edition: February 2001

10 9 8 7 6 5 4 3 2

*To Christie and to my parents*

# CONTENTS

ACKNOWLEDGMENTS      ix

LIST OF ILLUSTRATIONS      xi

INTRODUCTION      1

1: ORIGINS      11
     THE FIRST WAR?      11
     THE FOCUS ON BIG GAME      17
     THE FAT OF THE LAND      21
     THE MALENESS OF THE BIG-GAME HUNT      25
     SIGNS OF THE HUNT      27
     THE COMMUNAL IDEAL      29
     MEGAFAUNA "OVERKILL" AND THE GENESIS OF WAR      34

2: PRIMITIVE WAR      41
     THE NEW FACE OF WAR      41
     LETHAL SOCIETIES      45
     DISCIPLINE AND DANCE      52
     CANNAE, PAST AND PRESENT      55
     LEADERSHIP AND THE "LOOK" OF POWER      57
     RED QUEENS OLD AND NEW      62

3: COMMANDERS      65
     IDENTIFYING THE WAR COMMANDER      65
     VISUALIZING DOMINANCE      71
     SUBVERTING THE WAR COMMANDER      78
     VOLUNTARY INVERSIONS      84

4: COMRADES 89
    SEEKING COMMILITO 89
    THE WARRIOR PROCESSION 93
    BUDDYHOOD AND BUDDY POSING 105
    LOYAL BROWNIES AND MULTICULTURAL PLATOONS 110
    FEAR ITSELF 116

5: ENEMIES 121
    THE USEFUL ENEMY 121
    THE DEFEATED ENEMY 124
    THE HATED ENEMY 133
    THE OFF-CAMERA ENEMY 141
    THE AMBIGUOUS ENEMY 146

6: HORRORS 153
    HORROR AND SYMPATHY 153
    NOBLE DEATHS 159
    THE "JUST" HORRORS 164

7: LIVING-ROOM WARS 175
    REAL-TIME WAR 175
    WAR IN EVERYDAY LIFE 181
    COMMUNAL VIEWING 187
    REALISM 192
    THE EFFECTS OF WAR IMAGES 203

8: FUTURES 211
    SEEK 211
    HIDE 216
    VIRTUAL WARRIORS 220
    INREALITY AND DISENGAGEMENT 226

NOTES 233

BIBLIOGRAPHY 259

INDEX 287

# ACKNOWLEDGMENTS

Although the bylined author must take responsibility (and ensuing blame) for any book, a volume of this kind is obviously a communal enterprise in several ways.

First, I want to thank those scholars with whom I began my education in visual culture and whose questions and ideas stimulated my thinking toward the present work. They include: Michael Griffin, Charles W. Haxthausen, Carolyn Marvin, Paul Messaris, Dona Schwartz, Joseph Turow, Amos Vogel, Katti Franz, William Hammond, and especially Larry Gross.

Second, I am grateful to other scholars who assisted me in this project specifically. They include: Hannah Gourgey, David Grove, Anne Jett, Lawrence Keeley, Thomas Kehoe, Thomas Knieper, Matthew Lalumia, Joyce Marcus, William Murnane, Paul Taçon, P. Willey, Ken Zagacki, and Larry Zimmerman. Special thanks is given to Paul Bahn and Harvey Bricker for their critiques of the work on primitive and prehistoric imagery.

Third, I want to express gratitude to those who helped in obtaining some of the images for this book. Of this long list, one name stands out: Madame Yvonne Vertut, who allowed me to reproduce her late husband's magnificent pictures of the prehistoric cave paintings.

I am grateful to the series of assistants I had during the long tenure of the writing of this book and to other graduate students who read and reacted to the manuscript: Hattie Baker, Bonnie Bauman, Angie DelCambre, Jie Lin, Jane Perrone, and Caroline Zhang.

At St. Martin's Press, solicitude and apologies are extended to my patient and long-suffering editor, Michael Denneny, his assistant, Christina Prestia, and to Sarah Delson for designing the cover.

George and Meredith Friedman were godfather and godmother of this project: they made it possible for me to submit the proposal to St. Martin's. Also, I am indebted to Captain Scott Belgarde, U.S. Army Reserve, for his careful verification of facts dealing with both ancient and modern military technologies and tactics.

Finally, and perhaps most important, this book was a family project. My parents raised me in a home of books, and I grew up infused with the appreciation that the past is present and that history guides our every thought and footstep. Crucially, my wife, Christie, devoted three years of her life to the book's research, organization, and editing.

# LIST OF ILLUSTRATIONS

1. *Alexander Mosaic*, Pompeii     4

2. *The Death of General Wolfe*, Benjamin West     6

3. Man with bird head and bison in shaft of Lascaux cave     13

4. Man pierced with arrows, Cougnac Cave     16

5. "Chinese Horse," Lascaux cave, near Montignac, Dordogne     22

6. Wounded bison, Niaux cave, near Foix     30

7. Rock painting, Arnhem Land region of Northern Territory of Australia     42

8. Five archers (or dancers) marching, rock painting, El Cingle shelter     47

9. Crow Creek site bone bed, south central South Dakota     50

10. Shield-bearer combat scene, Writing-On-Stone site, southern Alberta     51

11. Archer battle scene, rock painting, Morella la Vella     56

12. Archer battle scene, Sefar site in Tassili, Sahara     58

13. Battle for a bull, Khargurtahl, Libya     62

14. Rameses II at the battle of Kadesh     69

15. Presidential candidate Michael Dukakis on M1A1 tank     70

16. Elamite king Ummanigash is greeted on his arrival at Madaktu     74

17. Ummanaldash, king of Elam, and his attendants     81

18. *Commander-in-Chief of the British Forces in the Crimea*     83

19. "Don't mention it, lootenant. . . ," Bill Mauldin     85

20a/b. Roman legionnaires (a) enter; (b) depart Babaorum camp in Gaul     93

21. "Warrior vase," Mycenae     97

22. "Odessa Steps" sequence, *Battleship Potemkin*     102

23. Achilles and Patroclus, Athenian cup     106

24. *L'Entente Cordiale,* Roger Fenton                                          110

25. Marines raise the American flag atop Mt. Suribachi, Iwo Jima              114

26. *Sir David Baird Discovering the Body of Tipu Sultan,* Sir David Wilkie   122

27. Palette of Narmer                                                         127

28a. Bonampak, Room 2, Mayans battling enemies                               130

28b. Bonampak, Room 2, Mayan ruler, officers, and their victims              131

29. Castrated, mutilated prisoners carved into steps of Monte Albán site,
    southern Mexico                                                          132

30. Film still from *Starship Troopers*                                      134

31. *Boer Treachery,* R. Caton Woodville                                     143

32. "Is it you, Mother?" Louis Raemaekers                                    148

33. "Fresh, spirited American troops . . . ," Bill Mauldin                   151

34. *Canada's Golgotha,* Francis Derwent Wood                                156

35. *The Dead at Antietam*                                                   162

36. Roman soldiers destroy a Gothic village                                  167

37. Boy and other civilians with hands raised at gunpoint in Warsaw Ghetto  169

38. Audience watches war, Albert Robida                                      176

39. Man videotapes a line of soldiers at Gettysburg battle reenactment      183

40. Saigon execution, Eddie Adams                                           204

41. Screen shot of *if22* video game                                         222

# INTRODUCTION

The idea for this book began with a single picture of war that is fascinating to me. It is a small, sepia-toned photograph, probably taken in the summer of 1920. There are four objects in the image: three officers of the Royal Hellenic Army and a tent. Below them is flat, dusty ground, and above, a colorless sky. The man seated in the center is short, no more than five feet eight inches, thin but well built; he has a neatly trimmed mustache and is noticeably balding. He is my maternal grandfather, and my family has noted the resemblance between us. But there is one aspect of the image that marks it as of interest to the historian of visual culture as well as to a descendant of the man: he is smiling. Actually, he is *grinning*, his legs casually pitched forward, his arms dangling loosely. In contrast, flanking him are two other officers assuming stiff, Napoleonic poses, complete with hands tucked into tightly buttoned tunics. My grandfather, then, is subverting the millennia-old genre of the war image known as the "commander portrait," where gravitas and a dignified stance are as important as level epaulettes and gleaming boots.

As with many pictures of war and warriors, the origins of this photograph's composition are cloudy. In other portraits, my grandfather cuts a fine, commanding pose. The man I knew as *papou* was no antimilitary radical; he rose to the rank of colonel before retiring. He was also perhaps the most decorated soldier in the Greek army during World War I. He won the croix de guerre, the French medal of valor, rarely bestowed upon a foreigner, especially on a battlefield distant from the western front. He fought again in 1920 in the failed war of liberation in Anatolia against the Turks. (The Turks also call it a war of liberation, but from the Greeks.) He was a hero to every veteran who spoke of him. In the ruinous *anabasis* to the Ionian Sea, he was the last to leave the dock, making sure every enlisted man was aboard the evacuation ships; yet he also had issued the injunction that he would personally shoot any soldier who committed atrocities against Turkish civilians. He was, in a word, a warrior, but as the photograph shows, he was willing, on occasion, to reject the ritualized peacock-ishness of so much of military affairs.

This incidental, obscure picture of war suggests wider principles. People within any culture and era have expectations about what is appropriate in the visual images they create or view. To understand the place of any image within a system of images, and any culturally specific system within an array of varying historical traditions, we must inspect both the details and the "big picture." One photograph can represent a genre; a deviation from the code of the genre (for example, a grinning officer seated between two stiffly erect comrades) calls at-tention to the norms of war imagery that can be studied and compared. The problems for us are to penetrate the veil of time, culture, and circumstance; to identify what is familiar and appreciate what is different; and to understand the minds behind the canvases and film. How can we see what someone else meant?

This quandary is instructively exposed in another picture from a war fought between Greeks and Central Asians, but created some 2000 years before my grandfather fought his battles. It is from the *Alexander Mosaic*, found in a villa at Pompeii. Historian Michael Wood deems it "one of the greatest of all war pictures" showing the chaos and terror of combat.[1] [**Fig. 1**] The mosaic is a Roman copy of a Macedonian painting that has been dated to about 330–300 B.C.E.[2] Now heavily damaged, the image shows a probably fictitious scene from the Battle of Issus between the forces of Alexander the Great and Darius II, ruler of Persia. In the battle, Alexander and his compact, unified, and well-trained Macedonian army of 47,000 defeated a Persian force of some 100,000. To save the day, at a wavering moment of the fight, Alexander, at the head of his elite Companion cavalry, charged directly into the center of the Persian line toward Darius.[3] The Roman historian Arrian claims that Darius panicked when Alex-ander approached and "incontinently fled—indeed, he led the race for safety."[4] Although hard fighting continued, when the Persian troops learned that their king had abandoned them, they began to scatter as well. In the pursuit, Darius' chariot, baggage, tents, and family were captured.

The picture, then, is a compression of a moment rather than the recording of a geographic fact: no written account describes Alexander and Darius in such proximity. In truth, the two kings probably never came within shouting distance. Here, the figure of a blond and bronzed young King Alexander on horseback is at left; directly in front and behind him are two generals, most likely his favorites Hephaestion and Antigonos. On the right, in a chariot, is Darius. The confidence of Alexander's stance and the uncertainty captured in the eyes of Darius II—exalted ruler of all Egypt, the Levant, the Middle East, Anatolia, Mesopotamia, and Iran—are unmistakable. We do not need to be literate in ancient history to see who is victor and who is in flight.

According to another interpretation, though, Darius' representation is more apologia than castigation. While the chariot driver steadily forges the team ahead, the king reaches out, ignoring Alexander, toward a young Persian noble who has fallen in front of the Macedonian charge. If the point of the picture was to praise Alexander, why was Darius' gracious gesture highlighted? The image may have been copied from a painting created in the service of Alexander's successors, his generals. Some of these men were not interested in contributing to a full visual hagiography of their former master—after all, they had killed his children and carved up his realm upon his death. Part of those territories included the Persian heartland. Perhaps this "noble Darius," forced to depart the field against his will, was a nod toward better relations with Persian subjects in the new order. Clearly, how we understand the image is a mixture of innate inference and cultural-historical knowledge. Darius' expression, pose, and gestures reach across the millennia; the why and wherefore can only be understood through extravisual scholarship.

This conflation is crucial, because images of war are *pictures* first and foremost, and understanding the physical and mental importance of seeing is fundamental to studying any particular genre of imagery. We are *Homo iconis* by our very nature, sight-driven animals that receive 90 percent of the data we collect and organize about the world through our eyes.[5] Visual images, artificially created on physical surfaces such as stone, canvas, or film, are the domain of humanity alone. Although elephants have been observed making lines and circles on the soil,[6] and some birds and insects build their homes in elaborate designs that would please the eye of the most exacting civil engineer,[7] and our closest relatives, chimpanzees and gorillas, can draw and paint when taught and prompted, it is imprecise to call such behavior pictorial or natural. Painting in other primates, for example, only comes after instruction; it is as artificial a cultural behavior for them as wearing diapers or riding a tricycle. More revealingly, other creatures do not attempt to create realistic images, that is, pictures that resemble the things they depict.[8] Finally, human beings go to great lengths and expend much time and resources to construct art that has nothing to do with shelter (as in the case of insects and birds) or survival. The cave art of the stone ages is an example. The caves were not inhabited by men; for what purpose they were decorated we will never know, but it certainly was not to house a family.

Many pictorial conventions seem natural and extra-cultural. To photograph characters from a low angle, for instance, is to imply that they are powerful ("big"), while to shoot them from a high angle is to imply that they are weak ("small").[9] That "bigness" is a sign of power is long recognized. A story from the court of Alexander is illustrative. After the battle at Issus, the conqueror, along with Hephaestion, met the mother of Darius in the captured Persian camp. The woman, Arrian describes, was "in doubt, owing to the similarity of their dress, which of the two was [Alexander, and so] prostrated herself before Hephaestion, because he was taller than his companion."[10] In antiquity, and still

1. *Alexander Mosaic*, Pompeii, copy from painting by artist Philoxenus (c. 300 B.C.E.?). *Naples, Museo Nazionale*

today, the "big man" view was and is created by constructing large-scale images of rulers, such as the colossal statuary of ancient kings and modern despots; the viewer is forced to "look upon" the works of the mighty from an insect's viewpoint. The effect is owed, perhaps, to the universal fact that all people spend the early years of their lives being smaller and shorter in stature than adults on whom they are dependent for sustenance and direction. Such conventions are

so only in name because they mimic the way all human beings process visual data.

Yet, despite the common use of the two verbs as synonyms, "to see" is not "to understand." Realistic pictures reflect the way we see; we thus infer that because they are realistic, they must also be truthful and fairly represent what is seen. As Berthold Brecht pointed out, however, "less than ever does a simple *reproduction of reality* express something about reality."[11] An oil painting such as *The Death of General Wolfe* (1770) can show a realistic scene. [**Fig. 2**] The landscape may be a credible rendition of a section of the Plains of Abraham outside Quebec, where a battle was fought in 1763 to decide the fate of Canada. The men who stand around the dying commander of the victorious English forces may be in correct period costume. The weapons they hold are likely the correct caliber. The lines and tones of face and cants of body are sharp and clear, almost photographic in their realism. The elements, then, may be accurate; in this case, however, the painter Benjamin West has created a scene that never existed. General James Wolfe died with only a few attendants, behind a ridge, out of sight of the battle, and was more bloodily wounded than shown here, including an unheroic shot to the groin. The picture is a Romantic fantasy, however faithful the contours of the shoe buckles or the facings of the miters.

Battles produce this kind of deception regularly. Sun Tzu, the fourth-century B.C.E. Chinese general, argued that "the whole of the art of war rests on deception." Samuel Johnson stated mordantly, "Among the calamities of war, may be justly numbered the diminution of the love of truth, by the falsehoods which interest dictates, and credulity encourages." But in *The Death of General Wolfe*, the deception is accomplished by the words used to describe the picture, and the implication that the image is the rendering of actual events. If the artist had

2. *The Death of General Wolfe*, Benjamin West, oil on canvas, 1770. *National Gallery of Canada, Ottawa*

stated, for example, that "It is a shame General Wolfe died lightly attended, so this painting is a fancy of what his reception should have been in a proper world," then it would no longer be deceiving. The lie arose from West's representation of the scene as factual when he assured viewers that "the same truth that guides the pen of the historian should govern the pencil of the artist."

Pictures, thus, *cannot lie in the same way that words can*; rather, we use words and implications to lie through pictures. "[T]he terms 'true' and 'false' can only be applied to statements, propositions," writes Ernst Gombrich, and "a picture is never a statement in that sense of the term. It can no more be true or false than a statement can be blue or green."[12] If a picture of a corpse-filled ditch, captioned "Dead Hutus Killed by Tutsis in Burundi," is recaptioned "Dead Tutsis Killed by Hutus in Rwanda," one or both sets of words may be partly or wholly false. The photographed human beings, however, remain just as dead. The picture, too, is the same; it is only the context of interpretation that has changed.

This universality of seeing coupled with the relativity of visual relevance is explored in Akira Kurosawa's film *Dersu Uzala (Dersu the Hunter)* (1975). The story follows a Russian army troop mapping an unknown region of eastern Siberia at the turn of the century. Early in their travels, the soldiers meet the title character, an aged woodsman. His family has died long ago and he has spent all his life in this beautiful but savage land. The Russians, in contrast, are newcomers, naive observers of the strange world they have entered. Realizing their helplessness, Dersu agrees to guide them. During the trek, both he and the soldiers scan the surroundings, but they select different data for processing and, thus, interpret the same world differently. Dersu sees water-filled indentations in a boggy road and determines that Chinese men have passed days before. The Russians do not notice the signs until he points out and explains them. And so it goes with many other items in the visual field of the woods to the point where Dersu occasionally becomes irritated at the Russians' "blindness." "How do you not understand?" he demands in halting Russian. "Look well! . . . You the same as children. Eyes not see!" He knows through experience that some objects indicate things beyond their mere physical presence; the naive observers are unaware of such connections.

This is the *hunter's eye*, which in times of interhuman conflict becomes the *warrior's eye*. It is an inheritance from the distant past when our ancestors relied completely on vision for distinguishing food, friends, and foes. It is also the learned ability to discern aspects of the visual field, whether in life or in an image, that are of greater relevance to the viewer. All seeing humans have such an eye, but it is influenced by culture and place, situation and character: the accountant spies a missing figure on a ledger; the art historian recognizes the brush strokes of Michelangelo; the mother discerns the unique contributions of her daughter in the dance troupe; the paleontologist spots the tooth of a *Homo erectus* on the seemingly featureless dust and rocks of the Olduvai Gorge; the drill sergeant is apoplectic at the sight of a recruit's unbuttoned collar. Pictures of war thus speak equally clearly to all who view them across the centuries; at the same time, many nuances are dependent on cultural awareness and individual expertise.

This metonymy—one thing symbolizing a greater condition—is the most intriguing aspect of visual imagery and will be implicitly or directly discussed in much of *Visions of War*.[13] Journalists and historians often employ images to stand for, encapsulate, or serve as exemplars for entire wars, eras, or even cultures. A typical instance was witnessed by viewers of the CBS News program *See It Now* on December 29, 1953. The camera showed a close-up of an American GI shoveling dirt from hard ground. Host Edward R. Murrow narrated, "This is Korea, where a war is going on. That's a Marine, digging a hole in the ground. They dig an awful lot of holes in the ground in Korea. This is the front. [Picture of Murrow behind sandbags] Just there, no-man's-land begins, and on the ridges over there, the enemy positions can be clearly seen. [Picture of Murrow looking at opposing ridge]"[14]

Each shot in this sequence was a metonym. Yet, because the imposition of metonymy is so ubiquitous and its inference so natural, we forget that it is an artificial construction. One way to think of pictures, then, is as visual anecdotes. They show one place at one time; even a long motion film cannot display every part of a battle as experienced by every soldier. Fixing a lens in one location, publishing the resulting frame, and claiming or implying that it "summed up" what happened in the battle is always a political act, even if the image makers are unaware of or deny it. The real question is who decides that any particular photograph (or any other kind of picture) is the "essence" of any war. Who rules the metonym? How does it define the "us" and the "them" in wartime? Why are we so willing to jump to a conclusion on the evidence of one vivid example?

These observations and questions led to this book, an exploration of the relationship between warfare, the men and women who fight and suffer from it, and the visual media that claim to capture it. The topic is vast, but I have restricted my investigations in this initial volume by time, space, and type.[15] Foremost, I examine *representational* images of the people and objects of land warfare. Maps, graphs, and charts, which are under the general category of graphic image, will be excluded. Neither is the choice of wars, personalities, artists, and illustrations comprehensive, nor an attempt to highlight the great war images of history. Sometimes culturally popular, politically important, socially revealing, and aesthetically pleasing visualizations of war are ignored or mentioned in passing (such as Ken Burns's *Civil War* television series). For the same reason, whole eras are ignored, and wars unmentioned—the pages are too few to cover everything.

Another limitation is the number of actual illustrations. A book of this kind would be impossibly large and expensive if it referred to every interesting picture of war and included a print of every picture to which it referred. In the cases of images unseen but spoken of, the reader, no doubt, will yearn to see the real thing—the original image—but that is the point. One goal of this book is to encourage its audience to seek out or review pictures of war with questions prompted by the discussion offered.

The pictures that are referred to and shown include specimens of the arts of the civilizations of the Mediterranean and the Near East, and especially those of Greece and Rome, as well as the pre-contact peoples of the Americas and Polynesia. After the time of the Renaissance, my study turns largely to Western art, that is, images produced by those working in European and later post-contact American traditions. Just as in Western Europe after the fourteenth century we find the most remarkable innovations in the technology of warfare, so too will we see the most influential developments in the technology of depicting war, continuing to the satellite imagery of the present day.

As for the subjects of the pictures, these too will vary, for "war" is not a creature of one scene or space. "The battlefield is the epitome of war," wrote American general S. L. A. Marshall.[16] Yet, however we define war, it involves many activities and locations besides the exact point of contact between armed men. Wars have been won in the training camps of Roman legions, on the playing fields of Eton, and in the factories of Detroit; the war experience includes death camps, the mess hall, and short-arm inspections. War can be, as the military theorist Antoine-Henri Jomini described, a "terrible and impassioned drama," but also a series of dull routines. That parts of war are shown in pictures and are deemed "realistic" or fantastic, true or false, powerful or irrelevant, is one of the biases of selection enforced by cultures, patrons, artists, historians, and audiences. Indeed, many common (and militarily decisive) events of war have never appeared on canvas or screen.

Finally, "fascination," as Hannah Arendt wrote, "is a social phenomenon."[17] What we want to see in pictures is a cultural indicator of our hopes and nightmares; likewise, theorists should never pretend to stand outside their theory, and cultural historians must recognize that they are products of their culture. The fortnight before completing this manuscript, I watched a recent war tale, Steven Spielberg's *Saving Private Ryan*. At the end of the film I cried—real tears for the loss of young Americans, and the grieving and self-questioning of the survivors. That I had seen similar incidents on screen and in thousands of other kinds of pictures of war many times before, that I was aware that these were not flesh-and-blood people dying before me but highly paid movie stars, that all the explosions and gore were the counterfeits of California wizardry—all this did not matter. Somehow the film worked on me, at that moment, and I cried, pulling my cap down and my sunglasses up, rushing out of the theater to avoid the gaze of others and to seek the healing radiance of the sun.[18]

Thus, at both the beginning and the end of this journey, I was reminded that pictures of war *matter*, to societies and to individuals. A stone relief carving of an Athenian hoplite deploying his long spear, a Hollywood movie of U.S. Marines storming the beach of a Pacific atoll, or a computer game's endomorphic hero blasting aliens into glowing debris, are projections of cognition as well as physical objects. As Stephen Jay Gould notes, "The pictures we draw betray our deepest convictions and display our current conceptual limitations."[19] Images of war reflect and refract the way we think about war; their study is a means to understand the place of the institution of war in human history and the human mind. Yet wars and images of war do not breed fascination in the same way, to the same degree, or with the same result to all audiences. As I left the theater showing *Saving Private Ryan*, a pack of teenage boys loped out alongside me, and I overheard the comment: "Neat stuff. Just like *Doom!*"

# 1

---

# ORIGINS

*THE FIRST WAR?*

War, said the philosopher Heraclitus, is the father of all men and all things.[1] Every nation, people, and institution, contemporary or past, has in some way been shaped by war; many have been extinguished by it. From 1496 B.C.E. to 1861, as one writer described, there "were but 227 years of peace and 3130 years of war; in other words thirteen years of war for every year of peace. Considered thus, the history of the lives of peoples presents a picture of uninterrupted struggle. War, it would appear, is a normal attribute to human life."[2] The social historian Pitirim Sorokin found that most of the nations of Europe had engaged in some form of war for at least half their existence.[3]

Nor is war a historical anachronism: the immense, unparalleled losses of life in the last hundred years have made the twentieth century a "century of blood" (Eric Hobsbawm), a "stinking" century (A. L. Rowse), and the "Black Century" (George Steiner). Even though there has been no worldwide or cataclysmic war, there have been only 26 days of world peace since 1945, and some 150 wars[4] have been fought or continue to be fought under such guises as traditional wars between nation states, border clashes, preventive incursions, punitive expeditions, revolutions, civil wars, "dirty wars," police actions, state terrorism, peacekeeping missions, anti-insurgency campaigns, ethnic cleansings, and humanitarian interventions. In all it would take 4,000 Vietnam Memorials to inscribe the names of the victims of the wars of this century alone.

War is also a uniquely human enterprise. In the activities of social insects like ants, many of the strategies and outcomes of battle as we know it are visible. Weapons of a kind are used by some animals; for example, polar bears will push blocks of ice onto sleeping walruses.[5] Among chimpanzees, our closest genetic relatives, there are fights between individuals and gang assaults on isolated members of other communities.[6] Human beings, however, fight planned, sustained, complex battles over years and over wide areas, employing up to tens of millions of combatants and hundreds of millions of workers in the war economy and using technological devices designed to kill enemies. Expressed motivations for war such as fulfilling treaty obligations or defending a faith are limited to *Homo sapiens*. Alone among the planet's fauna as well, we create images to memorialize, celebrate, understand, or decry our wars.

Yet the origins of war are obscure. We do not know when the first group of men began to kill their neighbors, kidnap the women, steal possessions, or seize land; nor do we know whether the aggressors considered these activities necessities of survival, points of honor, or ethnic imperatives. The Egyptians under Rameses II fought the first major battle (recorded in writing) against a Hittite army at Kadesh in c. 1300 B.C.E., but civilized warfare, between cities and states, reaches back much further. The initial motives for wars of smaller scale, between families, groups, and tribes, are even more distant. There are signs of murder, organized and individual, among the archaic populations, such as *Homo erectus*, living a million years ago.[7] Among the nearest human subspecies to our own, the Neanderthals, violence was widespread, though it is unclear whether from accidents, animal attacks, or fighting. In one study, 40 percent of Neanderthal individuals in Europe and Asia show signs of traumatic injury to the head.[8] Among the remains of the later stone ages in Eurasia and Africa, weapons, and tools to repair and improve weapons, are common, but we do not know whether those weapons were used by men on other men.[9]

Neither do we know the idea, era, provenance, or medium of the first artificially created visual image.[10] Some recent discoveries are tantalizing: geometric shapes on Australian rock surfaces date to about 40,000 B.C.E.; specimens of rock art in Tanzania are placed at the same time; a piece of bone upon which one of our ancestors inscribed what may be the outline of a horse's head dates to 70,000 B.C.E.; a 230,000-year-old pebble carved in a rude human shape was found in Israel. However, we will never find a "picture zero," only those that may date earlier than other samples. What is understood is that the first picture-making *industries*, the first instances of a widespread cultural practice of making representational images, appear among anatomically modern humans in the Upper Paleolithic (Old Stone Age) era about 35,000 to 12,000 years ago.[11]

This art does depict battles—but not the ones a historian of war art might seek. For example, in the Lascaux cave in Dordogne, France, on the wall of a barely accessible shaft are several figures painted around 14,000 to 18,000 years ago.* [**Fig. 3**] As no natural light penetrates the cave's depth, the images must

---

*As an archeologist interviewed for this book noted with considerable understatement, "dating prehistory is a messy problem." Most dates are probably too recent and based on uncalibrated radio carbon dating, a technique that measures the amount of radio carbon (C14) in plant or animal material which has been absorbed during the organism's life and then decays over time at a known rate. For example, after 11,460 years the amount of C14 in a piece of burned wood will be 25 percent of the amount present when the tree was cut down. Immense problems exist in using the technique, however, most no-

3. Man with bird head and bison in shaft of Lascaux cave, near Montignac, Dordogne, France (date not certain; perhaps around 12,000 to 16,000 B.C.E.). *Photo: Jean Vertut*

have been viewed with stone lamps that cast a dusky, flickering glow.[12] The shapes themselves seem relatively straightforward. A giant bison, evidently wounded, appears to charge a fallen, stick-figure man wearing a bird's-head mask. Below the bison is what may be an arrow or spear. Nearby is a staff with a small bird figure at its hilt. Farther below may be an atlatl, a hooked instrument with which ancient and modern hunter-gatherers launched a spear with improved speed, accuracy, and power. (To the left, out of frame, a rhinoceros departs the scene; six dots extend from its rear.)

The first great student of prehistoric art, whose interpretation defined it for half of the twentieth century, the French priest Henri Breuil, saw such visual imagery as the initial signs of a spiritual florescence in the Stone Age. In his summa, *Four Hundred Centuries of Cave Art*, the *abbé* reflects: "[F]or the first time, Men dreamed of great Art and, by the mystical contemplation of their works, gave to their contemporaries an assurance of success in their hunting expeditions, of triumph in the struggle against the enormous pachyderms and

---

tably the contamination of the sample by material from other dates. (See Renfrew & Bahn, 1996: 132–138.)

grazing animals."[13] Breuil argued that cave painting was sympathetic magic, or "la magie de la chasse," reflecting the fertility of prey creatures and illustrating the process that would lead to the success of the hunt. Through this prism, every sign, squiggle, line, and shape on the cave walls became an element within a magical realm.

Yet, in many ways, the Lascaux scene is atypical of the art from which it sprang; the cave imagery of the Ice Age rarely displayed overt violence or pictures of men or small animals like birds, and nothing of social customs and traditions. The actual weapons presumably used in hunting prey are commonly seen impacting or lying near the great animals.

In fact, the duel of the bird-man and the bison reflects the early prevalence of the habits of body and mind that give us the capacity for the warfare that we picture and practice to this day. This interpretation can be disputed, however, and is not provable. To use words from one culture to describe the activities of another is always a political act. It is an ethnocentric value judgment to impose the term "war" to describe the activities of hunters of the Ice Age. The peoples of that time probably had no word for war and would be amazed at the concept. Yet the actions they engaged in were the genesis of those that later human beings applied to war, and the state of mind that sustained the hunter is identical to that which drives the warrior, even when the opponents and victims are of different species.

The art, ideas, and folkways of the Upper Paleolithic are of great interest to understanding who we are because so much that distinguishes us from the rest of the animal kingdom first appeared or became common then. The era has been called one of the "big surprises" of history,[14] a cultural revolution,[15] and a creative explosion.[16] Even if the achievements of the time had earlier origins and precedents, the era's art, as paleohistorian Paul Bahn puts it, "constitutes a dramatic qualitative and quantitative advance on earlier evidence for symbolic activity."[17]

The greatest flourishing of Upper Paleolithic cave art—or rather, the area in which we have found the most evidence—is Franco-Cantabria, what now comprises the northern coastal region of Spain, the Pyrenees mountain range, and the Dordogne and Rhône River valleys in southwestern France. Here, archeologists have found the most sites of habitation, the greatest amount of statuary, cave and rock paintings and markings, carved bones, antlers, and stones, the most elaborate burial sites, and the most signs of social and technological complexity.[18] In size the art ranged from tiny statuettes of women to immense wall paintings of the fauna of the prehistoric peoples' world. The main period of the production of art occurred during the last great peak of glaciation, the Ice Age. Despite harsh conditions, the hunters enjoyed their own version of an "affluent society,"[19] among one of the richest accumulations of megafauna (large animals) in the natural history of the world.[20] It is likely, then, that the character of the region encouraged different groups to cooperate, albeit temporarily, to fully exploit the environment. War among humans may have been unnecessary because cooperation (in seeking and killing game) brought about the best return from violent effort.

The end of the Upper Paleolithic world came when the glaciers retreated to their present position north of Europe. In Franco-Cantabria, thick forests replaced the tundra and steppe landscapes. The modern observer who associates open spaces with barrenness and the forest with life cannot understand the calamity this was for the peoples of the time. When any society makes the transition from exploitation of wild game and plants to a cereal economy, acute and chronic nutritional disasters—ranging from famine to iron deficiency, degradation of dental health, rise in infectious diseases, increased infant mortality, and a reduction in life span—are the inevitable results.[21] The newly created woodlands could only support about 20 to 30 percent of the animal life that existed in the previous era. The cultures that produced much of what we associate with prehistoric art changed or collapsed. The caves were forgotten and abandoned, the paintings not to be uncovered for 10,000 years.

It is also from the Ice Age that we have the first unambiguous evidence of men slaughtering each other. This image from Cougnac in Southeastern France shows a human figure pierced by either spears or arrows.[22] [**Fig. 4**] Yet, in the fossil record, what we find barely fulfills the definition of war as "all organized forms of intergroup homicide involving combat teams of two or more persons, including feuding and raiding."[23] In an Italian site, the skeleton of a child was found with an arrow or spear point buried in the spinal column.[24] Other fossil remains bear the marks of arrow wounds as well. For example, the right ilium of a human pelvis from the San Teodoro site in a cave in Messina, Sicily, is pierced by a small flint flake. There are currently twelve other sites from the Upper Paleolithic era that show evidence of arrows used to kill humans.[25] In the few excavations outside Europe, interhuman violence is also apparent. In the northern Sudan, at the site of Jebel Sahaba dating to about 10,000 B.C.E., we find evidence of a "lethal society."[26] Fifty-nine skeletons were uncovered, of which more than half indicate extreme violence, such as crushing, cutting, and blows to the skull; weapon points are imbedded in some of the bones. The violence crossed lines of age and sex, and was thus probably not the result of hunting accidents or personal feuds.

Nevertheless, evidence of interhuman violence in the Upper Paleolithic is more scarce than for any other period in modern man's time on earth. In the next eras, the Mesolithic-Neolithic (c. 9000–4000 B.C.E.), and during the subsequent rise of urban civilization, evidence of systematic warfare becomes frequent, indisputable, and immense. Moreover, in the record of the bones, there is one curious fact about injuries suffered in the Upper Paleolithic: there are more wounds found on the remains of women than of men.[27] But male-female ratio may be a spurious statistical anomaly—the sample size of the injured dead is tiny. Furthermore, these wounds are not necessarily the result of personal violence or war, but may be due to natural calamities in the harsh, rugged environment and the relatively thinner bones of females. In any case, after the end of the Upper Paleolithic, the ratio is reversed (with men having more wounds

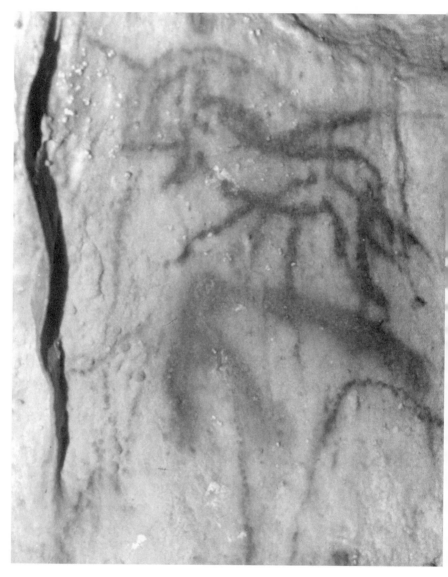

4. Man pierced with arrows, Cougnac Cave, France (date not certain; perhaps c. 18,000 B.C.E.).
*Photo: Jean Clottes*

than women) and, moreover, violent injury is frequently associated with weapons; combined, these are certain signs of offensive or defensive violence. We can speculate, therefore, that although there was violence between people in the Upper Paleolithic, organized, purposive warmaking as we know it existed only on a small scale or was directed not toward other men but toward other species.

Pictures of interhuman violence are rare, though we should not assume that this reflected a generally pacific state of society. To find the more important and revealing pictures of war, we should look at unlikely figures, the many images of animals on the cave walls. To the modern eye, they are bucolic, like photographs in a nature magazine or scenes from a wildlife documentary. Arther Ferrill, like most historians of war, largely dismisses the Paleolithic as not being of interest to his field. "The cave paintings," he writes, "reflect very little evidence of warfare or of advances in weapons technology. There are several thousand scenes of animals, and, on the whole, they are idyllically peaceful."[28] But the absence of overt violence (people killing each other or gutting animals) in art does not necessarily correspond to the absence of violence in society. Many peoples, from the Spartans[29] to the Yuan[30] dynasty of China to our own contemporary Western culture, may display visual arts that have no concordance with or are unrepresentative of actual warmaking practices.

In fact, the cave images were the first art of war, a war whose stakes were no less life and death than the battles of Roman legions or U.S. Marines. These were the images spawned from a culture whose most important component—to the exclusion of almost all other aspects of social life—was the killing of big game. To understand the origins of the vision of war, we must engage these images, and try to appreciate them through the hunter's eye.

## THE FOCUS ON BIG GAME

Because we lack any written sources, eyewitnesses, or even the most tenuous myths or traditions from the time of its creation, cave art may serve as a Rorschach test for the fancies and agendas of competing researchers. How can we adopt the warrior's eye when the artist-hunter and his culture have been dead for at least 12,000 years? The almost three hundred decorated caves and shelters that have been uncovered and explored thus far display a version of reality that seems to defy sense—our sense, that is. The people of the Upper Paleolithic Franco-Cantabria were hunters and gatherers; over the millennia their environment varied, but generally it was dominated by lush tundra covered with game, rivers and seas teeming with fish, and skies filled with fowl. The people mated, bore and raised children, fashioned clothing and shelters, hunted and gathered food; no doubt they also told tales of their own lives, weaved legends of the supernatural, and organized themselves into interlocking family groups. Their art varied too, from body tattooing to necklaces of beads and animal teeth, wood carvings, clay sculpture, and the famous cave paintings.

But the art upon which the Stone Age people expended their greatest labor, resources, and time—the cave paintings—is largely limited to only one subject: big game. The French prehistorian André Leroi-Gourhan conducted a survey in the late 1960s of some 90 caves and 1,955 portrayals of animals.[31] He recorded that about 93 percent of the pictures were of large game such as reindeer, horse, bison, aurochs (the giant prehistoric bovid), red deer, ibex, and mammoths. At the Font de Gaume cave near Les Eyzies (Dordogne), France, for example, the galleries display some two hundred images, of which there are eighty bison, forty horses, twenty-three mammoths, and other large creatures, the fewest of which are predators; only one of the images is of a human figure.

How much does such a view represent or distort the world in which the artists lived? One way to answer this question in part is to compare the imagery to the archeofaunal records—the bones of animal species existing at that time found in association with the caves. Simple counts produce incongruities. At the Ekain cave in northeastern Spain, 57.6 percent of the animals depicted are horses, but no bones of horses have been uncovered; at Tito Bustillo in northern Spain, the surface art is about evenly split between horses and red deer, with some ibex, but the fossil record overflows with the remains of red deer.[32] In France, at the Comarque site, horses make up a majority of the cave paintings and sketches, but of the bones found from nearby sites, three-quarters are from reindeer.[33] At Lascaux, there is only one identifiable picture of a reindeer, yet this creature's bones account for 90 percent of those found near the cave; at La Vache, horse bones are rarely logged in the archeofaunal record, yet horses are represented by 25 percent of the drawn figures.[34] The huge Rouffignac cave, known locally in Dordogne as "La Grotte de Cent [100] Mammouths" (actually now 158 and counting), is crowded with paintings and engravings of the now extinct pachyderm, but no mammoth bones (only a few teeth fragments) have been found anywhere near the site.[35] Almost every known cave that has been investigated presents such discrepancies.

Body counts alone, however, do not reveal the intent of the artists. To this end, two researchers, Patricia C. Rice and Ann L. Paterson, have made an exhaustive study of the correlation between the cave art and the bone remains.[36] Their comparison is regulated by the type and size of the species in question. They found that small creatures, such as fish, reptiles, and rabbits, were drastically underrepresented in the paintings. Medium-sized animals, especially the red deer and the reindeer, which some researchers believe were a staple of the diet in much of the Upper Paleolithic, were "portrayed in rough relation to their prevalence in the archeofaunal record."[37] Larger species, such as the horse and the bovines, were overrepresented in the cave imagery. Rice and Paterson conclude that the decision to record a creature on the cave walls was perhaps linked not to the frequency with which it was hunted and eaten, but its meat yield; that is, the economic contribution of big-game animals was the primary stimulus for the imagery.[38] The art portrayed animals that were preferred as sources of food and other materials, such as hides for use in clothing.

In addition, the imagery could be interpreted as displaying the animals that were most feared by the hunters. To address this question, Rice and Paterson asked a panel of animal and hunting specialists to rate the species shown on a scale of perceived danger. In most cases, such as the mammoth, bovines, and horses, the more dangerous the species, the more likely it was to be represented in cave art. The combination of practical nutritional value, utility, and perceived danger from these animals that are overportrayed on the cave walls suggests an important link between the prestige of the big-game hunt and its benefits for society. Notably, in later periods (such as the Neolithic), when the large game had disappeared, the focus of art was no longer on animals at all, but on human interaction.

Other parts of the natural world, from the heavenly bodies to the mountains and rivers and sea, make few appearances. Painted animals run and stand without sky, sun, cloud, or moon backgrounds—not even a horizon or earthline. More interesting, there is no evidence on the cave walls or in the mobiliary (portable carvings and statues) art of gathering plant food. There are only a few shapes that some researchers interpret as plants of a kind. This is remarkable considering the role of plants in daily life. Absent as well are flora that may have been used as medicine. We also know that juniper-bush wood (which burns aromatically for long periods) played a role in illuminating the caves. Its charcoal has been found at Lascaux.

Missing as well are the smaller animals; no flocks of quail or colonies of rabbits line the cave walls. Reptiles are rarely pictured. Eggs and fish roe, which would have provided additional dietary protein, are never shown. Birds make up less than 0.2 percent of displayed cave art and fish only 0.3 percent.[39] It is possible that smaller creatures actually did make up very little of the Paleolithic diet. Ethnographic data suggest that when societies find a high-yield food source, they tend to concentrate on its cultivation or procurement to the exclusion of lower-return foods.[40] Largely unpainted as well are salmon, which may have comprised a substantial part of the Upper Paleolithic diet at times and in certain locations.[41] In any case, the smaller creatures' absence suggests that the artists were not making a statistical survey of biodiversity.

Variations in the animals shown are also infrequent. There are few images that display baby animals or young adults.[42] Neither are there many images of old, lame, or dead animals, though some of the animals shown may be in forms of distress.[43] These are particularly interesting missing pieces; the young and lame animals are attractive targets for predators because of their relative weakness, slowness, and, in the case of the newborn or unweaned animals, undeveloped survival instincts. Some of the painted, sculpted, incised, and carved creatures appear swollen, perhaps pregnant. This would have added to their nutritional value as a kill and perhaps made them more susceptible to the hunter.

More revealingly, the visual imagery of the caves portrays very few fantastic—what we would think of as mythical—creatures. Only 0.4 percent, according to Leroi-Gourhan's account, are not identifiable and could be imaginary beings. Rarely is there anything approaching a unicorn; there are none of the griffins, winged horses, plumed snakes, flying bulls, or chimeras of other visualized iconologies. Neither are there three-headed gods or giants. When men are shown wearing animal masks, it is almost always clearly just that—men in shamanistic costume, not part-human/part-beast creatures. The imagery, whatever its magical connotations, was of the world; people drew what they saw, or what they expected to see. If the art *was* magical, it was a grounded, practical magic.

The final and most intriguing absence in the cave imagery, and to some extent in the mobile art, is that of the artists and their society. Where are the people? The big animals have crowded out almost every activity or scene of human life. No more than two hundred vaguely identifiable human figures are shown on the cave walls;[44] some are therianthropic figures (half human and half animal), or men wearing animal heads or masks. There are in other caves outlines of human hands, many of which are mysteriously missing some or all of their digits. We also have in the mobiliary art the "Venuses," those obese women which may have been either fertility goddesses or real women suffering iodine-depletion-induced cretinism. But compared to the vast numbers of pictures of animals, especially large game creatures, the sketchbook of the human figure is threadbare.

More important, in 20,000 years of art, we have only a few images that could pass as *realistic* portraits of individual people. This was not for want of talent. Animals were often drawn with such striking clarity, vitality, and faithfulness to the original that they seem an early version of photography. Also, we see nothing of society save some hints of incidents from the hunt, and a few sketches that appear to be couples engaged in sex. There are no hikes in the woods, no feasts, no group or individual dances, no children at play with fathers and mothers, no mates asleep together, no gathering of berries, no celebrations of births, no panoramas of funerals. A visitor from another planet would not infer from this corpus that human beings were the authors of the images.

What can we make of this seemingly skewed vision from the ice ages? Referring to the Rice and Paterson study, we can see a pattern and a unifying theme in the art of the caves. The animals painted were the "best catches," which also provided the most fearful challenge and the greatest prestige to the hunter.

## THE FAT OF THE LAND

George Orwell once commented that, whatever one's feelings about such things, it was impossible to look at some animals' "hindquarters without thinking of mint sauce."[45] The visual imagery of the Upper Paleolithic is almost always of big-game animals that weigh over 100 pounds. The animals invariably appear in the prime of life; one might even say, from the point of view of a meat-eater, that they are plump and juicy. For example, there is from the Lascaux cave probably the single most famous animal image, that of the so-called Chinese horse.[46] [**Fig. 5**] In its original color, it is a bright orange-red. It is painted as if about to begin a gallop; several lines, possibly spear points, aim toward its back. It is in the peak of health, and fat, either with pregnancy or with autumn's accumulation for the winter. The plumpness is exaggerated to the point of absurdity. Only the most determined vegetarian, of which probably none existed in the Upper Paleolithic, could look at such a beast and not think of the steaks and solid layers of backfat it would provide. These images border on a form of food pornography.

The health of the animals in the cave paintings would have also signified another nutritious resource that again must be viewed through the hunter's eye: the marrow. Two researchers, one of whom, Jean-Philippe Rigaud, spent months examining the food preparation and cooking habits of the Nunamiut natives of Alaska—whose diet consisted largely of game meat—made a remarkable discovery about the food preparation of the Upper Paleolithic. In most healthy animals, bone marrow is one of the richest sources of fat. The Eskimos, like most modern circumpolar hunters, not only cracked the long bones of the big-game animals that they killed, but also smashed the smaller bones, which they boiled into a nutritious, if greasy, soup.[47] The researchers discovered among Paleolithic sites the same intensive use of small bones.

Why the importance of fat from meat animals? This question seems puzzling to those of us who benefit from the contemporary version of the affluent society. Approximately one-third of Americans suffer from some sort of eating disorder; one-quarter are clinically obese, that is, at least 20 percent over average body weight for their sex, age group, and height.[48] Paradoxically, the media of our culture are replete with indications that avoidance of fat and the attaining of a lean build is our main cultural obsession. On the other hand, the obesity is related to the legacy of the caves. In the 99 percent of human history that preceded our affluence, food was not instantly accessible at the local supermarket, nor was it as calorically rich as the products of the fast-food chains. In the early

*(overleaf)*
5. "Chinese Horse," Lascaux cave, near Montignac, Dordogne, France (date not certain; perhaps c. 12,000 to 16,000 B.C.E.).
*Photo: Jean Vertut*

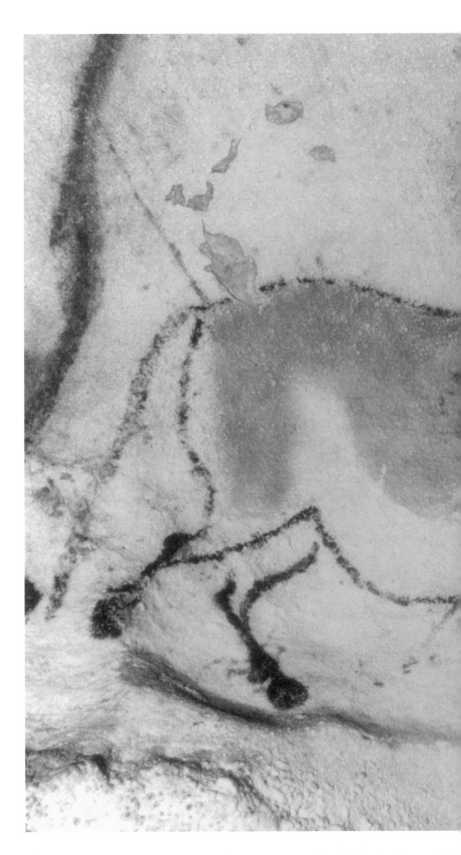

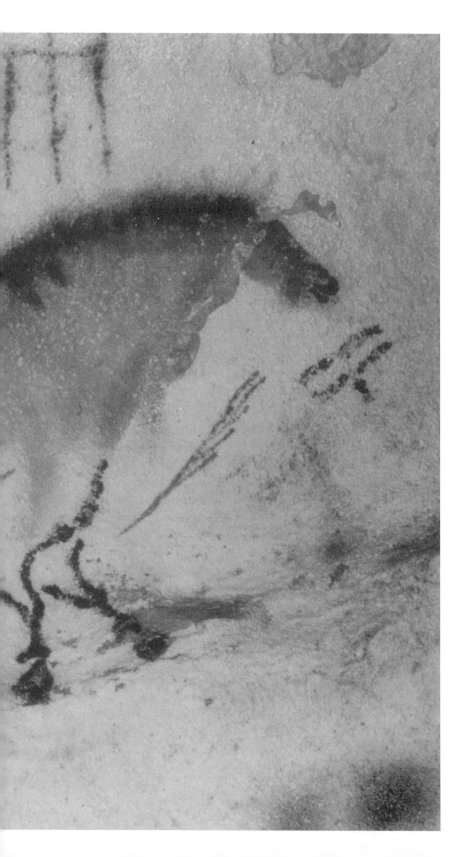

agricultural era, and to some extent today, as anthropologist Marshall Sahlins put it, "starvation [was and] is an institution." Our bodies are designed to store fat, men at the waist, women in the buttocks and thighs. For the modern middle class, the fat is deposited in the endless progression of what people of other lands and prior times would have seen as rare feasts, but we just think of as cheese-burgers and fries.

So we have forgotten, our eyes obscured by the mounds of food on our plates and tables, how the subsistence hunter's eyes scan game. Caloric consumption needs are highly correlated to a person's level of exertion and the climate. The hardy nomad Inuit of the circumpolar region had the heaviest required food intake in the ethnographic record: about 3,100 calories a day. Every pound of muscle increases by 100 calories the body's energy consumption. Meat is the most efficient caloric food per unit of weight, with the exception of some nuts. One kilogram of marbled meat provides 2,700 calories in a neat package.[49] Meat also provides the most balanced food in terms of essential amino acids.[50] It is no surprise, then, that voluntary vegetarianism is the product of sedentary cultures seeking to control access to certain types of food for various practical or religious reasons. No foraging peoples pass up a good steak. Also, the evidence suggests that hunter-gatherers who efficiently exploited their environment, especially in game-rich areas and eras like the Franco-Cantabria of the Upper Paleolithic, were able to avoid periodic starvation.

But meat can be a tasty trap if it is not in the correct fat-to-lean ratio. The fat on game—wild animals store fat subcutaneously—is its crucial attribute for the hunter in the temperate or cold climate. Most game meat simply does not provide adequate nutrition; overconsumption of it will lead to protein poisoning. Historically, hunter-gatherers have been known, even in times of scarcity, to avoid or disdain the killing of meat animals—like the bison—during seasons such as in the late winter and early spring in which the meat is stringier and the animals have little fat under their hides.[51] Many explorers and travelers in the western United States noted the debilitating and possibly deadly effects on men produced by eating too much lean meat (a phenomenon known as "rabbit hunger").[52]

Farley Mowat, the Canadian naturalist, emphasized this danger in his account of the year he spent with the Ihalmiut Eskimos in the late 1940s.[53] These inland hunters, who called themselves "the People of the Deer," depended almost entirely on the reindeer migration. However, at only one time of year, in autumn, were the reindeer at their choicest nutritional level. The bucks, especially, stored a layer of up to two inches of fat on their backs. Misguided attempts by the Canadian government to supplement the Ihalmiut diet with cans of beans or by lending them fishing nets proved tragic; the People of the Deer needed the white, rich fat of the healthy bucks and the pregnant does to survive. Fat, in their culture, was the greatest prize of the hunt.

The elongated and bloated animals of the cave walls should be seen through such an imperative. The strongest evidence that this was a hunter's art is that these great beasts seem to be dedicated to the god of fat. The smaller, leaner animals, such as the rabbit, are largely unpictured because they were relatively unimportant and unsought by the hunters (and, of course, there was no danger-bought prestige attached to their killing).

Finally, meat is more than food for the individual, as suggested from ethnographic data, taking into account all its complexity and lack of correspondence to the Paleolithic era. When meat is shared, the benefits are mostly social; reciprocity of meat is a tool of community integration and individual prestige.[54] The prestige the great hunter obtains as a "meat-winner" may also purchase, through his renown as a provider, that basic coin of biological success, greater reproductivity. In some studies, contemporary hunters who excel at procuring (and sharing) meat are better able to provide for larger families, with children more likely to survive to adulthood.[55] Moreover, among modern-era hunter-gatherer people, rates of infidelity are extremely high and these liaisons often result in pregnancy.[56] When married women have affairs, they prefer to do so with higher-prestige partners—literally the big catchers.[57] In summation, the implications for all of human activity, then and now, are obvious and vast: talented, successful aggression is rewarded.

In the cave images, practical dietary and nutritional requirements are intimately linked to a culture dedicated to the *aggressive* tracking, pursuit, and killing of big game. While it is possible that early human ancestors collected meat from the kills of other animals, it is obvious that the development of behaviors, including tool use, which would allow the direct procuring of meat would be highly favored by evolutionary forces. As one researcher notes, "Hunting returns for hunters using traditional technology are from 10 to 200 times greater than that observed for baboons, with an average of about thirty-fold higher returns for male human hunters than adult male baboons."[58] The killing was rewarding. That those same activities would be directed against other humans to obtain commodities such as wealth, land, and power is a natural derivative of the mental, physical, and material skills developed for hunting. The cave paintings showed both death and dinner; in the Franco-Cantabria of the Ice Age, the twain did meet.

## THE MALENESS OF THE BIG-GAME HUNT

The art of the caves is of such beauty and attention to realistic detail that the creators must have been intimately familiar with what they were picturing. The subjects were not carcasses dragged home to the camp by others or scavenged in the field, but represented vibrant, living, hunted creatures. Hunters' eyes saw them and painted them.

These artists must have been male.

The chain of logic to support this claim is not driven by politics but by fact. The pictures on the cave walls are of big game; big-game hunting is a male activity.[59] As one writer has noted, "The only form of division of labour by sex found universally is that women do not have established roles or equipment for hunting."[60] In a survey of over two hundred farming and foraging cultures, researchers found that in 99.4 percent of societies that hunted large terrestrial game animals, only men were sanctioned to engage in the hunt.[61] In another study of nontechnological societies, it was found that only in 10 percent were males involved in any way in child-care activities, while in 96 percent there was no tradition of intimate nurturing relationships between fathers and their children.[62] Men's work in tribal cultures has traditionally been the long-range, high-energy food procurement involving considerable physical effort, danger, and time spent away from the home base.[63] Women's work involves gathering activities—including capturing small game animals—child care, and the preparation and maintenance of clothing and home shelters. More decisively, women's work also tends to be more routinized and less subject to the variability of the hunt.[64]

This is not to say that women are wholly absent from the imagery of the Upper Paleolithic. On the cave walls there are pictures of women, but almost none are as detailed as we might expect. More prominent are the so-called Venus figurines, small statuettes of corpulent women.[65] Yet, in not a single one is there a hint of vitality or action. These are contemplative statuary, perhaps tokens of fertility, and in a culture that valued fat they could have signified prosperity. It is very difficult, moreover, to imagine such ungainly persons hunting bison on the tundra. In contrast, the big animals are captured in poses of action and tension. Whatever the economic contribution of women's work to food procurement, it was not documented in Paleolithic imagery, at least in a way that we can understand. No one should read this chapter as a slight to the economic contribution of women to prehistoric society. The archeofaunal and archeological records as well as analysis of historical tribal societies suggest that horticulture and gathering—traditionally women's activities—can yield a majority of the food obtained. Women have also participated in communal hunting such as the driving of herds of large game off cliffs.[66] But violent, weapons-based, confrontational fighting against big, dangerous game is historically and was (we infer from all evidence) prehistorically an overwhelmingly male activity. The cave peoples, in the art that remains to us, chose to depict only the animals hunted as big game. Plant foods, small animals, indeed almost any hint of gathering activity is absent. Because the art was an investment of resources, this means something. The people of the Upper Paleolithic displayed what was important to their society; we do the same with our visual media. More important, what we see of humans themselves in the art betrays the divisions of activity. Although there are nonobese women displayed in the paintings and portable sculptures, as one researcher points out, "Men by contrast are often depicted in conflictual or dramatic situations fighting against animals or carrying their trophies, equipped with weapons or opposing other human creatures."[67] This statement could equally be applied to almost all the art of war throughout history.

There is no reason to think that the cave artists were not divided either by sex or by task. If the images were used in a system of information exchange, and this information was vitally important, it makes sense that those who would be privileged with wall space and would be given the time and resources to create the images should also be the most trusted and wisest sources of information: the hunters themselves. Contemporary studies of nontechnological peoples have noted that though handicrafts are the province of both men and women, at least until very recent times the carving of figures was exclusively the domain of males.[68] It is clear that since the dawn of recorded history the creation of visual imagery, as with hunting, has overwhelmingly been a male interest and vocation.

The sexual division of labor which has arisen in almost all societies, whereby women were largely accorded the tasks of gathering while men engaged in big-game hunting, suggests that there were what might be called pride networks operating in both worlds. Big-game hunting, like warfare in the pre-computer era, puts a premium on strength and aggression; it must have created its own culture of distinction and value. While it is true that in many subsistence hunter cultures there is an egalitarianism that frowns upon any hunter boasting of his skills, at the same time the more successful the hunter, the more likely he is to be rewarded with prestige within a group, and possibly more successful mating. Hundreds of thousands of years of hunting created a male culture in which skill in risk taking, in tests of strength, endurance, bravery, against often gigantic odds, was valued. These engagements were subsumed in a struggle of life and death—the killing of other creatures or the wounding, incapacitation, or death of the hunter. It is no surprise to find that in most of human history (with exceptions), soldiering too has been a male activity.

## SIGNS OF THE HUNT

The circumstantial case for the cave imagery's link to the male activity of hunting is weak. Here are images of big, dangerous game; but where are the images of hunting itself? A largely missing element of the society of the period is the connection between the human figures and weapons.[69] Yet there are hints of killing and the hunt shown by slashes, lines, and points driven through some of the cave imagery. One interpretation holds that these are intended as wounds, darts, spears, or arrows. Such marks have also been found on the Upper Paleolithic mobiliary art.[70] In many statues, though, it is difficult to tell whether a mark is a separate object such as a spear, or is a sign denoting the length of the animal's fur or its color.[71] The marks may also be signs of environmental phenomena, such as the direction of the wind. Another interpretation holds that they are magical eminences, vectors of power or force, either erupting from an animal or penetrating it.

It is also interesting that most of the animals are shown in profile, not from the rear or head-on. This cannot be purely an artistic convention. To attack a grazing or a predatory animal from the front is obviously the strategy of least efficiency and most danger. In addition, the flanking shot would be most likely to impact a vital organ.

Consider an image that suggests such an iconography of hunting. This speared bison was drawn on a wall of the Niaux cave near Foix in southern France, whose paintings are thought to date from about 14,000 to 12,000 B.C.E.[72] [**Fig. 6**] What are we to make of the straight and diagonal lines superimposed on the creature's body? Through the hunter's eyes we see a very healthy animal, its back ridged with the fat of autumn, marking it as a choice prize. Arrows hit the side, chest region, where an impact that crashed through the rib cage would be most likely to pierce a vital organ. In the original, the second, wider point is lighter in color. Several conventions are possible. Perhaps the second spear has impacted on the other side of the animal; or, it could be deeply imbedded in the flank—the killing blow. The short arrows thus may score deep hits while the longer ones may have only grazed the hide.

The spears of the time could be deadly; one researcher deduced from their exit points that they were "shaped so that they can pierce the hide of an animal, penetrate muscles and internal organs, and inflict a life-threatening wound."[73] Notably, the Niaux bison is surrounded by the parts and bodies of other bison and a horse, some of which also contain arrows. Was this a "kill"? We know from the archeofaunal record that the ancient bison was a larger creature than its modern descendant. A healthy bull, such as the one depicted here, could easily weigh 2,000 pounds and measure 12 feet in length; they were fleet-footed animals, capable of climbing rocky ground easily, jumping across wide ditches with a stride of up to 11 feet. They were "brave and strong, difficult to surprise and kill."[74] A series of accurate, deep spear hits would have been required to bring a healthy bull down.

If these signs on the cave scene are weapons, they would signify the teamwork required by multiple hunters to corner and kill such a great beast. The spears have all impacted in a rough line, suggesting a unity of effort, a sort of firing squad or ambushing team. The different colorings may also suggest a third dimension, the lighter colored dart hitting from the other side. This implies regulation and coordination between men, to fire at the same time and to hit roughly the same area. If these were vectors of power, the interpretation would differ little. Either the bull is being impacted by shafts that operate like spears, or it is releasing lines of force from open wounds in its body.

However such beasts were brought down, it must have involved teamwork—men operating not as independent agents but cooperative killers. All hunting involves, besides physical skills, social organization. The megafauna of the Upper Paleolithic were dangerous beasts, whether hunted as individuals or as a herd. The hunters developed systems of tactical command, control, coordination, and communication. From these demands arose the genesis of leadership and ca-maraderie. That such a system focused on killing without hesitation or mercy should not be forgotten. The art suggests that in the hunting experience, man developed the techniques that would serve him equally well in battle against other men. As we shall see, in rock art the hunting party marching to seek out game and the war party in procession to battle are visually indistinguishable—and indeed the same resources and frames of mind may drive and sustain both activities.

## THE COMMUNAL IDEAL

Hunting and warfare reward both individual skill and cooperation with oth-ers. Recreating the training of the American Indian hunters of the Great Plains for the buffalo drives (where herds of animals were stampeded by groups of people, including women, off cliffs), anthropologist Thomas Kehoe explains:

> These communal hunts were planned, and usually they were preceded by ceremonies to increase the chances of success. During the communal hunt, individual hunting was prohibited. Chance was minimized in communal hunting through the prehunt ceremonies which taught the skilled partic-ipants exact, prescribed drive methods. The difficult feat of manipulating and luring a herd of animals into a trap at a prearranged spot was carefully plotted.[75]

Descriptions by ethnographers of such ceremonies and practices among bison hunters are common.[76] The identical nature of the training for a military cam-paign is self-evident; cognitive and physical skills that allowed better cooperation were obviously survival skills in hunting bison just as they are in attacking a fortified machine-gun post. Victory, however, was not the capture of scalps, the

(overleaf)
6. Wounded bison, Niaux cave, near Foix, France (date not certain; perhaps c. 12,780 to 14,050 B.C.E.).
Photo: Jean Vertut

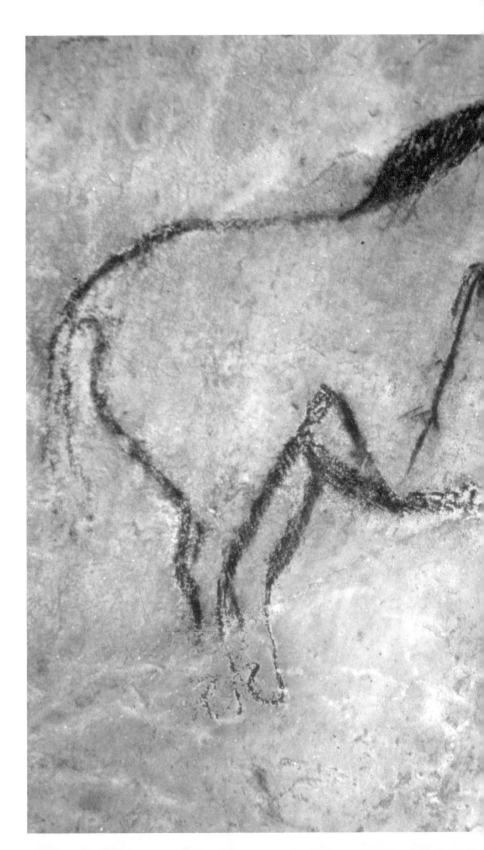

sack of a city, or the securing of a grid square, but meat, the coin of survival. Thus, we have a social version of man's Janus face: the link between community bonding and mass killing, with conflict not the antithesis of cooperation but its foundation.

The evidence of fossilized bones tells this story. George Frison, an archeologist who spent a lifetime researching and in some cases reenacting the hunting heritage of the Paleo-Indians in the North American Plains, has identified several cases where he associates ritual activity and bison jumps.[77] In one 1,700-year-old site in Wyoming, Frison found a small complex near a drive corral that was apparently roofed by bison skulls. He hypothesized that the structure, which contained no remains of domestic use, was employed for religious purposes associated with the hunt. Other evidence of shamanistic activity has been found in a bison kill site dated to about 10,000 years ago.[78] The importance of ritual was of relevance to the kill itself but also to the ordering of the social structure that allowed the collective action of individuals to result in a successful animal drive. The drives were associated not only with the kill, but with a large temporary outdoor production line of butchering and processing the meat.[79]

Such communal activity implied organizational structure and hierarchical leadership. As Frison argues:

> Communal hunting reflects the need for some kind of temporary authority in order to ensure success since a careful coordination of activities of a number of individuals was necessary in order to locate a buffalo herd of proper size, maneuver it into proper position, stampede it into the corral, and then kill the animals. At any of the stages, except possibly the last, the possibility of failure of the venture was always present.[80]

Any expedition, from a small cadre of kin-based hunters to the larger alliances of families suggested by the animal drives, would have required an authority: a leader. American Indians in the buffalo hunt, while stressing the importance of communal planning and executing of the attack, still required a single man "to guide the animals in the right direction [who] was held responsible for [any] failure."[81] Attributes of wealth familiar to us—such as money and land—were absent as rewards for such leadership. In this activity, however, we see the origins of the stricter hierarchies that were developed in sedentary village life in the Neolithic, later in the ancient civilizations, and through to the present day.[82] In the leadership of the small band of hunters or the larger group of drivers, we find the first instances of military-type command and castes.

What does such social organization suggest about the art itself, and its relationship to what may be called the first war, the war on nature? Within the record from the last century of patterns in the rich hunting areas of Africa, there are reports from, among others, the missionary Stanley Livingstone, that hunters would deploy to prearranged locations, waiting for game to pass by.[83] Notably, only in areas of rich, diverse populations of game is such a strategy regularly successful; we know that the Franco-Cantabrian region was just such a location. Intriguingly, even in regions of less faunal plenty, hunters can burn down the tree cover and create an artificial boom in small plant growth that attracts small animals, which they can in turn hunt.

These patterns of social organization and hierarchy underscore the importance of community in the hunt. A great deal of social science research in the last fifty years has concentrated on the effects of "groupness" on people. The utility of groups, in offense and defense, in procuring the basic substance of life, is apparent in the animal kingdom as well. Studies of bird[84] and primate behavior[85] suggest that information transfer is one of the crucial elements of group cohesion and a benefit of living in a community. No individual has total knowledge of the world, hence the utility of a group, where one learns not only by ostensible messages passed between members, such as birds' calls, or language and visual imagery among humans, but also by direct observation of fellow members. Birds in a flock, for example, will often learn of food and bodies of water by observing and following other birds from the same flock. Likewise, the youthful human hunter, artisan, or army recruit can be trained not only by listening to his veteran elders but by observing them as well.

Visual imagery is an extension of the individual, but it is also a projection available to inspection by an entire community; it acts as an intermediary between the character of the self and the group. A picture on a cave wall served as a source of community, a shared vision of the important goals of daily existence in the Ice Age. That those shared, visualized goals included the killing of big game tells us much about what was important to that community, just as our television screens reflect the chief concerns of the mainstream culture (or, to be more accurate, what is important to the power-holders in a society, past and present). In this way, too, the images were a technological innovation. From that moment, our ancestors had an avenue besides language and gesture through which to exchange ideas with other individuals. Of course, interpretations of the images would vary, but perhaps less so in such tightly knit kinship groups, or between hunter families that shared an identical visual world and life experience. For the first time in history a man could actually "see" what another man meant about something—significantly, an animal that he wanted to kill—which was not physically in front of him, but only projected onto a medium.

Finally, the features of the animals served as a grammar of key signs of the environment and the battles to come. The exaggerated and distinct horns in many paintings, for example, may signify the animal's state of health and its sex.[86] In addition, focusing on certain characteristic parts of the animal such as the head and back would allow hunters to recognize animals from a distance.[87] For the paleoartists, the genius (and the genus) was in the details, such as the arc of the horns, the slant of the nose, the curve of the haunch. To this end, one writer commented that if someone erased the entire bodies of the bison on the walls of the Altamira cave in northern Spain, an experienced hunter would be able to recognize the creature by its hooves alone.[88] Such cues and rewards are sought out by the eye of the hunter in an effort to control his world and feed his family. Entire communities of the Ice Age peoples shared this vision and the values that shaped it.[89]

## MEGAFAUNA "OVERKILL" AND THE GENESIS OF WAR

The vision of the Upper Paleolithic is the prologue to the rest of the story of organized human aggression. Pictures which, on their surface, appear to be utterly placid and devoid of any signs of human combat are actually traces of humanity's first and oldest violent struggle: that with nature. Moreover, the images present the first stage in developments of warfare. These include the importance of small-group cohesion; the stalking, ambush, and driving of an enemy; the attack on the flank; the rituals and tacit knowledge of war-related skills; the spirit of training and discipline; and the vitality that must infuse the soldier. Here too is the macho celebration of the "big kill." This early, primal vision of hunting was simply transferred to battles fought against other men once the large herds of herbivores and competing predators had been destroyed near the end of the Upper Paleolithic. As humankind turned to agriculture and horticulture, as populations increased and became more sedentary, as great hierarchies developed and lasting wealth was accumulated, as rivalries for land and other resources increased, men turned the tools and the ideals of the war against nature to the war against other men on a much larger, more systematic basis.[90]

The results of the war on megafauna are invisible because we do not see what is missing from the landscape. The turn-of-the-century Welsh naturalist Alfred Wallace observed, "We live in a zoologically impoverished world, from which all the hugest, and fiercest, and strangest forms have recently disappeared. . . . [I]t is surely a marvelous fact . . . this sudden dying out of so many large Mammalia, not in one place only but over half the land surface of the globe."[91] In 1967, researcher Paul Martin explained this phenomenon based on a chilling observation: in every place on earth where human beings first arrived during the post–Ice Age period, large mammals died out rapidly. Moreover, almost unprecedented in the history of evolution and extinction, the large *species* (animals with a common gene pool that can interbreed) and *genera* (groups of interrelated species, such as mammoths and mastodons) of mammalian herbivores and carnivores became extinct without other creatures filling their ecological niches.[92] In all, 72 percent of existing large animal species in North America became totally extinct at the end of the Ice Age.[93]

In Europe and most of North Asia, the extinction of the great creatures was associated with increased human population, but the centerpiece of Martin's case is the Americas. When the Spanish conquistadors arrived riding horses in the early sixteenth century, the native peoples had never encountered the equine or imagined such a use for an animal; they were, until the arrival of Europeans, a pedestrian culture. Many tribes, especially in the north-central plains, readily adapted their subsistence patterns and folkways (including their style of war) to this new creature. The horse, however, as well as other animals including mammoths, giant beavers, sloths, and saber-toothed cats, had previously existed in the New World.

Martin suggests a scenario he titles the "blitzkrieg." The first Americans found a continent that, like the Franco-Cantabria, was full of large game. However, unlike the animals of the European, African, and Asian regions which long ago became wary of men, the megafauna of the New World had no experience avoiding human hunters. As their population rapidly increased, the Clovis people (known collectively by their particularly powerful spear), Martin theorizes, spread out from the Bering Sea to the tip of South America, killing large animals as they went. This expansion need not have been precipitous. A mere 1 to 2 percent growth rate in population, expanding sixteen kilometers per year, would have easily conquered all of the Americas in less than a millennium. In this model, Martin described human beings as superefficient predators who saw no reason to stop killing plentiful game, nor felt any compunction to engage in conservation. The Paleo-Indian hunters "preferred killing and persisted in killing animals as long as they were available." Unsurprisingly, the genera of megamammals that existed at the time which are now extinct are specifically the big game that would have been targeted by hunters (or competed with hunters) for food.

Martin's thesis has generated controversy to this day, but has found many champions, ranging from the anthropologist Jared Diamond to the sociobiologist Edward Wilson.[94] As Diamond notes, the best evidence for human culpability in the extinctions is negative. Islands like New Zealand and Madagascar, which underwent human predation last, were also the final stands of the archaic giants. The north and south islands that make up New Zealand today, for example, were apparently uninhabited by humans before the arrival of the Polynesians about the year 1000. Their ecosystem was dominated by moas—giant flightless birds, relatives of ostriches and emus—that grew up to 12 feet in height. When the Europeans first arrived in the 1700s, they found beds of bone assemblages that resembled the kill sites of the Americas and Europe; also, the culture of the native Maori people was permeated with tales of heroic moa-hunting. The fauna that the Europeans discovered in New Zealand was extremely impoverished and devoid of any large creatures, including the unfortunate moa; the only mammals were two species of bats.[95]

Another piece of evidence in favor of the overkill hypothesis is ethnographic.

Aboriginal peoples, if given the opportunity for an easy kill or if suddenly enabled with superior killing technology, do not hesitate to use it with destructive
efficiency. One case was that of the Ihalmiut people, who at the turn of the
twentieth century hunted caribou in north-central Canada and numbered about
7,000 people.[96] In these frozen barrens, which seem inhospitable to human life,
the People of the Deer carved out a proud and independent existence. Though
they only employed weapons made of antlers, bone, ivory, and stone, each year
they were able to cull enough game from the great migrating herds during the
summer and early autumn months to survive the devastating winters. The Ihalmiut would seem to have been an example of a native people who were "in
balance" with the land. Even though they did not overexploit the deer, the
Ihalmiut had no word for hunger in their language.

The destruction of the Ihalmiut, their culture, and their ecosystem began
when white merchants started trading them guns and bullets for the prized furs
of the white fox. An Ihalmiut with a rifle could kill in minutes what would have
taken weeks using bow and spear. Within a few years, the People of the Deer
abandoned their former hunting techniques, forgot how to construct traditional
weapons, and no longer trained how to use them. Thus the trap was set for the
hunters as well as the hunted. When the market for white fox collapsed, the
traders left. Without bullets the guns were useless, but no one knew how to
return to the old ways. Moreover, in the days of the gun, the Ihalmiut and other
neighboring peoples had conducted a great slaughter of the reindeer herds.
Whereas before the natives had a good chance of encountering at least one of
many migrating herds, now a single trail of reindeer moved on the land; when
the Ihalmiut missed it, they starved. This and the diseases that opportunistically
followed hunger reduced their numbers so that by the late 1940s only a few
dozen of the people of the barrens remained. That this was a great crime by the
traders and the Canadian government is certain, but the lesson of relevance to
our study is that the Ihalmiut enthusiastically took up the new technology of
overkill with no regard for the long-term results. This is a trait of mankind,
primitive and modern.

Thus may have been the mechanism that ended the Old Stone Age. Certainly,
the overkill hypothesis has its detractors. Perhaps the aridization of much of the
world at the end of the Upper Paleolithic 13,000 to 11,000 years ago was the
primary cause of the disappearance of large mammals. Moreover, the Clovis
people may not have been newcomers; in the Americas, sites of human habitation provisionally dated to before 13,000 years ago have been found. Yet Clovis
may have represented a technological advancement or a cultural shift rather than
human immigration. The climatic changes set off increasing competition among
Paleo-Indians for dwindling big-game resources. Increasingly efficient human
hunters sought dwindling populations of big game and the result was the ani-

mals' extinction. This spiral of speciescide may have occurred throughout the world at the end of the Upper Paleolithic. However, criticism of the overkill hypothesis misses the point. That human beings were not in all cases successful in wiping out entire fauna from any given area does not mean that they did not try, regardless of the consequences. As the case of New Zealand illustrates, when entering an area, human beings exploit the environment to its limits and beyond. They kill whatever is easiest to kill, and plan no more than a season into the future.

Nor does it mean that every single aurochs, cave bear, giant sloth, and mammoth was hunted down and killed. All species have a minimum viable population: if the number of individuals falls below this level, the species has no chance of survival.[97] This apparently is the case of the mammoth and mastodons of North America, which became extinct by about 9000 B.C.E.; these animals disappeared from Europe by 10,000 B.C.E. and from Siberia at about 8000 B.C.E.,[98] but survived in a dwarf form—isolated from human hunting—on Wrangel Island, in the Arctic Ocean northeast of Siberia, until almost 2000 B.C.E.[99] The bones of individuals dated to the time of the extinction of the species, about 11,000–10,000 years ago, show no signs of being victims of climate change, that is, of the disappearance of their food stocks. They were "fat, fit and well fed."[100]

But one unusual feature is evident in the tusks of the females, where growth patterns reveal intervals between live births. Studies of African elephants have shown that females under stress because of high rates of predation by humans respond by giving birth more frequently; they are trying to make up for losses. The last mastodon and mammoth females show clear signs of this sort of birthing stress. Since they were healthy in every other respect, the only independent variable that may have caused them to step up their rates of pregnancy must have been the pressure by human hunters. This pressure, of course, may have come about because arid conditions were making the human inhabitants also more desperate for food; hunting pushed the vulnerable megamammals to extinction.[101]

Indeed, evidence that the activities of early humans sometimes had unanticipated large-scale negative impacts on their environment is accumulating from many regions. Climate researcher Gifford Miller and his colleagues have reconstructed the rate of rainfall over the last 150,000 years from field evidence around Lake Eyre, in central Australia.[102] They found that the amount of rainfall declined sharply after the arrival of human beings some 60,000 years ago. Their experimental tests as well suggest that aboriginal burning of vegetation may have been one cause of this decrease. The ancient, low-relief landscape of Australia is the most nutrient-depleted in the world and may have been particularly sensitive to burning by early immigrants, with the nutrients released lost to wind and water erosion. Finally, at about the same time that the rainfall weakened, all of the largest marsupials of Australia became extinct, and as most browsed on vegetation, conversion of tree/shrubland to desert scrub may have inadvertently led both to the extinction of animals and to the area's becoming desert.

The same apparently is true of the surface of Easter Island; its once dense forests were destroyed by the Polynesians who colonized the island.[103] Such cases also suggest the ambiguity of the term "natural." So much of the world we see around us was shaped by the predation on flora and fauna of primitive man that we mistake it somehow for a natural, non-man-made existence. It is a distinction without a difference. The clear-cutting of an entire continent and the extinction of an entire species have a similar result, whether it is by the hand of a primitive tribesman holding a spear and a firebrand or a rancher riding a bulldozer.

A final example, an overkill in miniature, is found in the archeofaunal records from one island in the California channel. Eight hundred years ago, pre-contact Indian people settled, and within a decade exterminated almost all creatures of land and sea nearby. The ethnobiologist who studied this tediously familiar exercise in human consumption noted:

> The evidence on this island shows that any species that these people could get their hands on—if it were vulnerable—suffered. It's not an attack on Indians. It's a statement about human beings in all times and all places. I think we are so disappointed by ourselves, about what we as a culture have done to the environment, we would like to think that someone has been more responsible. We want a moral example and Indians fit the bill.[104]

That the aborigines and natives were not more admirable than we are is disappointing but unremarkable. As Edward Wilson has noted in assessing the long record of extinctions brought about by human beings in the past, the ethos we still practice is: "What counts is food today, a healthy family, and tribute for the chief, victory celebrations, rites of passage, feasts."[105]

Today, we are exterminating large and small creatures and poisoning and paving over habitats at an alarming rate. At this time, with the earth's population at about 6 billion, there exists roughly 1 hectare (10,000 square meters, or 2.471 acres) of non-desert, uncultivated land for every person on earth. Only 29.4 percent of the earth's surface consists of land classified as being in a state of nature.[106] As our population increases, this quasi-natural area is destined to decline, perhaps precipitously. We are in fact the only species that by predation alone can cause another species to become extinct.[107] If we want to arrest this destruction, we cannot look to the tribal peoples or their art as offering alternatives or solutions; there we see only a reflection of our own impulses in the war on nature.

This accounts for why small, young, and weak beasts—not to mention insects, vegetation, and almost everything else—are missing from the illustrated menu of the choicest dishes of the Upper Paleolithic. Every vision of war is guided partly by a system of values that defines the honor, glory, and prestige of the warrior. The big game—the fat, healthy bison, horses, aurochs, mammoths, and deer—were the grand prizes, the ones that delivered the maximum payback in terms of weight of food and nutrition, but also brought the greatest praise upon the hunter and his "team." It was, then, precisely because the Upper Paleolithic was an affluent society that the hunters expended considerable time, effort, and resources to portray those beasts that, by their reckoning, brought the most honor to kill.

But meat is not the only measure of man. As one anthropologist has noted, "modern human teeth show no obvious adaptation to specific foods."[108] We are the ultimate dietary generalists. Although in Western civilization meat has been considered a staple of existence, other cultures have derived most of their protein intake from creatures unlikely to leave any trace in the archeological record: insects.[109] Such omnivorous tendencies are a powerful survival tool. In contrast, specialization is the "tender trap of evolutionary opportunism."[110] Specialization occurs when a creature overcommits its survival to the exploitation of a single food or habitat resource. Modern examples are the koala, which eats only eucalyptus leaves, and the giant panda, which depends entirely on bamboo shoots. In the short term—and this may be thousands of years—species thus specialized can thrive, yet they live in a perilous state. If, for example, as is happening in China, the bamboo forests disappear with the encroachment of human cities, roads, and agriculture, then the specialized panda is doomed.

Because humans are omnivorous, it follows that we are omnibehavioral as well. In examining the Ice Age and its imagery, we do not find Jean-Jacques Rousseau's "noble savage," nor do we see Calibans "not honoured with human shape." Rather, especially in Franco-Cantabria, the Janus face of man is revealed: man the creator of beauty was also man the killer. Human beings can be found living in the arctic wastes hunting reindeer and caribou, or shopping in grocery markets in Manhattan, or planting rice knee-deep in the paddies of Thailand. We can survive in the foothills of the Himalayas, the jungles of the Amazon, on a Los Angeles highway at rush hour. But more than this, our behavior can be modified not simply to fit the environment but to shape it. Our ancestors lived in open camps—venturing into caves to create art and for other reasons—and kept fires at the entrance to warm themselves and to keep out predators; we now live in houses and, with a minor adjustment to the thermostat dial, alter the room temperature to our exact comfort.[111] Individuals, even entire nations, may not adapt, but the human race can, though perhaps at the cost of all other species.

Moreover, drastic changes may occur even in the individual; an accountant can, with training, become a fierce warrior. Likewise, a soldier may wage war for years, but eventually return to his tranquil farm. It is part of our range of behaviors that we can cooperate with, challenge, or destroy our natural enemies and each other. The big-game hunts of the Upper Paleolithic were a microcosm of such warlike behavior—cooperation and killing, altruism and ruthlessness, the egalitarianism of shared dangers and the male prestige cult of the "big kill." In the training, the ritual celebrations, the bonding, the tracking, stalking, and the killing of elusive, mobile big game, we fought a war—one of life or death. The lessons learned about the importance of teamwork, timing, training, cunning, leadership, bonding, and achieving a communal vision of goals continue for warriors of all eras. The world of the Upper Paleolithic was not unconnected to our own; we are its progeny.

# 2

---

# PRIMITIVE WAR

## THE NEW FACE OF WAR

In Australia's northern Arnhem Land, about 10,000 years ago images began to appear that showed duels between individual men.[1] [**Fig. 7**] These constitute the oldest scenes of interhuman combat thus uncovered. They suggest a global phenomenon of increasing competition for scarce resources. The environment was deteriorating, once fertile areas were growing more arid, and big game was disappearing. In later stages, advancing toward historic times but still before contact with Europeans and state-based societies, human conflicts evolved, with large groups depicted in battle. In this early example, about 6,000 years old, a total of 68 warriors are painted on a cliff face. Certain universal conventions of war are present. First, there are two "sides": the figures are divided into distinct groups, facing each other. Second, they are almost all armed with spears and stone axes. Third, there is differentiation between the ranks of the combatants. Those in the front of both armies have different clothing (or larger heads) than those in the rear; they are likely the leaders of the battle line. Most important, this is not mock combat, or ritual play between compatriots. Spears are suspended in midflight, about to impact. The "commander" of the right army is wounded, pierced by one spear with others about to hit him. Unlike the nature portraits of the Ice Age, whose connection to human violence is only inferred, this Australian painting is unambiguously a picture of war.

Such images were produced in another era, by a different society and ethos, than the cave paintings of the Franco-Cantabria and the Upper Paleolithic. The last glaciers receded from mainland Europe and North America about 12,000 years ago. In their wake, the environment changed; the world became hotter and drier, the sea levels rose. Within a thousand years, most of the megafauna depicted in cave art disappeared from the northern hemisphere. Human predation, overkilling, and culling played a significant role in these extinctions and continued wherever human hunters arrived. At the same time, the New World occasioned new folkways. The caves (and their wall art) were largely abandoned.

7. Rock painting, Arnhem Land region of Northern Territory of Australia (date unknown; likely c. 4000 B.C.E.).
*Photo: Paul S. C. Taçon, Australian Museum*

THE AUSTRALIAN MUSEUM

Populations spread north and east. The subject matter of the art of the period no longer centers on the big mammals but on men (and women). Moreover, while not a single image dated to the Upper Paleolithic shows interhuman combat, such imagery becomes commonplace during these new, harsher times.

Why did organized warfare flourish? What evidence from bones, tools, and art do we have about the new ways of war, their scale and causes? What role did imagery have in reflecting and affecting these processes? The focus of our gaze here is on a type of human social grouping rather than a definite era. The prehistoric period encompasses the Middle Stone Age (the Mesolithic, beginning in Europe about 12,000 years ago), the New Stone Age (Neolithic, starting c. 4000 B.C.E.), to the rise of great cities, agriculturally based hierarchical civilizations, and nations as the dominant mode of human life. The onset of urbanism is variable, because the development of human settlement patterns did not follow the same routes or clock everywhere. The city of Jericho in the Near East, for example, was first encircled by stone walls, probably as a defensive measure, around 6000 B.C.E.[2] In parts of the Americas, Australia, Polynesia, and Africa, the Stone Age endured until the arrival of the Europeans in the fifteenth century and onward, and is better known as the "precontact" era.

The social groups of the so-called primitive (not a pejorative in this case) peoples were tribal societies. These are defined by what they are not: the conglomeration of people into urban centers; the extreme stratification and hierarchization of society, with kings and peasants, warriors and priests, merchants and craftsmen; the erection of monumental architecture and art; and the prevalence of organized warfare on a massive scale. In the ancient "civilized" world, entire societies accorded considerable resources to building weapons and supplying armies, fighting and conquering their neighbors, and engaging in battles not on the scale of the individual or family group but in tens of thousands of armed men on either side.

The "war before civilization," as anthropologist Thomas Keeley has written, can be studied as a subject in itself.[3] But in considering war among tribal societies, we can also dispel one of the most prevalent and delusional visualized myths of our own age. The exposition of this myth is widespread, from the effusions of new-age prophets to Hollywood films like *Dances With Wolves, Pocahontas,* and the latest version of *Last of the Mohicans.* All three films show inter-Indian and intra-Indian violence, but in each case it is the arrival of the white man that sets off the brutality. Even the darkest character of the films— Magua in *Last of the Mohicans,* a sinister figure who commits appalling acts of butchery—is no natural-born killer: it turns out that his children were slain by other Indians in the employ of the British. Thus, when he tells a French commander of his intention to continue killing—"Magua took the hatchet to color with blood. It's still bright. Only when it's red, then it will be buried"—it is a cry of aggrievement: he is a victim. So Nathaniel, the white man raised by Indians, demands of the Huron war chief in *Mohicans*, "Would the Huron kill every man, woman and child of their enemies? Those are the ways of the Yankees and the français traders, their masters in Europe infected with the sickness of greed. Magua's heart is twisted. He would make himself into what twisted him [i.e., the white man]." Likewise, the Disneyfied shaman of *Pocahontas*'s tribe proclaims: Europeans "are not men like us. . . . They prowl the earth like ravenous wolves, consuming everything in their path."

This portrayal is a product of our disgust with the destruction of nature and the bloodshed wrought by the civilizations from which we descended. Observing our own century of trench warfare, death camps, ever-sprawling suburbs, poisoned wetlands, devastated rain forests, mercury-stained oceans, and collapsing biodiversity, we project onto the tribal peoples a face of interhuman peace and genteel ecohumanism, the myth of the "green native," the primitive tribesperson spiritually in touch with the natural world, respecting it, not overtaxing its resources, in tune with the "colors of the wind." And indeed, some present-day primitive groups, living on the fringes of the industrial world or trapped in small, impoverished pockets, have shown their ability to survive without destroying the flora and fauna with which they share space. They also have avoided warfare as we know it. But as art, the evidence of archeology, and protohistorical tradition testify, these are peripheral (and recent) exceptions to a general rule. As we have seen in the previous chapter, tribal peoples have exhibited no less destructiveness of the natural world than have we—only our scientific ignorance and political discomfort has kept this fact obscured. Primitives have left the bones and scorched earth to prove that they had and have no less inclination for genocidal warfare and violence than do civilized peoples of contemporary and previous eras. The difference is in scale, not performance. We can look at primitive war not as an example of an alternative to our own way of war, but rather as its first flowering.

## LETHAL SOCIETIES

In Europe, the Mesolithic era lasted to about 4000 B.C.E. It is during this time that, in contrast to all the ages of human and humanlike creatures before, two new trends occur in the record of fossil remains. First, we have many discoveries of people who were unambiguously killed by weapons; there is ample evidence of murder and massacre.[4] Second, the ratio of male deaths to female tilts dramatically: whereas before, women made up a modest preponderance of violent deaths, now men account for 80 percent.[5] Both of these trends suggest an increasing frequency and regularity of violence. In the ethnographic record, such biased mortality reflects greater numbers of young men dying in battles.[6] Gender preference is also confirmed by significant absences in the visual imagery of the later stone ages; there are no figures of female warriors or weapons carriers in any of the art of the tribal era. In fact, the maleness of tribal warriors is typically emphasized by the visual convention of bulging muscles and huge, erect penises.

The major question about the early visions of human war, however, is: to what extent was it warfare as we know it? This is a difficult problem both to define and to answer from the visual evidence alone. Within the anthropological literature, "ritual war" is described as low-level, low-intensity combat, in which the object is generally to display bravery to a traditional enemy and to one's own group. Such "showing off" in warlike displays, which do not necessarily lead to war, or mock battles with low casualties, is a behavior of many uncivilized peoples. In the Americas, for example, among one period in the history of the Crow Indians it was "meritorious to kill an enemy, but the lightest tap with a coupstick was reckoned higher. Obviously the idea was not primarily to reduce a hostile force but to execute a 'stunt.' "[7] Similarly, Saukamapee, a Cree Indian, in 1787 described a "battle" with the Shoshone that took place almost half a century earlier:

> Both parties made a great show of their numbers, and I thought that they were more numerous than ourselves. After some singing and dancing, they sat down on the ground, and placed their large shields before them, which covered them. . . . Our iron headed arrows did not go through their shields, but stuck in them. On both sides several were wounded, but none lay on the ground; and night put an end to the battle, without a scalp being taken on either side, and in those days such was the result, unless one party was more numerous than the other.[8]

Another potentially confusing aspect of tribal war is that the society may seem overtly militaristic, yet not actually engage in warfare. The anthropologist Avi Almagor notes, for example, that the reputedly "fierce" Magay tribe of East Africa has both warrior organizations and long-standing feuds with neighboring tribes.[9] The warrior organizations have an internal leadership hierarchy, engage in rituals and celebrations, and utilize imagery and symbolism that exalt their machismo, *esprit de corps*, and warrior status. Yet in many cases these are superficial attributes, employed more for purposes of show and deterrence than in aggressive engagement. Their fierceness may be facade rather than reality; they strut, rally, and pound shields, but engage in few battles. Our dilemma as viewers is that such displays, lacking accompanying written sources or anthropological reports, would look much like preparation for and conduct of warfare.

Without ethnographic accounts and testimonies of men like Saukamapee, a rock art image of such battles would look lethal enough. How, then, do we analyze visual images of "war" without written histories to explain them? For example, this is a scene from rock paintings of the Gasulla Gorge in what is now Cástellón, Spain.[10] [**Fig. 8**] Its date is uncertain, but it most likely comes from the Neolithic era, about 6,000 years ago. The question is, who are these men? Are they dancers, hunters, or warriors? Is this a prancing display or a march to war, or both? Is the first man in line a shaman or a drill sergeant, or, again, both? How can we tell play warfare from real war? This is not an esoteric question. War is in the eye of the beholder, but for our purposes the kinds of wars that were fought matter very much. Do we see in the imagery of the prehistoric, pre-contact era pictures of war or what the Romans called "kiss and clang"? If the latter, then we must look beyond the Neolithic and the Mesolithic for the ascent of true, territorial, genocidal warfare between peoples.

The question is even more relevant if we are concerned with the political reality behind the visions of war. In the last ten years, some researchers have advocated—much like the "Indian contact with white men" movies listed above—that we regard tribal warfare almost totally as the product not of universal human attributes or general environmental pressures, but rather as arising from the impact of expanding states, especially the European colonial powers.[11] The mechanics of this impact are as follows. A state-based society enters a new area, undermining and breaking up the networks of alliance and trade that existed among the pre-contact tribal groups. In addition, some tribes are pushed off their land, forcing them to fight with neighboring tribes for reduced space. Often the state-based societies' representatives bring with them diseases to which the tribal people are not immune, as well as plants and animals that disrupt the native ecosystem. Finally, even if the outsiders are more benign

8. Five archers (or dancers) marching, rock painting, El Cingle shelter, Gasulla, Castellón, Spain (date unknown; perhaps c. 4000 B.C.E.).
*After D. Mazonowicz, 1974*

and only interested in trade, such trade—which is usually for guns—upsets the power balance and the systems of value and work of the tribal people.

The Americas seem to be a classic case of this deadly contact. In Central and South America, conquests of tribal groups were accompanied by plagues, enslavement, destruction of the aboriginal cultures, and the destabilization of existing polities. In North America, introduction of firearms, gradual displacement by colonists, and competition for trade goods such as beaver pelts inaugurated fratricidal wars among the tribal people. One researcher who focuses on these disruptions suggests that "genocidal warfare," where one group assaults, slaughters, and destroys another, was an offspring of European contact.[12] Pre-contact aggression, in this scenario, was lower-level, and largely ritual in nature—play war.[13] Other researchers who take a less extreme view still stress that it was contact with the expanding European states that precipitated the increased level of violence in the "tribal zone."[14] One of the leading proponents of this view, R. Brian Ferguson, argues that "the wild violence noted by Hobbes was not an expression of 'man in the state of nature' but a reflection of contact with Hobbes's Leviathan—the states of western Europe. To take the [post-contact] carnage as revealing the fundamental nature of human existence is to pass through the looking glass."[15] Furthermore, this genocidal warfare effect occurred almost immediately and spread rapidly throughout the Americas from nearly the first moment of Columbus's arrival.[16]

Theories of tribal war that minimize its scope and lethality or blame excesses on the influence of contact with colonial Western or urban-centralized civilizations have an intrinsic and traditional appeal to anthropologists. As Keith Otterbein has pointed out, "not one important anthropologist has devoted more than a small fraction of his [or her] professional life to the study of warfare."[17] He suggests three possible reasons for this extraordinary fact. First, when anthropologists began the in-depth investigation of tribal people in the late nineteenth century, the tribal era was already declining, and all tribes to some extent had been affected by contact with encroaching civilizations, both native and Western. Second, anthropologists avoided studying war because they morally opposed it. Third, many of the small tribes the anthropologists observed in the field had long before given up their warrior folkways; notably, this occurred under the management of colonial powers. In addition, an uncharitable outsider might conclude, though Otterbein does not, that this failure of vision was due to willful blindness: the anthropologists wanted to promote a view that man is, by nature, a peaceful creature. The result of this hundred-year dearth of studying tribal war is that the ethnographic record is skewed against both recording primitive war and exploring its causes, institutions, and effects. Any generalization that most primitive tribes do not fight wars must be viewed through this prism of politically motivated suppression and falsification.

Indeed, it is now clear that the tribal zone theory fails accurately to describe early societies; there is strong evidence that warfare as we know it flourished long before Columbus, and even before the rise of urban civilization itself.[18] Intergroup aggression was not an anomaly in North America but thrived for at least a thousand years before the arrival of Europeans.[19] For example, in west-central Illinois, around 1300, the homicide rate in the Indian communities was twenty times that of present-day Washington, D.C., the murder capital of America.[20] In Australia, traditional warfare between tribal groups resulted in a death rate higher than that of any European country of the last three centuries.[21] New studies of recent tribal societies also suggest that fierce, violent intergroup conflict was typical.[22]

Archeology has not only provided grisly proof of authentic interhuman warfare before the contact period but also suggested its causes. This picture shows some of the bones of over five hundred men, women, and children in Crow Creek, south-central South Dakota.[23] [**Fig. 9**] All were killed by weapons in about the year 1300, two centuries before the voyage of Columbus.

Details of the massacre are worth exploring. The attack was apparently not unexpected. The village of about fifty dwellings was ringed by stockades, earth ditches, and bastions, and stood on an imposing ridge. As expected in tribal war, in all the younger age brackets, from fifteen to thirty-four, the remains of males outnumber those of females two to one. In the older age brackets, from forty-five to fifty-nine, females outnumber males two to one. The possibility is strong that the young women were captured as trophies of war. Ninety percent of the skulls show evidence of scalping; tongues, hands, and feet were cut off as well. Finally, animal teeth marks on many bones indicate that the bodies were not immediately buried, but left strewn about the ruins of the village. This was a pre-contact case of genocide.[24]

It is difficult to look at this picture and not make a connection with other, similar photos of the aftermath of slaughters of our modern era. The Crow Creek photo is reminiscent of the marshes of Babi Yar, when in 1941 German soldiers and Ukrainian sympathizers massacred 100,000 Jews. The photo could equally recall the killing fields and alleys of Cambodia, Smyrna (Anatolia), El Mozote (El Salvador), Vukovar (Bosnia), Hama (Syria), or Rwanda. The scene of piles of human bones stripped clean, laid out in a pit, is ubiquitous in the history of war. This was not only a massacre of American Indians by other Indians, but of humans by other humans: an activity also unique among all other species of fauna on the planet.

The cause of the little holocaust on the Missouri is unknown but can be inferred. Analysis of the remains shows almost all the people killed had also suffered from several periods of extreme malnutrition. This was before the Spanish introduced the horse in North America, and long after the megamammals had disappeared. The people would have been that most wretched breed of human, the subsistence farmer. The massacre likely came at a time of increased population pressure coupled with reduced crop yields. The defensive barriers are a strong indication of ongoing hostility. That a people facing starvation invested such effort, materials, and time in fortifying their village is significant. The killing may have had an economic cause: competition for scarce resources. That does not mean that other reasons for war and mass killing were absent; honor, ethnic hatred, rivalries among chieftains, religious disputations, lust for goods and women may have all contributed to the calamity.

We have no art depicting the massacre at Crow Creek by the victims or the perpetrators. The petroglyphs and rock paintings from the period and the region, however, are similar to those from the Arnhem Land. In the "Writing-On-Stone" site, south of the Saskatchewan River on the border between Montana

9. Crow Creek site bone bed, south central South Dakota (c. 1325).
*Photo: Courtesy of P. Willey*

and Alberta, is an example of the late prehistoric ceremonial art, which persisted from about A.D. 1000 to 1700, when the introduction of the horse radically changed Northwest Plains culture and warfare. Characteristic of this art were the shield-bearing warrior motifs.[25] [**Fig. 10**] In this phase, the scenes tended to be static, showing duels between individual warriors or small groups. The warriors square off, facing each other. This is signified by the direction of the feet and the heads of the shield totems. The combatants also bear distinct weapons, raised against each other. One fighter has a different headpiece from another. Arms are upraised; it could be either the moment before combat begins or part of a ceremonial mock combat. Each opponent, strikingly, has a unique identifying motif on his shield—as do the warriors described by Homer in the *Iliad*—in this case two separate types of birds. It is a heroic portrayal of warfare.

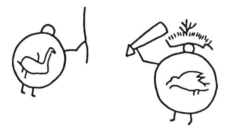

10. Shield-bearer combat scene, Writing-On-Stone site, southern Alberta, Canada (late prehistoric period, c. 1000?–1700).
*After J. Keyser, 1986*

There are no rock art images of warriors killing old women or scalping babies. This may have reflected a social compunction, such as shame, or the unimportance of such events in the more honor-bearing prestige of warfare between fighting males. The art displayed, as do all arts of war, only part of the wartime experience: the Crow Creeks, the scalping of old women, the decapitating of babies, and the rape and kidnapping of young women were not chosen for artistic depiction (presumably by the victors of the battles). Here, too, we see a link between tribal man and most of the worldwide art historical tradition. Warriors encourage the view of themselves that they idealize, typically heroism, endurance, or their own suffering. That is the definition of war that they claim as "reality."

But the rise of warfare among tribal peoples raises another important issue: why such extreme violence in the new eras? Evidence of the arrival of larger-scale warfare—lethal societies—in the Neolithic coincides with the development of sedentary agricultural existence.[26] The staking out of land and the resultant growth of property gave people something to fight for, but agriculture also allowed increases in and greater concentrations of population. Thus, wars were not necessarily dysfunctional to the human race. Most animal species could not survive fratricidal war on the scale that people have practiced it. On the other hand, human beings have shown remarkable abilities to recover the losses of war through natural and purposely increased fertility. Despite the vulnerability of females during pregnancy and the fragility of children and dependence on their parents for survival for a longer period than any other animal on the planet, human fertility for the species as a whole, if not for individuals, has defeated any attempt of war to suppress it in the greater scale.

This intensified fertility response (which failed for the mammoths) can also be seen in smaller societies. Among the aboriginal Barí of modern-day Brazil, losses of young men have been extremely high due to attacks by gun thugs hired by local ranchers and oilmen seeking to clear the land for exploitation.[27] In various battles the young men died at a very high rate trying to defend the community, the women and children. Remarriage was rapid, probably as a response to the high numbers of widows and orphaned children. The increasing death rates of men are suggestive of warfare as the cause. The smaller the society, the less able it is to recover its losses, and the closer extinction of the culture looms: the more reason then to form larger groups that can deploy bigger field forces.

Societies under threat produce males to counter the threat; hence the organization, even among so-called primitives, of lethal societies.[28] Wherever a response is called for to a threat of attack from outsiders, the sexual division of labor becomes more severe.[29] The war art was produced then for the same reason the Upper Paleolithic artists painted pictures of big, meaty game. In the Old Stone Age, the greatest immediate economic return (and consequent prestige) was bestowed on the killer of the largest protein and fat package. This was only reliably obtained by hunting; hunting required cooperation. The lower rates of homicide and intergroup violence in the Upper Paleolithic probably reflected cooperation in the killing of big game. In the tribal eras after the die-off of the great megafauna, a new factor entered the equation. In the competition for arable land and the grain and trade goods of a neighbor, war was a risky but potentially profitable enterprise. By killing their neighbors, the communities prospered, or at least survived. This was and always has been the basic impetus for a lethal society. Contact with Europeans did not instigate it, though prehistoric art may not have always showed it.

## DISCIPLINE AND DANCE

Oppositionality—two armed groups facing each other with weapons in flight—is the Arnhem Land image's clearest convention. In some ways, the invention of photography limited the scope of an artist to depict combat. Military art has produced only a handful of factual photographs and films of combat where both opposing parties are equally shown within the frame. Military, news, and documentary photography generally manages to capture only the implication of the enemy: one group of soldiers firing out of the frame at an unseen foe. This absence is not mysterious; few news photographers stand in no-man's-land with a wide-angle lens as opposing regiments collide. The only expedient is, as demonstrated in the Persian Gulf War (1990–91), to place the camera within a bomb or missile, but even then we see only the object to be destroyed. In the Arnhem Land image, the artist is able to extrapolate from a chosen angle a revelation of the battle. The two sides are parsed so that there is no doubt that they are in opposition. This makes the image easily readable, even though we cannot share the culture and the artistic heritage of the painter.

But what else is structurally implied by the opposition of groups? In the Arnhem Land battle, each "side" is moving against the other; each army has unity and unidirectionality. Although a great deal of prehistoric warfare involved not so much battles between units as duels between individual warriors, still it is obvious from this image that there was a very early conception of what modern military planners call "unit cohesion." Military historian John Keegan has written, "Inside every army is a crowd struggling to get out, and the strongest fear with which every commander lives—stronger than his fear of defeat or even of mutiny—is that of his army reverting to a crowd through some error of his making."[30] Historically, armies—from the Macedonian phalanx to the Roman *testudo* to the Napoleonic column—were combined to hold men together as much as defend them or wield them for attack.

But prehistoric armies were not, as might appear to the modern commander, purely amorphous masses. Commanders of the time would also have needed the degree of rank discipline required to achieve certain basic goals. These were, first, to gather their men to jointly attack some object; second, to stage elementary tactical maneuvers and *ruses de guerre*, such as feigned retreats and ambushes from flanks; and third, and most important, to bond the men into a cooperative fighting force.

These objectives can only be met through training. In the art of the Neolithic, the simple division into sides suggests that this basic step was achieved. But what of cohesion and tactical control? It is revealing that many students of the rock art of the Neolithic comment that it is often difficult to tell the difference between images of dance and of battle. In the Upper Paleolithic, men began to don animal costumes, developed and honed hunting tactics, and engaged in community-building rituals. Dance is an amalgamation of all of these, the most regulated and coordinated example of joint movement. In the rock drawing from the Spanish Levant mentioned previously [**Fig. 8**], the meaning is ambiguous—these could be soldiers marching to battle or a line of dancers. The figures' legs are coordinated in the same motions, their powerful thigh and calf muscles taut and

starkly defined; they march or dance literally in lockstep; each man carries a bow
and a clump of arrows; bows are held high like rifles in a modern platoon on
parade. Throughout Eurasia and Africa we see similar images. From the Indian
subcontinent there are rock paintings depicting similarly attired, attenuated, and
armed bowmen in procession.[31]

That we cannot tell whether these armed men are dancing in a ritual or
marching to battle is relevant and revealing. Each activity overlapped with the
other. As William H. McNeill has noted, the connection between dance and drill
is powerful and long-standing.[32] Moving in coordinated steps and motions of
torso, arms, and head creates a sort of "muscular bonding" that arouses a "eu-
phoric fellow feeling."

To regulate the body of the soldier necessitates three different types of training. First, the physical body—the muscles and tendons—are made to use certain
types of motions, building their strength and coordination. Second, dance trains
mind and body to work in rhythm and step with *others*—this is the objective of
military drill as well. Both subsume the principle of tacit knowing—doing something without consciously thinking about it—that is so important to athletic
achievement. Third, dance may help warriors build a "communal vision." The
anthropologist Roy Rappaport argued that for the Maring people of New Guinea,
mass displays of dancing created a cohesive symbolism that served to unify the
tribe in times of tension with neighboring groups.[33] The dances also ostenta-
tiously showed off the strength of the tribe. The value of such displays helped
recruit allies and intimidate enemies.

Dance, in other words, both creates and defines community, and as suggested,
the tribal age was the time when communities first came into lethal, organized,
and genocidal conflict. Whereas a picture can create a communal vision, dance
(like drill) produces communal action. The dancers, in their frenzy, try to reach
altered states, singing, clapping, often dressing with animal hats or masks.[34]
Dance not only trained the minds and bodies of young men for war but also
reinforced within them a sense that they were part of a community, a village, a
tribe, a band of brother warriors.

Neuroscience has recently addressed this condition. Serotonins are chemicals
in the brain that attach emotional meaning to incoming data. Manipulating
levels of serotonin through drugs such as Prozac radically alters people's moods
and even life views. But levels of serotonin can be naturally boosted by engaging
in ritualistic, repetitive motor activity. The repeated pacing, hand washing, or
other behaviors of depressed or obsessive-compulsive people may in fact be
instinctive self-treatment. Community rituals of such behavior perform a similar
function, and may promote in a Pavlovian fashion positive association between
coordinated group activity and the individual's participation. No matter how
exhausted the dancer is after the dance, or the soldier after the drill, he may be

getting "high" on the activity. Hence the exhilaration, almost joy of battle seen in the pictures of tribal warriors; they literally danced to war.

Finally, the superb muscle tone, agility, and sculpted physiques of the men in the rock art emphasizes (visually) the importance of *male* youth.[35] A basic definition of war, after all, is the mass killing of teenagers by other teenagers as directed by their elders. The emphasis on action and fitness in the art was self-generating: to be part of the warrior caste of young men was, as it is today, to be among the "few, the proud," or, as described by the recruiting motto of Rhodesia's Selous Scouts, to be "a man among men." That pride in belonging, the *esprit de corps*, is generally seen in military history as a fundamental attribute of the successful army unit. Interpreting the ideas of George Patton, British soldier and historian H. Essame summed up the feeling of many war commanders in asserting that "life in the Army, at any rate, tended to be an extension of boyhood . . . the leader must appeal to the vanity of the youthful male."[36] The young male joining the Spanish Levant warrior band, Caesar's legion, or a modern-day street gang would have felt that same projecting of loyalty in the service of violence. In this vein, the director of a program on refugee trauma commented that most of the genocidal killings in Rwanda of minority Tutsi peoples were committed by packs of teenage boys. "Young males," he lamented, "are really the most dangerous people on the planet, because they easily respond to authority and they want approval."[37] Such menacing creatures make their first appearance in the war art of the Mesolithic and Neolithic eras.

## CANNAE, PAST AND PRESENT

The cave images of the Upper Paleolithic typically showed animals in profile. To hunters, this was a fortuitous angle of view and attack: the flank was the region offering the biggest target for the spear and the most soft tissue and vulnerable organs. Associated tactics are also documented in the tribal era. One such scene is enacted in a Neolithic battle between two groups of archers at Morella la Vella, in Castellón province, eastern Spain.[38] [**Fig. 11**] An enemy is hit on two flanks, and at the center of the attacking force is the man who appears to be the leader. Such a plan of battle required personal leadership, a unified purpose, and the knowledge of the wisdom of the flank attack to trap the enemy in a crossfire. The man at center—who sports a large, distinct head covering—faces three enemies. In prehistoric combat, this central position would most likely be held by the bravest and best warrior, the leader. He would stand to receive the frontal attack of the enemy while his compatriots maneuvered to the enemy's flanks.

This double envelopment tactic is omnipresent in the history of war and achieved its prominence, in recorded history, as the most famous and influential military stratagem. On August 3, 216 B.C.E., a Roman army commanded by the rash Consul Varo met the Carthaginians under Hannibal. The latter, whose army had crossed into Italy over the Alps, decided to fight near a small Apulian town named Cannae. The Romans, on their home soil with greater numbers of infantry, were confident of victory. The Carthaginian leader, however, who had more cavalry, pinned the Romans in a frontal attack with his center, while he struck at both their flanks and rear with his more mobile troops. The Romans fell into a "sack" where they were crushed. It was the greatest defeat in the history of the republic, though the Romans eventually won the war.[39]

Cannae was perhaps one of the most important battles ever fought, not because of the issues it settled, but because the "Cannae concept" so mesmerized future generals and statesmen. It was into such a sack that war leaders throughout history have dreamed of trapping their opponents. After Cannae, all who were schooled in the arts of war, from Caesar's camp to West Point cadets, would be told of a battle in which, by a simple division of forces, one side completely annihilated the other. In Hans Delbrück's history of the battle, the lesson drawn for a generation of German soldiers was that a numerically inferior army could defeat a superior one by this simple *ruse de guerre* if carried out with guile, speed, and efficiency. It was the dream of Cannae that was fixed upon the

11. Archer battle scene, rock painting, Morella la Vella, Castellón, Spain (date unknown; perhaps c. 4000 B.C.E.).
*After D. Mazonowicz, 1974*

German chief of staff Count Alfred von Schlieffen when he designed his nation's strategy of attack in World War I. "To win a decisive, destructive success," he wrote in 1900, "it is necessary to make a simultaneous attack on two or three points at once—that is, on the front and against one or both flanks." In World War II, the German *Blitzkrieg* that confronted an enemy with an infantry force and encircled him with tank spearheads was simply a mechanized version of Cannae. Colin Powell, in describing America's plan for defeating Saddam Hussein in the Gulf War, summed up yet another repetition of Hannibal's strategy: "First we are going to cut [the army] off and then we are going to kill it."[40]

In the art of the era of war before civilization we see another precursor of the warfare of ages to come, a Cannae in miniature. The tactics that the artists thought important enough to map out on the walls of stone were simple prophecies of those that would one day govern the fates of national armies. This is a crucial distinction, and revolution, in the history of warfare. In personal heroic combat, catching an enemy "not looking" and hitting him in the flank is defined as cowardice; in organized warfare, such a tactic is considered genius. What was "lily-livered bushwhacking" in the disputes of the Old West is masterful generalship in the struggle of nations. We have improved on the means of achieving that end in battle—modern airpower can be said to have simply added a vertical component to the outflanking strategy—but the objective has not changed in thousands of years.

## LEADERSHIP AND THE "LOOK" OF POWER

In tribal society, leadership was no longer an expedient but a fixture. Its guise and principles, if we look through the warrior's eye, are strikingly familiar. Consider the marching soldiers image from the Spanish Levant. [**Fig. 8**] The chief is distinguished by being first in line. This is not just an inference, for the artist elaborated the leader in other ways. He wears a different headpiece from that of his "men." He is also physically larger, taking up more surface area on the rock canvas. This is a widespread convention of the vision of commanders in many cultures. Finally, in contrast to the men of the squad, he carries the bow in his left hand and the arrows in his right. This could be an indication of his dexterity, but it could also be seen as yet another sign of leadership within that culture. For these ancient warriors, even as for the modern college lecturer, the arrow is a tool for pointing and directing.

In the picture of the battle from the Arnhem Land, the role of the leader is even more distinct, dramatic, and related to combat. [**Fig. 7**] At the front line of the fighting, on both sides, the leading figures have larger, rounded headdresses. In contrast, the back ranks of both groups have smaller heads or headdresses. The only man who is definitely wounded is the right group's first figure: four spears fly toward him, while one already has struck deep through his

12. Archer battle scene, Sefar site in Tassili, Sahara (date unknown; perhaps c. 4000 B.C.E.).
*After D. Mazonowicz, 1974*

abdomen. It is difficult not to read this contrast as signifying that the elite fighters or the leaders on both sides were placed in the front ranks. Again, this casualty seems familiar—such is the risk of leading men personally into battle. Neither does this seem a work of imagination. It is almost certainly an anecdote of battle and the first of a genre of visualizations of the deaths of war commanders such as Leonidas at Thermopylae, Roland at the Pass, General Wolfe at Quebec, "Stonewall" Jackson at Fredricksburg, or Sergeant Striker on the sands of Iwo Jima.

A more complex vision of heroism and leadership is displayed in another battle from the Neolithic, at the Sefar site in Tassili in the Sahara. [**Fig. 12**] The warriors are depicted in vigorous movement; their legs are stretched nearly to horizontal lines. It is almost a cinematic frame. As one analyst of this picture describes, these men seem "no longer subject to the law of gravity."[41] At the southeast corner, the bowmen charge en masse. The leader, although he has no distinctive dress except perhaps for his light-colored arrow quiver, is the largest man in the attacking force. Also, of all the warriors in the left-hand battle group, he is the only one with his arrow unexpended. Was this because he fired first as a signal to attack? Then he would have had time to rearm while his men vollied their arrows, which fly toward the army on the right. Or is he waiting for a better shot? In either case, he is clearly leading his men in a charge. The right-hand squad's actions, however, are harder to read. Several of the men run away, literally in headlong flight, but others seem to rally. Is this the beginning of a counterattack, a last stand, or perhaps even a trap?

Whatever the events, visually these are hypermen, with calves and thighs bursting from the rock canvas, V-shaped torsos, and broad, strapping shoulders that would be welcome in any logging or football camp or marine recruiting office. This was not only a sign of youth and vigor but of power. Overt masculinity is simply an accentuation of a biological fact: the "pumped" musculature is the feature of the human male that most distinguishes him from the female, except for genitalia—which often protrude like weapons from the dancing warriors of the tribal eras. Today, we use the term "big man" in much the same way. Size is not just a metaphor for power, but in a society that puts a premium on physical strength and athletic achievement—as is the case in the hunting of big game or battles with other men—it makes sense that these are the features most sought after in the leader, or those used as conventions for his representation in war art.

Was the big man a pretense, a stylistic formula? In confrontation, animals puff, raise hackles: bigness is a form of implicit and explicit intimidation. Were many of the warriors and leaders actually stringy but feisty, short but ferocious, dumpy but crafty? If so, then this is another instance, as with the fattened animals of the cave paintings, of depicting expectation rather than reality. Warriors throughout history have been of varying sizes and shapes. The ancient Mayans depicted their terrible men of battle as being squat and fat, with fleshy chins and slack arms. The armor makers of the Renaissance were careful to build "belly-holders" to accommodate the girth of captains and commanders whose paunches were better developed than their trapezius and deltoids. Frederick the Great, the Prussian king and general, allowed only the tallest men to join his guard. On the other hand, promotion to Napoleon's Imperial Guard was based upon achievement and ability. Paintings and commentary of the time reveal how diminutive men who were fierce fighters looked overwhelmed by their heavy uniforms and three-foot bearskin *shakos*. Pictures of the Zulus from the Victorian era are similarly deceiving. In photographs, the hardy warriors of Southeast Africa appear without muscular definition and with ample stomachs, but they could run forty miles in a day and fight a battle immediately afterward. In the *Rambo* film series, Sylvester Stallone's brawny body stands in stark contrast to the gaunt, almost skeletonlike physiques of the Long Range Recon Commandos—the unit in which his character fought—that we see in photographs from the Vietnam War.

We do not know, then, whether in the Neolithic there was a divergence between fact and representation, reality and style, or between the codes of different tribes. In small societies where intelligence and strength would be tested daily, it is perfectly logical that the big man of the tribe, or at least the big man who led the warriors to battle, would also be physically the largest person. It is only in later ages that the most decrepit, obese kings and lethargic, frail commanders would employ the art of war to erect paintings and sculptures that distorted their physiognomy and made them seem bigger, greater, more powerful than they really were.

From such images another convention of the representation of military command is born. The leaders we distinguish here are literally "up front": they lead, act, and direct in battle. It is a characteristic in any army that the hazards of elite unit leadership are greatest. Among the Cheyenne dog soldiers, war chiefs were "chosen to be killed"; those who outlived their four-year tenures were considered to be failures and an embarrassment.[42] Battlefield leadership must be by example and in person. The Neolithic cadres shown in the rock images were, in a sense, elite strike forces: small, tightly knit, loyal to each other, highly skilled and trained, and under the direct guidance of leaders who had risen to power by means of strength and ability. Each man knew that his commander was sharing his risks.

The legendary commanders of civilized armies understood and exercised this practice. If not at the front all the time, they at least arrived at the moment in a battle when the leader's visible body was as necessary as his spoken orders (and the fresh troops he usually brought with him). Caesar's narratives of his war in Gaul are full of moments where his appearance on a tall charger, distinguished by the flowing "scarlet cloak which he always wore in action to mark his identity," was what turned the tide of a battle, what excited the men to effort and rallied sagging fortunes.[43] The Duke of Marlborough was likewise "famed for his ability to overcome the problems of distance and obscurity, and for his knack at appearing at critical points to rally the men as if guided by superhuman knowledge."[44] Napoleon's bravery was the stuff of barracks and broadside legend: at Rivoli five horses died under him; at Borodino the soldiers of the Grande Armée threatened mutiny because he was getting too close to the gunfire. In the American Civil War, Confederate general Thomas J. Jackson earned his immortal title when another commander saw him standing, wounded, in the thick of the fight and proclaimed, "Look! There is Jackson standing like a stone wall! Rally behind the Virginians!"[45] George Patton too believed that the "living presence" of the commander of an army should be visible to troops in inspections and sudden drop-ins, but most of all on the battlefield "to show the soldiers that generals can get shot at."[46]

But there is another implication of a leader being a "big man" who is "up front." Being noticeable, visible to enemy and comrade, forces rapid decision making in combat. The one fatal mistake of a commander is not necessarily to make a bad decision, but to make no decision. Indecisiveness on a battlefield is a form of communicable disease that is easily transmitted to the men and exploitable by the enemy. The same advice is given today to ROTC candidates of the U.S. armed forces. Faith in a leader's knowledge of the correct path, and his will and determination to overcome all obstacles on that path, serve as a rough definition of charisma. The British psychologist Antony Storr perceived that this was the magical quality of Winston Churchill in 1940, on the eve of total defeat in the Battle of France. "Churchill became the hero that he had always dreamed of being. It was his finest hour. In that dark time, what England needed was not a shrewd, equable, balanced leader. She needed a prophet, a heroic visionary, a man who could dream dreams of victory when all seemed lost."[47] Similar statements can be made about almost any leader who seems to attract a dedicated following, whether religious, military, or political. He believes absolutely, perhaps contrary to all other evidence, that providence will ensure his success, and that the path that he has chosen to found a faith, to lead an attack, or to win an election, is the only way. The visionary leader's power is to compel others to share in his personal vision.

What drives men to obey other men, to follow leaders, even to their own death or that of others? In the 1960s, psychologist Stanley Milgram conducted a series of famous experiments where upon orders of a researcher, subjects repeatedly inflicted electric shocks on people they did not know, but who they were told were other subjects. (The shocks were not real; the "victims" were researchers, although the subjects did not know this.)[48] The person giving the orders in the experiment was an authority figure. As many of the subjects later explained, they assumed that he "knew what he was doing." Also, the willingness to apply increasingly painful—to the point of death—electroshocks on other human beings was justified as an act of submission that relieved the participants of responsibility: "I wouldn't have done it by myself. I was just doing what I was told."[49] Milgram concluded that this defense was not posited ad hoc but rather revealed "a fundamental mode of thinking for a great many people once they are locked into a subordinate position in a structure of authority. The disappearance of a sense of responsibility is the most far-reaching consequence of submission to authority."[50] It is also the characteristic most eagerly exploited (or rather, redirected) for use by military leaders of any era who expend considerable effort in word, deed, and image to convince soldiers (mostly young males with the least developed sense of personal responsibility) that "I know what I'm doing." In the Neolithic, obedience was by example, as these images attest.

Finally, a rough rule of art and society is that the greater the hierarchy, the greater the trouble elites take to create their portraiture. The most powerful leaders, at least in the early civilizations, either achieved their power or maintained it through military force or the threat of military force, and often ordered the construction of gigantic monuments or complex works of art to memorialize themselves. Such forms of art betray cults of personality or of kingship. The more important an individual, the more resources of manpower, time, energy, materials, and wealth are expended in displaying his image or commemorating his achievements in some way. In contrast, in the rock art of the San peoples—the "bushmen" tribes—in southern Africa, there is almost no differentiation of individuals; no great chiefs are accorded separate space or extra effort or given distinctive features in the art.[51] The subsuming of art to the service of promoting a single leader above all other men was the symptom and perhaps the cause of the civilized warfare of the ages to come in the empires of Assyria, Rome, and the Nile. War threw down such leaders, but it also brought even more power, prestige, and goods. The distinctions first apparent in the rock art—the different headdresses, slightly more accentuated musculature, and front-rank position of Neolithic leaders—were a prologue to the vast monuments to come.

## RED QUEENS OLD AND NEW

The visual record of the era "before civilization" attests that interhuman warfare was not only present but a celebrated aspect of life wherever it arose. Searching the evidence of primitive war we survey, as Lawrence Keeley puts it, "an all-too-familiar catalog of deaths, rapes, pillage, destruction, and terror."[52] We can even see, in some cases, what there was to fight about. For example, in Khargurtahl, Libya, there is a rock painting of a "battle."[53] [**Fig. 13**] Although the warriors are stylized, it seems that the three "triple-white-line" men on the left have formed a defensive perimeter around a choice bull. The "black-line" men, in turn, close in on the prize. At the center of both sides, the two largest figures face each other. The captain of the whites stands squarely in front of the bull; the captain of the blacks, at the crux of the arc of his men, charges. This is

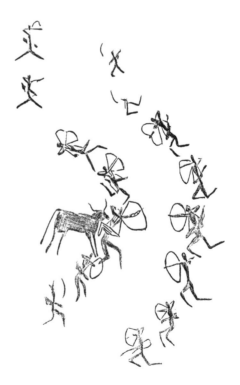

13. Battle for a bull, Khargurtahl, Libya (date unknown; perhaps c. 4000 B.C.E.). *After L. Frobenius, 1937*

a dispute over property, over a thing that is accorded value to the point that killing other men is an acceptable price to pay for its seizure. No pictures of this kind appear in previous eras of human history; they are common in the Neolithic, however, and become a staple of the art of war.

In surveying the arts of tribal peoples, it is clear that the rise of interhuman warfare was simply an extension of previous habits, skills, and ideas inherited from long-standing hunting traditions. The concept that others, whether wild creatures or strange tribes, are the enemy and that their killing is sanctioned in the struggle for survival is one such notion. It has strong resonance; human beings have often created elaborate justifications for killing, but the simplest is that the enemy was "less than human." The development of this situation in the Mesolithic and Neolithic can be blamed on a changing environment which, through overpredation, human beings may have helped to deplete. Megafauna overkill and warfare are related phenomena. ". . . it takes all the running you can do, to keep in the same place," shrilled the Red Queen to Alice. As resources dwindle, competition increases; so men waged battle for a bull, and eventually enacted massacres like those at Crow Creek and others of the present day.

Yet it is misleading to cite environmental pressures as the first and last cause of war. To do so absolves the culpability of man, transforming him into a puppet of the elements; it suggests an "aridization defense" to replace the alibi of Nuremberg. There are many causes of war. Propaganda, visual and verbal, plays a crucial role in inciting group violence. Wars can be popular, at least in their initial stages, but few wars are wholly unplanned. Massacres typically have an ideological underpinning or are encouraged by the powers that be. Two thousand years of anti-Jewish doctrine stoked the ovens of Auschwitz. The mobs of young killers in Rwanda were organized and underwritten by the elders in the government, media, church, and commerce. It is unlikely as well that the Crow Creek massacre was the result of a spontaneous argument between formerly friendly (but ultimately hungry) native communities. We do not know to what extent images on the rock surfaces served the purpose of rallying for war. The cave art of the previous era could be considered hunting propaganda in that it exalted the value and attractiveness of those creatures that our ancestors were preparing to kill. In the visions of interhuman warfare from the later stone ages, we may see memorials to victories (or defeats) that displayed a communal memory. Perhaps these served as reminders for vigilance and incitements to vengeance as well as celebrations of the cult of the warrior.

We do know, however, that this was the era in which differentiation between people in society was growing. In the Neolithic we see the first appearance of monumental art—the great stone menhirs that dot Europe and the Near East. We find the first traces of sacred buildings, elaborate graves, and vaults for the dead. And in the images we have the first indication of leaders. Moreover, it is unlikely that these were the temporary leaders produced in cultures wholly devoted to the hunting of big game. In such a society, the power of the leader dissipated quickly after the hunt because the "wealth" had to be distributed immediately. The "big men" were big only as a consequence of the wealth they dispensed, not that which was collected and kept.[54]

The key difference that may have produced an upsetting of this egalitarianism was the delay in food procurement and distribution brought about by settled status.[55] Sedentary peoples do not share food from the gathering immediately, but rather store it, suggesting a mechanism whereby cliques of the powerful may gain control over the process of allotting grains and goods (and of course, by extension, booty from war). The link between this system and the grain "dole" of the ancient emperors and even the disbursement of government funding by today's elected officials is self-evident. We know from the ethnographic records that such societies, like those on the northwest coast of North America, are also characterized by violence and warfare. In almost every society ever studied, "the indigenous category for exploitation," notes Marshall Sahlins, "is reciprocity," where the big men find ways to take "better than the proportionate share" of communal items.[56] Thus, the rise of the lethal society may have a circular connection to the nascence of powerful individuals. The more war, the more likely that through war successful leaders will rise to prominence and influence; the more territories and goods that are divided among competing leaders, the more likely the leaders will use war to advance their interests.[57] Leaders thus both instigate war and arise from it. As expressed to her diary by a fourteen-year-old nascent philosopher whose life was cut short by war:

> I don't believe that the big men, the politicians and the capitalists alone, are guilty of the war. Oh no, the little man is just as guilty, otherwise the peoples of the world would have risen in revolt long ago! There's in people simply an urge to destroy, an urge to kill, to murder and rage, and until all mankind, without exception, undergoes a great change, wars will be waged, everything that has been built up, cultivated, and grown will be destroyed and disfigured, after which mankind will have to begin all over again.[58]

# 3

---

# COMMANDERS

## IDENTIFYING THE WAR COMMANDER

Incised into one of his reliefs, Esarhaddon, king of Assyria (r. c. 680–69 B.C.E.), proclaimed: "I am powerful, I am omnipotent, I am a hero, I am gigantic, I am colossal."[1] Throughout history many rulers have been concerned with asserting verbally and implying visually this sentiment. In the film *Monty Python and the Holy Grail* (1975), King Arthur and his servant pass through a narrow street where plague victims are tossed in wheelbarrows. One of the collectors pauses his chant of "Bring out your dead!" to remark, "Must be a King." A townsman asks, "Why?" The answer is perfectly sensible: "He hasn't got shit all over him." This observation encapsulates a paradox we face when surveying the range of poses, expressions, costumes, props, backdrops, and actions that captains and kings adopt in times of war. On the one hand, pictures of war leaders across human history use varying styles, media, and situations. Assyrian princes were carved in reliefs; English generals at the Crimea posed for the daguerreotype; in an oil painting, Napoleon rode to glory in the Alpine valleys; General H. Norman Schwarzkopf led reporters on a guided-missile video journey. On the other hand, all such portrayals employ a limited menu of visual techniques and conventions to attain a single purpose. In most visions of war leaders, the Monty Python peasants' view was the one intended: to make the commander stand out, if not like a diamond in a dungheap, at least distinguished from all other men.

What separates the battle leader from ordinary men on the field and on canvas or film? Maurice de Saxe, the seventeenth-century French general, said that the three main qualities of command were intelligence, courage, and health. Napoleon (echoing Julius Caesar) believed that luck, the goddess Fortuna, was the mistress of success in battle. While the definitions of the first two qualities and the final one have remained relatively fixed, the third has undergone visible changes. In the Neolithic, the robustness of the leader was occasionally suggested by his physique; the commander of the Stone Age platoon was not always the biggest man, but never was he portrayed as the runt. At that time, when all war was personal, and all combat tested endurance and strength, it is not unlikely that the "big man" really was greater in stature than all those around him. The convention of making the leader into a larger figure may have reflected physical fact. In the history of the vision of war, no culture, no style of art, no genre has chosen to reduce war commanders to smaller figures than they were in real life—the exaggeration is always toward making a "big man" bigger.[2]

The Neolithic artists had only three techniques within the limited range of their medium of paint on stone to signify who was the war commander. The first distinction was position: the leader took the front rank in battle, or was the linchpin of a defensive perimeter or a Cannae envelopment. The second path of differentiation was of dress; the head covering of the leader stood out in size, shape, or style from that of his followers. Finally, in the Stone Age leaders we see the hypertrophy of the human form. While many warriors appear to be superbly conditioned men of action, leaders may be broader in shoulder and greater in height. Because these paintings had no relative sizing between objects closer in the foreground and more distant in the background, the only way to present differences in size was to increase a figure's surface area on the rock.

In the ages of bronze and iron, the rise of great urban centers and rich empires that followed, and almost until the present day, artists serving king and fatherland were commissioned (or ordered) to produce icons enhancing the dominance of the war commander over nature, the soldiery, battle, and the picture. The history of the vision of the war commander is a checklist of imparting qualities of dominance to often unlikely subjects. It was no accident that much of the canvas of war, at least until recently, was focused less on the horrors, indignities, and miseries—and even bravery and stalwartness—of ordinary soldiers than on the veritable and feigned achievements of war leaders. In base terms, the goal was to laud the war leader and thereby praise the system of government, the institutions of society, and the hierarchy of people that created, supported, or was embodied by that leader.

Indeed, to *control* images of war was, in a political sense, an expression of power. But even if total, that control may backfire on the patron of the images. Two examples delineate these issues, one from the distant past and a culture radically different from our own, the second from the recent past of our Western culture.

When the Aztec emperor Montezuma heard of the arrival of strangers (Spaniards) from the eastern sea of his kingdom, he sent a delegation of greeting and inquiry. Accompanying his ambassadors was a squad of artists. While preliminary and rather amicable negotiations were going on with the newcomers, the artists set to work copying the Spanish camp. The diplomacy lasted several weeks, so the artists had the leisure and the cooperation of their subjects to finish. Every last horse, dog, and piece of armor was painted. "The cannon and cannon-balls, and indeed the whole of our army, were faithfully portrayed," observed one conquistador.[3] Upon completion, the paintings were duly packed off to Montezuma.

The artists were not simply gathering data, nor was the Aztec emperor merely an art collector; the art had another purpose. When the conquistadors finally arrived at Montezuma's palace, for a time they were honored guests and were shown the magnificence and wealth that the Aztec empire had acquired. Particularly fascinating was a room in which a picture or a sculpture of everything in the kingdom—from enemy tribes to jungle jaguars—was kept. Hernán Cortés, in one of his letters, noted that "all the things of which Mutezuma [sic] has ever heard, both on land or in the sea, they have modelled, very realistically, either in gold and silver or in jewels or feathers, and with such perfection that they seem almost real."[4] With these likenesses, Montezuma expressed an ancient conviction: to picture a thing was to control it. The emperor conceived, falsely as it turned out, that paintings would exert power over his foes. After the Spaniards kidnapped him, when he was stoned by his own people in anger at his weakness, and as he lay dying—the Aztec Empire months away from destruction—perhaps he understood that images cannot exert magical control over the reality of war. Montezuma's artists did not fail him in depicting the conquistadors realistically, but he could not divine the hearts and minds of the subjects, and the results were fatal. The meaning of data, visual or otherwise, is never self-evident or self-explanatory.

The circumstances were different but the outcome was similar in America's greatest short-term military catastrophe—the only time an American army has been driven back, had to abandon its equipment and wounded, and then never regained the lost territory. The time was late 1950; the place was North Korea. Earlier in the year, North Korean divisions had suddenly attacked the South. South Korean and American forces retreated to a harried beachhead, and were threatened with expulsion from the peninsula. General Douglas MacArthur and his staff conceived of a bold stroke: an invasion into the enemy rear. The subsequent Inchon landing was successful; American and allied forces routed the North Koreans. Within a month, American spearheads approached the Chinese border. MacArthur announced that the war was all but over. The one worry was intervention by the newly installed Communist government of China, but MacArthur and almost the entire American military command reassured President Harry Truman that such a thing was either impossible or, if it occurred, would be thrown back easily. So, with supreme confidence, American and allied armies began what MacArthur called his "final drive to end the war." In one week in November, however, the situation collapsed. Over one million Chinese soldiers crossed the border near the Yalu River. American forces incurred heavy losses; units were reduced to what one veteran described as "small bands of desperate men." The blow to American pride was tremendous. A military force backed by lavish supplies, complete command of the air and sea, and the finest, most modern military equipment had been defeated.

In the years after the war, the truth, as much as it can, has come out. The Chinese believed that "Korea was a pistol pointed at the heart of China—her industrial heart, just North of the Yalu River."[5] From the Chinese point of view, intervention was the only option. Nor was the Peking government reticent about its plans, as warnings were given through diplomatic sources.[6] Chinese soldiers were even captured in Korea shortly before the attack. Most important, Chinese troop movements were photographed by American reconnaissance planes. The visual evidence was clear. Why then were the U.S. commanders, all seasoned soldiers, taken by surprise? The assumption made by the American authorities was that mainland China was irrelevant, that Chinese troops would prove as poor fighters as the North Koreans, or that the Chinese presence in the North was defensive; rationalizations were concocted to deny the obvious, as preconceived belief was imposed on pictures and the visual facts were reinterpreted to fit the assumed wisdom.[7]

Neither were American media (and therefore the public) aware of the dangers involved, since the Pentagon frame of mind (imposed by the power and prestige of MacArthur, the previously successful war commander) was essentially replicated for public consumption. In many maps of the war zone printed in newsmagazines before the intervention, the land north over the Korean border was not even labeled as being "China," but "Manchuria." On such maps, the third-party enemy was the Russians. The United States tried to impose its vision on the world; the world overturned it. This lesson is perennially lost. People interpret what they see based upon their expectations. What is crucial in inspecting images of war is the claims that are made about their truth and their representativeness, and to what extent the audiences of the images are prejudiced to accept, ignore, or reject the offered interpretation. Deception works because the viewers are eager to be duped; often, in our eagerness to celebrate a leader's ability to save us, we overlook the possibility of the failure of vision.[8]

Nevertheless, the leader's vision of war is still the most likely to be replicated in physical images. The clarity of this dominance imperative in pictures of military command is highlighted by a simple experiment. Show naive viewers—young children—a painting, carving, or sculpture of a martial scene. Ask them: Who is the most important man in the picture? Whether facing a Mayan tapestry, a Roman relief, or a Victorian oil painting, the children's eyes will penetrate the veil of culture, time, and space. They will extend a finger almost immediately to a single man and proclaim, "That one's the king." They do so invariably because the techniques of arranging objects in the frame of an image, of differentially sizing or lighting them to please the artists' masters and patrons, are sometimes subtle and other times direct, but are not spurious. The human brain

14. Rameses II at the battle of Kadesh, Ramesseum (mortuary temple, West Thebes) (c. 1300 B.C.E.).
*Photo: William Murnane*

processes visual information and accords importance and relevance to things within the visual field. The king's image hijacks hard-wired patterns of cognition and subverts them to the cause of his superiority.

Such continuities and conventions are demonstrated in two images, which are separated by 3,300 years and a vast gulf of culture. At first glance, their subjects and settings seem to make their juxtaposition absurd. In one picture we see the Egyptian pharaoh Rameses II steering a chariot, annihilating a Hittite army; in the other, Michael S. Dukakis, the 1988 Democratic candidate for the presidency of the United States, rides on an M1A1 Abrams tank. The original conceit behind the creation of both images, however, is similar. The men have placed themselves, for propagandistic intent, on the premier land war machines of their day. Each man commissioned the image, to confirm in the first case and propose in the second case, status as commander in chief of his nation's armies.

These pictures, as well, sum up some of the basic themes of the visual portrayal of war leaders through all eras. Rameses II, the autocrat who led his chariot armies to war in what is now northern Syria against the forces of the Hittite empire, had carvers record his visage and explain in hieroglyphic writing his exploits on the 60-foot walls of a great temple dedicated to himself.[9] [**Fig. 14**] He became the "Ozymandias" who, in Shelley's poem, boasted that all should "Look on my works, ye Mighty, and despair!" The pictures and the accompanying words (in the picture-writing) constitute one of the first visual and written records of any battle, that at Kadesh, c. 1300 B.C.E.[10] In these and other monumental images—"mass" communication channels of the ancient world—the sovereign of the state radiates his authority and prowess to all who view him, from a low angle or from a great distance. In the original work, Rameses is bronze-skinned, broad-shouldered, long-armed, resolute of face, wearing the twin crowns of upper and lower Egypt, and literally a giant smiting pygmies. In the written records accompanying the images, Rameses boasts that he routed "every warrior of the Hittite enemy, together with the many foreign countries which were with them." In contrast, the Hittite king, Rameses tells us, "stood averted, shrinking, and afraid."[11] Even Rameses' troops get short shrift: "You have done a cowardly deed, altogether. Not one man among you had stood up to assist me when I was fighting . . . not one among you shall talk about his service, after returning to the land of Egypt."[12] It is clearly intended that all who surveyed the pharaoh's

15. Presidential candidate Michael Dukakis on M1A1 tank, television advertisement by campaign for George Bush, 1988.
*Produced by Greg Stevens with Roger Ailes on behalf of the Bush for President Campaign (1988)*

works and read of his deeds would believe that he was the paramount war leader, at the expense of everyone else present on the field of Kadesh.

In contrast, the Dukakis image represents a failure of the dominance imperative. [**Fig. 15**] The original picture was a pseudo-event, a publicity stunt staged by his campaign consultants and staff to associate their candidate, who had been cursed with the brand of "liberal" and criticized as "soft on defense," with a powerful and vivid symbol of America's armored might. But in a democratic age, where images can be appropriated or recaptioned by other competing leaders, and when the authority of a war chief is not absolute, the best intentions of visual propaganda can go awry. The image shown here was appropriated from news video for a political advertisement on the preeminent mass medium of our day, television, produced by the opposing campaign of incumbent president George Bush. Dukakis, diminutive, with an Alfred E. Neuman grin and an overtightened tie, looks faintly ridiculous on the tank. The sardonic voice-over and video text instruct us that this is not a case of positive association, but jarring juxtaposition, and that Dukakis is antidefense and likely to weaken America's armed forces.

Something else, however, unites these two images: the ambiguity of their facticity. What was not made clear by the news media in Dukakis's case, or by Rameses' stone carver publicists in nineteenth-dynasty New Kingdom Egypt, was that both visual texts, the relief and the advertisement, are used to misrepresent what happened. At best, the battle on the plains of Kadesh was an indecisive draw; Rameses retreated southward and eventually ceded in a treaty to the Hittites all the lands he boasted of conquering. On the other hand, Dukakis's original photo op was an honest metonym of his campaign position: to decrease America's nuclear arsenal but strengthen conventional forces such as armored divisions. As communications scholar Kathleen Hall Jamieson notes, Dukakis was losing in the polls and so the press framed the story as desperation, and allowed the Bush voice-over to define the event.[13] In sum, little of what Rameses claimed to have happened at Kadesh seems to have been accurate, or rather, to praise their god-king, his masons and scribes exaggerated his military acumen as much as his physical proportions. Likewise, very little of what Bush's campaign claimed about Dukakis's antidefense policies was true. But legends, however false, can glitter more brightly than fact, and in both cases the vision of the commander endures—the former of glory, the latter of foolishness.

## VISUALIZING DOMINANCE

There is a photograph that shows Dwight Eisenhower talking to men of the 101st Airborne Division on the eve of the Normandy invasion. The image was widely circulated during the war and reappears often in historical texts. The jaunty commander-in-chief vigorously addresses the strapping young men who are in full battle gear complete with painted faces. All the men's eyes are attentively locked on the general. A film of the same meeting where Eisenhower shakes hands with individual soldiers was also popular. Yet it was not until historian Cornelius Ryan undertook a meticulous investigation that the names of the paratroopers were revealed.[14] This is a compromise between longstanding tradition—where the commander is distinctive in appearance and identification from all the men—and the more modern trend of paying homage to the ordinary soldier. Indeed one of the simplest indications that the subject of an image is a man of power is that the image is created at all. The war commander is set apart in a picture, either as its entire subject or "standing alone" in separated space within it. Individualized portraits could be tiny yet numerous (such as coins) or, as we have seen, colossal and singular. Such visual conventions used to laud the leader are natural analogs of human vision. They are transhistorical and cross-cultural because they were created to be so. Rameses II, for example, whose name is proverbial for monumental self-aggrandizement, was not producing images only for personal satisfaction and private delight. They were mass communication, or rather, massive communication, in plain sight for people—from scheming temple priests to potentially dangerous generals to ordinary peasants whose taxes and labor supported the great artifice of the state—to appreciate and to understand. These images were meant as messages to foreign ambassadors and visitors as well. Few cultures are isolates, and the Bronze Age of Rameses II was an era of international trade and cosmopolitanism. The pharaoh's artists painted and sculpted him so that every Hittite, Edamite, Babylonian, Canaanite, Nubian, Libyan, or Mycenaean observer, even if ignorant of the meaning of hieroglyphics, would absorb the basic message: The king is great and powerful and dominates the battlefield.

In life and in art, war commanders have also been distinguished by their dress. The degree of decorative disparity represents a very real problem that leaders in war have faced since the Neolithic, and that is the question of command and control. To lead, one must be able to instruct, to tell troops what to do, to govern in some way their movements. In the earliest battles, when armies consisted of scores of men rather than hundreds or thousands, the leader could yell commands and take actions which could be heard and seen by his men. With the rise of agricultural civilization, however, the challenge of command and control became greater. Leaders identified themselves by dress on the battlefield so that they would be recognized, obeyed and followed. Yet ostentation to display valor and authority was a cultural convention. Among the ancient Aztecs, the greater the warrior, the more decorated he was with elaborate and colorful feathers and costume.[15] This system of differentiation was meant to strike fear and awe in opposing armies and to reward warriors by according them higher heraldry of rank. The conquistadors of Spain, however, found the Aztec plumage to be ludicrous, and reacted with contempt and laughter.

In other instances, honor may be bestowed on the uniform at the same time that its occupant is scorned. Such was the fate of imperial Russia's hapless minister of war, General Vladimir Sukhomlinov. Always carefully preened, with a breastplate of jangling medals, the general was well known at court as a popinjay, and indeed wormed his way into the good graces of the quixotic last tsar of Russia more because he made a good dinner-table guest than because of his organizational skills. Like many of Nicholas II's appointments, he was the worst man for an important job. As Barbara Tuchman writes, Sukhomlinov, "having won the Cross of St. George as a dashing young cavalry officer in the war of 1877 against the Turks . . . believed that military knowledge acquired in that campaign was permanent truth."[16] As a result, Russia was made ready for war against German modern radio communications, rail systems, heavy artillery, airplanes, and machine guns by a man who thought horse and saber would conquer Berlin. He also, to satisfy his own vanity and the material desires of his young wife, misappropriated war funds. Following the catastrophic defeats of the first year of the war, he was dismissed. After the war he wrote a book of self-vindication, revealingly dedicated to the emperor of Germany. His most lasting gift to the visualization of the war leader is the so-called Sukhomlinov rule: the more dazzlingly dressed a *modern* army, the worse it is likely to fight. In reaction to such ostentation the armies of the Bolshevik Revolution exhibited almost no distinctions of rank display—yet within a generation Russian generals again adopted the heavy coverings of ribbons and medals as signs of achievement and hierarchy.

The war commander can also be distinguished in images by the actions and attention of those around him: by gestures and glances of dominance and subordination; varying contrasts of height and depth; and the distinction between himself as individualized leader and the formless mass. An example is this Assyrian image, from the wall reliefs of the palace at Nineveh in what is now Iraq. [**Fig. 16**] The scene is of an incident in the neighboring nation of Elam, a sometimes ally but often enemy of the Assyrians. Ummanigash, king of Elam, arrives at his palace and is greeted by soldiers. The leader is distinctly higher up in the picture, standing above his men: metaphor recapitulates ideology. Each soldier is lined up in an identical pose, indistinguishable in manner or dress. Each as well gives an upper hand salute betokening subservience. The look and pose of all present cross times and culture: "Absolute authority," wrote the film historian Siegfried Kracauer, "asserts itself by arranging people under its domination in pleasing designs."[17]

The parallel between war leadership and its artistic representation is that whereas in the former, commanders seek to control the physical environment, in the latter they need to dominate the symbolic landscape. This is often accomplished by such juxtapositions of mass as placing the leader in the foreground of an image where he dwarfs the mountains and the regiments behind him. But

16. Elamite king Ummanigash is greeted on his arrival at Madaktu. Assyrian relief, South West Palace at Nineveh (c. 635 B.C.E.).
© *The British Museum*

in the immediate personal space of the leader, it is important that he be seen exacting control over the machines of war and the natural world as well. Rameses II fires his arrows while directing his chariot, the reins tied about his waist. This is improbable, but it sums up the godlike status accorded to the pharaoh. Michael Dukakis, as well, did not choose to ride a jeep or a military truck, but the most powerful war chariot of our era. More typically, the visualization of the control of an instrument of war and of nature is the ubiquitous painting or statue of the equestrian war commander. In many cases, the leader is gesturing, saluting, or making commanding sweeps of the hand while restraining a powerful horse with a light squeeze of his knees.

Even in death, the war leader can be lauded by the visualized rituals of atten-

tion, demonstration, and focus. A famous case is that of Benjamin West's *The Death of General Wolfe* (1770).[18] [see **Fig. 2**] The image refers to a factual event but portrays a fictional scene. General James Wolfe, commander of the English forces at the Battle of Quebec against the French (1759), died at the moment victory was assured. The painting, which to today's eyes looks staid and proper in its form and theme, was revolutionary. The dictates of the time were that paintings of battle scenes should be transposed to the classical era. It was perfectly acceptable to paint the demise of a Spartan or Roman prince, but to show the death of a modern commander in contemporary robe was considered to be in bad taste. When King George III learned that West was creating a nonclassical scene, he reprovingly said that it would be "very ridiculous to exhibit heroes in coats, breeches, and cock'd hats."[19] Watching *The Death of General Wolfe* in progress, the director of the Royal Academy of Art, Sir Joshua Reynolds, also cautioned West not to paint war in its modern guise, but to hold up instead "the classic costume of antiquity, as much more becoming the inherent greatness of his subject than a modern garb of war." West's reply became legend, a credo for a new standard of art for a century to come:

> [T]he event intended to be commemorated took place on the 13th of September, 1759, in a region of the world unknown to the Greeks and Romans, and at a period of time when no such nations, nor heroes in their costume, any longer existed. The subject I have to represent is the conquest of a great province of America by the British troops. It is a topic that history will proudly record, and the same truth that guides the pen of the historian should govern the pencil of the artist. I consider myself as undertaking to tell this great event to the eye of the world; but if, instead of the facts of the transaction, I represent classical fictions, how shall I be understood by posterity![20]

When the painting was finished, Reynolds reversed his judgment and proclaimed it would "occasion a revolution in the art."[21] He allowed it to be displayed at the Academy, and *The Death of General Wolfe* became a great sensation, the most popular single picture of its era. King George revised his opinion as well and commissioned a copy from West, who went on to paint thirteen largely identical versions for aristocratic collectors. He created a genre that continued well through the era of photography: the heroic death in battle of a contemporary commanding hero. It served the interests of the state (which was the patron of art) by transforming men who had died for the honor of their prince into worthy residents of Valhalla.

The arrangement of the painting and its elements both inherited a tradition and introduced one. The pose of the war leader, General Wolfe, is borrowed from previous pictures of Christ after he was taken down from the Cross. All of the thirteen main figures besides Wolfe in the image train their gaze upon him. Their variety—one is a mountain ranger, several are officers, some are in the army, some are navy marines—conveys his coordination of the different services of the English forces during the battle. On the left, several figures point away, trying to direct the dying Wolfe's gaze toward the victory that he has won. In the background we see the storm clouds of battle, the shifting masses of armies and the tall cathedral spire that marked Quebec. Facing Wolfe directly is an Indian. He is the incarnation of the noble savage: tattooed, with leather pouch and gun, superbly fit and strongly countenanced; he adopts the classical pose of the thinker contemplating the scene before him. "Prior knowledge" is little required to understand the basic theme of this picture, because the "monumental dignity" of the arrangement of the subjects recalls a universal theme of martyrdom.[22]

The parallel between Christ's sacrifice and that of Wolfe was not mere sentimentality but West's keen sense of a great emerging nationalist consciousness. The painting struck such a popular chord, both with the general public and the aristocracy, because Wolfe's story "had been well ingrained in the national mind as the rallying cry for British patriotism."[23] Wolfe was canonized by the nobility and the public almost immediately after his death. An epic play written some years earlier than West's painting has Wolfe falling, uttering as his epitaph:

> My Glory's Race is run!—My country's serv'd!
> Quebec is conquer'd!—Great George is Victor!
> I wish no more; and am compleatly satisfy'd.[24]

In a romantic biography by King George's own private physician, Wolfe is cited as the general whom Britons "love best."[25] Monuments were erected, other paintings produced, and writings penned in his name and image. West's picture itself was both a fantasy and a realization; it ignited public appreciation and captured the mood of the times.

Yet it was not, as West claimed, an image that showed the "facts of the transaction." *The Death of General Wolfe*, as art historian Theodore Crombie wrote, was "one of the best known and most copied historical masterpieces of all time ... [but] also one of the least accurate."[26] Wolfe personally involved himself in the fighting, sometimes directing his soldiers from the front lines. He was wounded twice, first in the wrist and then in the groin. A third and final wound, to his neck, came as he was ordering several regiments to fire point-blank at the advancing French. West correctly represents the wrist injury, but there is no hint of the groin wound—this was not a noble enough place to suffer, in painting at least, the fates of battle. After the last, mortal blow, Wolfe allegedly stated: "Let not my brave soldiers see me drop. The Day is ours. Keep it." John Knox, a captain of the army, saw him carried off, "to the rear of the front line."[27] Still conscious, Wolfe was placed about 300 yards from the fighting in a small hollow where he continued to give orders briefly before dying, his last words those of exalted gratitude for victory. Although up to fourteen people claim to have been present at his death, only four are confirmed: a lieutenant, an artillery officer, an ordinary soldier, and "a private man."

It is significant that although many other versions of the death of Wolfe portray this probably more factual, smaller scene—a few men in an ignored corner of the battlefield—none of these achieved any renown. They did not find a willing market of patrons. Here is no niggling sideshow, but a grand epic scene, where the dying general, mourned by "an entire chorus of admirers," is center stage under the proscenium arch of heaven.[28] "Many heroes lived before Agamemnon, but all are oppressed in unending night, unwept, unknown, because they lack a dedicated poet," intoned the first-century Roman poet Horace. West, who knew classical history and literature intimately, understood that the death of heroes must be witnessed by many. Indeed, in almost all the "death of" paintings in oils of the eighteenth and nineteenth centuries, the central prone figure, whether Admiral Nelson or some subject from antiquity, is surrounded by a circle of officers and men who reflect upon him in admiration and sorrow.[29] For a century, when heroes died in battle, their demise was restaged for public display, a ritual that became so important and so sacred that not even death could arrest the war commander as the actor from playing out his final role.

## SUBVERTING THE WAR COMMANDER

In the hands of contrarian artists, conventions of honor or dominance become parody or subversive visual commentary. The medium of film in the twentieth century, the era of the greatest public cynicism about the war commander, provides several such examples. From David Lean's adaptation of *Dr. Zhivago* (1965), there is a scene in which a Russian officer—in pristine greatcoat and uniform, visibly in contrast to the rags of his men—stands above a trench exhorting the soldiers to charge the enemy lines, shrieking, "Come on, you bastards!" It is late in the disastrous Russian participation in the war, a year before the calls to arms would have harked to "tsar and holy motherland." Now, the soldiers remain silent, immobile, and dour. Then, Tom Courtenay, who plays a young intellectual who volunteered for the army but would later become a revolutionary, jumps up above the trench and cries, "Come on, comrades! Come on! Come on!" They rise up to follow him—to their death. It is a presage of the revolution to come. More brutally, in a later scene, a column of soldiers mutinies. An officer who has stood on a barrel to address them falls into the water when the barrel cracks and breaks; as the men laugh, one shoots him.

The fall from height, the emptiness of the usual slogans, and the laughter are subversions of the proper social order. Certainly, war commanders have laughed *with* their men, and caused the men to laugh at jokes. Julius Caesar's speeches before battle consisted of ribald tales of his own dubious sexual exploits and poking fun at his baldness. George S. Patton, Jr.'s lurid and expletive-laden lectures to his troops drew reactions ranging from astonishment to the laughter of comradeship—this was no old fuss'n feathers martinet! But ridicule can also puncture the facade of awesome power. The struggle to be all-highest, for example, is parodied by Charlie Chaplin in his film *The Great Dictator* (1940). The leader of Tomania, Adenoid Hynkel, played by Chaplin, confronts another dictator, a Mussolini look-alike. Each is determined to be the "big" man, so using barber chairs they engage in a battle to lift themselves farther up until they almost crash into the ceiling. In a few seconds of screen time, all the would-be giants, from Rameses II to Hitler, are symbolically laid low.

Is this kind of subversion new? It is conceivable that a hobbled Egyptian veteran of Kadesh—who, contrary to what the pharaoh's inscriptions claimed, "had stood up" in the fighting—scoffed (perhaps in lowered tones) at Rameses' egomaniacal monuments. Nevertheless, all the images we have examined so far—no matter how complex the context, no matter how its propaganda goals may have fallen short (as, for example, the picture of Michael Dukakis in the tank)—followed dutifully the dominance imperative. They were designed to make their subjects look good. The reason for this is that the leader and his class are those who throughout most of history supported the production of art and supervised (or at least funded) war. One can scan the entire corpus of Assyrian, Egyptian, or Roman art and find not a single image which makes a big man "look bad," that is, inept, cowardly, unworthy of command according to the standards of the time. Leaders who were in fact ignoble have certainly been depicted, but in a positive light. Nero on his coins appears like the effeminate artist he thought himself, yet his pose in gold relief is as regal and noble as his more virile forebears. The modern viewer, looking through a civilian, nonmilitaristic and nonheroic eye, will see in many such pictures vainglory and puffery, and that in itself is an interesting development in the way pictures of war are appreciated.

In contrast, the symbolic throwing down of an *enemy* war commander by the inversion of the dominance imperative is ancient. This display, from the North Palace of Nineveh, shows Ummanaldash, another king of Elam. The contrast to the triumphal greeting from troops for Ummanigash in the previous panel is stark.[30] Ummanaldash was defeated by the Assyrian army in a great battle in 639 B.C.E. In a victory tablet, the Assyrian king Ashurbanipal gloated,

For a (distance) of a month of twenty-five days' journey I devastated the provinces of Elam. Salt . . . I scattered over them. . . . The dust [of their cities] I gathered together and took to Assyria. . . . The noise of people, the tread of cattle and sheep, the glad shouts of rejoicing, I banished from its fields. Wild asses, gazelles and all kinds of beasts of the plain, I caused to lie down among them, as if at home.[31]

Special humiliation was saved for the vanquished ruler. It is a visual "before and after" lesson on the penalties of stoking the wrath of Assyria. Whereas all attention was on Ummanigash, in this image an ordinary Assyrian soldier who grips the defeated King's hand gazes forward, toward Nineveh. [**Fig. 17**] Ummanaldash, still decked in his robes and bulbous, attention-drawing crown, looks backwards. The interpretation given by Assyriologists is that he is reproaching the mountain tribes from whom he had sought asylum but who instead turned him over to his Assyrian enemies.[32] In any case, he is not the center of attention. He is not larger than any other man. He does not grant the king's touch; rather, an ordinary soldier clasps him. His own captured men adopt a pose of supplication as they walk behind the horses, this time not aimed toward their leader but toward the capital of the empire that crushed them. In a later panel, an Assyrian soldier pushes Ummanaldash into the cart while another struggles with him, yanking on his beard. Successful war leaders are not subject to such indignities. This picture is a reminder that the fortunes of war, what the medieval peoples called the "wheel of history," can as easily raise the star of an obscure man as ruin a king.

Displaying enemies in such a fashion was common. But at a critical juncture in human history, a new kind of picture appeared, designed not to laud one's own leader but to lampoon him, not to praise but to parody. This shift is intimately linked to three developments: the rise of citizen armies in the Napoleonic period; the growing enfranchisement of the middle and working classes in industrial democracies; and the infiltration into the officer caste of people from humbler backgrounds. When Carl von Clausewitz wrote that "war is a mere continuation of policy by other means," he replaced the medieval and Renaissance paradigms of war as the isolated game of professional gentlemen and mercenary armies with the post-Napoleonic vision of war as "the sum of available means" and "the strength of the will" of an entire state.[33] In such an undertaking, the cooperation or consent of the governed was sought rather than taken for granted.

New populism and democratizing was reflected in the changing public discourse about the soldiery. The duke of Wellington often referred to his men— the ordinary musketeers of the line—as the "scum of the earth." To be a British officer in that time was to share, as Robert Hughes describes, the "army's assumptions about human nature; and the chief of these . . . was that the motley rabble who comprised the rank and file could only be turned into soldiers by unremitting discipline backed up by summary flagellation and the threat of the firing squad."[34] Wellington's appraisal and the officer's prejudice was not unwarranted and was shared by most civilians. Recruitment was largely from among the wastrels of society, what an eighteenth-century aristocrat might call the criminal class. But during Victoria's reign, by midcentury, more and more sons of the working and middle classes were entering the armed forces. These were not "scum" but citizens, and the British public regarded them as heroes and comrades.

The crisis that revealed the new reality of war commandership was the Crimean conflict. Lasting from 1853 to 1856, the war began between the Russian and Ottoman Empires over jurisdictional rights to the holy places of Christianity in Jerusalem. In the "great game" of politics of the time, Turkey was seen by

17. Ummanaldash, king of Elam, and his attendants captured in the mountains. Assyrian relief, North Palace at Nineveh (c. 645–640 B.C.E.).
© *The British Museum*

Britain as a check on Russian global expansionism. England and France joined forces to prop up the Ottoman war effort. In September 1854, an allied army of British, French, Turkish, and Sardinian soldiers landed in the Crimea in a bid to carry the fight to Russia itself. The allies won several battles and captured the Black Sea port of Sebastopol. Russia sued for peace. This slim historical outline, however, cannot adequately convey the misery of the soldiers and the foolishness of their commanders. J. B. Priestley noted that what saved the allies, besides the sturdiness of the common British foot soldier, was that the Russians "were even bigger muddlers than their invaders."[35] Walter Savage Landor summed up the events in his poem, "The Crimean Heroes": "Hail, ye indomitable heroes, hail!/ In spite of all ye generals, ye prevail." Such a sentiment may have been expressed at the time of Rameses, but we have no record of its being published.

The war is little remembered today save for the praiseworthy activities of Florence Nightingale and the infamous Charge of the Light Brigade, where "someone had blunder'd." However, a single perceptive war correspondent, William Howard Russell, representing *The Times*, created a historical precedent. He was shocked at the hardships endured by the troops—hunger, thirst, disease, abysmal living conditions—and appalled at the callousness and ineptitude of the aristocratic officer class, especially the English generals. There was much horror to be seen; ten times as many English soldiers died of dysentery as from combat.[36] He wrote about what he saw, not only outlining for his readers in detail the disasters and horrors he witnessed but also noting how they were undermining the war effort itself.

The Charge of the Light Brigade was also a topic for Russell's sharp criticism; unlike the poet or the dragoon, he had the acuity and time to "reason why." He explained to the public how the charge had resulted from an archaic staff system better suited to knights in armor than modern war. Although he called it a "glorious catastrophe," he spared no one's reputation in outlining its causes and failures. Characteristically, the British government accused Russell of treason. Russell's pen, however, triumphed. *The Times* was the largest-selling and most influential paper in the country. The British government in charge of the war's · prosecution fell from power in the wake of the revelations.[37] Substantial reforms later occurred within the armed forces. Field Marshal Sir Evelyn Wood, who served in the Crimea as a young man, even gave Russell more credit than the generals for the eventual success of the campaign, claiming that "by awakening the conscience of the British nation to the suffering of its troops, he saved the remnants of those grand battalions. . . . [He] caused the heart of the nation to go out to its soldiers as it had never gone out before."[38] Russell's sympathies and the public's reaction suggested that a new dictum of war commandership and coverage (in words and images) had arisen: *woe to the commander or journalist who defames the ordinary soldier.* Russell's dispatches heroicized the suffering common warrior, which made attacks on him as a traitor seem foolish; but an equal reaction was that audiences were now receptive to heroicizing the ordinary man-jack of the line. From the Crimea to the present day, Western audiences of war news and fiction have been squarely in sympathy with the men in the trenches.[39]

The Crimean War was also the first ever photographed. Roger Fenton, a barrister-at-law and the son of a member of Parliament, was one of the "gentlemen" photographers of his day. Fenton traveled to the Crimea with letters of introduction to the general of the allies, and under the royal patronage of Prince Albert, the consort of Queen Victoria. Fenton was under strict military supervision. The only pictures to emerge from his camera's negative plates were of soldiers placidly sitting near their tents or allied generals in conference. The result of his picture taking, therefore, was hardly stirring. As Gisèle Freund recounts: "After about three months of strenuous work, he returned to London with nearly 360 plates. These images, showing only well-groomed soldiers behind the firing line, give a false impression of war. Fenton's expedition had been financed on the condition he photograph none of the horrors of war, so as not to frighten the soldiers' families."[40]

These pictures, which at the time could not be printed directly onto news pages, were recut as woodprints and appeared in the *Illustrated London News.* Fenton, however, showed no evidence of chafing at restrictions. He enjoyed a good life at the dinner tables of the generals. He felt it was a bore to be always asked to do portraits of the officers and men, "yet if I refuse to take them, I get no facilities for conveying my van from one locality to another."[41] In fairness to Fenton, he was also handicapped by the intricate and time-consuming process of midcentury photography. It took up to several minutes to fix an image. Battle scenes were out of the question, and indeed it would not be until World War I that a photographer could take pictures of soldiers in live combat. Technology, censorship, and lack of initiative then conspired severely to restrict the vision of war and commandership in the Crimea. No photographs of the problems of the campaign or the suffering of the allied soldiers were shown to the British people during the war. Fenton's camera to some extent perpetuated the dominance imperative.

But a new kind of imagery followed in the wake of the war. An example is a drawing of the supreme commander of the British forces, Fitzroy Somerset, Lord Raglan. As we saw with Benjamin West's hagiographic vision of General James Wolfe, an artist can borrow from the historical conventions of representation to bestow immortal glory on the war commander. But as propaganda can fail, so too can other methods be employed to ridicule and denounce a commander whose leadership has failed his men and his nation. This caricature by the great illustrator Joseph Noel Paton is sardonically entitled *Commander-in-Chief of the*

18. *Commander-in-Chief of the British Forces in the Crimea* [caricature of Fitzroy Somerset, Lord Raglan], Joseph N. Paton, 1855.
*Illustration courtesy of Matthew Lalumia*

*British Forces in the Crimea* (1855). [**Fig. 18**] Drawn a year after the ending of the war, but not shown publicly until many years later, it depicts Lord Raglan as Death, the first horseman of the Apocalypse.

Paton borrows the conventions of the heroic to ridicule the decrepit. The death figure is stripped of his uniform, an emperor literally naked to the bone. Only the items of pomp and ceremony remain: a feathered hat, overstuffed epaulettes, and an unused sword. He points in a victorious pose, not toward a battle but toward undelivered supplies, including medicine and winter clothing. The horse itself is a skeleton, though in the brilliant details of realism that are essential to caricature, the equestrian pose is instantly recognizable from thousands of heroic oil paintings and statues of war leaders. Scattered about the horse's hooves are not the debris of an enemy, but the dying men and horses and ruined guns of Raglan's own army. In the background are two other shadowy horsemen identified as "Famine" and "Disease." It would be impossible to create a more devastating attack upon the character of a war commander. As historian Matthew Lalumia notes, "The pose and gesture of Paton's skeleton mock the breed of military portraiture showing victorious princes and generals. . . . No other work of art emerging from the Crimean War so clearly demonstrates the radically altered perception of the martial elite."[42] Freed from censorship, the caricaturist's pen lacerates the failed war commander as effectively as any reporter's prose. The 10,000-year-old rules of glorifying leaders can be, in the brushes and pens of their critics, weapons to topple the mighty.

## VOLUNTARY INVERSIONS

Are contrarian images of war leadership always dysfunctional or products of resentment that undermine commanders' ability to conduct a war? Is the dominance imperative sacrosanct to accomplished management of men in battle? Should war leaders always try to suppress satiric, parodic, or nonlaudatory views of themselves? There is an intriguing middle ground between the dominance of Rameses II at Kadesh and the humiliation of Ummanaldash, between the heroicism of *The Death of General Wolfe* and the subversion of *Commander-in-Chief of the British Forces in the Crimea*. That middle ground is occupied by acceptable or even purposive inversions. Many of these involve humor, seemingly at the expense of the war leader. But the voluntary nature of the exercise, when considered in the context of the war, is functional. It strangely acts to preserve the status quo rather than to challenge it.

This aspect of allowable inversion is illustrated by a cartoon entitled "Don't mention it, lootenant."[43] [**Fig. 19**] The artist, Bill Mauldin, worked for *Stars and Stripes*, the official U.S. Army newspaper, and accompanied the American forces throughout World War II into North Africa, Sicily, Italy, France, and Germany. Mauldin was known as the GIs' cartoonist. In his work, which followed the exploits of Willie and Joe, two fictional but prototypical infantrymen, he displayed a puckish delight in puncturing any vaingloriousness that existed in the military spectacle. He also underscored the indignities, miseries, and terrors of warfare. These are sharply drawn in this cartoon: Shells explode in an angry sky, and bullets whiz by. In the background there is a destroyed town; in the foreground is the moonscape of a battlefield, including the obstacles of bent posts and barbed wire. Here, too, is an event that would be recognizable to a Neolithic artist: the burly soldier, his legs braced, carrying a wounded officer to safety on his back.

This description is the script of an episode of heroism. But the basis of laughter is the reversal of the expected. Neither the soldier nor the officer plays the traditional hero. Their uniforms are nondescript, baggy, dirty. Both are unshaven, scowling, and hunchbacked. The only distinction of command is a single

19. "Don't mention it, lootenant. They mighta replaced ya wit' one of them salutin' demons." World War II cartoon, Bill Mauldin.
*Reprinted by permission of Bill Mauldin and the Watkins/Loomis Agency*

bar on the collar and the helmet of the "lootenant." The officer is wounded in the foot, not in that traditionally noble place of injury, the chest. In another age, in the era of Napoleon or Queen Victoria, on the canvas of an oil painting, or perhaps even today in a Hollywood movie, this situation, with almost identical staging, would be one of romantic, or at least gritty, valor—as it was even within the comedic storyline of *Forrest Gump* (1994). Mauldin has reduced it here to farce, while preserving the matter-of-fact bravery of the dogface.

Then there is the wonderful caption: "Don't mention it, lootenant. They mighta replaced ya wit' one of them salutin' demons." Despite the wretchedness of the conditions of the soldiers, and the visual stripping away of any of the colors, costumes, and trappings of glory, this *is* a heroic situation. The ordinary man saves his officer from what we assume would be certain death. Yet the soldier's proffered reasons are not protestations for king, fatherland, honor, or duty. There is nothing in the caption that might serve as a motto for schoolboys, senators, or cadets. Nor is there any personalization of affection or loyalty between men. Willie the GI is simply stating, "I'm saving your life because you're not so bad as officers go, and if you bite the dust we might get a worse one." The worse one, the saluting demon, would be, of course, a Lord Raglan. In a very American way, Willie was being both heroic and humble, shrugging off his virtue as necessity. He is a hard-nosed, cynical wit, who ends up doing "what's right" in the honorable tradition of the tough, street-smart wiseguy. The quip could accompany the stony sneer of Clint Eastwood, the wry smile of Mel Gibson, or the curled lip of Bugs Bunny with equal success.

The sentiments expressed in this cartoon were probably also muttered among Caesar's legions, Charlemagne's axemen, and Napoleon's *chasseurs à cheval*. Only in the modern era, however, were such delicious subversions of the displays of public order in wartime allowed to be visually expressed in print, to be mass-communicated. Again, this cartoon appeared not in an antiwar poster but in the official army newspaper. Mauldin himself comments, "Many old line officers are no doubt shocked at a spirit of passive rebellion which occasionally shows itself in this citizen army. That's the whole answer. It is a citizen army, and it has in its enlisted ranks many men who in civil life were not accustomed to being directed to the back door and the servant quarters. To taking orders, yes; but to taking indignities, no."[44] Such humor, then, was functional, an escape valve for discontent that allowed men who risked their lives every day to feel slightly empowered. In the right circumstances, humor can contribute to unit cohesion and fighting effectiveness.

Such inversions of rank and subversions of the dominance imperative could be publicity efforts in themselves, not simply allowed but propagated. The English newspaper *Sphere* on May 20, 1916, printed a photograph of some flooded army barracks. In the picture, we see an oblong building that is up to its windows in a currentless river, while a few men in uniform stand on the roof gazing at the camera. The caption in the newspaper reads:

ONE OF THE HUMOURS OF CAMPAIGNING IN THE DESERT—
AN OFFICER'S CAMP FLOODED OUT.

During the flood season in Mesopotamia, wash-outs are of frequent occurrence. The country is one of extremes—the weather is seldom moderate, either the country is baking in the sun or it is deluged by waterspouts and floods. Accompanying the floods high winds are often experienced, which heap up the water and send it over the river and canal banks, to the intense discomfort of such troops as are unhappily quartered near the centre of the disturbance.[45]

The image was taken and printed during one of the darkest hours of Britain's involvement in World War I. The last English and Australian forces had been withdrawn from the beachhead of Gallipoli to the west, showing no profit from the gamble that cost the lives of almost half a million men. Here, in the Middle East, the British had been defeated once again by the Turks in an epic siege of the city of Kut, Iraq, where a British garrison surrendered only twenty days before this story ran. "The 'picnic' in Mesopotamia was probably the biggest muddle of all," writes historian A. J. Barker. "The facts present a picture which is one of political ineptitude and mismanagement."[46] British forces in the "land of the Two Rivers" were the least funded, worst equipped and supplied, and most poorly led of the war. In a region of little vegetation, the soldiers fought with antique rifles, faulty ammunition, and surplus hardtack. Kut was a special humiliation: the British commander had endeavored to bribe the Turks to withdraw, and this offer was publicized. Ultimately, however, the white flag flew and 2,000 British troops spent the rest of the war in captivity. The government in England tried to put the best face on the disaster; uplifting rhetoric flowed in from allies in Australia and France.

The photograph was but one attempt to obfuscate "one of the greatest mistakes in British military history."[47] The implications are that the miseries that the soldiers were forced to undergo were not caused by the incompetence of a British government that did not allocate adequate supplies or men to the Eastern enterprise. Nor is blame assigned to officers who stretched their supply lines and underestimated the Turkish resolve to fight. The spin placed on the story is that "humour" is the result of nature: this was nothing worse than a bad camping trip. We see that being the butt of a joke can serve the interests of the war leaders, when it appears to demonstrate their parity with the men and diverts attention from their failures as commanders. Humor at the expense of military authority thus serves two purposes for that very class. First, it reinforces the ideal of a democratic army. Second, an officer, and an officer class, that can "take a joke"—unlike Lord Raglan and the marionettes of the Crimea—is humanized; this removes from the man, the uniform, and the class the stigma of elitism. The humor here, of course, is a very mild one, a token of indignity, not a surrender of power.

In all, commandership and its visualization have assumed various rules of presentation. For pictured prehistory and history these conventions were remarkably similar, repetitive, and easily read. Later eras and sentiments overturned the rules and broke them, ridiculed and lampooned them, but always referred to them. The fundamental change from the Stone Age tribal society to the urban empires was one of scale and economy: the more recent kings and emperors invested huge resources of time, material, and money to convince their armies and people visually that they were worthy war commanders. This dominance imperative did not markedly alter until the Renaissance, and was not overthrown until the nineteenth century in concurrence with democratizing social change. In the era in which we live, commanders can still glorify themselves, but they must do so in less blatant, boastful, and ostentatious ways. Most important, at the end of the Middle Ages in Europe and during the rise of mass democracy in the West formally established by the time of the Crimean War, a new hero appears in the visions of war. He is not a king, often not even an officer; he is the ordinary soldier of the line or sailor of the deck. It is he who will be the central object of focus of war photography in the twentieth century and of the most contemporary mass medium, that of film. As evidence, even the most dashing and celebrated Axis and Allied commanders of World War II have been featured in only a handful of movies, while the personalized account of ordinary soldiers in a squadron or platoon is an established genre, common to the point of cliché. The war commander who does not in word and image pay these men their due is doomed to fail, both on the battlefield and in the crucially influential eyes of the public.

# 4

---

# COMRADES

## SEEKING COMMILITO

A television public service announcement begins by showing a young man sprawled on a couch watching TV, his sneakered feet up on the coffee table; it is a study in slacker disengagement. But then an uplifting tune drifts from the set: *"When the heavens thunder/When the nation calls/You can make a difference/ And be a part of it all."* On the screen, National Guardsmen load sandbags, protecting some town, we infer, from flooding. The boy plants his feet on the floor, looking wide-eyed and drop-jawed, as one of the guardsmen points to him through the TV, breaking the fourth wall of the medium. The man bellows: "You, come on!" and jerks a thumb in a "follow me" gesture. The boy flies headfirst into the TV set and joins the sandbagging team. Various scenes follow of junior guardsmen planting crops, inspecting a helicopter, and saluting the camera. The voice-over intones: "Find yourself in the Army National Guard, serving one weekend a month and two weeks a year, and you'll find an extra paycheck, money for college and a great way to serve your community. Call 1-800-Go-Guard!" The audience for this ad is obviously meant to be the older Boy Scout, not the would-be combatant.[1] The special effects are impressive, made to appeal to a video game generation.

Thematic appeals, slogans, and visualizations of "joining up"—where a young man is invited to become part of a band of comrades—are essentially unchanged from the Stone Age. The act of recruitment in the National Guard announcement is made by a future comrade; variations use other types of persons. In a U.S. Army ad, a young man riding an M1A1 Abrams tank recalls in a flashback the small-town adults who encouraged his ambitions: "To Mr. Phelps, the teacher who taught me . . ." In a U.S. Marine recruiting video, a young man returns from boot camp in uniform; the narration declares, "You'll prove yourself to those who had their doubts." At these words a gray-haired father nods approvingly at the uniform. And, of course, for men throughout history, women have been both a direct and indirect incitement for enlisting. In World War I, a famous poster showed a mother, sister, and fiancée waving off their young man accompanied by the slogan, "Women of Britain say Go!" Finally, the inducer to "sign up" can be the war commander himself. The sandbagging officer in the National Guard PSA gives a variation of the beckoning signal used in the portrait of England's Lord Kitchener in World War I, the "I Want You" gesture of the United States' Uncle Sam, and the "follow me" forward wave of the U.S. Army in Action poster of infantry commander Aubrey "Red" Newman exhorting his men to "get the hell off the beach" of Leyte Island after landing.

Such recruitment strategies underscore that men fight for other men as well as for leaders, causes, countries, booty, and adventure. The bond between the effective leader and his men is often forged by what the Romans called *commilito*, or "fellow soldiership." Its diverse aspects are visually expressed in the column of the Roman emperor Trajan (r. 98–117). No Roman prince achieved as great military success as Trajan, and in histories of peoples as disparate as the Turks and the Indians he survived as the model of the warrior ruler, the *optimus princeps*. Toward the end of his life or shortly after his death, a 100-foot stone column was erected in Rome commemorating his campaigns and the conquest of the Danubian kingdom of Dacia. From the base of the column to its peak, reliefs are laid out like an unfurling scroll, dense with scenes and peoples showing major and minor events of the wars: sieges, field combat, capturing of prisoners, and the subjugation of towns. These panels stretch 200 meters and hold about 2,500 figures. Yet, most of the activities shown are the soldiers at work, setting up camp, laying bridges, erecting fortifications, constructing siege works: the necessary and the mundane tasks of warfare, but also those which distinguished the Romans from their barbarian enemies. If the disciplined *manipul* (the Roman platoon) and unyielding *testudo* (the turtlelike formation of legionaries) were manifestations of the cohesion of the Roman fighting unit, then the pick and the spade were symbols of a Roman army machine that tackled all obstacles, man-made and natural, to achieve its direction and desired result.

But why should a monument to the glory of a war commander contain so many incidents of less than glamorous busywork? The Greek writer Hermogenes instructed: ". . . [I]f we are describing a war, we shall first of all mention the preliminaries such as the generals' speeches, the outlay on both sides, and their fears; next, the attacks, the slaughter, and the dead; finally, the victory trophy, the triumphal songs of the victors, the tears and enslavement of the victims."[2] Missing from this catalogue—whose events are shown on Trajan's column and make up part of the agenda for most war artists—is the "grunt" work before the battle. This is the cutting and digging, polishing and sharpening, hauling and slogging that characterize the life of the ordinary soldier, from the V-chested men of Neolithic Spain to Willie and Joe: the endless hours of waiting and preparing that precede and follow the "moments of terror" in battle. Trajan's column illustrates all that Hermogenes cites and the labor of the spade as well.

The first scene in the panel confirms this establishment: the god Neptune gazes approvingly as Roman soldiers bridge the Danube. It was no easy task. To cross into the Dacian heartland, Trajan had to build a series of bridges across the river strong enough to withstand floods and the weight of the ten legions he assigned to the wars. The historian Diodorus Siculus claims that Trajan's bridge was the newest wonder of the world. More trials were to come. To safeguard themselves in hostile wooded terrain, legionaries cleared forests and built fortified camps. To crush the enemy, the Romans engaged in a series of massive and precise sieges like that which precipitated the fall of the Dacian capital of Sarmizegethusa and the flight and suicide of their king. But such construction projects had not only a practical intent; their visualization was in itself an act of propaganda that the Roman viewer would have understood. The mark of a disciplined army with faith in its commander is that it will endure the tedium and indignities of preparing for war as well as the shock of battle. Among what the Greeks called the *klea andrön* (glorious deeds of warriors) was their ability to march, dig, build, and toil in the company of their leaders and their comrades. And throughout the panels, the emperor, strapping in body, fine muscles carved deep into the stone, is there among the troops, watching over them and addressing them in speeches, the *adlocutios* that were standard fare of commander-soldier contact.

More important, here was a prince who kept his soldiers from engaging in the more wanton acts that had plagued many Roman armies in its past: mutinies, looting of friendly towns, drunken upsets of every kind, and insubordination. Such excesses are conspicuously cited as being absent under the firm hand of Trajan. The historian Dio Cassius remarks that "pride and arrogance on the part of the soldiers" was checked in his reign, "so firmly did he rule them."[3] The script of Trajan's column is read in this light. The emperor's glory was enhanced by showing the troops undertaking dull and dreary labors, which was a testament to their discipline and their loyalty, and to the skill of the commander who could require of them not only to face death and retain cohesion and *sang-froid*, but to work each day "nine to five" in the ordinary tasks of the army.

These are precisely the characteristics cited by ancient historians and biographers of Trajan. Pliny wrote in his *Panegyric*, as if addressing the emperor, "it was your habit to inspect your comrades' tents before you retired to your own; the last man must go off duty before you would take a rest yourself."[4] Trajan was a great leader, participant, and observer: "Nothing escaped your direction or your observant eye . . . you can call nearly all your soldiers by name, and know the deeds of bravery of each one, while they need not recount the wounds they received in their country's service, since you were there to witness and applaud."[5] Dio Cassius tells us that the emperor personally expressed concern for wounded soldiers, gave medals to the brave, and spoke in the name of the fallen.[6] Another Roman writer compared him to the good shepherd.[7] There are stories that, even if they are not true, express what most soldiers would have readily believed about their general: that Trajan tore his own clothes to make bandages for wounded soldiers.[8]

The basis for the images of camaraderie in war is so intimately connected to success on the battlefield that little has changed in how comradeship is shown from the Neolithic age to today in ads aimed at recruiting the "Net" (born after 1979) generation. In interviews conducted after World War II, researchers found that, "More than any other single characteristic, veteran enlisted men mentioned helpfulness toward their men, and the display of personal interest in them and their problems, in describing the characteristics of the best officer they had known in combat."[9] Indeed, "takes a lot of interest in what his men are thinking" was the most frequently cited quality of the sought-after commander, and the lack of which was the most crucial detriment to morale.[10] The biographer Plutarch detailed 1,800 years ago the preference of any grunt when he described what gratified a legionnaire and what visually marked this satisfaction: "It is the most obliging sight in the world to the Roman soldier to see a commander eat the same bread as himself, or lie upon an ordinary bed, or assist in the work in drawing a trench and raising a bulwark . . . [for they admire] those that partake of the same labour and danger with themselves."[11] In this vein, Pliny adds of Trajan: "They saw how you shared their hunger and thirst on field manoeuvres and how their commander's sweat and dust was mingled with their own; with nothing to mark you out save your height and physique."[12] Such was the tradition, which remains with us, at least symbolically.

Sometimes, however, a commander will retain the tradition but project a culturally tailored view in his representations. At the Battle of Blenheim in 1704, the duke of Marlborough ranged the length of the field, personally intervening in the hot spots. His front-line leadership was instrumental in defeating the French, who were led by a commander no less valiant, but slightly less capable, and cursed with extreme nearsightedness. In the *Marlborough Tapestries*, however—the series of cloth paintings of the duke's exploits created for and still hanging in his palace—Marlborough is pictured at a proper distance from the battlefield, according to the dictates set for the gentleman-commander of the early modern era. He stands upon a hill and gazes at the far removed maneuvers of chessmen infantry; but the commander broke the rules in the actual battle when victory and not courtly propriety was at stake. In modern armies, junior officers play such a role; the expectations for their behavior by the men have not changed since the Stone Age.

Such ties go under many names: *commilito,* but also charismatic ties, *esprit de corps*, camaraderie of the trenches, loyalty to buddies, and, in the language of twentieth-century sociology, primary group attachments and reference group orientation. Each denotes somewhat different degrees and distinctions of the same concept. Mutual suffering can breed contempt, divisiveness, sniping, pettiness, and panic, but it can also produce close friendship and bonding. If war consists of battles, commanders, enemies, horrors, and power, it also includes intimacy between hoplites, legionnaires, yeomen-at-arms, *condoratti*, grenadiers, *poilus*, frontoviks, Landsers, and GIs. These bonds are eternal, and can be deduced in the Neolithic and in Augustan Rome, at Iwo Jima and before the gates of Troy. Of the two types of bonding, between soldiers and other soldiers, and between officers and men, the former, the comrades-in-arms, have not changed at all, in depiction or in expression. Wise commanders thus seek to encourage and to be part of these ties, because comradeship is the universal basis both of unit cohesion and success in battle. Though the ordinary soldier as a main subject of imagery is absent until the late Renaissance,[13] his role as a supporting player has always been indispensable.

## THE WARRIOR PROCESSION

As we have seen, caricature can better sum up in an image or set of images the rules of a genre than a long exposition by art historians. Representative are two panels from *Obélix et Compagnie*, a cartoon adventure of the series *Aventures d'Astérix* produced by the writer Goscinny and the artist Uderzo.[14] [**Fig. 20**] No

20. Roman legionnaires (a) entering; (b) departing Babaorum camp in Gaul.
Goscinny and Uderzo, *Obélix et Compagnie*, 1976.
*Paris: Dargaud Editeur © Les Editions Albert René/Goscinny-Uderzo*

ancient picture, no history book, no film has probably more affected the image of the Roman Empire and ancient Gaul than the output of these two pens. Astérix is a diminutive Gallic warrior. The period is 50 B.C.E., and as the introduction to every book in the series tells us, "Toute la Gaule est occupée par les Romains. Toute? Non!" One village on the Breton coast remains undefeated, for the villagers are empowered by a magic potion that makes them invincible in battle. Since this is a cartoon for children—but also beloved by adults in and beyond the francophone world—the battles consist mostly of roughhousing and tumbling; no one is killed, but by the end of every episode, another Roman legion has been reduced to a limping shambles by the super-powered Gauls.

In the first panel, the beginning of the adventure, a new Roman detachment arrives to garrison one of the forts permanently stationed around the Gallic village. In a catalogue of the elements that made the Roman army so often victorious (and would have been approved of by a Neolithic artist), each soldier is a perfect replica of the others. The angles of foot, expression, packing of kits, lines of fingers and arms, grip on weapons, deployment of shields, are all in perfect harmony. Leading the soldiers is the massive-chested war commander, his face like an eroded cliff, his muscles bursting from under his brass chestplate. Even in caricature the portrayal expresses the discipline of the Roman legions, which enabled them to defeat armies many times their size. That discipline was perfected in campground marches and duties. As Edward Gibbon pointed out, "so sensible were the Romans of the imperfection of valour without skill and practice, that, in their language, the name of an army was borrowed from the word which signified exercise."[15] The result was a killing machine—a base augmentation of the aim of the hoplite phalanx where every man worked for the whole. The Jewish historian (and former rebel) Josephus asserted that the Romans prepared so thoroughly for war that "It would not be far from the truth to call their drills bloodless battles, their battles bloody drills."[16] The warrior procession, and its deployment in regulated ranks and files in camp or in battle, was the ancient marker of the trained and thus potent army—and no one excelled at warrior processions like the legions of the Caesars and Trajans.

But in this *bon geste* cartoon, the well-honed warrior procession awaits a chaotic future. Confronting them is the commander of the garrison that has been stationed here for the last year. Whereas the new commander is strapping and vigorous, the old one has declined into a pear-shaped, unshaven wreck, the antithesis of Roman public presentation. A few panels later, the old garrison staggers out, an amusing mixture of decrepitude and joy. Faced with an invincible enemy, Roman discipline has collapsed; the army has become the opposite of its former self. The real conceit, known to fans of the series, is that by the last page of the book the smart, fresh Romans will be reduced to the slovenliness of their predecessors.

The orderly march (or ride), of course, is greatly favored by history's war artists and generals—and it can imply unity in the most trying circumstances. For example, at the end of *Fort Apache* (1948), John Wayne has just completed a press conference after taking command of a U.S. Cavalry unit whose former commander died Indian-fighting. A journalist comments that in war only the leaders are remembered. Wayne, disgusted, turns away to look out a window; framed by a setting sun, his face is then superimposed on a long train of blue-coated, yellow-kerchiefed cavalrymen riding obliquely into the camera. His voice-over narration intones, "They're the regiment. Their pay is $13 a month. Their diet beans and hay, maybe horse meat before this campaign is over. They'll fight over cards or rot-gut whiskey, but share the last drop of water in their canteens—they're the regiment, the regular army." The scene and the sentiment reveal a physical and a spiritual ideal of the warrior, at least according to artists and generals: correct formation embodies *commilito*. Thus this warrior procession, the oldest stock *mise-en-scène* that displays the unity of fighting men, serves many purposes. It instills the discipline of unified, regulated movement. It allows commanders to watch over their soldiers; for practical reasons, desertions are less likely to occur when soldiers move in one group; psychologically, the uniformity of soldiers allows commanders to resolve their expendability and interchangeability; and it reinforces the bonding of soldiers as part of a unit that maneuvers and, it is hoped by the generals, fights as one. Machiavelli advised that when an army scattered, its only hope of battlefield resurrection was to "flock to the banner." Military parades are held for the benefit of the home-front audiences as well; they display the utility of tax dollars at work and reassure the public that they are guarded by crisply aligned legions.

The vision of war, in Roman reliefs or classic Hollywood movies, typically both actualizes and comes to define such ideals. Yet the connection between "buddyhood" and "warriorhood" is hardly symbiotic or linear. Buddies can desert together, freeze up together. The generals' ideal can break down before the kinds of conditions war buddies face. In the example cited above, even veteran Roman troops could mutiny or ignore commands as a unit. Such mutinies, frequent in the Late Republican period, and even more so in the Imperial third century, are largely unexpressed in Roman art. Unmentioned, too, in *Fort Apache* is that in the real-life U.S. cavalry on the western plains, the men—faced with terrible isolation, punishing freeze-burn weather, bad food, tedious routines, and other miseries—deserted at a rate that approached 50 percent. Such a flood out the back door of Fort Apache would not, of course, have fit into the John Wayne mythos.

Indeed, warrior processions can be exercises in deception; the concerted tromp and clank of rank upon rank, file upon file of men, horse, and machine can obscure the organization's decay. For example, in the Paris Bastille Day parade of 1939, the French army, complete with glittering blocks of cavalry, marched in procession, along with tanks, squadrons of planes, and 35,000 infantry. The cavalcade had been specifically designed, as William L. Shirer notes, "to instill confidence in a populace which had doubts about the capacity of France to stand up to Hitler's Germany."[17] The show was convincing; one writer exclaimed in reaction: "How could one fear Germany?" Unseen were the archaic leadership skills and war plans of the French command, its rigid doctrines of defensive war, the obsolete systems of communication, the shortages in planes and heavy guns, the poor quality control standards of its armaments. In greatest irony, the army massed some 350 tanks to impress the multitudes of citizens, foreign reporters, and ambassadors. The machines rumbled down the Champs-Elysées with great effect. Yet French tactical doctrine in warfare defined the tank as an infantry support weapon. In the Battle of France to come in the next months, those mass tanks would be dispersed into piecemeal forces. The Germans, on the other hand, though they possessed fewer tanks, compacted them into Panzer divisions, the foundation of the *Blitzkrieg*.

This does not detract from the utility of the warrior procession for show, maneuver, and training. The procession is the most efficient mode of travel, for wildebeest or for human beings. In the chapter on primitive war, we viewed a scene dated some 6,000 years ago from the Gasulla Gorge in southern Spain [see **Fig. 8**]. Despite its antiquity, it displays the similarly canted bodies, unidirectionality, equal pace, and "uniform" gear and weaponry that mark a warrior procession. The combatants may be easily compared to the modern rifle platoon, marching in formation, weapons held high, circumspect spacing between each soldier. Such warrior processions reappear in many civilizations. From ancient Lagash, the city-state kingdom in central Mesopotamia about 2500 B.C.E., a mural shows the marching figures of infantry, all with identical expressions, shaven heads, grass skirts, spears held in perfect presentation. In the Assyrian reliefs, as well, there are many images of identically attired and bearded soldiers, marching, fighting, enacting siege works, all with a uniformity of expression, direction, and action. These mathematically precise alignments reflect the seriousness with which the state applied itself to war. From the Hittite capital of Begazcoy in central Anatolia from around 1400 B.C.E. there is a similar procession of warriors carved on a stone wall. Each is dressed identically in the characteristic Phrygian cap of the Hittites; all march together in lockstep, almost arm-in-arm. They are dressed as warriors, but there is a controversy among researchers as to whether they are among the 1,000 gods that the Hittites worshipped or simply soldiers.[18] In any case, whether they are deities or the king's guard, the visualization of their unity is self-evident; a sociological insight is expressed: only through war is there national unity.

One interesting example of the procession display is a vase from an ancient Greek fortress of Mycenae. [**Fig. 21**] Sixteen inches high, overprinted with black lacquer, it is dated to about 1200 B.C.E. The time and style associate it with the palace of the legendary King Agamemnon and the era of the Trojan War. Uncovered by Heinrich Schliemann, the vase's decoration shows a startling analogy to any modern scene of the first days of a war. A procession of warriors, moving from left to right, all similarly attired and shaven, of uniform racial features and body cant and pose, march off to war. They are, in fact, hoplites from 750 years before the hoplites were said to have existed, according to traditional historiography. Was this a private army, a citizen's militia, a mercenary force? From their spears hang what are probably bags of food prepared by their womenfolk, who see them off on the other side of the vase. These men do not match in any way the vision of the warrior suggested by Homer's descriptions. Indeed, they look rather insipid—more Gomer Pyle or Beetle Bailey than Achilles or Sarpedon. This, of course, is a view through modern eyes; perhaps their ungainliness was an accepted convention of the time. Possibly the images were meant to be humorous. Clearly, though, they are not individualized heroes. Each man not only looks the same, from the slant of his nose to the point of his chin, but carries the same kit and armor; even their shields are not distinctive. Unlike the display of heroes in vases of the later centuries, no inscriptions identify individuals.

This does not suggest that the society of Mycenae, the wellspring of the Trojan

21. "Warrior vase," Mycenae (c. 1200 B.C.E.).
*National Museum, Athens. Courtesy of the Hellenic Republic Ministry of Culture*

War legend, was egalitarian. To the contrary, Schliemann also found the graves, festooned with gold masks and votive objects, of what was unmistakably a dynasty of powerful kings. War was their main business enterprise, the sacking of cities their career and the basis of the royal economy. From the written records we find meticulous bureaucratic details of booty captured, slaves distributed, spears and chariots allocated. Powerful rulers, war commanders, sent these marching warriors to battle. If heroes did live in those days, we have no pictures of their exploits that are clear to the modern eye. Even in the allegedly Heroic age, the ordinary men in regular marching formation are an integral part of the experience and the vision of war.

Yet the warrior procession need not be synonymous with the suppression of the individual. This is visibly so in the most spectacular warrior procession (in terms of size and enduring beauty) in the world's history. It was created some 2,500 years ago by the Chin emperor, the first ruler who unified all the warring kingdoms of China, and who gave his name to the nation. Although his reign was short-lived and most notorious for his tyranny, no warlord in history expended so much effort to acknowledge those who sustained his power. Near the ancient capital of Xi'an, archeologists have uncovered as many as 1,400 statues of the soldiers of the Royal Guard. Each terra-cotta warrior wears greatcoat cloth armor; many hold weapons of various kinds. They are deployed in units of archers, halberdiers, spearmen, and charioteers; officers stand silent vigil in front of their platoons; stone horses await near their masters.

Incredibly, the buried Chin army was not a work of mass production. The statues were made of conjoined pieces with some body parts cast from a central mold, yet in the face and head, each soldier is an individual, almost certainly patterned after a real fighting man. Distinctive nuances of face and gesture and even body height and shape mark every statue. The men, utterly lifelike, are shown as they probably were, muscular, strapping, resolute. It is impossible to look at their grim faces and not recognize the veteran professional soldier. The statues are tall, averaging about five feet ten in height. These were tough, brawny men of war who were honored by a vast enterprise of their king. Altruism was of course not his objective; the bonding between commander and soldier is often cemented by personal addresses, the *adlocutio* of the Roman emperors, medals and trophies, and, on a monumental scale, memorializing for the ages. It is also quite possible that the Chin emperor, who spent much time and attention seeking an elixir for eternal life, believed that these men would follow him into the next world as his immortal retinue.

The most common visualization in antiquity of the massed soldiers moving in formation, which then in battle deployed in massed ranks, was the Greek phalanx. Art, iconography, and literature proclaimed its beauty and virtue. The hoplite, long javelin extended, armored with helmet or without, standing in battle, is the dominant image of the Greek warrior. The formation is omnipresent in classical, fourth-century art, the era of the Peloponnesian War. Phalanxes appear on vases, frescoes, mosaics, and above all on reliefs and sculptures. Membership in the formation was also a matter of considerable pride. The Greek poet Aeschylus, renowned in his time and awarded many prizes and much praise for his tragedies, asked that the only notation on his gravestone be that he had fought with his fellow Athenians at Marathon.

Why were these warriors so exceptional, making membership among them an honor? Consider first their kit. The term for all the equipment used by a soldier of a phalanx was *panoply*, which implies its variety and complexity. The round shield of the hoplite, the *aspis* (thirty inches in diameter), was the standard defense weapon, designed specifically for the phalanx in classical Greece. Each man in the phalanx held his shield by the left arm, attached by wooden pegs and leather straps.[19] His offensive weapons were the spear and the short sword. The spear could be thrust or thrown, but the sword, like the *gladius* of the Roman legionaries, was a short stabbing weapon meant specifically for close combat in crowds. With his helmet, greaves, shield, and weapons, a hoplite would typically carry 75 pounds of equipment to combat. So great was this burden that often a servant was employed to carry the shield and three days' worth of food.

The weight and the type of armor and weapons had several implications. The first was that the hoplite defense system was constructed not for a hero fighting in single combat with wide room for acrobatics and swordplay, but for a man among a mass. When in unbroken formation, in his armor, partly covered by his own shield and those of his comrades, a hoplite was almost immune to being killed by an arrow, though he could be wounded in an extremity.[20] Second, the Greeks assumed the cavalry of the day—which did not have stirrups—could not ride down a mass of hoplites that *stayed in formation*. Third, the hoplite could change directional orientation, but he was not highly maneuverable. Essentially, the hoplite warrior was an instrument of stubborn defense and dogged thrust. Finally, the phalanx was deployed in formations of eight to ten ranks, or up to sixteen ranks deep in the Macedonian version. The hoplite mass thundering forward could build up a great deal of momentum, with the intention of shattering the lines of an enemy. The porcupinelike spread of spears interlaced with shields and the slit-eyed Corinthian helmets might also serve as a visual display terrorizing into flight lighter-armed and less resolute opponents. Packed like bronze-armored sardines, they literally had no room to run; for successful retreat, flight had to be wholesale.[21] Plutarch described the formation as "some single powerful animal, irresistible so long as it is embodied into one, and keeps its order, shield touching shield, all as in a piece; but if it be once broken, not only is the joint force lost, but the individual soldiers also who compose it lose each one his own single strength, because of the nature of their armour; and because each of them is strong, rather, as he makes a part of the whole, than in himself."[22] To break ranks was to betray those around you, and considering that many battles were fought near the walls of the city, perhaps before your relatives and womenfolk as well.

Such an ethos and equipment of war had social ramifications, indicating that Greek society favored such a soldier and explaining why he and his fellows were the heroes of so many reliefs and vases. First, they were largely men of the middle and upper classes. Businessmen and landowners, political opponents, poets and master craftsmen would take their appointed place in a line. According to Thucydides, the hoplite class in Athens of men of military age numbered 30,000, compared to only 1,200 members of the equestrian or knights class who could afford a horse and its stabling. Those they stood next to were not strangers nor even recently acquired buddies from training camp or the trench, but brothers, fathers, uncles, and next-door neighbors in the city-state. Thus, for the citizens of Athens, the army was not some separate body quartered in a distant land. Rather, the people were the army, perhaps in a way never seen in any civilization before or since. This form of equality, whereby every male citizen of reasonable age was equally liable for sacrifice and responsible for security, was, the Greeks believed, irrevocably tied to the maintenance of a democracy. Yet, as the warrior vase of a thousand years before Athenian democracy displays, the mass did not in fact require an egalitarian social order to sustain it.

The politics of the procession can both unify the participants and terrify the observers. In all the above examples, uniformity of appearance, direction, and action is probably under these circumstances a positive symbol, that is, it connotes willful and approved camaraderie in a fighting force. Men who will endure the discipline of marching together in perfect step will, it has been assumed since the beginning of warfare, deploy and fight with equally skillful coordination. However, the warrior procession can also, depending upon the audience and the intention of the creator or stage manager, have malevolent implications.

Consider the contrast between two very similar warrior processions in film. In Leni Riefenstahl's film *Triumph of the Will* (1935), the warriors on procession are the men of the SS (*Schutzstaffel*, or Black Shirts). Initially, these units were formed as Hitler's personal bodyguard. Heinrich Himmler, a master of intrigue and bureaucracy, gradually expanded the organization, so that many historians eventually characterized it as a state within a state. Himmler was deeply infused with the mythology of *Volk*, Satanism, and astrology. Although he himself looked no more threatening than the bespectacled chicken farmer that he had been in his civilian existence, he insisted on an elaborate system of visual symbolism to costume the men of the SS. Entire volumes are devoted to the elaborate genera of shoulder cuffs and heraldry the SS imposed on itself; a thriving hobby industry is still dedicated to its collection. Most striking were the parade-ground black uniforms, whose sleekness was only interrupted by silver piping and unit markings. For the letters "SS" Himmler borrowed the lightning-flash runes of the ancient Nordic language. The overall effect was imposing. The soldier himself was a living canvas whose frame was transposable to other media: the silver on black responded well to photography, even in poorer quality newsprint.

*Triumph of the Will* was the world debut of the Nazi movement in general and the black-shirted SS in particular. There is one sequence that seems to sum up the racial mythos upon which the SS was grounded. A long chorus line of black-clad, black-helmeted, hip-booted SS men marches down a set of steps; the music is ponderous and thumping; the iron heels of the soldiers' boots click on the marble. They are, to use a metaphor of which the Nazis would have approved, like gods temporarily descended to mingle with ordinary men. The sequence is obviously intended to be a warrior procession of ageless clarity and beauty, yet it is often employed in contemporary documentaries, beginning with Frank Capra's *Why We Fight* series, as an example of the *threat* of the unity of an evil enemy.

How such a warrior procession can be seen as an indication not of positive camaraderie but as a symbol of the troglodytic values of an enemy "other" is more clearly demonstrated in the most famous warrior procession in the history of film, that presented by Sergei Eisenstein in *Battleship Potemkin* (1925). [**Fig. 22**] Known to every film buff, the sequence is much copied, both earnestly (*The Untouchables*, 1987) and in parody (*Naked Gun 33⅓*, 1994). The setting is the 1905 revolution. In the wake of Russia's defeat by the Japanese in war, protests and mutinies erupt throughout the country. Among the most legendary occurred in the Black Sea fleet on the battleship that gave the film its name. The revolution was crushed, but to Communists like Eisenstein it was simply a precursor of the greater rebellion to come a few years later following the disasters of another war.

In the climax of the film, ordinary citizens are trapped in the ocean-front gardens of the city of Odessa. The tsar's troops, in crisp white uniforms, advance with bayonets fixed. People panic and flee. A woman whose son is wounded carries him back up the steps toward the soldiers, pleading "Don't shoot! My boy is very ill." Another woman, pushing a pram, is shot in the side. She collapses, her fingers letting go of her precious charge. The baby carriage begins rolling down the steps, and downward behind it come the soldiers of the tyrant. The film is silent, but the boot clicks are easily imagined. These automatons of authority are enacting a warrior procession, but rather than signifying brotherhood or camaraderie, in the efficiency of a well-coordinated fighting force they present purely negative implications. These men, in their unity of direction, uniform, expression, and action, are removed from the human race. They lack pity and any vestige of connection with the people of their own country. In contrast, however, Eisenstein saw the rebellious sailors of the *Potemkin* and the people as "moral victor over the guns of tsarism."[23] The bloody warrior procession, the descent down the steps of Odessa, signifies the eventual downfall of the regime that would employ such cruel robots against its own people.

The warrior procession can also be injected with pathos and irony if, as so often happens when we view an image, we impose context on it that would have escaped its creators. We see a narrow moment in time within the frame of an image, but because we know the end of the story, if the results are fatal, our interpretation of the warrior procession cannot be admiring. Such is the case with many images of World War I. During the war, governments allowed the taking and filming of pictures, staged or real, of troops "going over the top," men clambering over the lips of trenches, heading toward an off-camera or out-of-focus enemy on the horizon. When they appeared in the pages of the *Berliner Zeitung*, *The Times* (London), the *New York World*, or *Paris Soir*, such images were meant to call up the same feelings of martial glamour, admiration for the camaraderie of men, and the *élan* of the charge to battle that any warrior pro-

22. "Odessa Steps" sequence, *Battleship Potemkin*, director, Sergei Eisenstein, 1925. *Photo courtesy of the Museum of Modern Art, Film Stills Area*

cession image would have suggested since Agamemnon mustered the Mycenaeans to march toward the ships that sailed to Troy. But a modern audience, and
indeed any audience in the last year of the war or afterward, would not have
"filled in the blank" in the same way that the generals could have wished. We
know that these soldiers were typically charging to their deaths, that beyond the
mist or the edge of the camera frame there was mud, barbed wire, and rows of
machine guns and artillery that transformed the warrior procession from a time-
honored formation for battle to a butchered carcass.

This is the tale painted by Peter Weir in *Gallipoli* (1981). Much of the film is
devoted to exhibitions of *commilito*. Excited young men—bucolic "lightfoot
lads" as described by the poet Alfred Housman—volunteer to fight in World
War I, exerting themselves in training, in play, in marches, and in mock battles.
The virility of these Anzacs, the doughty young warriors from Australia and New
Zealand, is impressed on us and them. With a change of uniform, their shapes
could be painted on Neolithic stone galleries or carved onto Trajan's monument.
But in the final scenes of the film the warrior procession is subverted; a dismal
coda is adjoined to the brilliant column. Whereas typically the warrior procession shows us the paths of glory, here we are presented with the edge of the
grave. Landing on the Turkish coast, the young soldiers muster and go over the
top. They are unified, a well-honed machine of battle, their bodies sculpted by
a life of exercise; indiscriminately, they are slaughtered, for the machine guns
do not distinguish between the bold and the timid, the unified and the irregular,
or the strong and the weak. We now can see the irony in glory; the warrior
procession can, in the hands of inept generals and under the guidance of overly
rigid doctrine, especially that which fails to take account of the dispositions of
the enemy, lead to catastrophic failure.

This is the morally correct, modern view of the warrior procession: the actual
seeking of battle is considered a pathology. But we must remember that those
who participated in the conflict may have had very different views before, during,
and after it. The real-life Anzacs were, by many reports, proud of their "magnificent achievements." As historian Bill Gammage notes, the Gallipoli survivors
were "a select fraternity, which could never admit new members, and for the
rest of their lives they would take pride in their distinction."[24] A warrior procession, then, may be but a march to the grave, but the ideals and spirit which
led that march may survive in art and in human memory. To obscure such a
reality is not to serve the cause of antiwar; to expose it is to better understand
war itself.

The instances of such events in the last two hundred years of military history
are legion, sufficient to underscore the driving power of the procession. Two
thousand British regular troops were cut down as they marched in neat rows
toward Andrew Jackson's sharpshooters behind a stone wall at the Battle of New
Orleans (1814). At Waterloo (1815), French cavalry regiments unsupported by

artillery or infantry launched themselves against British squares but could not break them. In the Crimea (1854), the Light Brigade sallied into the valley of death against Russian artillery. "C'est magnifique," commented a French general observing the scene, "mais ce n'est pas la guerre." In the Austro-Prussian War of 1866 at the Battle of Königgrätz, the Austrian 1st Corps, in tight ranks with flags flying and playing the regimental tune, threw itself into the Prussian lines. In less than half an hour, almost 300 of its officers and 10,000 of its men—half its complement—lay dead. Four years later, in the Franco-Prussian War, the French Guard Cavalry charged the German lines. "Ah, les braves gens!" cried out the king of Prussia as he watched the enemy mowed down by his riflemen. In turn, the assault of the Prussian Guard lost 8,000 men in ten minutes. In Pickett's charge at Gettysburg (1863), a Confederate division was destroyed as it met the reinforced center of the Union line. In African colonial conflicts, Zulus, unable to adapt their rigid tactics of frontal assault, were cut down by British machine guns, cannon, and rifle fire at Roarke's Drift and Ulundi (1879). In 1944, during a battle in New Guinea, David S. Rubitsky, a United States Marine sergeant in the 32nd Division, killed as many as 400 to 500 Japanese soldiers who were trying to charge his position at the head of a steep, broken ravine. At the Normandy coastal ridge of Verrières on 25 July, 1944 the elite Royal Highland Regiment (the "Black Watch") of the Canadian army was ordered to repeatedly attack a heavily fortified German position across an open plain without air, armor, or artillery support and under pouring rain. They incurred 400 dead and 1500 wounded. (It was not until 1994 that details of the disaster were released.) Modern small-arms fire, artillery gunfire, and aerial bombardment have necessarily relegated massed formations of men marching in rigid unity to parades, not to combat.

This does not mean that the symbolic impact of the warrior procession cannot be clear to a modern audience. As the film *Glory* (1989) illustrated and its title underscored, even we can honor the death charge unfazed by cynicism. The film depicts the training and battles of the 54th Massachusetts Colored Infantry during the American Civil War. As is typical in films about black revolutionaries, the main protagonist is white: Matthew Broderick plays Robert Gould Shaw, the commander of the regiment. Certain scenes seek to establish that black soldiers did—contrary to the expectations of many white Northerners—train and fight as well as any, but this is not a film about the camaraderie of victory, or how pulling together produces a happy result. The 54th faced their own Gallipoli on July 18, 1863, in the attempted storming of Confederate Ft. Wagner in South Carolina. Along a beach, in procession, superbly conditioned, uniforms crisp, boots polished, flags snapping, the black men and white officers and sergeants of the 54th march forward in quick step. White soldiers cheer them on: "Give 'em hell, 54th!" It is the moment of acceptance, of union, of glory.

Nearly all the film's main characters die—in real life, the regiment sustained

50 percent casualies—halted by the defense works, slaughtered by enemy guns. In the final scene, the bodies of the "defeated" men of the 54th are thrown into a pit. In the charnel trench, black bodies mingle with white. It is a powerful visual moment, which the filmmaker does not sentimentalize by heavy-handed voice-over. These men indeed gave the last, full measure of themselves, and divisions of class or education or region between the black soldiers or between black and white die with them. The warrior procession may be doomed, yet the point of the scene and the film is obviously not to exploit the outrages of war, but to praise the gallantry of such men. The greatest intimacy among comrades-in-arms is that of shared suffering unto death; this is the unspoken caption of most warrior processions.

## BUDDYHOOD AND BUDDY POSING

Another subgenre of pictures showing comrades-in-arms is the buddy pose. On a red-painted Athenian cup from around 500 B.C.E., we see one of the icons of intimacy between fighting men. [**Fig. 23**] The soldier at the right is identified as Achilles. His patient is his friend Patroclus. In Greek, one meaning of *Achilleus* is "grief," which, second only to anger, is the hero's defining emotion in the *Iliad*. When Achilles refuses to fight as a result of his argument with Agamemnon, it is Patroclus who eventually dons his comrade's armor to drive back the Trojans. The cup displays a moment not cited in the epic, but it conveys the poem's essence—that the two men are the best of companions. When Achilles is first told of his friend's death, Homer tells us, the hero, womenfolk in the camp, and goddesses all join in the heart-wrenching despair:

> . . . the black cloud of sorrow closed on Achilleus.
> In both hands he caught up the grimy dust, and poured it
> over his head and face, and fouled his handsome countenance,
> and the black ashes were scattered over his immortal tunic.
> And he himself, mightily in his might, in the dust lay
> at length, and took and tore at his hair with his hands, and defiled it.[25]

Later, when Achilles rescues the body of Patroclus—which has been stripped naked—from the Trojans by routing them three times and killing "twelve of the best men among them," he weeps "warm tears as he saw his steadfast companion lying there on a carried litter and torn with sharp bronze."

These are extraordinary words to the modern viewer, accustomed to the Hollywood tradition of the man who does not cry. Such a high-pitched reaction to the consequences of war would be inconceivable for the stony characters played by John Wayne or Clint Eastwood, although the emotional depth might be implied by a lowering of eyes or a curl of lip. But in the definition of manhood

23. Achilles, right, bandages a wound for his friend Patroclus. Red-figure scene from Athenian cup (c. 500 B.C.E.).
*Bildarchiv Preussischer Kulturbesitz, Germany*

posed by the *Iliad*, near-hysterical demonstrations are natural and not taken as contradictory to one's status as man or soldier. Nevertheless, it is interesting that in other traditions and later interpretations, the Achilles-Patroclus relationship is sexual. More important, Achilles' manhood is challenged and his effeminacy is suggested. According to one version of the story, the hero tried to avoid serving in the war by dressing as a woman. Shakespeare's *Troilus and Cressida*, another tale of Troy, features an Achilles who is downright prissy.

But the intimacy of the trenches need not be sexually driven or expressed. As the late Randy Shilts outlined in his history of homosexuality in the U.S. military, many of the signs and rituals of camaraderie among soldiers, from mock-fornication hazing rituals to shared tears of terror, would, in a civilian context, be read as "gay."[26] Men in groups form dynamics of kinship and connection that transcend the individuals who belong to them.[27] It is in the military unit—whether a Neolithic squad or a U.S. Marine platoon—that such bonding and behavioral changes are most regulated and encouraged.

Numerous testimonies of war veterans recount the special attachments—indistinguishable from the Homeric description—that exist between men in camp and field of battle. One World War II veteran recalled, "The men in my squad were my special friends. My best friend was the sergeant of the squad. We bunked together, slept together, fought together, told each other where our money was pinned in our shirts. . . . Whatever belongs to me belongs to the whole outfit."[28] In Erich Maria Remarque's antiwar novel, *All Quiet on the Western Front*, he testifies that his buddies were an indispensable support in World War I: "These voices . . . are more to me than life . . . they are more than motherliness and more than fear; they are the strongest, most comforting thing there is anywhere: they are the voices of my comrades."[29]

This camaraderie is a universal element in warfare. For some, like German World War I veteran Albrecht Mendelssohn Bartholdy, it offered succor beyond that available in ordinary society: "The men in the trenches had camaradership to comfort them, while the people at home, as soon as the blockade made itself felt, had to face competition and struggles for life in its ugliest forms. . . ."[30] In all, veterans of the Great War (as in many others) found that they lived in a self-contained world, with small numbers of fellow men as their only companions in suffering. Historian George L. Mosse describes the situation as follows: "[C]ommunications with the rear were often difficult and dangerous. Soldiers fought in small units as they held their segment of the trench. . . . Members of a squad were thrown upon each other's company, often for weeks at a time, bored with interminable guard duty, sniped at from the opposite trenches, and sometimes forced to go over the top."[31] It is the dark truth of military history, well known to commanders and students of war, but unexpressed on recruiting posters and war bond rallies, that the misery that begets company is considered a sine qua non of military effectiveness.

Such a concept is drawn from a nonheroic vision of war: groups will defeat individuals. The tenet was astutely worded by the Arab philosopher Ibn Khaldun: "Victory, or even the mere avoidance of defeat, goes to the side which has most solidarity and whose members are readiest to fight and to die for each other."[32] Similarly, S. L. A. Marshall, General of the Army in World War II, commented, "I hold it to be one of the simplest truths of war that the thing which enables an infantry soldier to keep going with his weapons is the near presence or the presumed presence of a comrade. . . . [H]e is sustained by his fellows."[33] In theory, that sustaining ability is what distinguishes the victor from the defeated, in campaigns of assault and attrition.

But is buddyhood really the foundation for successful warfare? The first principle of group cohesion is *propinquity*: people living together tend to band to-gether. Early sociological studies, such as on the neighborhood gangs observed by Frederick Thrasher or the "boys on the corner" studied by William F. Whyte, showed that identity in a gang was and is largely based upon what might be called "personal geopolitics."[34] People who live in the same area usually share the same burdens and have similar ethnic identity, background, and folkways. In addition, because of employment, limited funds, or restricted territory of movement, they tend to identify with each other, and even spontaneously form groups to celebrate this identity and to defend their territory. Charles H. Cooley, the social scientist who first used the term "primary group," suggested that intimacy was its basis, where people encountered each other and interacted every day.[35] Such intimacy builds dyadic empathy. The fate and fortunes of the buddy are personalized; the friend is the extension of the self. The training or battle platoon, therefore, was the perfect location and grouping to foster such attach-ments.

But simply placing people into a group does not necessarily make them loyal to each other or transform them into a cohesive instrument of battle. The in-dividuals must be inculcated to work together, and part of that unification occurs as they find relationships within the group, if they are willing to do so, and above all if they are guided by a leader they respect and trust. Men may not select their primary groups in an army, but they do choose their friends, and it is to those, not necessarily the group itself, that they have the greatest loyalty. The crucial task of the good war commander is to employ the many intricate relationships within a group in service of the aims of the group itself, of war, and of his own leadership. The ultimate expression of that successful attachment is often only revealed after a leader's death. Manfred von Richthofen, the Red Baron, wrote in his diaries of a flight leader who was shot down over France: "everyone who came to know Boelcke imagined he was his one true friend . . . indeed was *the* one true friend. Men whose names Boelcke never knew believed they were es-pecially close to him."[36]

The dyads of buddyship, however, can work at cross purposes with the mil-itary function. Those who argue against the presence of women in the military will often claim that the protective instinct of men would interfere with the combat effectiveness of a mixed fighting group, that men would spend more time trying to protect the women than performing their duties. Whether or not this is correct, the feelings of protectionism and mutual sympathy shared be-tween men and women do not outweigh the buddy intimacy that always arises between men against fire. The loyalty to one's bunkmate—between Willie and Joe, or Achilles and Patroclus—may serve the ends of war, but may interfere with them as well; the revenge of Achilles, after all, did not place the Greeks a single step closer to winning the war.[37]

So men in war live, work, eat, sleep, fight, and die in close quarters. These relationships are easily visualized, the simplest being the most common war image of the photographic era: the buddy posing. Typical of these were the very first photographs of war, those produced by Roger Fenton in the Crimea. Such images were not new: ordinary soldiers as specified subjects of art first appeared during the wars of religion in Europe, beginning at about 1500.[38] The relative cheapness of materials, however, later allowed photographers to create images for the first time *for use by the soldiers*. A majority of Fenton's images of war are similar to this one, entitled *L'Entente Cordiale*, which shows British and French troops in camp together.[39] [**Fig. 24**]

Similarly, and on a greater scale in the American Civil War, the individual and group posing became something of an industry for independent photographers like the roving cameramen of the Mathew Brady Company. These pictures were produced en masse cheaply and relatively quickly. In addition, the realism and novelty of the new medium must have been attractive. The choice of the posing, however, was both a commercial ploy and a practical imposition. The fastest developing process of the time could not fix pictures in fewer than twenty seconds—it would have been impossible for Fenton, or any of the Civil War photographers, to shoot a battle. Photographers could only "capture" men and objects that would not or could not move—the inanimate, the staged, and the dead. In any case, the invention of photography engendered countless posed warrior images in the catalogue of the vision of war. Today, every American family with a son or daughter in uniform has a color picture of him or her, usually including a flag, on the mantelpiece. Every soldier retains somewhere a picture of his buddies or the standard platoon photo with nameplate taken and distributed by the army itself. Photography in a sense allowed the ordinary soldier to own a vision of war (or warriorhood) for the first time in history, and that vision's implicit message was one of camaraderie.

The intimacy of that relationship held no pretense. The buddy posing is the memory of war that most soldiers keep on their mantel because it is that which they most treasure—a metonym for the most positive experience of the war. Those who demand greater realism from war imagery should keep such a sentiment in mind. No old soldier keeps pictures of enemy dead or disemboweled buddies on the wall of his den. In some ways, unlike filmmakers who often seek out the most dynamic and sensational scenes of warfare, the soldiers themselves and their families tend to prefer the most mundane and sedate. The buddy posing should not be classified as simply a piece of propaganda by the war office to make the battlefield less grisly. On the contrary, it is rightly honored by men and survivors who know the many realities of war, but choose to retain one treasured vision of it.

24. *L'Entente Cordiale*, British and French troops in the Crimea, Roger Fenton, 1855. *Gernsheim Collection, Harry Ransom Humanities Research Center, The University of Texas at Austin*

## LOYAL BROWNIES AND MULTICULTURAL PLATOONS

Friends and enemies are often, in the conventions of war art, distinguished by stock character stereotypes of "us" and "them." On Trajan's column, there is no ambiguity as to who is a Roman and who is a Dacian. But the exposition of camaraderie need not be with people who are dressed alike or even who are identified as having the same kin group. War has created strange comrades in the trench line. It has often served the propagandists of war to produce visions of what today might be seen as multicultural unity, especially when juxtaposed against a monolithically evil and visually uniform enemy.

Allied posters from World War I, for example, often extolled the hardiness and virtues of colonial troops—Indians for Britain, Africans for France—fighting for the empire. Such a figure in Western visual culture might be called the "loyal brownie." The brownie's role is largely mute; he marches, charges, and dies for the Western cause, but his status as a true "Englishman" or "Frenchman" is equivocal. The loyal brownie is typified by the figure of Gunga Din. In Kipling's poem, the native water-bearer is "a limpin' lump o' brick-dust," but he works hard in the heat of battle and dies loyally to save a British soldier. His dying words are, "I 'ope you liked your drink." In the 1939 RKO film *Gunga Din*, the heroism is the only aspect of the story that remains. Sam Jaffe, a white American who plays the title character, complete with turban and shoe polish skin coloring, is obsequiously loyal to the soldiers of the British Raj, led by Cary Grant. Din bows, scrapes, accepts any abuse, and offers no protests about his "regimental bhisti" status except in the wish to be of more service to his masters—to fight for the British as a soldier. In the end, he dies blowing a bugle warning of an ambush, and is given a soldier's funeral by the leading white male stars. In the Gunga Din motif, it is always the loyal brownie who dies—usually cheerfully—for the white man, never the reverse. Whatever assistance he gives to the white leaders, it will never be enough to bring him to center stage except in the moment of death.

Gunga Din is *not* a fantastic stereotype but the symbol of a vastly important social fact. "The sun never set" on the British Empire because of the superior material resources, training, and equipment of the English armies and navy, but also because wherever the English went, especially in India—a land of hundreds of millions—they were able to recruit generally loyal and efficient native workers and soldiers. The loyal brownie was also useful self-congratulation for that imperial dignity. The existence of so many hundreds of thousands of dependents, soldiers, laborers, and lower-level bureaucrats allowed colonials to claim that they did not rule others for selfish motives, but rather ruled in cooperation with the best elements of the native land. Without the presence of the Gunga Dins, British India would not have lasted four hundred years.

The markedly radical shift in the composition of the warrior group came in the twentieth century, and found its most extreme visualization in American film. Certainly, mixed units were not unportrayed in the cinema of other nations at war. In British World War II films like Noël Coward's *In Which We Serve* (1942), the group of warriors varied, including men from different class and regional backgrounds, from the cockney to the university man, from the city shopkeeper to the small-town Scotsman. In Jean Renoir's *La Grande Illusion* (1937), set in a World War I German prison camp, the three main characters, Maréchal, Rosenthal, and Boïeldieu, are from (and stand for) different sections of French society: a factory worker, a capitalist Jew, and an aristocrat.

But it was in World War II Hollywood's casting of the warrior group that the

112 VISIONS OF WAR

true "multicultural platoon" came into full flower as a stock method of displaying groups of warriors and tools of war ideology. They were common fare
in movies like *Bataan* (1943), *A Walk in the Sun* (1945), and *The Sands of Iwo
Jima* (1949). The formula was simple. A group of GIs would be introduced: the
drawling (white) southerner, the tough-talking Bronx native, the Jew, the Italian,
the Pole, the Irishman, and so on. *Saving Private Ryan* recapitulates the lineup.
The multicultural platoon of the World War II film was an unambiguous statement about the war itself. Yet in each of these films, whatever heroics and supporting efforts the ethnic or regional character offers, almost invariably the star
is the most (visually) Anglo-Saxon of them all: John Wayne, Gregory Peck, Gary
Cooper, Charlie Sheen (*Platoon*, 1986), and Tom Hanks (*Saving Private Ryan*).
Still today, ethnics follow—they rarely lead.

The film which visually painted the broadest cultural tapestry was *Sahara*
(1943). To effect its display, the story—written by John Howard Lawson, an
avowed Communist who was later blacklisted—sets up an improbable convergence. It is 1942 in North Africa; an American tank is wandering the desert
separated from its unit. Its commander, Humphrey Bogart, encounters British
stragglers, including—a conspicuous absence from other multicultural platoon
World War II films—a black man (a Sudanese in the British service). Among
the Britishers' prisoners are an Italian and a German. In a plain metaphor, the
hodgepodge international army fortifies itself in an abandoned colonial outpost
at the only oasis for hundreds of miles. A much larger German force surrounds
them and lays siege. The events are unimportant; it is the visual display which
is a fascinating partial break with the stereotype but also a form of its reinforce-
ment, so typical in the ambiguity of many Hollywood films about the war. Each
ethnic representative makes his own brief speech, revealing his perspective on
the war, while the camera shows him in close-up. A Frenchman "has been killing
Germans since '36." The Italian decides he no longer wants to fight for Hitler
and dies heroically warning Bogart that the German prisoner has escaped. The
black soldier, Tambou, is a Dersu of the desert, even though his homeland is
about a thousand miles away. He knows where all the oases are. Brave, obedient,
he dies in Gunga Din style, killing the escaping German. His last act is to give
a cheerful "thumbs up" sign to Humphrey Bogart.

But this variation among racial types is only meaningful in contrast with the
opponents. No distinctions are made between enemy soldiers in *Sahara*. All of
them are traitorous, brutal, scheming: in a word, stereotypical Germans. The
message of the film is hammered home less by what people say and do than by
who they are. In the end, the multicultural platoon, because they stick together
and are loyal to each other, defeat their adversaries. This is a powerful ideal of
cross-ethnic unity that still resonates in America today, that the divisions that
exist among peoples can be transcended in the name of a greater cause. The film

*Glory* is simply a recent incarnation, complete with central white hero. In *Sahara*, the foregrounded cause is the defeat of the Aryan "superman." The connotation, however, is the support for old-fashioned ideals of Americanism.

It is revealing to examine the content and context of the most famous single real image of World War II, which is yet another register of the multicultural platoon, and subsumes the dichotomy of showing ordinary soldiers as unified and uniform, but also endowing them with individuality, heroism, and empathy. This is Joe Rosenthal's photograph of the second flag raising on Mount Suribachi on the island of Iwo Jima by American soldiers and marines.[40] [**Fig. 25**] Iwo Jima means "Sulfur Island" in Japanese, and the battle that took place in February 1945 would subsequently be synonymous with hell for 75,000 marines and support personnel who eventually landed on the island to unearth, crag by crag, its 25,000 Japanese defenders.

Early on the morning of February 23, Mount Suribachi, the highest point on the island, had been captured by marines. In many ways it was the most important symbolic moment of the Pacific War, the very first time an American flag had been raised over the sovereign territory of the empire of Japan. Two photographers, Joe Rosenthal, a civilian working for the Associated Press, and Bill Genaust, a marine employed by *Stars and Stripes*, missed the first flag-raising. When the photographers finally scaled the summit, they found a small group of marines ready to lift up a second flag. The first one had been too small to be visible from a distance, so the commander in charge of the Iwo Jima invasion had ordered the largest one his quartermaster could provide to be set up so that all the marines on the four-mile-square island could witness that victory was in sight.

Genaust's memories of the events will never be known; he was killed nine days later. But Rosenthal survived, and in interviews given to *Collier's* in 1955, he explained in detail the genesis of the photo. Both photographers saw some marines preparing a long iron pipe and another holding a flag. "What are you doing?" Rosenthal asked. "We're gonna put up this bigger flag," a marine answered, "and keep the other one for a souvenir." The new flag was much bigger, measuring eight feet by four feet eight inches. A few steps from each other, Rosenthal and Genaust lifted their cameras, Rosenthal a still Speed Graphic, Genaust a 16mm color Bell & Howell. The flag was lifted up, still on its pole, by five U.S. Marines and a sailor. Rosenthal continued to take pictures, and at the end of the day sent off several packs of film, including one that showed the flag-raising, to which he gave the following caption: "Atop 565-foot Suribachi Yama, the volcano at the southwest tip of Iwo Jima, Marines of the Second Battalion, 28th Regiment, Fifth Marine Division, hoist the Stars and Stripes, signaling the capture of this key position."

The picture achieved almost instant fame after being published in *Stars and*

25. Marines of the 28th Regiment of the Fifth Division raise the American flag atop Mt. Suribachi, Iwo Jima, February 23, 1945.
*Photo: Joe Rosenthal*
*© AP/World Wide Photos*

*Stripes* and elsewhere. Rosenthal was dogged for years by rumors that it was posed. This was largely due to the beautiful symmetry of the frame. An art critic called it "too phony to be real." However, as Rosenthal commented, "If I had faked it, nothing like the existing picture would have resulted." For example, he would have made sure that the men's faces were turned toward the camera. "Get faces, not butts and backs" is, after all, a standard dictum of news photography in war or in politics.

Yet the fact that the men are unidentifiable in the image, distinguished only by their uniforms and bodies, seems appropriate; thus they may more easily, in the eyes of the American public, stand for any son in uniform. It is a buddy posing and warrior procession of unknown soldiers. The publicity engine of war, however, requires that celebrities have faces and names, so almost immediately the identity of the six men was sought out. Three were killed in the subsequent fighting: Private First Class Franklin R. Sousley (nineteen years old, second from the left in the photo); Sergeant Michael Strank (twenty-six, just left of Sousley), and Corporal Harlon H. Block (twenty-one, furthest right). The three who survived the battle were Private First Class Ira H. Hayes (twenty-three, farthest left in the photo); Navy Pharmacist's Mate Second Class John H. Bradley (second from right); and Private First Class Rene A. Gagnon (nineteen, the man who carried the flag up Suribachi, only visible by his helmet near Corporal Block).

The survivors were withdrawn from action and paraded around the country on the Seventh War Bond drive, the war's most successful. The original group of six could have been cast by Warner Bros. Their professions included carpenter, factory worker, laborer, farmer, textile worker, and apprentice mortician. They originated from New Hampshire, Wisconsin, Ohio, Arizona, Pennsylvania, and Texas. Their ethnic backgrounds included Anglo-Saxon, Pima Indian, Czechoslovak, and French. Their diversity became one of the selling points of the image and its ideal—they *were* America, or rather how America wanted to see itself in olive drab in wartime.

The irony of this portrayal is that it mirrors almost exactly one of the visions of intercultural camaraderie that existed from our enemies: the German Nazis and the Japanese. In the latter case, it was political policy, although often not translated into military practice, that they too were the apex of a multicultural conglomeration. The conquered territories of the Philippines, Manchuria, Indonesia, Burma, and Malaysia were included in a "Greater East Asia Co-Prosperity Sphere." This economic and military union of all Asian peoples was juxtaposed against the American enemy "other." Yet the record of Japanese occupation was largely grim in China and the Philippines and Korea; imbedded in this propaganda of co-relationship was the Japanese self-image of being a master race, more top-down colonialism than leveled multiculturalism. Nevertheless, in each conquered nation of East and South, collaborationists of not inconsiderable numbers set up working governments.

An analogous multicultural identity was suggested by Nazi racial propaganda, and met with greater success. Though the Nazis were generally held to cling to the concept of a single master race, according to complex *Volk* racial category schemes, there were at least six subdivisions of the Germanic people. Many in the Third Reich believed that their mission was to unify all such peoples, which included the Scandinavians. Even the Japanese, after the sealing of the Axis alliance, were by twisted logic given the title "honorary Aryans." The physical and visual embodiment of such "inclusivity" was the Waffen-SS, the armed units of the SS. Foreign legions were recruited from Netherlanders, Norwegians, Danes, Finns, Swiss, Swedes, Flemish, Wallonians, Frenchmen, and a handful of Britons, Latvians, Estonians, Ukrainians, Croats, Bosnians, Italians, Albanians, Russians, Hungarians, and some Indians, as well as ethnic Germans from Alsace, Denmark, Czechoslovakia, Italy, Hungary, Romania, Poland, and Yugoslavia. As one historian suggested, at its peak, 950,000 soldiers served under the SS runes.

"It is quite possible that the Waffen SS was the largest multinational army to ever fight under one flag."[41] This diversity was played up visually, especially in the pages of *Signal*, the German wartime military magazine, translated and distributed for both a home and European audience. Typically, ethnics were featured joining in the fight against communism on the eastern front.

Motivations for enlistment in the SS ranged from high combat pay to desire for glory. Some men and boys were press-ganged; others volunteered. Still others reasoned that after the fall of France, the war was essentially over, and wished to buy prestige for their countries in the new Europe. However, postwar independence was a fiction deceitfully offered only on wall posters. Hitler stated: "When speaking to the Germanics of the North-west and North, one must always make it plain that what we're building is the Germanic Reich, or simply the Reich, with Germany constituting merely her most powerful source of strength, as much from the ideological as from the military point of view."[42] Yet the recruitment programs were successful—at least until the war was obviously being lost. Visually, and through the organs of propaganda, two images suggested the main inducements to "join up": the ideal comrade, and the common enemy, the Bolshevik-Jew symbolized by dragons and other monsters at the gates of Europe. The former image attracted Christian De La Mazière, a young Frenchman who volunteered to join the Charlemagne Division of the Waffen SS, and who remembers the recruiting posters glowing with "beings without defect or flaw who would never rot or decay."[43] The latter was the outer threat, and such imagery found strong sympathy across the Continent, from the Caucasus to Paris. Even more so than in Hollywood World War II movies, the purest racial type was the "hero" in the tale. Multicultural platoons or armies shown in print or on film may thus be signs of both tension and unity in the real armies they portrayed.

## Fear Itself

The unification of men in battle is taken as a prerequisite for military success; the stern drill sergeant of the Assyrian training fields outside Nineveh probably operated with a similar rationale to that of his descendant at Camp LeJeune. Common wisdom seems to dictate that men who fight together are more successful than those who fight as individuals. But is this so? In groups or alone, what do men actually do when faced with combat? This is an especially important question in the context of most modern armies. Save for a few Central Asian militias, there is no contemporary warrior caste in the ancient sense of Spartans, Samurai, Aztecs, Zulus, or dog soldiers inured from birth to battle. How do the majority of men in arms fight? The answer seems to be—they often don't.

The simplest quantitative way to measure fear on a battlefield is to gauge how well rifles were loaded and discharged. In the era before the breech-loading rifle—that is, for most of the Civil War—armies could actually count the failures of their troops by collecting all the jammed and exploded weapons after the battle. This exercise occurred at Gettysburg, July 1–3, 1863. Gleaners, working for the Union army, gathered all the discarded rifles, which were then sent to Washington for inspection.[44] The results were astounding: 37,574 rifles were recovered. Presumably more had been lost in the fields, mountains, and forests of the battlefield, or scavenged by retreating Confederate troops. At least two-thirds of the rifles had never been fired. Of the total, many were jammed, with two, three, or as many as ten musket balls crushed in the breech. One wonder weapon had twenty-three iron balls shoved into its barrel. This was a remarkable record of misfires, mishaps, and misloading by the soldiers of the armies of Northern Virginia and the Potomac. They were not found to be the result of mechanical failure. For a significant portion of the troops, the simple act of firing their gun, or of even loading it correctly, proved too harrowing or too complex. This is an unvisualized reality of war, from Mathew Brady photographs to recent films such as *Gettysburg* (1996). The movie, notably, was praised for its realism, but as always realism is selective. *Gettysburg* misrepresented what actually happened by showing thousands of men on both sides dutifully firing away with effect.

More comprehensive evidence of "freezing up" during combat surfaced during this century. In 1947, General S. L. A. Marshall published *Men Against Fire*, a summing up of studies of the behavior of soldiers fighting in World War II. His question was a simple one: What exactly did a man do when confronted with combat? The answers were depressing for any general who thought an army would replicate its training in the field. At most, a quarter of all men in battle fight; the rest do nothing. Only when compelled with threats, encouragement, orders, or begging will this silent and sluggish majority actually engage in combat. Even when it does, it will do so only halfheartedly and for a short time. The crucial aspect of this finding was that these were not cowards, men who purposely ducked or shirked duty. They simply would not fight—though they would assist in tending wounded—and could not find in themselves the motivation to be involved in what was occurring around them. Marshall concluded:

We found that on an average not more than 15 per cent of the men had actually fired at the enemy positions or personnel with rifles, carbines, grenades, bazookas, BARs [heavy machine guns], or [regular] machine guns during the course of an entire engagement. . . . [T]he man didn't have to maintain fire to be counted among the active firers. If he had so much as fired a rifle once or twice, though not aiming it at anything in particular, or lobbed a grenade roughly in the direction of the enemy, he was scored on the positive side. Usually the men with heavier weapons, such as the BAR, flamethrower or bazooka, gave a pretty good account of themselves, which of course is just another way of saying that the majority of men who were present and armed but would not fight were riflemen.[45]

Furthermore, the fighting minority, the fifteen to twenty men in every hundred who consistently engaged in combat, were also the same men who did so from battle to battle. Officers often were unaware of the passivity of most of their men, because of their distance from the battlefield or because of the difficulty of communication due to terrain or other considerations. Finally, there seemed to be no direct link between performance in boot camp and achievement on the battlefield. "There were men who had been consistently bad actors in the training period, marked by the faults of laziness, unruliness, and disorderliness, who just as consistently became lions on the battlefield. . . . They could fight like hell but they couldn't soldier."[46] In turn, on the parade ground and in the training camp, the nonbelligerent majority might perform and maneuver without flaw.

During the Korean War, the firing reaction rate increased markedly, up to almost 55 percent. In the Vietnam War, the sons of World War II veterans fired at a much higher rate, almost 95 percent. As veteran and military scholar Dave Grossman details, this "remarkable increase in killing" was achieved through training that scientifically stressed "desensitization, conditioning, and denial defense mechanisms."[47] Here reality and the representation of the vision of warfare for the combat platoon displayed in thousands of Hollywood movies about World War II—even those that made the claim to be "revisionist" and anti-heroic—separate utterly. In the average Hollywood film that depicts war and the activities of the multicultural platoon, there are only two possible options for a soldier: he fights or he shirks. In *The Fighting 69th* (1940), based on the exploits of the New York "Irish" division in World War I, James Cagney, reversing his standard tough-guy role, plays a coward and a malingerer. While the rest of the men fight and die, Cagney startles and bolts. But this stark contrast was not uncovered in General Marshall's research. The bulk of men neither ran nor fought, but simply sat quietly where they were, almost as if they were watching a movie and not participants in the battle.

This raises a troubling question about the vision of war: no entertainment war movie ever made has recreated such a scene. No multicultural platoon film has ever shown a sixth of its men fighting while the rest freeze up. Cowardice or inaction is always shown as a case of individual or group deviance from a brawling norm. The gray area of inactivity, of passive observation, seems to be unrecreatable on the screen, or perhaps it could not be adequately explained to the audience accustomed to the black or white alternatives of mainstream movies. But why has the passive majority not been shown in some other way, for example, in news or documentary footage? Marshall's findings have been known for almost half a century, but in almost every documentary of any war such visions of passivity are absent. Part of the reason may lie in the presence of filmmakers, still photographers, or videographers. Being shown on camera by, for example, a CBS News crew would no doubt incite soldiers to engage in some sort of activity.

It is intriguing that all histories of war are written as if the heroic era was a long-dead anomaly, an archaic memory of a time when the bravery of individuals made more of an impact than the organization of great masses of troops. The armies Marshall studied were made up of conscripts and volunteers from civilian life and few veterans of previous wars; presumably the deliberately warlike Aztecs—ritually told at birth by the midwives, "perhaps thou wilt receive the gift . . . [of] the flowered death by the obsidian knife"[48]—performed more spontaneously and aggressively. Certainly in the phalanxes of the Spartan army or the legions of Rome or the double rows of British grenadiers, generals, perhaps intuitively, understood that the passivity of the mass could be employed if properly coordinated. In modern armies and ancient, threats of prosecution or summary execution as well as desensitization through alcohol were also given as incentives to stay in the line and fight. A soldier who would not fight but would stay in place would at least maintain the integrity of the line. Also, by forcing him to remain in a formation surrounded by his immediate comrades, whatever dyads, loyalties to group or corps, personal honor, or compelling by commanders standing nearby might take hold and stir the most lethargic participant-observer into action. This is also why small units of elite, professional forces have historically defeated greater masses of poorly trained conscripts; the former's superior aggression may be due as much to their self-selection to be among the "fighting minority" as to their training.

One motivation, however, can induce comrades-in-arms to attack with greater gusto: the prospect of victory. Likewise, hopelessness can dissolve all bonds between men. This was revealed in research by Richard Holmes, a professor at the Royal Military College at Sandhurst, through interviews with members of the elite 2nd Parachute Battalion (2 Para) of the British Guards, who were largely responsible for the ground operations during the Falklands War.[49] In several battles, contrary to popular myth, the Argentine defenders were neither cowardly nor ill-equipped for combat. Although the British won almost every engagement, they were often checked by ferocious Argentine fire, and encountered young men who were willing to die to hold their positions; also, significantly, the Argentines outnumbered the British by three to one.

When the South Americans did finally, in each case, cut and run—abandoning their equipment, even their backpacks and shoes—it was not from innate timidity, but rather as a result of the collapse of the belief in their own unit. Officers, notably, were the first to flee (in contrast, the commander of 2 Para was killed, personally leading the assault on an Argentine position). A soldier on one of the positions taken by the 2 Para recalled, "We were just targets for their artillery: lots of times I felt like a duck on a lake, being shot at from all sides. I felt terribly helpless. We didn't feel like soldiers, we didn't want to make war."[50] As one British commander noted, "We decided to make this a noisy attack rather than a silent one because second-rate troops do not like being shelled."[51] The Argentines' flight, however, was illogical. British firepower, expressed through artillery and tank support, seemed, in retrospect, ineffective in doing the job that it was designed for: killing the enemy. The boggy ground absorbed most of the shells' explosions, but in the heat and cacophony of combat, logic and reason are largely unknown factors in the behavior of men.[52] On the other hand, as Holmes concluded, the British were "steeled by the display of the enemy being pounded by artillery." It made them feel metaphorically as if the gods of war were on their side and that victory was inevitable. They judged their own situation in relation to the position they imagined the enemy was in. So they charged up the hill together as would any band of Mycenaeans or Neolithic tribesmen. Certain victory enhanced fighting enthusiasm; charismatic, competent, and front-line leadership guaranteed it.

This is the last piece in the puzzle of the vision of war camaraderie from the perspective of the soldier. Social scientists studying youth gangs found that a key consideration within the formation of these gangs is the *exterior threat*: that some force, from the police to a neighboring gang, poses a danger, and that banding together is the only response possible. Military organizations since the dawn of time have artificially created gangs by taking young men and placing them in relative isolation in a training camp or barracks. They are forced to socialize with each other. Such results were found in a study by Sanford Dornbusch of the Coast Guard Academy.[53] Regardless of students' backgrounds, the intense discipline, severing of former attachments, and communal deprivation suffered by the cadets made them draw closer together. They created their own spontaneous community, with shared values and traditions often quite different from those that many of them left behind. What occurs in military training is a process of stripping away layers of socializing, and even what may normally be defined as humanity, and replacing it with a new group identity. This loyalty is greatly enhanced when the group is seen as "being in the same boat," facing a common opponent. Commanders hope that on the battlefield such a response will be evoked, with lethal results for a more threatening enemy. In sum, to make war—and images of war—comrades need not only each other but an enemy to hate, fear, and fight. As Clausewitz affirmed, "War is inconceivable without a clearly defined image of the enemy."[54]

# 5

## ENEMIES

*THE USEFUL ENEMY*

In the entire corpus of art from the Upper Paleolithic, there is not a single image showing duels or battles between men. The conflicts or confrontations depicted are either men against animals, such as the bird-headed man's mortal combat with the charging bull, or between animals.[1] In Mesolithic-Neolithic and tribal images, interhuman combat is common. In the prehistoric Native American petroglyphs from Writing-on-Stone, Alberta, for example, dueling warriors square off, each with his own distinctive shield pattern and headdress [see **Fig. 10**]. In the Arnhem Land battle scene, there are unambiguously two "sides" in a major tribal skirmish [see **Fig. 7**]. We know this because of simple visual cues that mimic the realities of the battlefield. The groups are in opposition; the men on the right confront the men on the left. The groups' uniforms—their headdresses—are of different types. We can even infer that the men at the front in different dress are the leaders. Yet there is one crucial detail of identification missing for the outside observer: *Who is the enemy?* From which band did the artist originate, or whose side was he on?

Pictures of war from the eras of civilization rarely offered such ambiguities. The oil painting by the Scottish painter Sir David Wilkie, *Sir David Baird Discovering the Body of Tipu Sultan* (1839), reveals one way modern peoples cast enemies in visions of war.[2] [**Fig. 26**] In the picture, the Indian prince lies dead, and whatever his former exalted position, by all the standards of visual laudation he is portrayed as "the defeated." He has been stripped of the centrality, superior height, and greater surface area that distinguish the glorified commander in a picture frame. Yet this enemy became a profitable subject for British cartoonists, sketch artists, and oil painters, and a sensation in magazines, galleries, and homes in England. "Tipu-mania" struck England shortly after the American Revolution's end, simultaneously with the rise of the cult of General Wolfe. Tipu's defeat and its aftermath "constituted by far the most popular heroic subject for painters in the entire [four-hundred-year] history of British India."[3]

As always, context is important. Tipu's father, Haidar Ali, was a general who took control of Mysore state in central India and placed the nation in a triangular rivalry between the Maratha kingdom and the British East India Company. Ali fought two wars with the British, and in both he acquitted himself well, once almost expelling the company from its headquarters. Tipu, on the other hand,

26. *Sir David Baird Discovering the Body of Tipu Sultan*, Sir David Wilkie, oil on canvas, 1839.
*National Galleries of Scotland, Edinburgh*

was a more rash leader than his father. In the Third Mysore War, 1790–92, he fended off three separate campaigns by the British and made peace only after half his kingdom was lost. Even then he flirted with an alliance with France, encouraging British suspicions. In the final war in 1799, Tipu was completely defeated, and was killed during the last stages of the storming of his capital, Seringapatam.

As a symbol, Tipu represented a wily and brave foreign prince whose dynasty had long troubled the empire's interests.[4] Moreover, the Mysore wars were avidly followed by the British public. Not only did they take place in an exotic locale full of strange and curious peoples, they were also a necessary series of victories to balance against the recent defeat in the American colonies. Artists of the time, almost in exact parallel to today's photojournalists, followed the campaign, but also for many years later returned to various related themes. Among these were the attacking of Seringapatam, the surrender of Tipu's sons, the recognition of his body, and the considerate treatment of his daughters, who were protected from soldiers' abuse by the conquering officers and pensioned off.

In Wilkie's painting, one of the English commanders (a former prisoner of Tipu) comes upon the scene of the prince dead, surrounded by his children and turbaned retainers. Here was an imposing enemy, beaten after a rough fight, adorned in all the splendors of Oriental glory. His sword and shield lie at his side, and a splendid bare chest is presented to the victor, who is posed with extended hand. In the background, the English climb over the walls and batter the sanctuary's gates. The nobility of the defeated reflects well on the valor of the victor. The themes and scenes struck by this image, then, were flattering to the commander Baird as well as to the audience.

Yet, as with *The Death of General Wolfe*, self-serving artistic license obscures fact. Baird—who commanded the divisions that broke into the city—and a grenadier company were the first to come upon Tipu's body; none of the descriptions of the time, person, or event, however, coincide with what we see here. The historical Tipu was short, fat, and very dark for an Indian of his caste.[5] Sir Wilkie portrays him as a lean, athletic, smooth-skinned young man. He suffered many severe wounds in the battle; the mortal blow was probably a "musket ball at close range through the temple."[6] But the mutilations—indeed, any obvious wound—are unseen in the painting. Moreover, as the British official history describes, in the heat of the fighting, "the body of the departed tyrant was thrown upon a heap of dead and dying, and the corpse, despoiled of everything valuable, left among the fallen Musalmans—naked, unknown, and unregarded."[7] Here he is like Wolfe, cleansed of unsightly blood and gore, and repositioned to be an object worthy of attention.[8]

As the case of Tipu suggests, if human beings in visualizing war create categories of comrade, then equally we impose an opposing category: enemy. The question of what is "enemyness" is intimately connected to the vision of war.

Wars are fought to attack and defend against enemies. Countries maintain great armies and devote considerable resources to protecting against both stated and potential enemies. And pictures, from the earliest images of the empires of the Near East to the most modern video displays of Gulf War commanders, depict as sine qua non of warfare who is an enemy, ascribing visually distinctive qualities that define him as "not one of us."

To the outsider, conflicts between groups often appear unnecessary and unproductive. However, sociologists like Lewis Coser and George Simmel have noted that conflict can have functional or positive benefits for groups.[9] Foremost is that a common enemy can reconcile a people to sacrifice and brotherhood absent in more pacific times. The group, finding itself in a situation of actual or perceived danger, draws closer together—the "circle the wagons" effect.[10] Groups in conflict will maximize the group-centric "good vs. evil" differences between them; events will be reinterpreted as justifying the virtue of the affiliated group and the villainy of the other. In times of life and death struggles between groups, the distinction will be sharpest and bitterest. As Freud explained, "hatred against a particular person or institution might operate in just the same unifying way, and might call up the same kind of emotional ties as positive attachment."[11]

Who the enemy is, what he stands for and how he is pictured, is often the way we define ourselves in war. The psychoanalyst Erik Erikson asserted that human beings form "pseudo species, i.e., tribes, clans, classes, etc., which behave as if they were separate species created at the beginning of time by supernatural intent, [each with] a distinct sense of identity, but also a conviction of harboring *the* human identity."[12] Yet, as the glorification of Tipu shows, the pictures we create of such enemies—their evil and virtue, ignominy and nobility—are often as distorted as the images we hold of ourselves and our war commanders. Though we assume that we are not like those we fight, the pictured enemy is a twisted refraction or reflection of the actions we take in war; his face may betray what we refuse to see about ourselves. Not only do they provide reasons for going to war, but the negative characteristics we assign to them (in contrast to those we believe exist in ourselves) support the continuance of the war. This is especially the case when leaders wish to focus the attention of their people away from domestic troubles. In seeking out the vision of the enemy, then, we must underscore his essential utility, no matter how evil we make him appear.

## THE DEFEATED ENEMY

The proper contrast of ally and enemy in the vision of war was the subject of a famous dispute in 1800 between the artist Jacques-Louis David and his friend and patron, Napoleon Bonaparte, then First Consul of France. The painting under discussion was David's *Leonidas at Thermopylae*, which the artist was working on when Napoleon visited his studio. In 480 B.C.E., a force of 300 Spartan soldiers and about 1,000 other Greek troops died defending a narrow mountain pass on the east coast of Greece against a Persian army vastly superior in number. Near the end of the battle, the Spartan king Leonidas was killed. Xerxes, the Persian ruler, offered Leonidas' remaining men their lives and freedom if they would surrender his body. The red-cloaked soldiers of Sparta refused and died where they stood in a circle around their king. Their Laconic epitaph—an eponymous term drawn from the name the Spartans gave to themselves, Lacedaemonians—later written in stone near the pass, was inscribed: "Stranger reading this, go tell the Spartans that we followed orders and died."

According to the Greek historian Herodotus, in his rage the Persian king ordered Leonidas' body stripped, and placed his head on a pike for display. Thermopylae became a national legend, a classical theme that found itself in poems, political speeches, and paintings throughout the nineteenth century. It was revived in a Hollywood movie, *The 300 Spartans* (1962), whose narration drew parallels between the Spartans' struggle against the Persians and the American War of Independence from Britain. Most important, in every known portrayal of the battle in image and fiction, sympathy was entirely with those who experienced defeat in the battle; no known Western picture was painted, nor any known "Persian version" penned, that lauds the temporary triumph of Xerxes.

However, Napoleon, the hardheaded general, saw no point in recasting Thermopylae in oil.[13] His verdict: "David, you will tire yourself out painting the defeated."

David defended the theme. "But, Citizen Consul, these are defeated men who have died for their country, and in spite of their defeat they have repelled the Persians from Greece for more than a hundred years."

Napoleon persisted. "That is not important. Only the name Leonidas is known to us while the rest is lost to history."

"All," countered David, ". . . except this noble resistance to an innumerable army. All! . . . except the devotion, to which there should be added, All! . . . except the ways, the austere morals of the Lacedaemonians, . . . it is useful to recall the memory of these soldiers."

Napoleon was unconvinced. His singular powers of concentration were attuned to crushing an enemy, not attaining martyrdom. Enemies, he maintained, must always be vanquished, in the field and in art. He saw historical facts made *vae victa*; the losers of war had no right to those facts.

History provides precedents for both opinions. Napoleon gained nothing from his eventual defeat except an immortal name, yet glorious defeat (and the accompanying spirit of *revanche*) has also been a potent catalyst of national unity. The cultural and political implications of martyrdom can be long-lasting.[14] Today, it is a common tale among the Greeks that Christ's return will be accompanied by the reappearance of Constantine XI Palaeologus, the last emperor of

Byzantium, killed in his city by the invading Turks (1453). Equally, after a series of Balkan wars in which Turkey lost most of its European possessions by 1914, a spirit of "never forget" aggrievement was fostered by nationalist leaders that eventually justified the genocide committed on Armenians and Greeks.[15] In the former Yugoslavia, many Serbs still define their national identity and mission from the defeat of their armies by the Turks at the Battle of Kosovo in 1389.[16] In American history, the defense of the Alamo during the 1836 Texas War of Independence was an event to "remember" precisely because it was the site of a defeat whose mythological status was immediately seized upon by Anglo rebels. Pearl Harbor, likewise, summed up such reasons for Americans to fight in World War II. Finally, much of Adolf Hitler's appeal arose from his insistence that the nation had been "stabbed in the back" by the harsh terms of the Treaty of Versailles after World War I. Such visions of glorious defeats play a role in legitimizing collective identity and justifying current enmity. For many peoples today, old wounds are never allowed to heal; pictures and stories refresh them.

    In the art of the Near East and the Americas, the iconographic formulas— the methods of representing enemies versus friends—could be based upon a single and almost unalterable rule that seemed to persist for most of human history through the Middle Ages, and still flourishes today. Identifying the enemy—on signet rings, reliefs, tapestries, paintings, or mosaics—is simple: *the enemy is always defeated.* Accordingly, if an army or a people is shown in such images as being defeated or humiliated, then they must have been an enemy of the patrons of the artists. One of the earliest images that shows the dyad of victorious friend and stricken enemy is the Narmer Palette.[17] [**Fig. 27**] It marks the transition between the "late prehistoric" and the "canonical tradition" of the commander in war and the treatment of enemies that would become the visual rule for several thousand years.[18] The palette encompasses four episodes (as described by Whitney Davis): (1) Enemy fleeing the ruler. (2) Ruler taking enemy citadel. (3) Enemies brought to the ruler for judgment. (4) Execution of enemies and celebration of the ruler. Its syntax of representation—the convention of relationship of victor to vanquished—is instantly comprehensible. Found at the Hierakonpolis site in Egypt, 80 miles south of Luxor, the palette is a 63.5-centimeter piece of dark green slate, with pictures and hieroglyphics carved on both of its faces. The central image of the obverse side is named within two characters of hieroglyphic as Narmer, the semilegendary king who united Upper and Lower Egypt and founded the first dynasty of pharaohs at about 3150 to 3125 B.C.E. Narmer set a pattern continued by all subsequent Egyptian rulers, including Rameses in the image that we encountered previously: he is a giant on the palette, at least twice as large in height and surface area as any other figure. The muscles on his forearms and legs are prominent. He holds up with his right hand a staff, and he wears the white crown of Upper Egypt. Groveling at his feet, arms spread in supplication, is a stripped prisoner.

27. Palette of Narmer, original at Egyptian Museum, Cairo.
*After W. A. Fairservis, Jr., 1991*

The captive's position, gestures, and nakedness are obvious and cross-cultural signs of submission.[19] One interpretation has it that this is a Libyan soldier or prince who has been defeated. In Mesoamerican, pre-Colombian civilization as well, the sacrificial victim and the war prisoner, often one and the same, were traditionally shown in art as naked and kneeling. The stripping of enemy corpses in almost all premodern war was both a practical matter of confiscating weapons and gaining booty and a symbolic gesture of power over an enemy. The forcible removal of regalia worn by decorated warriors was humiliating proof that they were no longer fighters. Such was also the custom among the Greeks of Homer's time (800 B.C.E.), and perhaps about the time of which he sang (1250 B.C.E.), for in the *Iliad* the stripping of enemy corpses was a common act of closure for a battle between heroes.[20] Theft from the dead was a heroic ritual.

In the warfare of classical Greece, the stripping of corpses was equally standard. Xerxes stripped the Spartan dead after Thermopylae. The Spartans them-

selves used display of their own bodies as an instrument of intimidating enemies
but, conversely, they used the bodies of enemies to contrast with their own.
Their king, Agesilaos, ordered that, when sold into slavery, captured enemy
soldiers should be paraded naked. According to the warrior historian Xenophon,
Agesilaos wanted everyone to note the contrast between the Spartan physique—
sculpted into "bronze muscles" by their strict regimen—and the paler, flabbier
"womanish" bodies of enemies from less militaristic city-states.[21] Stripping prisoners was also common among the Romans and their enemies. Livy wrote that
after the Battle of Trasimeno Lake in 217 B.C.E., the remnants of the defeated
Roman army surrendered to the Carthaginians on condition of being allowed
to depart "with a single garment each."[22] Hannibal honored the terms with what
the historian derisively called "true Punic reverence": the Romans were stripped
and draped in chains.[23]

The Assyrians, perhaps because their art and industry was so focused on war,
are emblematic of this tradition of emphasizing victory over enemies. Although
the empire suffered defeats, none was ever displayed as such in their art; indeed,
victories are depicted as decisive and absolute. For example, from the reign of
Tiglath-pileser III (744 to 727 B.C.E.), there are reliefs from the central palace of
Nimrud portraying the storming of a town. The beginning of the sequence shows
Assyrians under direction of their officers laying siege to the city; they have
surrounded it and propel giant spears from siege engines. Elsewhere, Assyrian
troops cross a moat and assault the town over ladders. The treatment of the
enemy in the panels is horrific. One Assyrian soldier decapitates a foe. Three
enemy soldiers are impaled on stakes. Two have been thrown or are jumping
from the walls of their city. Other unfortunates lie strewn about, their bodies
stripped of armor and clothing. Along the line of fortifications, still other enemy
soldiers raise their hands in an unmistakable gesture of surrender; nevertheless,
an Assyrian slays one of these. In another plate reminiscent of the story of Saul
from the Old Testament, Teumann, an Elamite king, is trapped by advancing
Assyrian soldiers and begs his son to kill him before being captured. We also
see victory parades, where prisoners are shown off; rivers filled with corpses and
discarded armor; Ethiopians, Arabs, Egyptians—a multicultural array—crushed,
burned, and tortured by the unstoppable force that was Assyria.

When compiled in this way, the impression of ferocity which the name of
Assyria evokes seems undebatable. In all, the reliefs at Nineveh, Nimrud, and
the other cities comprise a veritable *catalogue raisonné* of the mistreatment of
enemies. That enemies are always defeated and one's own kings are always victorious is indicative of the hierarchy of society in the ancient empires. For 5,000
years, human beings lived in communities where political power was extremely
centralized. When regimes were overturned or destroyed, it was simply the trading of one king, pharaoh, or supreme warlord for another. As one views the
Assyrian reliefs, the implications for the history of warfare and for the vision of

war are significant. The Assyrians were legendary for their destructiveness, and if this is a stereotype, it is one that they calculatingly proclaimed themselves. The litany of one early king, Ashur-nasir-pal, was a not uncommon description of the treatment of his enemies: "3000 of their combat troops I felled with weapons. . . . Many of the captives taken from them I burned in a fire. Many I took alive; from some (of these) I cut off their hands to the wrist, from others I cut off their noses, ears and fingers; I put out the eyes of many of the soldiers. . . . I burnt their young men and women to death."[24] Such meticulous detail is well illustrated by what is shown on the palace walls. No amount of revisionism can turn the Assyrians into Milquetoasts.

Yet it is always important to ask to what extent that which we see in the art of war is that which was useful to be seen. What we see can often be taken as representative less of a program than of propaganda. These bas-reliefs were displayed in the homes and halls of the kings of Assyria; they were not intended solely for private reflection. Ambassadors of the many peoples of the Bronze Age world would walk past pictures of mighty, muscular monarchs, regimented Assyrian legions, and sorrowing stripped enemies. The images not only served the ego of the king but reminded those he wished to awe and inspire that the powers of his god and his army were terrible indeed. In such hierarchical societies, the annihilation of the enemy ruling caste was a practical decision, an extension of diplomacy. These visiting ambassadors were the very people who possessed the ability to organize military efforts against the land of Ashur.

Even so, closer inspection of the reliefs also suggests that the Assyrians were capable of restraint. Although there were no formal rules of military conduct, such as those endorsed in the Geneva Conventions—the Bible amply testifies it was considered acceptable practice to slaughter men, women, and children— the Assyrians do not display cruelty for cruelty's sake. The main objects of their bloodlust in the reliefs are enemy soldiers, officers, and rulers, those who actually posed an unarguably real threat to the state. By contrast, in several reliefs which depict the displacing of populations, the refugees are shown carrying their belongings, and the women and children have been provided with special carts for transport. Moreover, we know that the displaced peoples were often resettled and integrated within Assyria—i.e., given the opportunity to become "Assyrian"—without prejudice or persecution; they were not, as is the practice with today's refugees, expelled to outside regions.

Finally, our quest for the social basis of imagery should never blind us to the private dimension of fascination as well. Assyrian kings who approved of the content of the reliefs would presumably have gained not a little enjoyment from reclining on a cushioned throne and gazing upon concrete evidence of their own hugeness and ferocity. Likewise, centuries later, Hitler kept a private film of the hangings and garrotings of those convicted in the July 1944 conspiracy to assassinate him at his headquarters. He would watch the film again and again,

28a. Bonampak, Room 2, Mayans battling enemies (c. 800).
*Photo courtesy of Peabody Museum, Harvard University*

enjoying the death throes of his opponents. On a movie projector still set up in Himmler's castle when it was captured was a reel showing the execution of Jews. The deliciousness of gazing upon tortured and defeated enemies may have been a simple motive of the absolute kings of the Near East. Since the official ideology was that the defeat of an enemy was a sign of his impiety, the torture of enemies may also have had an approved religious aura.

In Mesoamerica, similar scenes of a vanquished foe were displayed, sometimes with even greater ferocity. The central room of a Mayan building uncovered from the site of Bonampak (c. 790–800) shows a raid conducted by Mayan troops on a neighboring tribe, and its celebratory aftermath.[25] [**Fig. 28a, b**] The enemies are portrayed with long, bedraggled hair and dark skin, and appear to live in dense jungle. These may have been symbolic and actual signs within Maya iconography of "border" barbarians. Whereas the enemies are largely naked, the Mayans wear colorful robes and are highly decorated, attacking to the tunes played on wooden or bark trumpets. In the battle scene there are ten Mayan warriors for every enemy, each of whom is either running in terror or being trampled. In the final section of the panels, the naked, captured enemies are on display in a state of disarray and terror, and await the pronouncement of their new master, a Mayan lord. Their arms are stretched in supplication: blood spurts as their fingernails are ripped out. Other rooms within the building present scenes of human sacrifice; archeologists suggest that the depicted raid may have been purely to obtain sacrificial victims for rites to appease the gods. This hypothesis fits well with Mesoamerican tradition, but also with the visualization of the enemy. These nude jungle dwellers have no perceivable wealth or resources, nor is their land laden with pilferable crops. It is the ritual of the prisoners' defeat and their sacrifice to the gods that interests these conquerors.

28b. Bonampak, Room 2, wall 5, Mayan ruler, officers, and their victims (c. 800).
*Photo courtesy of Peabody Museum, Harvard University*

The Zapotec culture of the Mesoamerican highlands, which flourished in the mid- to late first century, also practiced the visual display of fallen enemies, but on a grander scale, perhaps the most striking in the history of the vision of war.[26,27] Typically, as is the case at the site known as Monte Albán, a bound, naked captive was carved in stone. [**Fig. 29**] Above him in the panel are glyphs of the picture-writing of Central America. Although the exact translation of the glyphs has not yet been made, archeologists believe they are the names of the individuals killed, along with a glyph for the concept or word "defeated." These carvings, which appeared on the walls of Zapotec cities, visible to citizens and to visitors, proclaimed in a sort of trophy advertising a listing of the victories of the home city. The bound miserable captive was the universal sign of an enemy's defeat, and " 'treading on the bodies of captives' was a powerful metaphor for conquest" later used in the iconography of the Maya.[28]

There is no indication at Monte Albán of bestowing nobility on or empathy for the defeated. The archeologists uncovering the site of one of the buildings comment that with three hundred or more carvings of sexually mutilated, naked enemies, "it must have been one of the most awesome displays of military propaganda in all of Mexico."[29] This enemy was not only stripped of his clothing and his dignity but also any semblance of "maleness." Such carvings add up to almost 80 percent of the city's public art. Because many of the figures are etched into the facings of steps leading into buildings, the enemies would have been tramped on by anyone visiting the complex. Unsurprisingly, Monte Albán and the other Zapotec centers were heavily fortified. The suggestion is that the tiny city-states

29. Castrated, mutilated prisoners carved into steps of Monte Albán site, southern Mexico, c. 300–100 B.C.E., Zapotec culture.
*Line drawing courtesy of Joyce Marcus*

were in constant warfare either with each other or with peoples from other valleys. In a land where city-states fought for control of narrow corridors of fertile valleys, public displays of the defeat of enemies may have served as billboards with a simple and cross-cultural message: "We are terrible to those who threaten us."

Similarly motivated displays were common in many regions and eras. Xenophon mentions Greek soldiers mutilating the bodies of Persians killed in battle "so that the sight of them might cause as much fear as possible among the enemy."[30] The practice of hanging bodies over the walls of a fortress was widespread in antiquity. Executed criminals in medieval England were left publicly to rot. The Wallacian prince Vlad the Impaler earned his bloodthirsty reputation and nom de guerre, Dracula (Son of the Devil), by impaling thousands of his enemies, both kinsmen and Turks, and leaving them in public view. In the civilizations of the nascent Nile Valley and Near and Middle East, and in Mesoamerica, the defeated, supplicating, and often stripped enemy, dominated by the victorious comrade or king, was a staple of the art of war. Such practices are another dubious distinction between humans and all other creatures, though one not often reckoned by biologists or priests. Only human beings make trophies of those they kill.

## THE HATED ENEMY

Wartime enemies need not actually exist or have existed; sometimes fiction delineates their types equally well. The notorious staple of sci-fi, the "Earth against Aliens" battle, sums up many of the mores and methods for visualizing an enemy. Recent effusions include *Aliens* (1986), *Independence Day* (1996), *Starship Troopers* (1997), the *Star Wars* film series (which is rather humans fighting other humans in space), and the *Star Trek* films and TV programs.

*Starship Troopers*, based on the 1950s Robert Heinlein novel, takes the alien war to its exponential extreme. [**Fig. 30**] Human soldiers are sent to fight a buglike enemy on a wasteland planet. In one scene, probably the most spectacular achievement of computer-generated war imagery yet filmed, a human fort is swarmed by thousands of alien creatures. Various bug castes are represented: flying insects, giant burrowing beetles, and artillery bugs that fire plasma from their anuses as antiaircraft defense against orbiting human spaceships. So accurate is their aim that they can divert asteroids, sending them careening across the galaxy to crash into Earth. The armaments of the troopers are similarly impressive, but the style is very World War II. The troopers are dropped on the planet by shuttle ships that deploy them exactly like the landing vehicles at Normandy and Saipan. Despite their advanced technology, the troopers are relatively lightly armored. Bug appendages can pierce their chest plates. Their guns are cartoonish in their seeming inability to run out of bullets; these, however, do little damage to the arachnids' armored exoskeletons. Most strangely, the humans have hand-held nuke weapons that they employ at point-blank range. We are not told about the effects of radiation (or the pressure of the blast) on the shooter. The film is a pot-luck of genres, *The Green Berets*, *Fort Apache*, and the 1950s army ant movies.[31]

*Independence Day* is the biggest (in box-office revenues and global scope of the battles) variant of the *War of the Worlds* scenario.[32] Aliens invade the planet; they are unyielding and have no interest in negotiation, only in our annihilation. Their technology is more advanced than ours. The best of our missiles, fighter jets, and even nuclear weapons have no effect on their defense shields. In the end, they are defeated by the modern descendant of the terrestrial flu that killed off the alien invaders in *War of the Worlds*. A human computer expert infects the aliens' mainframe with a virus that temporarily shuts down their defense system; this provides the opportunity to destroy their mother ship and to cut off the power to their attack craft. It is, at least in cinema, the first incorporation of future tech war with information war. The aliens are described as interstellar locusts, moving from planet to planet: "After they've consumed every natural resource, they move on."[33] They are totally without any virtue; purely evil enemies intent only on our extermination.

Enemies, of course, can be cast to order; the fiction film is not the only realm

30. Film still from *Starship Troopers*. Troopers battle giant insect.
© 1997 TriStar Pictures, Inc. All Rights Reserved. Picture: PhotoFest

of this kind of stereotyping. As turn-of-the-century social reformer and photographer Lewis Hine commented, "while photographs may not lie, liars may photograph."[34] The unsuspecting viewer, subscribing to a faith in the narrow literalism of photographic truth, may not understand the difference. In June 1943, *Life* magazine pictured on its cover a haggard, unshaven, bent-nosed man in a gray sweater and a German army helmet. The picture was emblematic, *Life*'s headline writers contended, of a master race in retreat: "This Hitler Superman is now a prisoner in Tunesia [*sic*]." The bleak visage of the defeated soldier seemed to illustrate the recent capitulation of a German army in North Africa; yet the picture, or rather the representation of its subject, was a complete fabrication. Upon British suggestion, the photographer had shot "the ugliest Arab they could find in the streets of Cairo . . . whom they dressed up in a sort of uniform."[35] The picture was printed on the cover of Britain's wartime *Parade* magazine, and then picked up, without any notation of the real identity of its subject, by *Life*. It is presented again in the 1977 compilation, *Life Goes to War: A Picture History of World War II*, but the untruth of the original caption is still not revealed to modern readers. This is often the case with miscaptioned photos; corrections are rarely as persistent as the deception or error.[36] On the other hand, the "Hitler Superman" was legitimately representative of a larger condition, the collapse of the Axis armies in North Africa. Words can lie, even while the implied visual metonym remains essentially correct.

Beastializing or "insectizing" an enemy, though, provides a convenient explanation for why and how other humans must die. In writing home to his parents to describe how his regiment helped exterminate the Armenians of eastern Anatolia in 1915, a young Turkish soldier stated, "I killed [the Armenians] like dogs. . . . If you ask news in this matter, we slew 2,500 Armenians and looted their goods."[37] Heinrich Himmler once harangued his chief henchmen: "Whether or not 10,000 Russian women collapse from exhaustion while digging a tank ditch interests me only in so far as the tank ditch is completed for Germany. . . . We Germans, who are the only people in the world who have a decent attitude to animals, will also adopt a decent attitude to these human animals, but it is a crime against our own blood to worry about them and to bring them ideals."[38]

Jews taken outdoors to be killed and piled in pits were stripped before being shot. But even in indoor facilities, the stripping seemed to accomplish a task of dehumanization, of turning men into animals to be funneled through an abattoir. With such language an SS training brochure instructed recruits about the nature of the regime's racial enemies: "To the outward eye the sub-human is biologically an entirely similar creation of nature; he has hands, feet and a sort of brain with eyes and a mouth. In fact, however, he is a totally different and a frightful creature, a caricature of a man with features similar to those of a human being but intellectually and morally lower than any animal."[39] A description of the spiritually similar Soviet system paralleled these ideas and practices: "the activists who helped the GPU [state political police] . . . looked on the so-called *kulaks* as cattle, swine, loathsome, repulsive: they had no souls; they stank; they all had venereal diseases; they were the enemies of the people and exploited the labour of others. . . . And there was no pity for them. . . . In order to massacre them it was necessary to proclaim that kulaks are not human beings."[40]

Animalization can work on its object as well as its perpetrators. People treated like animals can act like them, especially in dully accepting their fates. "We just walked like sheep, truly like animals," described a Hutu refugee of massacres on his people in Burundi in 1972.[41] Confused and unsure, many gave up hope of escape and returned to face certain death. Indeed, as Hannah Arendt pointed out, the apparent willingness to dig their own graves and await the bullet was common among victims of Nazi death squads, including Russian and American prisoners of war.[42] Thus, the twisted visage of an enemy is not just a projection of hate; it is also fundamentally a symptom of self-love. The enemy is shown as evil and of an inferior species so that we may bask in the knowledge of our own superiority.

But in the evils that are assigned to the enemy, there is a caesura between the modern world and the ancient. In the art of the civilizations of the Nile, the Near East, and Mesoamerica, enemies are crushed, tortured, dragged by the hair; they are most commonly seen losing battles, surrendering, and languishing in yokes. Nevertheless, in all the art of the period and the regions, there is not a single image reminiscent of what we today would classify as atrocity propaganda. It is the victors who boast and lavishly display the actions that we less bellicose observers see as atrocities, which are, after all, generally what happen to people who lose battles. No ancient king ever showed the suffering of his own people in war unless it was a minor detail of a larger canvas displaying the crushing of an enemy.

Nor are there instances in ancient art of enemies shown as subhuman, animal-beasts, or in any way as evil people. The Elamites were vanquished and, in accordance with Assyrian ideology, were justly punished by the gods for daring to oppose Assyria; but they remain as human as their conquerors. The same could be said for all of Roman and Greek art, even with its higher standards of realism. Greek soldiers fighting centaurs were painted on vases, but the centaurs are not bestialized real enemies; they are fantastic half-men, half-horse creatures of mythology. However badly an enemy army might fare at the hands of the Greeks or Romans, or however much it might be labeled "barbaric," in the art of their conquerors they would be shown as men. When compared to the portrayal of enemies in the modern era, then, the ancient empires and classical states seem eminently more restrained. Our brand of "evil enemy" imagery is not present in their visual vocabulary.

World War I was perhaps the most fertile field of hate propaganda. In many of the compilations of cartoon and poster art published during the war and thereafter, especially those produced by Britain and its allies, all varieties of the nefarious metamorphoses of the enemy are well represented: Germans become slithering beast-men, devils in gray, pigs stuffed into drab uniforms and spiked helmets; their atrocities were legion, from rape to torture to slaughtering Belgian babies. The images are repetitious, which, of course, is one of the bases of propaganda. Generally, they fall into two categories that often overlap. The first is those that show the enemy committing evil. The second twist the enemy into an inhuman form of beast or demon. Both are visualizations of threats to the kin group as well as flattering reflections of the artists. To display an enemy as inhuman is, by contrast, to award ourselves with humane (and human) status.

For effective atrocity propaganda, we need look no further than the most famous case of World War I, the death of Nurse Edith Cavell. Cavell, convicted of helping escaped Allied prisoners of war and Belgian youths find passage to England, was executed by German authorities in occupied Belgium on October 15, 1915. Allied cartoons showed the English nurse after her execution, lying crumpled under the smoking pistol of a gloating, porcine German officer. In some images, Kaiser Wilhelm himself wielded the gun, leering at the pale form of the fallen woman. Such visions were accompanied by vigorous polemics. In a sermon, the bishop of London asserted that "the cold blooded murder of Miss Cavell, a poor English girl, deliberately shot by Germans for housing refugees, will run the sinking of the *Lusitania* close in the civilized world as the greatest crime in history."[43]

Edith Cavell had been the headmistress of a school for nurses in Brussels. During the war, the school was converted into a hospital. The German occupation authorities, who were concerned with young men fleeing Belgium to fight with the British, arrested Cavell and charged her with aiding and abetting the passage of at least two hundred escapees. The Englishwoman, unlike some of the others who had been arrested before her, neither denied her activities nor feigned ignorance of their consequences. She proclaimed that her actions were in service to her country. She even admitted knowing that some of the Allied soldiers she had assisted would probably have joined fighting units. By making this confession, she had broken a published law of the occupation authorities: for "conducting soldiers to the enemy," the penalty was death. Most of her thirty-four co-defendants escaped the firing squad. The circumstances of Cavell's death became the stuff of legend. According to one story, all the soldiers in the firing squad had fired high or missed on purpose; an officer had to single-handedly perform the execution.

The German authorities badly miscalculated the impact of the event. The kaiser, who most people speculate would have pardoned Cavell if he had known of her case, was not informed beforehand. There were testy interchanges on the matter between different military and diplomatic jurisdictions. The marquis of

Lansdowne remarked that "she might at any rate have expected that measure of mercy which I believe in no civilized country would have been refused" to such a "brave and devoted" woman. Baron von der Lancken, head of the political department of the German occupation authorities, who had petitioned for clemency for Cavell, admitted that the whole affair was a "serious political error."[44] As propaganda historian James Morgan Read summed it up, the Germans had "handed to the English an atrocity story . . . which needed no embellishments or distortion to be as effective as it was dramatic."[45]

Political scientist Harold Lasswell argued that it was the German officer class's seeming inability to consider any situation outside of proper military viewpoints that crippled the nation's public relations efforts.[46] For example, shortly after Cavell's execution, two German nurses were shot by the French. The circumstances were somewhat different from those of the English nurse: the German women were actually paid spies. Yet the incident could obviously have been exploited, at least as a counterpoint to the death of Edith Cavell. An American newspaperman in Berlin, shortly after her execution, met with a German official in charge of propaganda efforts and asked him why he didn't "raise the devil about those nurses the French shot the other day?" The German official answered, "What? Protest? The French had a perfect right to shoot them!" Lasswell argued that this attitude demonstrated that people who were in charge of propaganda during wartime must not only understand what incidents are worthy of exploitation but also appreciate the intended audience. To the German officer class, the shooting of anyone who violated the laws and proscriptions of military expediency was perfectly justified; they were unprepared for disagreement, and unaware that in war other codes were extant. Such blindness is often born out of a sense of superiority, and what Barbara Tuchman notes was their "relentless talent for the tactless."[47] It was, after all, Kaiser Wilhelm who had exhorted his soldiers to make "their name equal to the Huns under their king Attila."

It reveals the human capacity for shifting blame and exuding self-righteousness that Germans too would emerge from World War I feeling aggrieved by enemy propaganda. A backfire effect of Allied propaganda may have been that it gave Germans the excuse not to engage in any introspection of guilt or doubt. Such externalizations were very well expressed by the Führer of the Third Reich, who understood and exploited his people's sense of victimhood. In *Mein Kampf* and his other writings and declamations, Hitler describes at some length how Germany did not follow the basic principles of propaganda in World War I, but certainly should in the next. Hitler stressed simplicity and repetition: make brief, uncomplicated statements, repeat them thousands of times, and burn them into the mind of the mob. The task of propaganda, he wrote, was "not to make an objective study of the truth, in so far as it favors the enemy, and then set it before the masses with academic fairness; its task is to serve our own right, always and unflinchingly."[48] The visual dimension was crucial: a person "will more readily accept a pictorial presentation than read a [newspaper] article.... The picture brings ... in a much briefer time, I might almost say at one stroke ... enlightenment."[49] This concept was the basis of the Nazi path to power and guided its vision of war: not to admit any crimes committed by colleagues, only to focus, repetitively, relentlessly, on the misdeeds, real or imagined, of the enemy. Adversaries must be made to "belong to a single category."[50]

Allied World War I propaganda probably was effective in the sense that it provided a rallying cry for recruitment and a self-justification for fighting. But the limits of that propaganda and its retrospective lingering aftereffects, not on prejudices against Germans but on attitudes toward propaganda itself in the Western democracies, are even more interesting and speak to some of the other factors which may guide the view of the enemy. Ordinary British and French soldiers, those who were actually fighting the "Huns," recall propaganda of this kind to have had little effect on them: because of the nature of the trench line, there were few encounters with any civilians, whether or not they suffered German oppression. Many Allied soldiers met and killed Germans who seemed as human as they were. In fact, Germans like the Red Baron could be seen as models of chivalry. In other words, the fighting men only encountered a routine enemy, not a hated enemy. At least as much resentment was directed toward home-front politicians and inept generals. Thus, many Western Europeans and Americans emerged from World War I with a deep suspicion of war propaganda. They had seen the enemy and he did not match the posters.

Lord Northcliffe, the British newspaper publisher who had been in charge of his nation's propaganda department, described in his memoirs how he had fooled Allies, Englishmen, and even Germans. Many Germans, especially liberals and social democrats, felt duped by promises of a moderate peace treaty if they ended the war. Englishmen, appalled at Northcliffe's admissions of outright lies about the enemy, considered such tactics to be "not cricket."[51] Americans were also inclined to listen with incredulity to fresh atrocity tales before and during the next war. As historians of propaganda describe, the oversimplification, factual distortions, and hysterical nature of anti-German propaganda in World War I "left a bad taste in the mouths of Americans. In turn this led to a justified suspicion of the power of organized propaganda, and ultimately encouraged the pacifist and isolationist tendencies that existed in the United States for the next twenty years."[52] As one British journalist put it in 1939, "In the midwest you have the feeling that men are waiting with shotguns to shoot down the first propagandist who mentions Belgian babies."[53] The political fallout was considerable. In the debate in the United States between those who advocated intervention against Germany or at least an anti-Hitler stance, and isolationists who believed that America should follow its original principles and avoid entangling alliances in Europe, propaganda became the worst pejorative to apply to someone else's political position. Colonel Tom McCormick, the owner of the *Chicago*

*Tribune* and an ardent supporter of the America First movement, accused the Roosevelt administration and the British of employing the propaganda tricks of World War I to manipulate America into another war. In a famous cartoon, a group of "ordinary Americans" was shown hunkered down in a trench while huge cannons bombarded them with British and Rooseveltian pro-war propaganda.[54]

The hate propaganda that caught hold and was most effective and popular in the United States during World War II was in fact against the newest enemy: Japan. Here was an alien who could be "reduced to a single category." The cartoons, posters, and cinematic portrayals of the Japanese were in many ways a restocking of the catalogue of images that the British employed against the Germans in World War I. Americans would, at least in retrospect, take up with delight the former but treat the latter with suspicion. A typical visual metaphor in poster art and cartoons was to portray the "Jap" as a rat, as vermin poisoning the world, deserving of extermination.[55] Physical differences too were highlighted or exaggerated for propagandistic purposes. Thick glasses, razor-brush haircut, buck teeth, diminutive size: these were familiar characteristics. In contrast, the Germans were a comprehensible, evil human enemy. The war in the Pacific was fought, as one historian put it, "without mercy"; in the opinion of many Americans and Japanese, the "others" were subhuman.[56] Hence the facility and non-controversial nature, at least at the time, of America's decision to drop atomic weapons on the Japanese cities. "This is the greatest day in history," exclaimed President Truman when he learned that the atomic bomb over Hiroshima had successfully exploded.[57]

But images like the "Jap rat" demonstrate another backfire effect of hate propaganda. Even before the war with Japan, the stereotype of the Japanese was negative, reinforced by images and stories of brutality in its war with China. These were based upon facts, but also without the context that Japanese colonialism was simply a latecomer to British, French, and American precedent. The Japanese were generally shorter and slighter of build than people of European descent; this condition was applied toward viewing them as not capable of flying bombers or operating tanks. Many Japanese did indeed wear glasses; many Americans thus wrongly concluded that the potential enemy could not fly or shoot straight.

At the same time, Japanese goods had a reputation for shoddiness; the American military ridiculed the notion that Japan could build efficient ships and planes. It never occurred to many Americans, because it was almost alien to the national ideology of consumption, that Japanese commercial goods may have been of a lower quality because most of the country's resources and efforts had been poured into building a military machine. The nation devoted 80 percent of its steel to manufacturing warships. Winston Churchill admitted in his history of the war that "The efficiency of the Japanese in air warfare was at this time greatly underestimated both by ourselves and by the Americans." Secretary of the Navy Frank Knox, a month before the attack on Pearl Harbor, had assured congressmen that if war came, "we could lick the Japs in two weeks."[58] In the wake of the raid, congressmen, generals, admirals, and newspaper editors continued to speculate that it had actually been coordinated or even flown by Germans. Secretary of State Henry Stimson and many other national leaders, in the words of historian Gordon Prange, found it difficult "to accept the fact that a military operation so swift, so ruthless, so painfully successful—in a word, so blitzkrieg—in nature did not originate with Hitler."[59]

There is considerable evidence, accumulated over the last fifty years, that many in the American political and military structure were quite aware that in early December 1941 there might be a Japanese attack on American military installations in the Pacific. Whatever prior warning Americans had about Japanese intentions—in fact, the United States had broken their naval code—they did not anticipate an attack so well organized or widespread. No one thought that the slight, faintly ridiculous little men from the East could defeat American and British armies and overrun much of the Pacific archipelago. So making the "Japs" into rats is less a reflection of the Japanese than of the American ego. Rats do their damage by stealth, cunning, thievery, by striking when the honest householder is not expecting it and where the larder is unguarded. Hence, the "surprise attack" at Pearl Harbor could be reinterpreted not as a blow to American pride and smugness but as treachery. Indeed, in Franklin Roosevelt's captioning of the events, it was a "Day of Infamy" to be avenged, not a humiliation to be suffered nor a case of incompetence and racial arrogance on the part of the American government and military. This is the double-edged sword of propaganda that reduces an enemy to a one-dimensional evil stereotype: hate may generate adherence to its cause, but it also blinds; prejudice may serve group solidarity, but it also clouds constructive self-criticism.

## THE OFF-CAMERA ENEMY

Some visions of the war enemy can be analogous to Sherlock Holmes's "curious incident of the dog in the night-time." "The dog did nothing in the night-time," stated his friend Dr. Watson. "That was the curious incident," replied Holmes. When, in the midst of war, the enemy is absent from a picture, this does not mean that his presence is unfelt, unrecognized, or irrelevant. In war photography, the enemy is almost always missing in the action. Few photographers are able to stand close enough to take pictures of unfriendly troops fighting hand-to-hand with the "good guys"; the painter, sculptor, and fiction filmmaker can, of course, recreate such scenes in relative safety.

The techniques of absence can be created, first, by simply not showing an enemy, by wiping him from the visual record. Second, most prominently the case in war films, the enemy may be present but his screen time severely reduced compared to that of heroes and friends. Third, and often in accordance with the second condition, the enemy is shrunk. Relative size, that useful indicator of the person of the war commander, helps distinguish friend from enemy; the latter is backgrounded in diminutive proportion to the lingering close-up accorded to those whom the artist serves or focuses his tale upon.

An absent enemy also can be inferred from the off-camera gazes of the subjects, or by evidence of the enemy's actions. In the Mauldin cartoon seen earlier in which the private carries his "lootenant" to safety [see **Fig. 19**], the Germans are indicated only by the tracers and shooting shells. In the cartoon, however, their role is mainly as pretext to the punch line, not part of a system of inference with ideological representation. A contrasting example is the drawing of "loyal brownies" by R. Caton Woodville which appeared in the *Illustrated London News* in 1899.[60] [**Fig. 31**] It was captioned: "Boer Treachery—Firing on Indian Stretcher Bearers in charge of a Wounded Officer." Two stalwart and evidently indignant Sikh stretcher bearers are scowling. We are not shown what they are looking at, and indeed it is unclear if they can see the enemy, but the implication suffices. The treachery has been committed by some foe, and in this case absence is terrifically significant.

The incident shown may or may not have taken place, but the scene is credible. In a series of wars from 1880 to 1902, the Dutch settlers in southern Africa fought against annexation into the British Empire. The Boers were mostly farmers living in scattered homesteads. Their numbers were small, but they were expert marksmen and riders, had much experience fighting in wars against the native population, and knew their homeland geography well. In combat, they rarely formed large field armies or offered themselves up to the British for set-piece engagements. They pioneered the hit-and-run tactics of indirect warfare— raids in the English rear areas, night attacks, sniping and retreating. Woodville's picture exemplifies the exasperation no doubt felt by British soldiers and their allies committed to fighting standard direct warfare. As always, one soldier's treachery is another's *ruse de guerre*.

But much more was happening off camera. The Boers were eventually overwhelmed because the British burned their farms and rounded up their families, who were conducted to special enclosures ringed by barbed wire: the first concentration camps. At least 20,000 Boer civilians died under conditions of privation that would resurface in another war, half a century later on an industrial scale. The *Illustrated London News* produced no picture spreads of these camps, but images like "Boer Treachery" fostered a climate of opinion that indirectly sanctioned their creation and maintenance. Moreover, the Sikhs in the drawing were colorful symbols of British imperialism, Gunga Din figures, the devoted natives. By implication, we might read that if these people from so alien a culture

31. *Boer Treachery—Firing on Indian Stretcher Bearers in charge of a Wounded Officer,*
R. Caton Woodville, 1900

are happy serving under the British colors, why should the white men of Natal refuse to accept English sovereignty? In short, in this image, though the enemy is not shown, the stares of the bearers and the declamation of the caption indicate his presence. The artists instructed us how to feel about the off-camera foe who refuses to "fight fair."

An unseen enemy, then, may have a palpable presence; but to shun portrayal of an enemy altogether, especially within the confines of certain forms of visual representation, is itself a symbolic act. One of the more remarkable features of the Nazi regime, for example, is only notable in retrospect, in considering the sum, kind, and focus of its visual texts. It is evident that, for Hitler personally and for the Third Reich in general, obsession with Jews as the source of evil and as a "problem" to be solved is pervasive. As Propaganda Minister Joseph Goebbels summed up the ethos of himself and many of his cohort: "The Jews are to blame for everything."[61] In newspaper, poster, and radio diatribes until the last days of the war, the Jew was identified as the abiding enemy of the German people. Even as the Jews of Europe had largely been deported or killed, the calumnies poured forth; Hitler's last will and testament, dictated days before his suicide and the fall of Berlin, was another parting agenda of accusations of Jewish perfidy. Yet, in the greater share of the visual arts, in the high-gloss photography magazines, in oil painting and sculpture, and with some major exceptions in film, especially of the later period, the Jew as war enemy is almost completely absent. Of the entire output of gallery paintings in the years of Nazi power, on those canvases approved by the state censors and displayed to the German people, there were but few images of the "great enemy." It is the vision of war's most chilling *lacuna*—those blamed for the war and all miseries felt by the German people, those on whom a campaign of meticulous extermination was being waged, are off canvas, off camera, and out of the frame.

The reason for this absence is again an implied one. Many of the top Nazi leaders were either previously failed artists, such as Hitler, or impoverished aesthetes like Hermann Goering. Probably no totalitarian regime in history accorded such importance to the fine arts. Hitler's aesthetic theory was sweeping and grandiose: "Art is the only enduring investment of human labor."[62] He further claimed, "The Germans are a people of soldiers and artists"; German art was the "proudest justification of the German people."[63] In contrast to Napoleon's almost boorish attitude toward artistic endeavors, Hitler respected and supported cultural production. Most civic projects, including roads and bridges, were justified for their artistic worth. The regime set up museums and exhibitions and generally encouraged the production of its approved styles and themes of art.

Such art, especially that shown in the galleries, was distinctly anti-Modernist; in fact, modern art and music, from surrealism to jazz, were held as prime examples of a degeneracy alien to the German people. The Jews topped the list of enemies projected as responsible for the decline of the arts into what Hitler called the "cesspool." In this *Kulturkampf*, the ranks of unapproved artists, whether Jews or Modernists, were to be removed, and indeed, the greatest purging of any profession that took place in the Nazi regime was in the arts. More important, Hitler felt, images displayed to the world should be free of all unattractive, modern, or unheroic themes, that is, *Judenrein* (cleansed of Jews).[64] The same applied to much work in film, and to slick publications like *Signal*, the German military magazine. In this latter medium, as historian S. L. Mayer notes, "Anti-Semitic propaganda, so virulent in the Reich itself, never appeared in a blatant manner; in fact the Jews were hardly ever mentioned. The impression given was that the Jewish problem had been solved, for according to *Signal* there were no problems in Nazi Germany."[65] Removal of Jews from the arts and physical living space was accepted and uncontroversial. A Jew-free photography and museum gallery was the prelude to an anticipated thousand years of a Jew-free Europe.

Such a mechanism is not unique to the Third Reich. Distance, in visual terms, lends disengagement. Again, these manipulations of the visual element are not wholly mediated creations—they work precisely because they are analogies to the way human beings see and think. Considerable research on how people, especially children, respond to visual images suggests that "Despite . . . differences in the nature of the information that is generally available about [screen] characters versus people, the cognitive processes involved in forming impressions of characters and real people appear to be highly similar."[66] One of the commonsense findings of such research is that people identify with characters they like: the more they like a character, the more they express concern with his or her fate.[67]

A basic way to relegate certain people to an unimportant status, to dehumanize an enemy, is simply not to show him in close-up. On-screen multitudes are created by long shots. Para-proxemic distance can influence para-social impressions, the feelings of identity with a screen character.[68] We like people we feel close to; we feel close to people we like. Hence innumerable western films of past generations in which "wild" Indians are not individualized, but rather are portrayed as a mass of shrieking savages, offered up to the guns of the white heroes.

Alternately, turning the enemy not into a howling mob but into a row of blurry shapes whose deaths then cannot be lamented can be achieved both by maintaining greater para-proxemic distance and by arranging their ranks in stiff, formal designs. This was exemplified in many early Communist films depicting the civil war against the "whites," or anti-Communist Russians. One such movie is *Chapayev*, written and directed by the Vasiliev brothers and released in 1934.[69] The great and subtle Russian actor Boris Babochkin played the title role of a legendary Red Army commander. The film was shown at the fifteenth anniversary of the Soviet cinema, and because its political stridency was overshadowed by an exciting story, appealing characterizations, and a poignant tale of humans trapped in a terrible war, the film was internationally hailed as a humane masterpiece. In one battle sequence, the "reds" array themselves in the modern style of war, hiding behind terrain, wearing camouflage clothing. They lie in wait for the attack by the enemy. The white guards (an "officers' battalion") advance in stiff-stepping ranks, appearing in the long shot to be so many windup toy soldiers—shades of their previous incarnation on the Odessa steps in *Battleship Potemkin*. This time, however, the reds slaughter the tsarists. The sheer numbers as well play some role in the detachment the audience is meant to feel at their deaths: it is less traumatic to kill a mob than a single man. Their mass, uniformity, and regularity undercuts their claim to humanity.

The absence of the enemy can also grant symbolic value to a war film, when it is contrasted to his former sinister presence. In *The Battle of Britain* (1967), we encounter some of the longest and most realistic aerial battles ever produced for a motion picture. The German pilots, while not given much individual screen time or the sympathetic details of home lives and family situations, are shown in their planes and air bases. We see Englishmen and Germans, as well as Poles, Czechs, and Canadians, fighting and dying in sky duels over England in the summer of 1940. By the end of the film, we have witnessed so many dogfights that they seem as much a part of the English skyline as birch tops, church spires, or swallows. It is all the more powerful when, in one of the final scenes, Laurence Olivier, playing the real-life commander of the air defenses Air Marshal Sir Hugh Dowding, emerges from his headquarters. It is a comfortable country building, with a well-tended garden beyond, reminiscent more of the land of Jane Austen than the Blitz. A pleasant sun shines on Dowding's face. Then the commander stands still as he realizes what has happened. The dog, as Holmes would have said, has not barked. Dowding looks up and the sky is absolutely clear, unblemished by smoke, flame, or tracer. No guns blast, propeller engines whine, or explosions sound. The battle is over. The Germans no longer fly against England; they have turned their gaze elsewhere, toward the East.

## THE AMBIGUOUS ENEMY

In some quarters, after World War I the disenchantment and bitter aftertaste left by propaganda reflected a revolt not only against war itself but the very idea of "enemy." One film, *All Quiet on the Western Front* (1930), based on Erich Remarque's novel, comments upon the nature of knowing an enemy. In the film, Lew Ayres plays a high school recruit in the German army. Like the youth of any country in the prewar era, he was indoctrinated in the notion of his own nation's natural supremacy and believed—what Wilfred Owen called "the old lie"—the Roman motto, *Dulce et decorum est pro patria mori*: it is sweet and honorable to die for one's country. Several years of trench warfare, of neither defeat nor victory but endless mud and stalemate, disabuse the German soldier of any of the glorious visions of war he began with in the first days of August 1914.

One scene draws into relief his conversion from reflexive warrior to reflective doubter, from certainty to ambiguity about who is the enemy he fights. In a particularly confusing battle, Ayres finds himself in a partly flooded bomb crater in the midst of a terrific artillery exchange. Bewildered by the smoke and gun blasts, he can hardly tell where he is. Suddenly, an ordinary French soldier, a *poilu*, stumbles into the same hole. The two men struggle, and finally Ayres stabs his enemy, inflicting a deep wound. The two are trapped in the trench for a night and into the next day while small arms and gunfire rattle continuously. The French soldier clings to life, groaning. Ayres alternately tries to help him, offering words of reassurance, and screams at him: "Stop it! Stop it! I can bear the rest of it; I can't listen to this! Why do you take so long to die? You're going to die anyway!" Almost always, the French soldier is shown in close-up or medium close-up. He is not "the enemy" anymore; he is a suffering human being.

After the French soldier has finally died, Ayres tells him, "You see, when you jumped in here you were my enemy, and I was afraid of you. But you're just a man like me, and I killed you. Forgive me, comrade. Say that for me, say you forgive me." Ayres then finds a picture of a wife and daughter in the dead man's jacket. The film thus not only visually places the enemy at the same level and distance within the frame as the "friend" but shatters the concept of protagonist and antagonist. This was, after all, an American film based on a German novel. Ayres was a young Everyman; the parallels between his character and the ordinary American doughboys sent thousands of miles away were clear, or would have been to the audience of that time. Having seen the Frenchman's family and above all having witnessed his drawn-out and painful death, we are unable to preserve the notion of an enemy as an anonymous, distant horde that serves only as extras for the macho prowess of the hero or as cackling villains who merit dispatch.

A similar scene was recorded in the early days of the war. This drawing is based on an event reported to the Dutch cartoonist Louis Raemaekers.[70] [**Fig. 32**] The cartoon, whose original caption reads: "Is it you, Mother?," shows a British Highlander wounded at the Battle of Soissons during World War I. In the delirium and blindness of approaching death, he mistakes a German infantryman for his mother. The notes of a postwar compilation of Raemaekers's work explain: "The German comprehended, and to maintain the illusion, caressed his face with a mother's soft touch. The poor boy died shortly afterwards and the German soldier, on getting to his feet, was seen to be crying." The vision of war here is noteworthy not just because it portrays the rarest of all representations of an enemy, that of kindness, gentleness, and pathos; it was in fact sketched by one of the most prolific producers of anti-German atrocity pictures. The Netherlands, unlike its neighbors Belgium and Luxembourg, was not invaded by the German army. The Dutch maintained a prosperous neutrality, trading with both sides during the war. Raemaekers, whose mother was German, had spent a good part of his life in Germany. Yet after he visited Belgium to

32. "Is it you, Mother?" (German soldier tending dying English soldier, World War I),
Louis Raemaekers, 1917

confirm atrocity tales, he became convinced that he had seen a "hell" and "a
terror unspeakable." Raemaekers began a brief career of drawing anti-German
cartoons that were eventually distributed all over the world, reprinted by Allied
governments in books and postcards, shown on exhibition, and translated into
languages from Arabic to Basque.

Typically, his cartoons were the most vitriolic form of propaganda, although in almost all cases he claimed they were based upon true incidents. Theodore Roosevelt said that Raemaekers "rendered the most powerful of the honorable contributions by neutrals to the cause of civilization." The German government put out an "arrest on sight" order for the cartoonist. It was Raemaekers's pen that incised several frames of furious indictment of the killing of Nurse Edith Cavell. The themes of the thousand or more cartoons he produced during the war are as unvarying as they are vituperative: Germany as the Grim Reaper; Germans slaughtering Christ; the kaiser executing women and children; German soldiers engaged in looting, spoiling, and pillaging. The Germans are the incarnation of everything corpulent, sadistic, scheming, uncaring, inhuman, bestial, and demonic, a veritable visual dictionary of the entire range of attack propaganda. "Is it you, Mother?" is almost the only exception. It expresses, in one panel, the entire thrust of a film like *All Quiet on the Western Front*: despite uniforms, flags, and the thousand-odd other symbols of division between people, there could come to pass moments of camaraderie. That these opportunities are fleeting, Raemaekers seems to be implying, is shown by the other German soldiers in the background who are in mid-march. There is no doubt that the compassionate infantryman will stay his tears, rise up and join his comrades, to fight, and kill, again.

But the "enemies" do not have to become buddies for us to infer that their worldviews and situations are or were like ours. That warriors may also share the same moment but see different parts of it as relevant is summed up by the 1969 film comedy, *If It's Tuesday, This Must Be Belgium*. One scene, in its understated way, says much about how we construct narratives of warfare. An American World War II veteran and a woman from his European tour bus are visiting the towering Bastogne war memorial, in northern France. They stand on one side of a long plaza, where he explains, "It was right here that we won the Battle of the Bulge. Hey! Now, you see down there where that couple is? Now, that was a German strongpoint. Come here!" The film cuts to "that couple," obviously Germans, the man complete with feathered hiking hat. He is evidently telling the same war tale as the American veteran, but from his own remembered perspective. The recreation is probably as old as war, or hunting: the Old Bullfrog reciting his battle adventures to an appreciative female audience.

The American continues: "After they thought that their barrage had softened us up they moved in with their tanks. Now what did we do?" "Moved in with our tanks?" his companion asks. "Yeah," he shrugs. The next lines are spoken by both the American and German veteran, in English and German, with rapid intercutting between them:

"We started down the hill . . ."

"every gun blazin' . . ."

"we hadda push 'em back or we were dead!"

"And then the Germans/Americans retreated!"

Slowly the two enemies converge, but in their reverie they are blind to the present engagement; they charge past triumphantly to seize the land on which the other had begun his pantomime. The same battle incident has been retold with the exact same plot, but with a completely different identity of victor and vanquished. Whatever the facts, the former warriors return to their respective tour buses, secure in their own vision of war—forever defeating phantom enemies.

But they are simply two sides of a coin. Their causes may have different virtues and vices, but their circumstances, and their ex post facto reminiscences, are identical. A similar point was etched by Bill Mauldin in his cartoon "Fresh, Spirited Troops."[71] [**Fig. 33**] This is justifiably renowned as one of the greatest cartoons of World War II, an achievement made all the more impressive because it was not a postbellum reappraisal or revision but a commentary produced in the midst of the war. Mauldin shows his genius by subverting the conventions of war propaganda as well as the distinction between enemy and friend. This is not, however, an antiwar cartoon. Mauldin's point, which he emphasizes in his written commentary, was not that the Germans were just like us. He argues that American soldiers realized who they were fighting, especially when they began traveling through the occupied lands of France and saw evidence of German war crimes. What he is stating is a universal in the history of war, often unexpressed in its visualization: rain falls as hard on the victor as the vanquished, and chasing a fleeing enemy is as exhausting as running in defeat. We may share certain conditions with the enemy yet still firmly believe that the fight is just.

What Mauldin is protesting here is what more recently Paul Fussell has called "the epidemic of BAD," the vastly inflated declamations of advertising and propaganda which put an upbeat "spin" on life's every facet.[72] To claim that "our side" is universally content and the enemy is uniformly discouraged probably serves to flatter the egos of generals as much as it did the pharaohs; yet in a people's war, fought not by aristocrats bred for the duty but by reluctant shoe salesmen and hog farmers, self-congratulation falls flat for the men asked to do the actual killing. Better rations, dry socks, more accurate air support, and fewer conceited new "lootenants" head the agenda of the common soldier's demands, not brassier slogans.

The idea that a warrior could be both good and bad, that the heroes could also be villains, that the face of the victim or of the evildoer could seem equally virtuous, is anathema to the simple doctrines of propaganda. But perhaps this vision of war and of the war enemy is closer to the truth than we would like to believe. As the enemy's motivations are understood, his philosophy explored, his history contextualized—or his foot soldiers seen face to face—the complexity that arises occasions neither beastification nor beatification. "We have met the enemy and they are ours," reported Oliver Hazard Perry after defeating a British

33. " 'Fresh, spirited American troops, flushed with victory, are bringing in thousands of hungry, ragged, battle-weary prisoners . . . ' (News item)." World War II cartoon, Bill Mauldin.
*Reprinted by permission of Bill Mauldin and the Watkins/Loomis Agency*

naval squadron on Lake Erie in the War of 1812. "We have met the enemy and he is us," observed Walt Kelly's comic strip character Pogo during the Vietnam War. It is rare that the visions of war *during* wartime itself make us face that possibility: the fury of the fight encourages categorical thinking, and ambiguity is relegated to afterthought.

# 6

HORRORS

## *HORROR AND SYMPATHY*

In March 1998, speaking in the capital of Rwanda—where four years earlier one million minority Tutsi people had been killed while international agencies and the U.S. government purposely avoided intervening—President Bill Clinton apologized for not having "fully appreciated . . . this unimaginable terror." In fact, in light of the visions of war we have seen from this century, and from most others, it is difficult to argue that enthusiastically executed genocide can or should be impossible to imagine.

Horrors, however they are defined, have always been part of the vision of war. The most prevalent has been the death of the soldier in battle. The bird-man of the Lascaux cave faced a charging bison, his spear and atlatl tumbling away; it seems most likely a moment of death in natural combat. In the Neolithic battle of archers at Morella la Vella, Spain, arrows pierce the "executed" figure. In the drawing of the battle from Australia's Arnhem Land, the captain of the army on the right is struck by a spear. It is unclear, however, whether the societies that fought these battles and created the images that represented them saw such visions as many audiences today would, for example, see the death of an American soldier on a street in Mogadishu, Somalia—as a "horror" of war. In all the images cited previously from ancient Middle East, Egypt, Rome, Greece, and Mesoamerica, death in battle is not withheld from the viewer's gaze; it is often the focal point—aside from the supremacy of the commander—of the scene. The distinctions between visions of the horrors of war lie in how they have been stylized and narrowed—made more or less palatable—and how sympathetically the victims and the perpetrators have been portrayed.

Certainly, many horrors of war have yet to find or be thrust upon an audience. For example, the diseases often enabled by the concentration of men in armies before the twentieth century have largely gone unpictured at all. Dysentery, the killer of ten times as many British soldiers in the Crimea as enemy guns, was never the subject of an oil painting. Even in modern films, the "runs" achieve no great prominence, and certainly no lingering close-ups. Such pictured horrors of war would of course, ironically, send audiences away or at least cause them to turn their heads in disgust at the poor taste of the image maker. No one wants to view such scenes, no matter how common they are in life. Again, the most realistic portrayal of war is still a selective one; no visual image shows *all* the horrors of war.

Of the ancient and classical civilizations of the New and Old World a simple generalization can be made, one that runs counter to the modern standards of propriety of public relations in wartime. When true slaughter was shown—massacres of foes and prisoners, and even killing of women and children—this was not a sorrowful memorialization, a cry to heaven for justice, or a sober record of war crimes. The horrors of war in Assyrian and Roman reliefs, for example, were interpreted as signs of divine disfavor for the victims. The revolts and rebellions of Elamites and Dacians were crimes against the king, the gods, and the empire. The same thoughts drive the visions of naked castrated enemies that adorned Monte Albán. The punishments were horrible, but fully justified in the ideology of the victors; the "victims" deserved what they got.

This is the difference of style between the ancient heritage and the modern view of the horrors of war that was established during the Renaissance. No contemporary military publicist, whether employed by the Pentagon or Saddam Hussein, would boastfully print or broadcast images of his country's own men killing prisoners, burning cities, or looting property. Such images would be suppressed, condemned as false or rationalized as being the result of accidents or failure on the part of lower-rank officers. For example, during the UN intervention in Somalia from 1992 to 1994, Canadian paratroopers were videotaped torturing to death a sixteen-year-old native boy.[1] The scenes were shown on Canadian media as a scandalous injustice; as one reporter put it, "these events shocked the entire nation. How could our boys behave so?" In reaction, the Canadian military denied that the act was officially sanctioned or encouraged by superiors, disbanded the unit—an elite regiment in the Canadian army—and initiated several courts-martial. Similarly, a Roman commander might very well have punished his men for torturing unarmed civilians who showed no evidence of anti-Roman activities. The Senate once ordered half a legion put to death because its men sacked the city that they had been sent to guard. But massacres, torture, mutilation, forced expulsion of rebellious or enemy populations were accepted stratagems; their representation in Roman art was unapologetic.

It is in the modern history of war, beginning with the full-scale innovation of firearms that developed during the Thirty Years' War (1618–1648) and the wars of Spanish Succession (1701–1714), that many visual images have been created to portray the horrors of war not as a boast but as an invocation of lamentation or blame. In the late 1500s, the French artist Jacques Callot created a series of etchings on the miseries of the wars in northwestern Europe, including his homeland, Lorraine. The resulting prints displayed torture, rape, pillage, and murder in detail.[2] Another series of works, on the Peninsular campaigns of the Napoleonic Wars, emerged from the pens and brush of Francisco Goya. In sketches bearing the same title as this chapter—*The Horrors of War*—he showed men, women, and children as monsters driven to mutual destruction. Grisly minutiae were unsparing and abundant: jagged bones, entrails, ripped limbs.

During World War I, imagery extolling the horrors of war, linked to the crimes of an individual state, was a standard of propaganda. Even after the war, in 1919, the same imagery could be deployed—but by then it could be challenged as well. For example, Canada's contribution to the New York War Art Exhibition was a 32-inch bronze sculpture titled *Canada's Golgotha*, created by Captain Derwent Wood, a veteran of the war. [**Fig. 34**] On a heavy wooden door, a Canadian soldier is crucified by barbed wire. Aping the role of Roman soldiers at the feet of Christ, two Germans stand below, taunting him.

*Canada's Golgotha* is significant because it straddled two traditions: it was emblematic of the "new realism," but still was part of the appeal to propagandistic myth. The sculpture itself, though seen by hardly any of the public, was reproduced in newspaper photographs. London's *Daily Mail* called it "Canada's sternest memorial to their sons' sufferings in the war."[3] But was it based on fact? In response to an inquiry, the Canadian Department of National Defense in 1930, after many years of leafing through files, found that "there are no drawings or photographs of the alleged crucifixion of Canadian soldiers available in this Department."[4] Yet there was sworn and written testimony given by two British soldiers that on April 21 or 23, 1915, near the town of Saint-Julien in Belgium, they saw "the corpse of a Canadian soldier fastened with bayonets to a barn door." The section of Saint-Julien where they claim the scene was encountered, however, was found never to have been occupied by German troops. Nevertheless, the incident became the subject of Allied war atrocity stories, and was shown in at least one fiction film. In a thorough investigation, a British major alleged that no German had been "less than 11,000 yards distant" from the area, and though a soldier tied up by barbed wire was seen, his tormentors were more likely to have been Belgian farmers than German troops.[5] Again, the views of *Golgotha* depend on the viewer, and realism on what was experienced as real.

During and after World War I, many images of combat and the soldiers' life in the Victorian Romantic vein—in painting, posed photographs, films, and posters—were produced. However, the discordance that was often presented between the realities of war shown to the public and those suffered in the field was made more stark and more widely known. Battles fought on moonscapes, covered in fog, by machine guns and artillery, seemed not to lend themselves to the sensibility and tactility of oil painting. Photographs could not capture such battles without endangering the cameraman. More important, the subjects themselves changed: modern armies, acknowledging the muddy battlegrounds, sub-

34. *Canada's Golgotha*, Francis Derwent Wood (bronze statue, 1919).
*Copyright Canadian War Museum, cat. no. 8940.*

stituted drab uniforms for striking combat dress, combinations of gray and brown and khaki. These conditions were known to art critics and artists alike. In the first year of the new century, reviewing art of the Boer War, the critic A. C. R. Carter noted that the very nature of war's "look" (for the artist and other viewers) had changed:

> How will the painter of modern warfare make up then for the rich uniforms the troops have left behind them? Let us hope that the future school will not rush to sensationalism to compensate itself for this deprivation of picturesqueness. Art has no home amongst the horrors of realism or of carnage. The warrior asks for no reminder of these. He hopes that they may be buried deep beneath the paths of peace.[6]

Lady Butler, the general's wife who was famous for her heroic compositions, reeled at the butchery of the western front in the first months of the war and immediately understood that her era had passed. "Who will look at my 'Waterloo' now?" was her rhetorical question.[7] Realism was the order of the day.

That realism, too, became defined not just by style and content but by medium. The *Golgotha* was one of the final celebrated statues of war. One of the last famous paintings was Pablo Picasso's *Guernica* (1937), created in response to the bombing of a small town in the Basque country during the Spanish Civil War. There is controversy to this day over who exactly bombed Guernica, but the evidence seems strong that it was Germans of the Condor Legion fighting for the Fascist forces in Spain. The picture shows a jumble of crazed figures—crying birds, broken horses, exploding light bulbs, screaming faces—meant to signify the horrors of a day when some nine hundred civilians were killed and an ancient city was destroyed.

But generally World War II's stock of horrors appeared in mass media, typically in news reels and print, and later in fiction film and television. The catalogues of horrors were now for the camera to reveal or censor. From China emerged pictures of the Japanese "rape" of major cities like Shanghai and Nanking. From Europe came the walking skeletons and the piles of corpses from the death camps. In Japan, human beings became outlines on the stone walls at Hiroshima and Nagasaki. Conflicts—from Korea to the shadow wars of colonials in Africa and Latin America to Vietnam, the Gulf War, and Bosnia—have been associated with and even defined by striking images that show death and destruction. What unites nearly all these images, besides the camera, is that they were displayed either in reporting of war, as evidence of the general horrors, or as accusations of war crimes: none encompassed visualized boasts by the victors.

But what does "realism" actually accomplish? Are we better able to stop or even understand the horrors of war now that we no longer take pride in them?

"Realistic"—that is, grisly—views of war do not necessarily shock and dissuade people from supporting or seeking war. Nevertheless, many "horror show" visions, in which an antiwar message is struck home with gruesome imagery, seem to assume telling effects. Such propositions are difficult to measure in everyday life—the effects of public imagery always are—but we can evaluate one example: reaction to a television movie, *The Day After* (1983), directed by Nicholas Meyer. Broadcast on February 20, 1984, it was authentically a political event as well as a piece of entertainment. At the time of its presentation, the antiwar movement in America and the West had largely coalesced into a single issue: the nuclear freeze. The program was a real-world test of whether showing war's horrors up close and personal helped to spur active antipathy to war.

*The Day After* is set in one of those "typical" American towns that is the favorite invasion target of aliens and runaway viruses. In this case it is the heartland: Lawrence, Kansas. We see the standard accouterments of a small town: ordinary people planning weddings, hustling to work, sharing the family dinner. Here, the herald of apocalypse is the television newscast. There are increasingly dark rumblings of an international crisis. The causes of the war are vague, but it is implied that the deployment of U.S. missiles in Western Europe precipitated the crisis. Yet the townsfolk are unconnected, both powerless to affect and disengaged from these events. All they can do is turn off the TV. A barbershop conversation includes a young man about to get married dismissing the idea of the bombing of his town "way the hell out here in the middle of nowhere." The answer: "There's no 'nowhere' anymore."

The crucial scene of the film is the college football game, that paragon of middle American normalcy. As the spectators watch, missiles soar overhead, and a girl student asks, "What's going on?" A man replies, "Those are Minuteman missiles." She wonders, "Like a test, sort of. Like a warning?" He responds, "They're on their way to Russia. They take about thirty minutes to reach their target." Another man adds, "So do theirs, right?" In another shot, as the missiles go off, a farmer runs upstairs to retrieve his wife, but she insists on making her children's beds; she struggles and screams as he drags her down to the fortified and stocked cellar. In a short time, the Russian missiles hit and we see the full kaleidoscope of nuclear effects: blinding light, mushroom cloud, electromagnetic wave which renders inoperative all machines based on transistors, from hospital incubators to most automobiles. The second half of the film is devoted to the decline and fall of the community; here is where the horror show begins: radiation burns and sickness, stacks of corpses, the breakdown of all social order, martial law, and the executions of looters.

Although ABC network officials went to some length to deny that the film had a specific agenda, accompanying the horror show are unambiguous intonations of who is to blame for the disaster: the political authorities. In one of the final scenes, the voice of the president, sounding like a *Saturday Night Live* parody of Ronald Reagan, ridiculously exudes a hopeful message that is in complete opposition to the dying community we have just seen. "There has been no surrender, no retreat from the principles of liberty and democracy for which the Free World looks to us for leadership."

*The Day After* was one of the most-watched TV movies of all time, attracting viewers in almost forty million American homes. It is unclear, however, whether the event had any real effect. Ronald Reagan, the unacknowledged villain of the film's nuclear war, did not suffer any drop in popularity in the wake of the program. In fact, one poll showed approval of the administration's defense policies actually rising slightly, and registered a similar increase in the perception that it was the United States more than the Soviet Union that was trying to avoid war. Nuclear freeze groups published viewing guides hoping to channel what they assumed would be a large audience into sympathetic political activism. Toll-free numbers were set up to allow people to register their support for the freeze and volunteer to assist in the campaign. The hot line received only a few calls. Public opinion scholar J. Michael Hogan suggests that the reason for this failure to translate attention into action or even reaction of any kind was because *The Day After* "lacked a key element of the apocalyptic tradition: the promise that we might be delivered from fear by faith or political commitment."[8]

We are all selective about defining, explaining, and absorbing the horrors of war, fantastic or real. Likewise, the relative nature of one's own definition of horror allows the idealist to behave with the greatest baseness and evil without troubling his or her mental balance. Pre-Columbian warriors of the Great Plains might sack a neighboring village and put its men (and many women and children) to the scalping knife, then define warfare as two heroes squaring off in duels. A soldier of Napoleon's army could plunder a manorhouse, rape the owner's daughter, and steal the down bedding, yet still gaze with approval at—and recognize the authenticity and accurate portrayal of—an image of a glittering hussar of the guard. Likewise, as George Orwell noted about the English leftist intelligentsia of the prewar years, they would swallow whole any atrocity story alleged against capitalist, colonialist, Fascist, or Trotskyite, but assume that any similar crime ascribed to the agency of Stalin's Russia must be false propaganda.[9] The same Janus face of accusation and sympathy has been taken up in the Vietnam War, the Soviet war in Afghanistan, the Arab-Israeli Wars, and the conflicts in Central America. Despite being real for the victims, the horrors of war we want to know about, believe in, and publicize as opposed to those we deny and hide are purely selections and projections of our ideology.

## NOBLE DEATHS

Much of the premodern and ancient art of war revealed the mechanics of how it was "sweet and honorable to die for one's country." Such nobility could be expressed by conventions with which we are familiar. The prime example is the warrior shot in the chest, hands clutching the air, with perhaps a line of flags fluttering beyond, or like Tipu Sultan and James Wolfe, lying in the hands of compatriots, body spared from real wounds in inconvenient places. Yet, even in the twentieth century, the details of how death is imposed may not be fully shown. An example is a scene in the World War II film *Breakthrough* (1950), recreating the advance of Allied forces into France in the summer of 1944. In the midst of furious battle in the "hedgerow hell" of the Normandy farmland, a GI—the Italian American representative of the multicultural platoon—climbs onto an enemy tank, knocks out its commander, and tosses a grenade down the turret hatch. Just after the subsequent explosion, his sergeant yells, "Dominic, jump! Jump, Dominic!" The hero, who had been partly obscured by the fire and smoke, wails, "I can't! I ain't got no legs!" He may not, but we *see* only tattered fatigues, not the jagged bone, the blood, or the severed limbs scattered across the road. The cleansing action here is not quite of the romantic totality imposed on General Wolfe by Benjamin West, but most of the horror is left to inference. It is real, but not fully realized.

Making death "noble" in Western art is often not censorship but sensitivity, a conscious decision to honor the dead by not dwelling on the forensic details of the death. Greek art of the city-state period is an example of this heritage. In Athenian drama, horror is not absent, and occasionally the audience of a play would see it in full close-up: a blinded Oedipus, or the head of a fallen king. Yet the Greeks largely kept the most horrifying murders and acts of violence offstage, out of sight, to be verbally recounted on stage. Likewise, a listener of the *Iliad*, the source of much battle imagery, would have been well aware of the damage that "tearing bronze" wrought on sinew, flesh, and bone. However, although pictures of hoplites and war heroes show the moment of death, rarely are there details of gushing blood or spilling entrails. This fact may be inferred tentatively from what survives of scenes of war on the red-figure and black-figure vases. Most show death in battle; to be more precise, they show one warrior prone before another. Typically, the only sign of death is a downward spear thrust to the chest. Seldom does a blade actually penetrate skin: rarest of all are blood and guts.

The modern critic could view such images and see in them censorship of gore and romanticism of death. This assumption ignores the social context of the image; it assumes a home-front audience ignorant of wars and the results of war. But no citizen of Athens, no Spartan, would have been fooled by such censorship into thinking that death in battle was heroic and sterile. In the course of their lives they would have either fought in battles or seen their consequences; these conflicts were pursued in proximity to the audience of the images, and the population of the images, even if projected as archaic heroes, was modeled after true fighters from the ranks of contemporary warriors. The noble deaths here were not attempts to deceive, nor to cover up the horrors of war.

Second, noble deaths were often military necessities, at least in the case of commanders. Wolfe's comment after his final, fatal wounding to the men who rushed to his aid, "Let not my brave soldiers see me drop," was similarly uttered by many others. In the Old Testament, King Ahab, cursed by God, yet still a responsible war leader, dies in battle; however, his men fasten the body to his chariot so that the enemy and the rest of the army do not see him fall. Likewise, El Cid, the Spanish warlord and mercenary, died in his battle with the Moors but held the line, strapped to his horse.

War images in the photographic era offer greater variation—often much more gruesome—in the styles of the depiction of death in battle. In the American Civil War, photographs of the dead and of wounded veterans, including those who had lost limbs, were seen by the public both during the war and afterwards. [**Fig. 35**] Even more sensational woodcut and engraving prints of such images did not spare audiences from the gore of combat. Yet the pictures were often reframed within the noble tradition. Oliver Wendell Holmes wrote in an *Atlantic Monthly* essay in August 1863 of his reaction to photographs of the dead at Antietam: "Let him who wishes to know what war is look at this series of illustrations." It reminded him of an earlier visit to the battlefield where he saw the carnage and debris of war and thought it "so nearly like visiting the battle-field to look over these views, that all the emotions excited by the actual sight of the stained and sordid scene, strewed with rags and wrecks, came back to us, and we buried them in the recesses of our cabinet as we would have buried the mutilated remains of the dead they too vividly represented."[10] These pictures— without color, pageantry, or noble posings—contrasted with the Romantic tradition that had dominated the visions of death in war on the canvas of oil paintings, but the Romantic *spirit* still prevailed.

Furthermore, even a pristine view of a living soldier may be horrifying if our minds fill in the fact of his death in battle. In June 1969, *Life* magazine published 217 photographs of Americans who had been killed in one particularly intense week of fighting in Vietnam. The photographs were all portraits, ranging from civilian graduation snapshots to the full military uniform and flag set-up. Almost all were provided by the young men's families. It is simplistic to claim that showing a young man in clean and pressed military uniform, slightly occluding an American flag, smiling, resolute, the incarnation of the strength of our youth, is somehow an attempt at evading the consequences of war. To know that "this gallery of young American eyes" was "one week's dead" was horrifying. Paul Fussell, in writing about the depiction of death in World War II, asserts that the real horror of ripped stomachs and headless corpses was carefully hidden from the home-front audience. Fussell also notes that soldiers constantly chafed at

35. *The Dead at Antietam.* Photo possibly by Alexander Gardner(?), September 17, 1862. *Reproduction courtesy of the Library of Congress*

what they knew to be their inaccurate portrayal at home: "[The soldiers held] the conviction that optimistic publicity and euphemism had rendered their experience so falsely that it would never be readily communicable. They knew that in its representation to the laity what was happening to them was systematically sanitized and Norman Rockwellized, not to mention Disneyfied."[11] Fussell's argument carries weight, but it is worth challenging as chronocentric, as a sentiment soldiers felt in the narrow trenches or during the slow pace of burial detail.

But do ordinary soldiers remain thus disillusioned long after the war? In commercial terms, the popularity of Rockwell and Disney has never waned; the sanitized view of war was and is perhaps the most tolerable, the easiest to bear. Governments may propose and fund it, but people also seem to want it; if it is propaganda, it flows from above and below. Veterans, whatever their cynicism during conflicts, eventually yearn for the John Wayne or Benjamin West idealization. *Cartes de visite* and military portraits are the displays that most soldiers of the photographic era have chosen to send to loved ones; widows and mothers who have lost their husbands and sons likewise recall them on mantelpieces in the portrait, not the autopsy photo. More revealing, almost all war memorials that display soldiers either portray some strain of victory (the marines raising the flag at Iwo Jima) or, commonly, the standing at attention or the equestrian portrait. At most, as is the case with the Women's Vietnam War Memorial, a victim is stretched out, wounded or dead, without excess gore or forensic detail evident. These are the memorials sanctioned by the state, but in almost all cases they are also the ones most popular with the public and veterans. The warriors themselves seem not to demand realistic horrors in their honor. "The warrior asks for no reminder of these," at least in his memorials—though he may sanction horrors in popular entertainment if he sees them as reminding new generations of his own and his buddies' sacrifices.[12]

Realists, those who claim that noble death is a cover-up of the truth of warfare, should answer this question, or rather reply to this vision: Would the survivors of the 54th Regiment, their families, and we today have been better served by a more gruesome memorial, such as that of naked men stained with lye stacked like cordwood in a pit? Such a *mise-en-scène*, whether in canvas or stone, would have been detested by almost everyone connected to the events. It is allowable, filmed in murky light, for a fictional movie; it would be unthinkable as a permanent memorial. The glory of the soldiers' fall was what was important; thus the men were memorialized in robust advance rather than in the mire of death. The difference between the grisly view of death and the noble one is more complex than simply a case of censorship by manipulative elites seeking to hide the public's view of the "reality of war." Certainly, visions of noble death obscure uncomfortable truths; they may also provide youth with expectations of a glorious entry into Valhalla. But such a vision was not impressed on resisting minds, nor did such young men of, for example, the Vietnam generation lack fathers and uncles who could, if they wished, tell them "what war is really like." If the noble death, or the concentration on moments of parade and pomp to the exclusion of sickness and amputation, is an illusion, it is one supported by popular demand as well as elite imposition.

Such a caution should apply when we hear people talk about images being realistic in a historical sense. When Steven Spielberg commented that viewing Oliver Stone's film *Platoon* was "just like being in Vietnam," he was defining realism as blood, gore, cynicism, and anomie.[13] Yet there are many realities of war, some sodden and plain, some horrific and grisly, some attractive and hopeful. Only about 100,000 out of more than 8 million Vietnam-era veterans ever spent time in the jungles fighting. The battles and slogging marches of *Platoon* were not common experiences; neither was the fragging of fellow soldiers; nor shooting civilians. Moreover, we can question if Stone's renunciation of the war was commonly shared among veterans. In 1980, the Veterans Administration conducted a survey in which 66 percent of respondents who were "heavy combatants" in Vietnam declared that they would return and fight the war all over again if this time they were unhindered by political restraints.[14] *Platoon* showed some realities of some soldiers in Vietnam, those that the embittered, left-wing filmmaker chose to display. The real question is to what end any vision of war presents itself, that is, who claims what about what aspect of realism. The biggest lie of all is that any picture can show *all* the reality of a war.

## THE "JUST" HORRORS

Margaret Mead argued that "warfare exists if the conflict is organized, and socially sanctioned and the killing is not regarded as murder."[15] War thus breeds a logic of killing that would not be acceptable in civilian life. It follows that horror, like every other aspect of war's imagery, is relatively assigned and valued. Tolstoy asserted that the machine of war desensitized those who participated in it, so that "there is no crime too hideous for those who form part of the government and the army to commit."[16] Orwell similarly commented that in wartime a man could murder another, but "never sleep any the worse for it. He is serving his country, which has the power to absolve him from evil."[17] The evils perpetrated by the enemy, however, are rarely absolved; on the contrary, they are magnified in visions of war. *Canada's Golgotha*, though displayed in one of the oldest media, thus is modern in a very important sense. The crucified Canadian is unambiguously a victim for whom the audience of the image was meant to grieve or feel outrage. The perpetrators of the horror were unambiguously the enemy for whom no sanction is offered and at whom all scorn is directed.

Today, as well, an issue that always surrounds a depiction of the horrors of war is that of *blame*. Allied patriots were quick to seize upon the sculpture as evidence of German brutality. The Germans, in their turn, denied the scene because it touched upon the activities of their own troops. By 1919, German officials had learned not to make any remark which might imply boasting over what world opinion defined as war crimes. Those on the Allied side who were disgusted or disenchanted by the overreach and overripeness of atrocity propaganda cited Captain Wood's work as an example of a preposterous event. The suffering was less important than "who did it." In the modern era, thus, choosing which horrors of war to visualize is a selective and partisan judgment.

The innocent, undeserving victim is in contradiction to the ancient vision of the horror of war, at least until the late Middle Ages. Of course, not all victims were deserving; many of the images from the Trojan wars depicted in Greek and Roman art show scenes of great pathos. Such art was drawn, from the view of the fallen Trojan women and children (and even the men), quite sympathetically by the Greeks, who considered themselves descendants of those who perpetrated the horrors. One repeated incarnation was the killing of Priam, king of Troy, and Astyanax, Hector's son, by Neoptolemus, the warrior son of Achilles, in the flames of the burning city after its capture by the Achaians.[18] In most scenes, the Trojan monarch, who lost all fifty of his sons to war, awaits passively for the expiation of his misery. In the *Aeneid*, Virgil claims that when Priam realized all was lost, he donned "his long-disused armour about his aged, trembling shoulders" and rushed to join the battle. His wife, however, restrained him. The deaths of child and old man, which are often combined in vase art, are symbolic of the destruction of the tradition and future of Troy. Though the Greeks have, to this day, identified with the victors—the *Iliad*'s Achaians—the plight of the Trojans and recognition of the essentially undeserved fate of the old man and boy are unmistakable. The war's terrible outcome was, as the poets and the heroes themselves remind us, the will of the gods.

The conception that the horrors of war are just and those who suffer deserve them is ancient and found in the theology of all religions. In the Hebrew testament, the prophet Samuel said to King Saul: "Thus saith the Lord of hosts, I remember that which Amalek did to Israel, how he laid wait for him in the way, when he came up from Egypt. Now go and smite Amalek, and utterly destroy all that they have, and spare them not; but slay both man and woman, infant and suckling, ox and sheep, camel and ass." (I Samuel 15:2–3) Essentially, God is instructing His people to commit genocide. Subsequently, Samuel removes the blessing of the Lord from the king for not being destructive enough, for sparing some of the sheep and herds of the Amalekites as well as their ruler.

Saul, by keeping the best farm animals of the vanquished people to distribute as booty to his own men, acted as a responsible war commander. Until the nineteenth century, in almost all armies, an instrument at the war leader's disposal to securing loyalty and bravery from his men was to promise them loot. From the Near Eastern city of Uruk, impressions of massacred and tortured prisoners decorate cylinder seals; the seals were probably used to fasten boxes of booty taken in battle.[19] On the Triumphal Arch of the emperor Titus, Roman soldiers carry off goods from the burning ruin of Jerusalem in the year A.D. 70; most notable among their prizes is the great Menorah of the Temple. In the British colonial army of the eighteenth century, the first soldiers entering a city typically had their pick of the treasures of the Oriental palaces. As late as the mid-nineteenth century, this practice "was universally accepted as one of the perquisites of being with the vanguard."[20] This is what happened at Seringapatam when Tipu Sultan's city was captured, though the traditional accompanying plunder of the city and rape of the women was discouraged. Even today, American soldiers surveying the Iraqi vehicles destroyed on the Basra "Road of Death" at the end of the Gulf War noted that almost all were stuffed with Kuwaiti merchandise.

The "just horrors" view of war is revealed in the narrative vision left by another of the Roman emperors. Forty years after Trajan came a ruler in whose memory the Romans erected a column that largely depicted his northern campaigns. The prince was Marcus Aurelius Antoninus (r. 161–80), the last of the so-called five good emperors of Rome of the second century. The column, which still survives today, shows scenes from his interminable wars against the Marcomanni and Quadi tribes of Germany.

Marcus is best known to history as the embodiment of the Platonic ideal of the philosopher-king: just, rational, temperate, learned, strong. Gibbon described him as "severe to himself, indulgent to the imperfections of others, just and beneficent to all mankind."[21] During his campaigns, he wrote a series of *Meditations* that survive today as a manual of the Stoic ideal of life and religion. Copies of Marcus' meditations have sat on the bed table of many a poet and king. President Clinton has stated that it is his second favorite book next to the Bible. It is perhaps one of the most gentle documents ever written by a warlord. Instead of stratagems or a horseback memoir, the meditations are instructions on how to live the virtuous life, to adopt "good morals and the government of my temper"; "piety"; "abstinence, not only from evil deeds, but even from evil thoughts"; "simplicity in my way of living"; "a benevolent disposition"; and "to love truth, and to love justice."

At first glance, Marcus' column and policies are in direct contradiction to the sentiments of his writings. In brief, Marcus' reasons for fighting in Germany and his plans for conquest would, if expressed today, mark him as a resurrected Hitler. His view toward solving the perennial problem of incursions into the empire by German barbarians was simple: he wished to conquer all the German lands of Central Europe and push the border of the empire through to what is now Poland. We do not know much about the details of his campaigns, but it was probably a war without mercy, in which complete and utter annihilation of the German people was part of his strategy. One of the great hypotheticals of history is to consider the consequences if he had survived to complete the enterprise. On Trajan's column, the Dacian enemy is portrayed with respect and sympathy. On Marcus' column, by contrast, the Roman soldiers have been transformed from individuals into a uniform, regimented killing machine. The Germans are slaughtered in heaps, and grimace in horror and pain. The column seems obsessed with bloodshed, whereas Trajan's monument concentrated on procedure. The latter displays the power and the glory; the former is a tour through the abattoir.

In this panel, for example, Roman soldiers destroy a Gothic village.[22] [**Fig. 36**] The scenes are horrible to the modern eye, and the ancients would have understood them as "horrible" as well. A legionary strikes a bare-backed villager who kneels on the ground. Another prepares to stab in the back a Goth who raises his hands to heaven in supplication. At center a burly soldier grabs a terrified woman by the hair, her cloak ripped aside to reveal a breast. One of her arms is extended in a plea for mercy, while the other clasps a frightened child. We must remind ourselves that this image was placed on a column of tribute to the man who commanded the soldiers who committed these atrocities. Romans were to look at such scenes and reflect upon the greatness of the empire, the legions, and the leader. By this light, the column of Marcus Aurelius is a truthful, if state-approved, vision of war. Those who erected the column in his memory may have been extolling his honesty with himself and those he ruled.

Is the "just" victim of the horror of war only an archaic view? The tortured Quadi woman and her flaming hut on Marcus' column have many modern analogs; do we see them any differently? There is a scene from a *CBS Evening News* documentary from August 1965 in which American soldiers set fire to the thatched huts of Cam Ne, a Vietnamese village; here too grieving peasants are shuffled off. Here as well we see the rousting of "a young woman holding a baby. The baby is crying. The mother is holding a filthy bloody cloth to its

36. Roman soldiers destroy a Gothic village, column of Marcus Aurelius (c. 193). *German Archaeological Institute, Rome*

side."[23] The wartime events are the same; even the poses of soldiers and victims are similar, although the Romans used torches and the modern GIs applied Zippo lighters. The difference exists less in the event itself—peasant villages are no less combustible after 1,800 years—or in what is shown than *why* it is being shown. The Roman image commemorated the event and lauded the commander who presided over it; it was also a warning not to defy the empire. The modern film, in contradistinction, was a criticism that infuriated the generals. The Pentagon denounced the story and its implications. Their tallies of enemy dead were much greater and houses burned much lower than those in press accounts; they claimed that Cam Ne was the site of Viet Cong activity and was destroyed in a battle. The visible messenger of these visions, CBS correspondent Morley Safer, was accused of being a KGB agent. Yet a marine whom Safer interviewed admitted that he had no "doubts" about the venture: "You can't do your job and feel pity for these people."[24] A Roman soldier would have given the same answer—but it is unlikely a scribe of the time would ask the same question.

A similar scene was acted out for the theatrical movie camera in Oliver Stone's *Platoon*, and has become a staple of the modern "realist" Vietnam War film. Charlie Sheen, the narrator, is among the young men of the platoon who burn down a Vietnamese village and terrorize the inhabitants, displacing them and destroying all their meager property. Again, in visual terms, such a scene looks much like that of the Goth village or Cam Ne. It is the presentation of the image, the caption, and perhaps our modern cultural reading that differ so greatly. But even in the supposedly antiwar *Platoon*, there is a strong echo of the ancient "this is what we had to do" sentiment. The platoon of GIs wipes out the village only after provocation: the ubiquitous incitement of retaliation, the finding of one of their own men slaughtered, tortured, and mutilated. Oliver Stone, a marine veteran of Vietnam, is criticizing what the soldiers did, but his sympathy is still wholly with them.

Or compare the Goths of Marcus' column and the harshly treated Vietnamese villagers to other women and children beaten down by circumstance. These are Jews of the Warsaw Ghetto expelled from their shattered hovels after a failed revolt in the summer of 1943. [**Fig. 37**] The events are similar to those described above; more in keeping with the column of Marcus, this picture was a boast, taken by SS photographers, and printed in a handsomely bound commemorative album by the commander of the brigade that crushed the ghetto. To him, no doubt, the frightened boy signified a great victory over a timid race, in the metaphor so frequently used in Nazi propaganda, the "rats" being flushed from their holes. It is disturbing to reveal this truth: one man's icon of outrage is another man's trophy photo.

It is irresistible to assume that images have fixed meanings that can be shared by all viewers; human experience, however, demonstrates the opposite. The case of the Nazi eye of the beholder is typical, not extraordinary. The Nazi league

Strength Through Joy organized tours by coach through the ghetto of Warsaw in 1942. One participant reported:

> Every day large coaches come to the ghetto; they take soldiers through as if it was a zoo. It is the thing to do to provoke the wild animals. Often soldiers strike out at passers-by with long whips as they drive through. They go to the cemetery where they take pictures. They compel the families of the dead and the rabbis to interrupt the funeral and pose in front of their lenses. They set up genre pictures (old Jew above the corpse of a young girl).[25]

Fritz Jacob, a German police captain who assisted in the mass killings of Jews at the eastern front, wrote to one of his friends of the "frightful Jewish types in Poland. I thank my lucky stars that I've now seen this mixed race for what it is. Then if life is kind to me I'll have something to pass on to my children. . . .

37. Boy and other civilians with hands raised at gunpoint in Warsaw Ghetto, 1943.
*Yivo Institute for Jewish Research*

These were not human beings, but ape people."[26] Commenting on similar visions, Nazi philosopher Alfred Rosenberg concluded: "The sights are so appalling and probably so well-known to the editorial staffs [of Nazi documentary filmmakers] that a description is presumably superfluous. If there are any people left who still somehow have sympathy with the Jews then they ought to be recommended to have a look at such a ghetto. Seeing this race en masse, which is decaying, decomposing, and rotten to the core will banish any sentimental humanitarianism."[27] For Rosenberg and his brethren, the images showed something very different than they would to other audiences.

Indeed, scenes similar to those witnessed by the tourists of destruction described above were in fact used widely by the Nazis, such as in *The Eternal Jew*, a documentary on the "Jewish problem." The filmmakers overlaid scenes of the shtetl and urban ghettos with carefully malevolent narration, concentrating on the supposed evil of the Jews being depicted. In one scene, we see extremely poor Jews in eastern Poland living in conditions of utter misery and poverty. The Nazi soundtrack instructs us that this is an example of Jews in their natural state before feigning civilization for the European eye.

> The home life of the Jews shows his inability to become civilized. Jewish homes are dirty and in complete disorder. . . . A surprising parallel to the Jewish migrations is offered by the migrations of an equally restless animal, the rats. . . . [W]herever rats appear, they carry death, spread leprosy, plague, typhus, cholera. They are cunning, cowardly and cruel and always appear in large numbers. They represent, among animals, the same element of treachery and destruction as the Jews do among humans.

Yet film scholar Amos Vogel notes perceptively, "It would be possible to take large sections of this film and provide them with a sympathetic commentary, stressing the Jews' plight in Eastern Europe."[28] So those same qualities (misery, destitution, squalor) which one viewer might see as cause for sympathy assigned for the Nazi viewer reasons for justified doom. The little boy of the ghetto and the Quadi mother were not visualized or viewed so differently.

The key distinction here is that the Nazi regime, or indeed any twentieth-century totalitarian government, did not officially approve of war crimes. Nazi propaganda portrayed the Allied bombing campaign as butchery of a high order, and the Soviets as mass murderers. During the attack on Russia, German troops overran those parts of Poland that had formerly been occupied by the Soviet Union. In the Katyn Forest, they claimed to have uncovered more than 10,000 moldering corpses of Polish officers. Most showed signs of execution. The Nazis proclaimed this a great war crime and tried to draw attention to the scene and lay blame on Stalin's regime. These charges were denied by the Soviets, and of course by the Western powers who were then allied with them. A year earlier the same American and British governments would have believed any war crime allegation against Stalin, who was seen as an evil threat equivalent (and at that time allied) to Hitler. In recent investigations, the German charges were largely confirmed: the Soviets were the perpetrators of the massacre. That the Germans regularly committed similar crimes against Russians, Poles, Jews, and others on a huge scale was irrelevant to their propaganda and, of course, unmentioned. If they had won World War II, we can be sure that American and British generals would be on trial for war crimes in, for example, the bombing campaigns against German and Japanese cities. Victorious armies also capture the moral high grounds.

A more recent confirmation of the relativity of how we judge the vision of war's horrors occurred during the Persian Gulf conflict. At 4:45 A.M. on February 13, 1991, two GBU27 electronically guided bombs were dropped on the Baghdad suburb of Al-Amariya by F-117 (Stealth) fighters from a U.S. tactical group. The bombs penetrated the steel-reinforced roof of a concrete building. CNN's Peter Arnett was the first to air the story, but without any images, simply reporting that "this is the worst of the civilian incidents we have seen in Baghdad so far." In reply to a question from a CNN anchor, Arnett also commented, "From what we could see, there was no immediate military target within miles of this place." In Arnett's autobiography, he recalls being amazed and emotionally disturbed by the story, but being warned by editors at the Atlanta studio to "cool down" before filing the first report.[29] Almost immediately, American and international networks scrambled to get visuals. These included burned survivors in the nearby Yarmak hospital and many images of charred bodies, unmistakably women and children, being pulled out of what was now identified as the Al-Firdus air-raid shelter.

The Iraqi government, and later many independent sources, maintained that the facility was a neighborhood bomb shelter, and as many as 2,000 women and children had been killed.[30] Margaret Tutweiler, then President Bush's press secretary, stated later, "The visual was horrendous. . . . A response couldn't wait three days."[31] Accordingly, the American administration and military mobilized for a coordinated diplomatic and press media campaign of denial and counter-allegation. The facility was, the U.S. government asserted, "a command-and-control center that fed instructions directly to the Iraqi war machine, painted and camouflaged to avoid detection and well documented as a military target." Indeed, more than a denial, the administration's line was a complete punting of culpability onto the Iraqi regime. White House press spokesman Marlin Fitz-water claimed that the presence of civilians indicated not that the building was a shelter, but that Saddam was using them as "human shields"—as he had done previously—for a military target.[32] The operations director for the Joint Chiefs of Staff concurred that he suspected a "cold-blooded decision on the part of Saddam Hussein to put civilians in facilities." The Kuwaiti ambassador and

American military officials gave interviews denying that the building was a shelter and reiterating Saddam Hussein's litany of previous crimes.

Interestingly, the counter-framing story, though it proved eventually to be false, resonated with public sentiment. Support for the war did not decrease as a result of this "horrendous" incident; public opinion did not waver because of burned babies. By rapid deployment of credible spokespeople and a plausible counterstory, the Bush administration demonstrated that even a flood of instant images of horror can be "managed." The spin placed on Al-Firdus by the Pentagon, however incorrect it proved to be, was generally accepted by the public, and even where it was not had little effect on opinion. The already demonized enemy was reduced to inhuman status; this meant that they could be killed without recrimination.

This is the coda of the vision of the horrors of war. How similar is the fate of the despoiled natives of Elam, the castrated enemies of the Zapotecs, the screaming Quadi woman, the starving Jews of Warsaw, and the charred babies of Al-Firdus? How different are the visions produced to classify them? If anything, the modern imagery of war is less revealing than the ancient. The Assyrians hid nothing from themselves or their enemies; we employ modern technology to occlude the very visions of war on which we congratulate ourselves as reflecting advanced technology. All this involves choices made by societies, but also by individuals who must be held responsible for their words and actions. As Daniel Goldhagen has described in his survey on ordinary Germans and the Holocaust, "The evidence that no German was ever killed or incarcerated for having refused to kill Jews is conclusive.... Germans could say 'no' to mass murder. They chose to say 'yes.' "[33] The record of such acceptance of killing "enemies of our blood," from cultures and locales as varied as Crow Creek and Babi Yar and El Mozote, from prehistory to yesterday's headlines, is so extensive that it calls into question the meaning of the word "humane" and the essence of humanity.

We can only conclude that there are potential horrors of war inside every human psyche. To claim that atrocities belong to only a certain type of person, government, army, or era, and that virtue and mercy are only within the province of ourselves, is to misunderstand completely the dualities of the human animal. All peoples perpetrate horrors of war; whatever their rationalizations, their victims are equally dead. Some horrors of war demand justice; others seem justified. The quality of justness is always filtered through and determined by our prejudices, and the quality of mercy is always strained.

Certainly, rhetoric has changed. Twenty-three hundred years ago, a Spartan mother might enjoin her warrior son to "come back with your shield or on it." Today, no middle-class parent of the Western world would be so bellicose. Still, no modern mother admonishes a son (or now daughter) going off to war to "make sure and obey the Geneva Conventions": we want our children to survive by any means necessary. Spectacularly evil actions are taken in the name of those means, and all societies to some extent sanction them. As Aleksandr Solzhenitsyn writes in *The Gulag Archipelago*, "If only it were all so simple! If only there were evil people somewhere insidiously committing evil deeds, and it were necessary only to separate them from the rest of us and destroy them. But the line dividing good and evil cuts through the heart of every human being. And who is willing to destroy a piece of his own heart?"[34] The horrors of war are visualized and appreciated through this broken prism; the horrors we see or do not see are determined by our flags and our sympathies.

# 7

## LIVING-ROOM WARS

*REAL-TIME WAR*

Of the Mathew Brady Company's pictures of dead soldiers on the Antietam farmlands, the *New York Times* wrote: "The dead of the battlefield come up to us very rarely, even in dreams. . . . Mr. Brady has done something to bring home to us the terrible reality and earnestness of war. If he has not brought bodies and laid them in door-yards and along streets, he has done something very like it." Yet wars have always been fought in the very rooms in which people have lived. If you want to know what civilization looks like, Seneca said, then gaze upon a sacked city. When the Romans sacked Carthage in 146 B.C.E., they left no stone upon another and salted the earth so that nothing would ever grow again. In the Thirty Years' War, when the forces of the Catholic emperor besieged and ravaged the city of Magdeburg (1631), only a fifth of the inhabitants survived. In World War II, bombing and street fighting left many of the cities of Europe and Asia, such as Stalingrad, Berlin, Rotterdam, Manila, and Shanghai, as moonscapes. In recent years, napalm might fall into the garden of a Vietnamese villager, a mortar shell shatter a Sarajevo street market, or a cruise missile sail past the balcony of a family in Baghdad.

The term "living-room war," however, implies not physical proximity—battle that can be smelled and felt a few inches away—but the para-proximity enabled by modern communications technology, especially the satellite.[1] Such a viewing experience was predicted in 1882 by the French artist Albert Robida, who, influenced by developments in photography, foresaw families sitting at home and watching wars unfold on a paneled screen while a synchronous phonograph played an accompanying soundtrack. [**Fig. 38**] Today, in this fashion we witness a living-room war on a television set from a couch or easy chair. The images that represent the war are beamed directly from the battlefield. Conflicts appear "live," bombs as they explode; it happens in real time. Despite the mediation of the camera and the screen, it is also a war that is tellingly realistic, seemingly unfiltered, that is, "up close and personal" in TV parlance. Most important, living-room wars are said to influence the decision making of government leaders and the opinions of the public about waging war and negotiating peace. The power of the living-room war originates in the fact that for most audiences, especially in the West where increasingly large populations have never served in the military, the mediated visions of war are the only ones ever experienced. Just as new generations learned about World War II not from grandparents who were there but from movies that interpreted the war experience, we gain knowledge about contemporary wars through television.

If these conditions and contexts are true, then the vision of war has entered a revolutionary age. Certainly, the contrast to more traditional ways of receiving news from the front, when the war was of some distance from the home audience, is sharp. In 490 B.C.E., Phidippides, a young Athenian warrior, entered the council chamber of his native city and proclaimed, "Chairete, nikômen" ("Rejoice, we are victorious").[2] He had run from the Bay of Marathon—140 miles in 36 hours—to announce the defeat of a Persian invasion force; the climactic event of the Summer Olympic Games celebrates this legend. His message delivered, Phidippides died of exhaustion. Although the distance and the runner's fate became famous, the occurrence was commonplace; messengers in classical Greece routinely proclaimed victory or announced defeat to the general in the

38. Audience watches moving picture of battle on screen.
Albert Robida, 1882

field or the elders of the state. Whether Phidippides, while panting through the city, notified merchants, slaves, and farmers of the victory, we are not told. Rumors of disaster and triumph in war could spread quickly through unofficial channels in the ancient world, especially by trading ships. Yet officially announcing news to the populace or the army was considered a formal, important ritual of state. News from the battle line traveled only as fast as boat, horse, runner, or perhaps pigeon.

More important, in heralding victory, Phidippides uttered two words; he did not draw a picture, nor bring one with him. In all the ancient accounts of messengers delivering news of battles and espionage on enemies, there is no mention of the use of pictures. The reason for this bias was simple. The ancients lacked the technology to reproduce images exactly, a method to imprint them quickly, and a medium to transmit them over distances. In a society without printing, every document is, in a sense, an original. Hand-copying is too imprecise; variations in style and penmanship can, for instance, disastrously alter a map.[3] As a result, the art of war was always created after the fact. In a Roman Triumph, large paintings of the general's victories would be carried in the parade so that crowds could view events of the battles. Historians might use pictures as well, as sources but not illustrations: the Roman emperor Lucius Verus advised the scholar Fronto that in writing a history of the former's campaigns, the latter should consult military paintings. It is unsurprising, then, that no military work of the classic era remains to us with any graphic or pictorial accompaniment. Pictures of war were only memorials, propaganda, entertainment, or decoration: they were not news.

For most ancient and medieval cultures, coins were the only medium through which martial themes, concepts, and scenes could be hand-distributed to the masses. When Julius Caesar defeated his enemies in the civil war, one of his first acts was to have loyal officers and his personal slaves take control of the mint at Rome.[4] They began an innovation in Roman politics and art. Only dead heroes and gods had heretofore appeared on coins, although it was customary in Eastern monarchies to imprint the likeness of living rulers. Each coin minted featured Caesar's head in profile on the obverse, with the reverse devoted to different images of Venus Genetrix, the goddess from whom the Julian family claimed descent. Caesar ultimately was marked for death because, among other incitements, he was the first Roman leader to engage in mass (as opposed to *massive*) visual propaganda. The Republican conspirators saw the coin as yet another confirmation of an impending Oriental-style kingship.[5] Here was a living man not only proclaiming his divine origin but also announcing plainly that he "*was Rome.*"[6] Despite Caesar's assassination, however, the practice of disseminating the ruler's visage on coinage endured for the entire history of the empire.[7]

The revolution of printing in the fifteenth century allowed pictures and text to be reproduced on a mass scale. The religious wars of the fifteenth and sixteenth centuries employed illustrated tracts of propaganda and training manuals of war, but delivery systems were hardly different from the commentaries of the past. There was no method of transmitting visions of war approaching what we today call "real time," especially from distant battlefields. Even the invention of photography did not herald an age of instantly viewed combat. So slow and cumbersome were the initial production and printing processes that most newspapers and magazines still displayed images printed from woodcuts and engravings. The Victorian magazines, for example, sent illustrators to cover all of the British Empire's "little wars" in its colonies. In the American Civil War, photographers' plates were rushed back to eastern newspapers and then converted to engravings. It was not until the first decade of the twentieth century that photographic images began appearing in news publications, and not until the late 1920s that photos could be sent "over the wire." The first live television broadcast was transmitted by Nazi Germany in 1936 to inaugurate the Berlin Olympic Games. The technology was too crude, however, to allow any part of World War II to be televised, and no homes were wired to receive it.

It was only in the late 1980s that pictures of war could be transmitted instantly to our living rooms. This process evolved over the last three decades with the growing dominance of videotape, the use of computers, and above all the launching of communications satellites. During the Vietnam War, news film took about twenty-four hours to be processed from the battle front to the TV screen.[8] By the 1973 Arab-Israeli War, improved satellite technology had reduced transit time to several hours.[9] In contrast, during the Persian Gulf War, visual news could be seen by viewers of CNN "live from ground zero."[10] As the size of camera and satellite dishes diminishes, it is increasingly possible for a single reporter (or soldier) with a laptop, a modem, and a digital camera to show a live episode of war to a home-front audience from any location under any conditions. The distance covered and exertions made by Phidippides have been compressed to almost nothing.

What arrives in real time are pictures, the dominant coin of journalism, and accordingly our main source of images of current wars. No modern political leader or citizen would be satisfied with a few words from a herald. News demands vivid, kinetic, "shoot-'em-up" visuals to draw audiences. As Edward Girardet suggests, "journalists, particularly television cameramen, are under pressure to bring back spectacular images to satisfy network appetites."[11] And NBC's Jim Lederman states, "Television news is enslaved to images. If an idea cannot be recorded in the form of an image, it will rarely, if ever, be given extensive time on a nightly network newscast."[12] The Los Angeles Times's David Shaw concurs: "Clear, dramatic pictures are the key to both 'good television' and to the impact a given story will have on viewers."[13] More than ever, the news that really matters is what is visually prominent. Accordingly, the media demand to be at the front—as with the invasions of the Falklands, Grenada,

Panama, and the Gulf War—and cry censorship if their cameras are denied full access to live war.

For self-evident reasons, war is the one subject that best fits the demands of the modern televisual marketplace. It readily provides kinetic visuals, dynamic action, the "bang-bang" and body count sought by visual journalists. War, through modern technology, is also more easily covered than ever before. A journalist can hitch a jeep ride to the battle front, get footage of a firefight, and transmit it live to a satellite dish the same minute. The prestige system of journalists—the ways in which they honor each other—also contributes to war being a favorite subject for the camera. Human violence is the topic that has been awarded the most Pulitzer Prizes for photography or videography. Most famous photojournalists have made their names covering combat. War also allows their relative self-perception of power and status to increase commensurately. For example, Peter Arnett's craggy face became an icon for broadcasting live from Baghdad during the Gulf War. Stories about dam construction, cultural festivals, or poetry competitions in foreign lands obviously do not lend themselves to procuring instant stardom for the journalist in the same way. Simply put, wars are made for TV.

But not all wars. Some conflicts are easier to cover than others. The many wars of Israel in its fifty-year history are an example of ideal conditions for photojournalism: a tiny country, with modern communication facilities, fighting on fronts about an hour's jeep ride from major hotels. Violence of some kind is almost always available, if not in war then in internal strife. Israel, while censoring to some extent the broadcasts of foreign journalists during wartime, still allows greater freedom than its enemies, a fact that many in the Jewish state bemoan. Small wonder that Israel has more foreign correspondents per capita than any other nation on the planet. Israel's enemies, on the other hand, simply ban foreign news coverage—unless the images favor them.

The result is a skewed vision of the scale and prevalence of warfare in the world. In 1982, a Muslim fundamentalist uprising in Syria was crushed by the government of Hafez al-Assad. The army reduced the nation's second largest city, Hama, to rubble, killing upward of 20,000–30,000 people. Only a few photographs of the events leaked into the news stream. In contrast, Israel's invasion of southern Lebanon a few years earlier was covered in lavish detail by thousands of foreign journalists.

This new pictorial order was first highlighted in the crucible of the Vietnam War. William Westmoreland, who commanded American forces in Vietnam from 1965 to 1968, noted in his memoirs: "With television for the first time bringing war into living rooms and with no press censorship, the relationship of the military command in South Vietnam and the news media was of unusual importance."[14] Marshall McLuhan maintained, "The war in Vietnam was lost in the living rooms of the nation." This belief became a commonplace in the

American military and affects its media and public relations policies to this day. In a survey of American officers who had served in Vietnam, more than 90 percent reported that they felt "negative" toward television news; the level of their hostility was matched toward only one other group: the North Vietnamese army.[15] Lieutenant General Lewis W. Walt of the U.S. Marine Corps stated:

> The camera, the typewriter, the tape recorder are very effective weapons in this war—weapons too often directed not against the enemy but against the American people. These weapons have a far greater potential for defeating us than the rockets or artillery used against our men in Vietnam. In a free society, in which the right of dissent is a sacred principle, an enemy has boundless opportunity to manipulate our emotions.[16]

Such attitudes and premises were absorbed by the Vietnam generation of junior officers, like Colin Powell and Norman Schwarzkopf, who made up the senior command in the Persian Gulf War. The military could no longer ignore or completely censor the press, yet they would wage war under the assumption that the battle to control the content and captioning of TV pictures was as decisive as campaigns in the air, sea, and sand.

The opening act of the American intervention in Somalia demonstrated the convergence (or collision) of real-time news, the race to get the best images, and the conducting of military operations. When navy SEALs and marines—in advance of main units—landed on the shores outside Mogadishu, over seventy-five reporters greeted them. It seemed a bizarre modern incarnation of the military dictum that victory goes to those who "get there first with the most." Laden in heavy gear, the troops deployed as they had been trained, in combat poses, ready for resistance and action. Their only danger, however, was tripping over cables or being blinded by klieg lights or camera strobes.[17] "Fellini-esque" was the description ABC's Ted Koppel gave to the scene, while Tom Brokaw likened the encounter to a "Dr. Strangelove movie."[18] The incident generated criticism from both the public and the political and military leadership. Defense Secretary Richard Cheney complained: "It was aggravating for our people to come in over the beach to find an army" of media.[19] CNN received hundreds of calls accusing the network of putting American lives in danger.

Yet the Pentagon had invited the media to cover the landing. As Michael Gordon of the *New York Times* pointed out: "All week the Pentagon had encouraged press coverage of the Marine landing. Reporters were told when the landing would take place, and some network correspondents were quietly advised where the marines would arrive so that they could set up their cameras. . . . But having finally secured an elusive spotlight, the marines discovered that they had too much of a good thing."[20] Nor were the media's moves a secret. The day before the landing, *USA Today* announced scheduled live coverage on its front page.[21] CNN's news director Ed Turner, interviewed after the debacle, recalled: "I was astonished to learn that 24 hours before the troops arrived, the State Department and the Pentagon were, in effect, saying 'Everybody come on down—here's the time, here's the location, we'd love to have the attention. Come visit us.' "[22] This incident illustrates that the rapid deployment of modern media surprises everyone, including those planning to exploit it; not only can we now see war as it happens, but the medium that provides our view can ambush the warriors themselves.

## WAR IN EVERYDAY LIFE

The art historian Ernst Hans Gombrich declared the late twentieth century to be "a visual age."[23] The average American watches up to six hours a day of television, but reads only one book a year. An American child will watch TV for about 27 hours a week—about 1,400 hours a year—but will sit in a classroom for only 900 hours a year. As of 1996, two-thirds of the world's households— 840 million—had television, more than have telephones, access to a physician, running water, or flush toilets.[24] From the screens in our living rooms, whether by cable, satellite, video player, or broadcast signal (and now even by modem), we can potentially receive millions of images a day of news and entertainment, fact and fantasy, advertising and features. Our roadside vistas are crowded with billboards using images to hawk products. We read newspapers and magazines crammed with vivid, kinetic pictures. We devote space in our homes to displays of living and departed loved ones, and scenes from vacations and weddings. Any ancient man, transported into our homes or downtowns, would be amazed by the movement, number, and especially the seeming fidelity to nature of the pictorial cornucopia.

It would be presumptuous, however, to carry the assumption of iconic ubiquity too far; other peoples, from Zapotec chiefs to Victorian householders, have lived with images playing conspicuous and relevant roles in their daily life. What is more remarkable in the modern West is the exclusion of visions of war in the minutiae of every day. The ancient Greeks and the Moche peoples of Peru, for example, ate and drank accompanied by images of war on pottery. The Greek drinking party, the *symposium*, was conducted while slaves or retainers passed out amphorae and cups of wine decorated with hoplites, episodes from the *Iliad*, and battles between the centaurs and heroes. No wedding china plates today or since the Middle Ages would detail such scenes. On other utensils that are still employed, like kitchen knives, or objects which we no longer use such as cylinder seals, warfare is also banished. In home furnishing, the carving or painting of war is largely undisplayed and unmade today. If they do exist, it is in a placid and (to our eyes) acceptable form: for example, a portrait of a loved one, living or dead, in uniform. Simply put, modern Americans, in contrast to the classical

Greeks, Romans, and many other archaic peoples, are more likely to have homes filled with dish patterns of flowers, statues of unicorns, and paintings of dogs playing poker than warriors in combat.

The visions of war in outdoor life, commerce, and government are also wholly impoverished. We have almost no analogous monumental art to weigh against the columns of the emperors of Rome, sculptured stairways of the Zapotecs, or the reliefs on Assyrian walls. We do not domicile the monstrous. We generally wish to avoid gazing upon the evidence of our own monstrousness, whereas previous civilizations, such as those of Monte Albán, saw the so-called horrors of war as a necessary political exposition, for themselves and others, and perhaps an aesthetically pleasing one as well. Our modern buildings contain little evidence of warfare except verbal allusions; none of the major monuments in Washington shows a scene of combat. In European cities, the vista is less pacific, but battle scenes tend to be relics of other ages. To see large-scale images of war, people must travel to museums or designated sites. Most revealing, coins are no longer a tool for celebrating war, or even warriors.

Buildings today are not owned by ruling nobles of the military caste, but rather by lords of business: banks, lawyers' offices, insurance agencies, and the like provide many walls on which to display art. In some cities, such as Philadelphia, builders must allocate at least 1 percent of their budget to public artwork. These creations are universally unwarlike. A huge mosaic of *Schwarzkopf's Triumphal Entry into Liberated Kuwait* in a Bank of America building would be unthinkable. Likewise, we will never walk past a Delta Airlines ticketing office and gaze upon a statue group of *Marines with Flamethrowers Routing Japanese from Their Dugouts at Saipan*. In plain sight, the remnants of war include the occasional POW or NAVY VETERAN tags that appear on automobile license plates. Only on certain days are people in military uniform even present on our streets—and then the occasions are wholly ceremonial, with no indication or expectation that the procession is marching to war.

One exception is historical reenactments, although these too are specialized events in out-of-the-way locations. In England, men restage their civil war as Roundheads and Cavaliers. In America, the refighting of the Civil War has become a significant social phenomenon. A July 1998 reenactment of the Battle of Gettysburg drew 20,000 men in Union and Confederate uniforms who bivouacked, marched, and restaged various moments of the battle, from the assaults on Little Round Top to the death charge of Pickett's division. [**Fig. 39**] The event provided many ironies: for example, would-be soldiers, whose uniforms were authentic in every detail, tossed down Pepsi and take-out pizza before marching to battle to the tune of fife and drum. Other incidents contributed to the reenactment's lack of faithfulness to the original conflict. During Pickett's charge, most "Confederates" declined to fall until they reached the edge of the Union lines; it was too hot to lie on the unsheltered ground for hours while the battle resolved itself. One participant was actually shot in the neck and had to wait almost an hour for an ambulance to carry him: his hour-long cries for assistance were assumed to be remarkably realistic acting. And above all, there were the crowds who sat or stood or lay watching the battles. Such spectatorship was not unknown in the early days of the real war, but by July 1863, civilians knew enough to stay away from battlefields.[25]

In terms of public militarism and monumentalism, the vestiges of the celebration of the warrior culture are most practiced in totalitarian regimes. Iraq is notable in this regard. Its major cities are adorned with posters showing events and idealizations of battles of the Iran and Gulf Wars. Marching soldiers are a daily sight. The largest public sculpture in the country—aside from the ruins of the Assyrian cities—is the so-called Victory Arch, which borders a processional walkway and pavilion in downtown Baghdad. Commissioned during the long deadlock of the war with Iran, it was erected in 1989 to celebrate "victory."[26] According to the official account, Saddam Hussein first sketched this landmark. Some 40 meters high, it consists of two 16-meter arms—modeled, it is said, from exact measurements of those of Saddam himself and enlarged by forty times—

39. Man videotapes a line of soldiers at Gettysburg battle reenactment, July 1998.
*Photo: Eric Mencher*

erupting from the ground, ending in bunched fists which brandish great swords. Supposedly cast from melted-down captured Iranian guns, helmets, and bayonets, the 24-ton blades curve toward each other, almost completing an arc. At the base of each arm are nets that hold 2,500 helmets taken from dead Iranian soldiers. The journalist Michael Kelly describes the helmets cascading out from the nets, cemented in place, "so that it is impossible to enter the pavilion without driving or walking over the helmets of the dead."[27] Naturally, the monument is the subject of humor among dissident Iraqis. One notes that it is structurally ill-positioned so that the warrior bearing the swords would have to be "squatting to get his arms in that position."[28] It is, however, an unmistakable thumping of the basis for the regime's power; such a bellicose memorial would not be constructed today for any Western leader, whatever his personal experience in war.

In the West, the war memorial as visual symbol has undergone two major shifts of display in the last hundred years. The first, fitting with the democratizing tradition, especially in Western Europe and North America, is that memorials, which used to be largely giant stone flatteries of mighty war leaders, are increasingly abstract, representational, or inscriptional praise to the ordinary soldier, regardless of rank or achievement, save mortality. For example, in five years after World War I, 36,000 war memorials were erected, appearing in almost every municipality of France. The second trend is that the modern war memorial is decidedly pacific. It almost never depicts battle itself.[29]

It is revealing to contrast the Baghdad Victory Arch to America's most famous war monument, the Vietnam Veterans Memorial in Washington, D.C. The project was undertaken with money publicly raised for a monument to be constructed on two acres on the Mall. A competition was held to determine the eventual design. Among the rules of the contest were that "the memorial will make no political statement regarding the war or its conduct. It will transcend those issues. The hope is that the creation of the memorial will begin a healing process, a reconciliation of the grievous divisions wrought by the war."[30] The winner of the competition was a Yale architecture student of Chinese American descent, Maya Ying Lin, who proposed a V-shaped wall, one side pointing to the Lincoln Memorial, the other to the Washington Monument. The latter stood for the American Revolution, the former for America's reunification.

The design was immediately controversial, partly because of its layout. It was not to be above the viewer—something to look up at—but at eye level. Its black marble was a departure from the white stone typical of war monuments. It also had no statue and no flag to focus the eye or stir the heart. Some veterans and conservatives thought it insulting; one called it a "black gash of shame." Ronald Reagan's secretary of the interior, James Watt, blocked the memorial's construction permit. Work began only after a flag and a statue group were added to the plans. Of the figures, a white soldier is flanked by a black GI and another soldier of indeterminate race—who, quixotically, carries a bandolier of bullets that point the wrong way, into his chest—symbolizing the racial mixture of the war. The GIs wear combat vests, baggy field gear, and uniforms, hold weapons, and look warily around, whether before or after a battle we cannot tell. Though depicted as in-country combatants, they plainly are not in combat. Again, there is no indication that veterans of the war wanted a grimly realistic monument—no patriot demanded, for example, that the statue group feature an American soldier screaming, his legs blown off by a mine.

The wall was dedicated on Veterans Day, November 11, 1984, "the first national war monument introduced to the public through television."[31] In time, the controversy over the structure faded. Protesters and proud veterans all have found the memorial a place for mourning, solace, reconciliation, or vindication. Visitors find names of comrades or loved ones, create drawings and etchings, tell stories to family members, or simply gaze silently. Within a few years of its creation the Vietnam Veterans Memorial attracted up to 15,000 visitors a day.[32] Perhaps one of its key components—only made possible by the polished black marble—is that the monument is itself a visual medium. Onlookers can view themselves in reflection, with flags and the edifices of Washington as background, and with the incised names of the honored dead superimposed across the picture.

But contemporary celebrity is no measure of enduring popularity. People do not forget wars they have lived through, only relegate and classify the memory in some way. Past wars, on the other hand, are forgotten; or rather, generations grow up with only high school history class mentions of them. The loss of personal connection is what dooms the war memorial to eventual obscurity.[33] Now, we are still living in the age of Vietnam; what will happen when the veterans grow too old to visit, the descendants have forgotten, and the nation moves past into other wars? Precedent shows the fleeting nature of public awareness, respect, and visiting of war memorials. All wars fade away and the passage of time is often symbolized by how peripheral the aging monuments become to daily life. As Rose Coombs documents in her study of World War I memorials, they slip from view, merge with the terrain, and we forget the links to the past—memorial markers are encroached upon by suburbs and farms.[34] The heroes and battles that were once headlines, then proverbial, are now erased; graves lie untended; tombs crumble; what was declared sacred earth has become beet fields; holy stones are reused for pavement. And only rarely, as the veterans have passed on, is there any controversy in these desecrations. "Memorials abide but a brief time," wrote the Roman historian Diodorus Siculus, "being continually destroyed by many vicissitudes."[35]

When one considers the tons of flowers, the rivers of eulogies in print, and the acres of canvas and screen dedicated to memorializing the dead, and of course the investment in the physical sites of the memorials themselves, the ephemeral nature of the monument to the warrior is especially bittersweet. This sense of loss is expressed visually in Akira Kurosawa's *Seven Samurai* (1954). The film is a statement on the universal fate of the warrior in the memory of countrymen. Seven wandering samurai defend a peasant village against a pack of bandits, and four of the heroes are killed in battle. In the final scene we glimpse their monument, four gleaming longswords plunged into a large grave mound, centered by the war banner of the seven samurai. It is a simple but stirring memorial to the fallen defenders of the village. But this, too, will fade. The villagers are in the fields, planting rice, singing songs, ignoring the living and the dead samurai. The wind blows dirt from the mound. Otomi, the veteran chief samurai, shakes his head at the sight, proclaiming: "We have lost the battle." And though we do not want to admit it, this may be one judgment for the fate of all warriors, no matter how spectacular their memorial. All things that stand will crumble to dust, and people will forget as the generations pass.

But ignored or not, war memorials encompass another act of symbolism that influences their place and boosts their immediate (if not long-term) popularity among the living: they homogenize the imagination about the war dead. Complex, personal events are visualized as uniform for public consumption. Inscribed with epitaphs—"to the fallen heroes," "to those who gave their lives," "to the brave," "to the honored dead," "to the unknown soldier who stands for all who fought"—the tens of thousands or millions who served in any war are cemented into one face, which in almost all cases is heroic or at least cleansed of war's grisly miseries. We have seen, and veterans know, that this is a misrepresentation. In war, pointed out Thucydides, a brave man will die, but so might a coward.[36] In every army, in every battle, there are heroes and cowards and men who were neither; there were those who were eating beans and were hit by artillery fire; others who tripped over a mine running away; those who froze to death loyally guarding a position; and those who died from fever in training camp. In the war memorials, they are all one. Bullets, viruses, and jeep accidents kill the brave, the cowardly, the indolent, and the unsuspecting indiscriminately; war memorials likewise make no distinction.

But signs of warfare are absent from other parts of daily modern life that would seem odd to the ancients. Our public leaders—Saddam, again, is a throwback—rarely exhibit martial tendencies in their dress. Today, a ruler will fly to a foreign station to visit the "troops," but his military visage is touristlike; he may sport, for example, a ball cap adorned with the name of the unit and a leather flight jacket. Though America has had presidents who were military men, none wore their uniforms in office, or carried a sword and pistol. In previous eras, rulers, even those who had little fighting ability or spirit (like Darius II of Persia), often donned the weapons and costumes of war in public. Roman emperors would wear breastplates or cuirasses with scenes of battles and military ceremonies carved on the facings.

To find a picture of war, we must seek it out in printed or transmitted media in a theater or library or on TV. Why this shedding and reallocating of the warrior heritage and existence? The archaeologist of 2,000 years from now, having no written or visual records of our culture—all our films rotted, videotapes demagnetized, CD-ROMs decomposed, acidic paper crumbled to dust— would conclude we were a people steeped in the arts of peace.

First we must admit that pretense contradicts fact. Our century is bloodier than any before. The United States has fought more wars in the twentieth century than were fought in the nineteenth, though we often describe them as "peacekeeping missions," "police actions," or "humanitarian interventions." We possess a military apparatus much greater in destructive power than any state in the history of the world. Within this decade, we fought a war in the shadows of Nineveh and Babylon and killed at least 100,000 of the enemy; in the 1960s and 1970s, at least 3 million natives died in the Indochina war, a sizable portion as a result of our actions; in the 1940s, we fought a war in which we killed more than 1 million enemy civilians by dropping atomic and conventional bombs on their cities. Also, of course, one-third of our national budget is devoted to "defense," and our leaders regularly reassure us that we are "the world's only remaining superpower."

The wars listed above were, we claimed, imposed by the enemy, and we acted in good faith to reduce casualties. This may be so, but we must keep in mind when observing ourselves as well as people of other cultures and eras that visions of war, or the lack of them, may reflect a society's self-image, not its practices. Again, psychologically this is a token of our wanting to assure ourselves that warfare is an incidental and unimportant function of the state; commensurably, the state is not supported or elevated by its occurrence. We like to project ourselves as a civilian federation, dedicated to commerce, the arts, humanitarian concerns—but not warfare.

## COMMUNAL VIEWING

The satellite and television (and now the Internet) allow us to watch wars and other events as they occur, in physically distant lands. No one, not even a political leader, is necessarily closer to the action than anyone else, except of course the soldiers and the cameramen. It follows that the exclusiveness of viewing war has largely been eroded. In previous eras, images of war in private art— floor mosaics, paintings, even some sculpture—were the property of the elite. This was largely true for the arts of most nations. The Aztec codices, for example, which colorfully displayed the history of the nation, "were created at the behest of elites for purely elite consumption."[37] The "great masterworks" of traditional

Chinese painting and calligraphy were inaccessible to those without connections, "for there were no museums of public collections," and it was not until the eighteenth century that pictures of paintings began to appear in popular books.[38] Most of the paintings now resident in the museums of Europe and the Americas, like *The Death of General Wolfe*, were owned exclusively by the nobility; peasants and urban laborers did not tromp through the galleries of the estates that displayed the canvases. The bas-reliefs of Nineveh were located in the royal palace, where only the ruling caste (and their guards and servants) and foreign dignitaries would tread. So when art historians speak of, for example, Chinese art of the dynastic period, it is likely that only a small percent of Chinese people have ever seen it before the modern era. At the same time, some of the art of war was public: the Zapotec steps, the great columns of Trajan and Marcus, the *Bayeux Tapestry*, and so on. The photographic era has radically democratized access to the art of war and the satellite news age has further erased the distinction between the elite and the ordinary viewer.

This is not to say that the politically powerful are not privileged with images of war unavailable to news organizations, such as photographs from spy satellites. The radical change is that the elite now prefer to consume the same images that ordinary folk witness. Politicians, like many of us, watch television (and read newspapers and magazines) to monitor the world environment. As communications researcher Jarol Manheim has noted, "in foreign affairs, even public officials can have a hard time gathering information, so even they may be dependent on the media for some portion of their understanding of events. They [in some cases] know little more than we know."[39] Anecdotal revelations of the attention policy elites pay to mass media abound. It is said that President Clinton—the first commander in chief who grew up with television—"prefers CNN to daily [CIA] intelligence briefings."[40] He also ordered the installation of a TV in the presidential bathroom. George Bush apparently faithfully watched the *Larry King Show* on CNN as a "barometer" to gauge "how the public was responding" to his actions and policies.[41] During the Persian Gulf conflict, the *Washington Post* noted, the "White House is preoccupied with the war," and that preoccupation was satiated by hooking up televisions in every office.[42]

Accordingly, it is quite possible that politicians state that they are watching TV so as to give the impression that they are dutifully "keeping up." Robert S. McNamara recalled that "during the whole two weeks" of the Cuban Missile Crisis in October 1962 when he served as secretary of defense in the Kennedy administration, he did not watch any television.[43] It would be extraordinary for a political leader to make that claim today; indeed, it would be taken as willful ignorance. Such is the importance of maintaining contact with world events through media imagery; to avoid it is to be "out of touch." Television news might be seen as the modern "great equalizer" where mighty and low all have, at least in the first minutes or hours of a major story, access to the same pictures in the same form through the same channel. As one CNN executive noted during the Gulf conflict, "Everyone with access to CNN, including the president, was receiving the news of the beginning of the war, from the very target, at the very same instant."[44]

But instant access is not, in visual or in informational terms, full disclosure: the subjects we all gaze upon together are limited, homogenous, and leave much out of the panorama of war. In no way does an evening newscast, or even the repetitive programming of twenty-four-hour news networks, provide us with complete views of what occurs in the world on any given day. Television news is less a window on the world than a peephole guided by selective pressures of what is and what is not newsworthy.[45] As we have seen, one of the principal elements for ranking a story or item as newsworthy is that it lends itself to a kinetic visual. Some items are more visual than others; some conflicts in certain parts of the world are less accessible to the camera. Even political leaders who may have access to other views still appreciate this fact; they know that what the mass audience is viewing is important precisely because it is all that the people get to see.

Nightly newscasts in the United States vary little in this regard; there is generally unanimity on what is the "big" story, which are the less important ones, and which are to be ignored. Likewise, the pictures that grace the covers of newsmagazine rivals Time and Newsweek show often almost the same shot. Studies of journalistic practice find that the definition of "news" among practitioners in major media organizations is universal, hence the product is identical.[46] Little outside the system is allowed into the marketplace of inspection, debate, and commentary. Anecdotally, the world's myriad famines, wars, genocides, and human rights disasters that have been largely uncovered by cameras seem equally to slip off the political agenda for action and response.

An example is the case of the American intervention in Somalia. The question can be raised: Why Somalia and not other locations where, if reporters had ventured, similar images could have been retrieved for international display? On the ABC Evening News of November 26, 1992, Forrest Sawyer began the newscast by observing, "The African nation of Somalia, where war and starvation have become a fact of life, has once again become the focus of the world's attention." On NBC's December 4, 1992, news broadcast, Jane Pauley similarly stated, "Tonight, Somalia has moved to the top of the global agenda." Her co-host Garrick Utley pointed out later: "Somalia is not the only place in Africa that faces famine caused by drought and war; there is also Mozambique and southern Sudan. But right now it is Somalia that is getting our attention."

In parallel, in Time's December 7, 1992, issue, the first after President Bush's decision to send American forces to the Horn of Africa on a "mission of mercy," a thin sidebar is accorded to "The World's Forgotten Tragedies." These, it says, were drawn from:

> the international relief group Médicins Sans Frontières [which reports] entire populations are at "immediate risk" from famine, war, disease or displacement. These groups [include] the reasonably familiar, the Muslims of Bosnia-Herzegovina, the Kurds of Northern Iraq and of course the Somalis, but they also include the South Sudanese, the Tuaregs of the Sahara, and the Rohingyas, "a Muslim group in Burma persecuted by the military government."

In *Time* of December 14, 1992, a photo montage of a series of starvation icons on the "Landscape of Death" in Somalia is introduced as follows:

> These are the images that have finally brought the world to Somalia's rescue. Why did it take so long, when some reporters have been telling the story for months? Such is the power of pictures: people are starving and dying in Liberia, Sudan, southern Iraq, Burma, Peru, yet no massive aid is offered. Humanitarian concern has no logical stopping point, but the world's attention is hard to capture. It is easy to argue that policymakers should not wait for gruesome television footage before they respond. But if images like these are what it takes to bring mercy to even one people in peril, so be it.

In similar insight, Ted Koppel noted: "*Nightline* went to cover Somalia and I was there and that meant bringing along our huge electronic tail. Now what are the chances of *Nightline* doing a story while we're in Somalia on Rwanda, or Latin America, or anyplace else? Slim or none."[47]

What unifies these observations is that they quite clearly signify a degree, but only a degree, of self-consciousness about the role of mass media. "The world" is personified and made into a sort of mythological figure whose "eye" of attention is randomly focused. Also, although the media note, with irony or pathos, that some tragedies are not being covered, they offer no concrete reasons why this is so.

Crucially, they provide no pictures of the other tragedies. The *Time* sidebar, for example, contains no illustrations; no Tuareg or Rohingya seems to deserve the presence of any of the thousands of journalists duly dispatched to cover the American soldiers who went to Somalia. The news camera, apparently, as Koppel seems to be admitting, almost always travels in a herd or not at all. Missing from this mild soul-searching is an indisputable fact: news organizations choose which stories to cover. Those choices are largely the result of economics, politics, and prejudices, but they are in the end still choices. Journalists have no one to blame but themselves if 3 million die unphotographed.

The distinctive feature of the system is the media's personification of indifferent providence. They admit, as CBS correspondent Tom Fenton wrote, that the race to be first with pictures of the big story no longer allows them to "wander off for a week in search of the mood piece or background story."[48] The failure to cover stories is not ascribed as a personal shortcoming, or even a sign that the news publications and channels do not give us "all the news"; or, if we give them thirty minutes they will bring us "the world." They cite focus as some sort of natural event out of anyone's control; we just happened to be paying attention to Somalia. Recognition of inattention by the media, therefore, is not intended as self-criticism. When journalists say that no pictures exist of a certain tragedy, what this actually means is that they did not go on location to take such pictures, or as is more often the case, news agencies and publications did not create an incentive to do so.

That our neighbors and the great para-community of television viewers share the same visual menu is the most dangerous aspect of this failure of vision. No one we know sees any different version of reality. We cannot call a friend in another city to compare and contrast the evening news; he or she has seen the same news, whatever the channel. The communal viewing and the TV visuals conspire to force us to accept the vision of war as defined by the satellite and the camera. The media, mass communication researchers often say, may not always tell us what to think, but are very effective in telling us what to think about. Today's headline is tomorrow's dinner conversation. Conversely, and perhaps more importantly, the media can ignore an issue or an event, including a war, and thus withhold it from the collective consciousness and attention of the world.

Such communal focus and ignorance affects what we see and what we think about it. Psychologists have shown that when people are presented with explanations for a phenomenon, they tend to assume that those explanations (and no others) must be the most likely candidates.[49] What is outside the living room is outside our mind as well as our sight. It follows, then, that news that does not lend itself to pictures is less likely to be covered prominently, if at all. What is not visualized is not news; the proverbial tree in the forest requires CNN to document its crashing. The ethnic cleansing of Bosnian Muslims is thus a tragedy, while the horror perpetrated on the people of East Timor is ignored. Newscasts are subjective filters that act to restrict our views of war (and other events) but also narrow the interpretations we may conceive of them. What we are shown is what we are told is important, and think it is important because it is what we are being shown. It is a circular, self-limiting system and a conflation of communal enlightenment and ignorance.

Finally, the "herd" nature of modern televisual journalism contributes to its powers of illusion. Because of the demand for the "money shots," and because most news organizations share the definition of what is news, there is fierce competition to procure visuals from the site of any photogenic conflict. Literally thousands of reporters will attempt to follow (or go before) American troops to a foreign land where they have been sent to fight or intervene. The resulting media feeding frenzy is a spectacle in itself. But the sheer numbers of journalists committed to one story means that any other news is largely impossible to cover—no cameras are available for disasters elsewhere in the world once the global press corps has been committed to one site. The mass of camera and satellite transponders combines with the huge flow of images to create an impressive feeling that saturation equals depth and thoroughness.

This is another illusion, but a profitable one for the press: quantity is confused with quality. As the British reporter Maggie O'Kane suggested about Gulf War coverage, "the presence of so many reporters and TV crews gave the public at home the impression that they were seeing and learning more than their parents and grandparents had, straining at crackling wirelesses to hear news from the front in earlier wars. They weren't."[50] The visions produced by the mass media were actually almost completely uninformative, whereas the single pen of an observant, honest, and irascible foreign correspondent in the Crimea about 150 years earlier had shaken a warmaking establishment to its core with the truth. That our neighbors, and even our rulers, essentially sit with us in the living room and share our view is a sign that technology has brought us, if not a radically new version of the vision of war, then a novel mode of communally seeing it. But that same new freedom also allows others, the powers that be of press and politics, to exclude from our communal viewing sights inconvenient to their interests. This practice is not new, but the pretense that we are better informed than ever in history about wars in distant lands is the big lie of the television age.

## REALISM

When Henry Fox Talbot published the first book of photographs, *The Pencil of Nature* (1844-1846),[51] he stressed the realism of the new medium: "The plates in the present work are impressed by the agency of light alone, without any aid whatever from the artist's pencil. They are the sun pictures themselves, and not, as some persons have imagined, engravings in imitation."[52] Each subsequent technological advancement in the photographic process was thought to have contributed to better capturing reality: the flash (first a magnesium taper in 1866); gelatin emulsion (1878); the halftone block (1880); the hand or miniature camera (1888); roll film (1889); aerial photography in wartime (1910 in the Italian-Turkish war); and the telegraphic transmission of images (1924). At its beginning, photography was a labor of amateur technology and gentlemen's enthusiasm. Talbot, Wedgewood, Niépce, Daguerre, and the other fathers of "writing with light" were all artists (and only the last was a professional); all were accustomed to the leisurely pursuit of the ideal view and the long preparation of materials. But their art was not in contradiction to their science, since both approaches sought the same prize. As one early (1843) reviewer gushed: "when the photographer has prepared his truthful tablet, and 'held his mirror up to nature,' she is taken captive in all her sublimity and beauty; and faithful images of her grandest, her loveliest, and her minutest features, are transferred to her most distant worshippers, and become the objects of a new and pleasing idolatry."[53]

Thus, photography began as an art form, or rather, as a means of attaining what had been just beyond the grasp of Western painters: fidelity to nature. So great was the achievement of these early photographs that the artist Paul Delaroche famously declared, "Henceforth, painting is dead." Indeed, the age of the great war painting, sculpture, and relief was drawing to a close. Only a handful of nonphotographic (or noncinematic or video) images of war would attain prominence in the twentieth century, the era of the camera.

Yet, surveying the work of the early photographers, one is struck by their similarity to standard themes of art such as posings, landscapes, and still lifes. These reflected technological limitations; until the late nineteenth century, photographers could not be called photojournalists. "Professional news photography," notes Michael Carlebach, "is a twentieth-century product with origins in the early history of the medium."[54] Revealingly, of over three hundred photographers who received special passes to picture military activity during the American Civil War, a large majority simply produced portraits or *cartes de visite* for soldiers.[55] At the same time, photography was the culmination of a practical Western quest to find what William Ivins calls "a way of making visual reports that had no interfering symbolic linear syntax of their own."[56] For the nineteenth-century photographer, then, there was no contradiction between the accomplishment of a realistic art tradition and the conception of a positivistic scientific and industrial revolution; photography answered ancient aesthetic and scientific yearnings alike.

In contradistinction, today we face an image world which is quantitatively and qualitatively different. On a surface level, all the dreams of realism (but certainly not of beauty) are answered. Still photographs and moving film and video seem to observe those distant lands for us, or as an eager photo editor of the midcentury, promoting the glory of his craft, contended, "The scientist, the engineer, the editor, the cameraman, are today linked in a united, and ever tireless, effort to speed the news photograph to the reader, so that when he scans the picture as he reads the accompanying story over his breakfast table, he can truthfully exclaim: 'This picture age is marvelous!' "[57] We may speculate, though, whether the new imagery machines have brought us closer to reality or perhaps rather forever obscured its distinction from what is representative. Is this new vision a liberation or simply a retrenchment? Does the camera bring us only an illusion of intimacy and understanding? These questions are rarely asked about the phenomenon of modern imagery called living-room war, so great is our faith in the truthfulness, verisimilitude, and "utmost fidelity" to nature of the video or photographic still. Are the pictures in our living rooms, of war and other subjects, truer than ever before was possible?

Realism in imagery is, of course, neither relative nor measured by an absolute standard. For example, the Greeks of 2,400 years ago thought their pictures as realistic as a CNN video is to us today. It is said that Zeuxis, a fifth-century B.C.E. artist, painted grapes so genuinely that birds flew down to snatch them.[58] The first multimedia artist, Theon of Samos, painted a hoplite in action and hid it behind a curtain; a trumpeter then sounded a charge while the curtain was withdrawn. So lifelike was the image, so convincing the sound effect, that unsuspecting viewers leaped back in terror.

The realism of news video is equally proverbial to us. No one looks at a magazine photograph of a distant war and thinks, "That's just someone's opinion." People may claim a photo was posed or staged; very few challenge the notion that photographs can express truth and falsehood.[59] For example, in a 1992 meeting of the UN Human Rights Commission, U.S. Assistant Secretary of State John R. Bolton attacked Serbia for sponsoring "concentration camps."[60] When the Serb ambassador to the United Nations claimed that the stories were false, Bolton held up a copy of *Time* magazine whose cover photo showed an emaciated man, identified as a Muslim held in a Serbian-run camp, standing behind a barbed-wire fence. "Pictures speak louder than words," Bolton said. "Is this fascism or is it not?"

Interestingly, it later turned out that the caption of the picture was "wrong" as to its major visual juxtaposition: the man in question was not *in* the camp, but outside it. Relatedly, journalists worry that the new techniques of digitalization will lead to an erosion of the authenticity of the news image. Fred Ritchin, former director of photography for the *New York Times Magazine*, reacting to several composite images that had appeared in major newsmagazines, commented, "Now the viewer must question the photograph at the basic physical level of fact."[61] But this sort of reservation masks the myriad standard distortions of the photograph and its editing. Photojournalism has its codes of production as much as any other part of the news industry.[62] These codes, however, are invisible because we assume that the camera does not lie, unless it is made to do so by nefarious intent. The "truth" of an image, whether or not it shows something that really happened, is less important than the struggle to define what the image means for national policy, especially in wartime. Paradoxically, the assumed natural objectivity of visual news undermines its adherence to journalistic ideals of neutrality. No newspaper is expected to show both *visual* sides of a story.

An example of such untruth telling through images was the bizarre shadow play of the Romanian revolution.[63] During mid- and late December 1989, a drama unfolded in Romania, with characters and events drawn from Hollywood Central Casting. After fifty years of Communist rule, and twenty-five years of oppression by the megalomaniac dictator Nikolai Ceaucescu, soldiers, laborers, religious leaders, and even many officials rose up in what seemed to be a spontaneous gasp and grasp for freedom. The dictator was delivering a speech from his headquarters to a huge crowd when suddenly voices rang out, calling for his downfall. Ceaucescu and his wife fled to a helicopter, only to be captured, tried, and rapidly executed. We saw, on our television screens, house-to-house battles between revolutionary soldiers flying the Romanian flag with its Communist hammer and sickle excised, and the blue-coated henchmen of the *Securitate* secret police. Blood ran in the streets; vehicles exploded; city blocks flamed. We also saw evidence of massacres of civilians in long rows of corpses. Then, abruptly, it was over; the people had won. It was a civil war in a fortnight, live, in color; it made great TV.

Yet, within months, a strange, indefinite context emerged: what had we really seen? Was the decision to depose the dictator actually made by top state officials weeks—perhaps years—before? It seems the first voices of protest at the big rally came not from the docile crowd but from pre-recorded tapes played through government loudspeakers near the rostrum. The massacres were sometimes real, sometimes suspect. The long rows of corpses were now purported to be recent dead from natural causes exhumed from the cemetery and requisitioned from morgues. Also, who had been shooting at whom? Many of the street battles, in retrospect, may have been staged. Why, in all the supposedly fierce fighting, was the fragile antenna of the television station, the alleged central focus of the revolution, untouched? Whose side was anybody on? It now seems that there were "good" *Securitate* who played a role in launching the revolution.

The controversy continues, but assuredly satellite feeds and videotape did not clear up the fog of war and the machinations of conspiracy. The tools of real-time war were employed to further the agenda of men within the regime who staged an internal coup that was transformed into a popular uprising. Andrei Codrescu, a Romanian poet and exile, astonished at being tricked, concluded,

> And hats must be off to the producers of the exceedingly realistic docudrama of the strategic military center from where, in a charged atmosphere reminiscent of *Reds* or *Dr. Zhivago*, generals with telephones on both ears

shouted orders at troops on vast invisible battlefields in every part of the country.

Today I stand abashed by my naiveté. Much of that Romanian "spontaneity" was as slick and scripted as a Hollywood movie. If I were in charge of the Emmys, I'd give one to the Romanian directors of December 1989.[64]

The mysteries of the Romanian revolution testify that the "reality" of war on video has no greater claim to truth than "realities" displayed in bronze, stone, or oil. Behind the curtain in the palace of the digital and satellite age may be potentially the greatest wizard of them all. Our susceptibility as viewers is drawn from the awe in which we hold the technology.

But we do not need to uncover secret policemen operating in the mists of the Carpathians to witness and listen to a certain degree of deceptive realism. Verbal lies are also relative to what pictures are being lied about, and it is often surprising how many of the seemingly factual pictures of war misrepresent in some way what is actually shown. A common practice in perfectly innocuous documentary films, for example, is the use of stock footage to illustrate specific narration: the words say this is one thing, but the pictures could be almost anything.

For instance, the documentary *The Unknown Soldier* (1991) told and showed four stories about American soldiers who died in the line of duty in World War II but whose bodies were never identified. One of the segments dealt with a famous "Peace Patrol." A squad of marines on Guadalcanal, led by Colonel Frank Goettge (a six-foot four, 240-pound ex-linebacker), set out to accept the surrender of starving Japanese laborers. The patrol was ambushed and massacred. Only a few survived; one swam six hours across shark-infested coral reefs to get help. When reinforcements arrived, as one veteran described it, "we killed every Japanese we found, some three or four times." Goettge's body was never recovered. *The Unknown Soldier* is a well-done, straightforward production, complete with all the standard devices of the documentary: personal interviews, voice-over, maps, photographs, and of course stock footage.

Where is the misrepresentation? Literally speaking, the documentary's narration was factual; what happened was what was described. The relationship with the images shown, however, is slippery. When we see a photo of Frank Goettge in a football jersey and the narrator tells us that Goettge was a college gridiron hero, we have a perfectly logical concordance between image and word. But what about when the narrator weaves the tale of the Peace Patrol setting out for the fateful island "on the evening of August 12, 1942"? We are shown Americans in green uniform, apparently marines, marching through what appears to be a jungle, or at least a grove of palm trees. The image-word juxtaposition is revealing:

| AUDIO | VIDEO |
|---|---|
| A few days after the American troops landed . . . | WIDE ANGLE OF AMERICAN TROOPS DEBARKING FROM LANDING CRAFT |
| A prisoner reported that | JAPANESE TALKING TO AN AMERICAN, SITTING IN A JUNGLE OR ON A BEACH |
| there were many Japanese laborers who were sick, disheartened, and anxious to surrender | SHOTS OF CROWD OF HALF-NAKED JAPANESE, NOT IN UNIFORM, LOOKING MISERABLE IN SUN |
| Colonel Goettge organized a patrol | MEDIUM SHOT OF COL. GOETTGE IN uniform WITH JUNGLE BACKGROUND |
| 25 Marines went out on the evening of August 12, 1942 | TWO SHOTS OF LONG COLUMN OF MARINES WALKING UP JUNGLE PATH |
| Only 3 would return. | |

Now, in retrospect, the Peace Patrol only became famous for its result, not its inception; it was unlikely that a camera crew just happened to be there on August 12, 1942, filming Goettge's men starting out, or that anybody filmed the exact Japanese prisoner who reported that comrades were at another island seeking to surrender. The footage shown is actually stock footage of "Marines in Pacific." The year may or may not be 1942—but the troop is definitely not the Goettge patrol. The aesthetic imperative of cinema and television decrees that a film must always show something visual; in most documentaries, the narration is written first and footage is found to visually match the words.

So the footage-narration association is a misrepresentation of what we are told about something specific; it is an ordinary falsehood that is part of the conventions of documentary. For this reason, this book includes no separate chapter on the deceptions of war images: all images of war are deceptive in some way because all images are both accurate and deceiving by their nature. But again, these are lies of representation; they are lies of *words*, implications that what we are being shown is truthful.

In general, the stage management of war news has become part of the code of modern visual realism, and those who wage war understand this fact. In reaction to the perceived power of media, military commanders of the Vietnam War generation attempted several counterprogramming strategies during the Persian Gulf War. These included: (1) censorship; (2) creating and distributing approved images; and (3) offering captions or news frames of discourse to guide interpretation of images that appeared in the press. The greatest impact was made when the military provided news organizations with gifts of kinetic, arresting video. These included montages of jets streaking off carriers and nose-eye views of "smart" bombs razing Iraqi bridges and neatly pinpointing tanks and missile launchers. Other images were captured directly by news cameras in rear areas in Saudi Arabia and Israel: Patriot antimissiles "taking out" Iraqi Scuds in nighttime displays. Both visions of modern war were spectacular. They also promulgated a stereotype and an agenda that the Pentagon deliberately cultivated: American military technology was superior and we were fighting a precise tech-war. These "captions" surrounding the many video clips of the bomb drops and Scud slams were repeated over and over; such repetition is the basis of establishing any idea as a commonplace. Newsmen and the public largely accepted the captions as factual because they truly seemed to match what we were seeing in our living rooms.

The visions were pre-interpreted by officials of state, especially war leaders. Three-star general Norman Schwarzkopf, commander of the Allied Coalition forces in the Gulf, was well cast as emcee for the war as variety show. Burly, ruddy, assured in gesture, speech, and manner, Pattonesque but also Everyman, he exuded an all-American can-do spirit and exhibited considerable wit in his presentations. In one instance he showed an aerial view of a bridge across which a truck was speeding. Seconds later the lens focused in as a laser-guided bomb hit the span—a direct hit, of course—and the bridge was bisected. Schwarzkopf noted the truck had passed over just in time and commented wryly, "The luckiest man in Iraq on this day, right through the crosshairs." With such bullmastiff charm, General Schwarzkopf fulfilled the observation of Bernard Montgomery (of Alamein) that a good war commander should be both a master and a mascot for his men.

He acted, thus, in the oldest tradition of command: appearing in person to deliver the *adlocutio* to the troops. But in a modern democracy, such rituals cannot all be enacted in physical presence; the press and the viewing audience—including political elites—constitute forces equally as important to rally as were the ordinary soldiers in ages past. The Pentagon understood the requirement to appeal audio-visually to public opinion. Kinetic images and authoritative commentary would attract the attention of news, the conduit to the masses. Schwarz-kopf's illustrations, persona, and words assured us that the reality we were shown was comprehensive and representative: "This is what the war is like." He also assuaged any doubts, insisting that "everything is great, under control."

There is no evidence whatsoever that these visions of war were staged or faked like some of what transpired in the Romanian revolution. A camera mounted in the nosecone of an electro-optically guided "smart" bomb or on the wing of the F-117A (Stealth) fighter that dropped it showed, albeit in grainy black and white, the scenes that passed before the lens in the moments prior to impact. The Patriot antiballistic missiles launched into the air in front of our eyes did result in explosions in the night sky. And whether through restrictions on targeting or new technology, the air war did mostly avoid numerous civilian casualties. *New Yorker* correspondent Milton Viorst wrote of postwar Iraq in April 1991: "There was no Second World War–style urban destruction, despite the tons of explosives that had fallen. Instead, with meticulous care—one might almost call it artistry—American aircraft had taken out telecommunications facilities, transportation links, key government offices, and, most painful of all, electrical generating plants."[65] Even Iraqis, describing Coalition bombings that had destroyed civil locations, "referred to them as 'mistakes'—conceding, in effect, that American pilots had occasionally missed their aim but had not deliberately sought out civilian targets."[66] This was also the conclusion of a cross section of outside observers, including CNN's Peter Arnett, who commented that the Iraqis "knew we were only going after military targets."[67] Joost R. Hiltermann, a reporter for *Mother Jones* magazine, also noted that "especially in Baghdad, the bombing was eerily precise."[68] Richard P. Hallion, in his detailed assessment of the military campaign, reviews such commentary and concludes that "the effectiveness and precision of coalition air strikes convincingly demonstrated that such results were not fanciful but, rather, the objective reality of modern war."[69]

Nevertheless, we now know, after the fact, that the dazzling visions of the Gulf War were neither comprehensive nor representative, nor accurately contextualized. For example, only some 5 percent of the ordnance dropped on Iraq during the war was electro-optically guided; only 27 percent of Coalition planes were even capable of carrying such weapons systems. "Precision-guided" munitions were rarities, not the majority.

Moreover, for various technical and political reasons, Coalition aircraft regularly did not hit targets with the full complement of explosives required for destruction. When we saw an image of bunkers exploding, it is quite possible that what we were really seeing was damage to the roof, not necessarily the tanks lodged inside. In military terms the job may have been "half-assed," but by televisual standards the pictures of billowing concrete and dust were impressive. The reality of future-tech precision existed, but was used only in a limited manner.

The "Scud hunt" as well was not all it seemed. The recorded demolitions of Scud launchers added up to 300 percent of the total Iraqi fleet. Many of the images we saw of "Scud missile launchers" being destroyed were miscaptioned.[70] The U.S. Air Force's own *Gulf War Air Power Survey* concluded that

> [I]t remains impossible to confirm the actual destruction of *any* Iraqi mobile Launchers by Coalition aircraft.... Most of these reports [of kills] undoubtedly stemmed from attacks that did destroy things found in the Scud launch areas. But, most of the objects involved—though not all— now appear to have been (1) decoys, (2) vehicles such as tanker trucks that were *impossible to distinguish* on infrared or radar sensors from mobile launchers and their associate support vehicles, or (3) objects that were unfortunate enough to have Scud-like signatures. [emphasis mine][71]

Scott Ritter, the marine colonel placed in charge of the final analysis of the Scud hunts' results, stunned the military by concluding, "all evidence indicates that no missiles were destroyed."[72] The true comprehensive reality thus was uncertain. The videos did not lie, but the claims made about the objects in the images were overoptimistic, inflated, or misleading.

The Patriot's story is even more confusing. What exactly were we seeing when a Patriot missile streaked into a dark sky, and seconds later there was an explosion and fireworks display? Was it truly the real-life video game that it appeared to simulate? Again, the image was not faked, but the context was complex and somewhat illusory. No incoming Scud missile was ever destroyed, that is, vaporized in the science fiction sense. Parts of them, including the fuel tank, would scatter at the nearby explosion of a Patriot. This fact should be posed against the efficiency of the Scud as an explosive-carrying platform. The Israelis themselves, in the words of Defense Minister Moshe Arens, drew the conclusion that "the Patriot may have caused as much damage as it prevented." It is also unclear how many Patriots actually hit Scuds. The Patriot would explode in the air even if no contact was made; fireworks would result in either case. In a review of the effectiveness of Gulf War weapons, Anthony Cordesman and Abraham Wagner painstakingly note that all sources on the subject seem "vague or conflicting."[73] Yet, the entertainment value of the fireworks display was so high that tough questions were not posed and doubts never raised about what exactly we were seeing.

But the false impressions telecast to the American public were not solely the product of military boosterism. Journalists wanted simple notations to accompany images; journalism specializes in black and white facts, not misty gray ones. Woe to the press spokesman who tells the public (honestly) that the facts are uncertain. Moreover, the huge corps of reporters in the Gulf was largely bereft of martial experience or education. This is true in any crisis where every television station and newspaper wants its own representative on the scene. In fact, early in the deployment, the Pentagon created a training program, available to journalists, to provide detailed information on all aspects of modern war equipment, technology, and strategy. Only a handful of the 2,000 reporters assigned to the Gulf over the next six months attended the classes.

This was not an anomalous happenstance born of an emergency situation. Studied ignorance is standard operating procedure for reporters covering military affairs. One of the few military veterans among the ranks of modern journalists, Fred Reed, recalled, "I once asked whether reporters could check out books from the Pentagon library. The librarian didn't know, she said, because no one had ever asked."[74] Such willful ignorance in a journalist covering hockey games would be intolerable to the public, his colleagues, or editors. As a result, reporters in the Gulf—even those who had some track record of covering military affairs—did not know how to question the pictures, but they also did not want to do so. Thus, it was not a case of the military forcefully manipulating the media; rather, the military provided the exact product the media required to serve their commercial interests.

It was no surprise, then, that public opinion surveys found little sympathy with carping by the press about military "restrictions." In effect, as James Dunnigan and Austin Bay suggest, the military played the "television briefing process card," which "expose[d] the foibles of the working press" and made Coalition military leaders into "sympathetic and credible figures," whereas the "sharp-tongued and cynical press became the bad guys."[75] The public also sensed, correctly, that the self-righteous utterances of the press were pretense, and that their claims of being tribunes of the people, only seeking the truth, were a mockery. In survey after survey, ordinary Americans labeled the press part of the power elite, separate from themselves. The public understood how ridiculous it was for news media to ask, as occurred frequently at Gulf War press conferences, for the particulars of the Pentagon's strategic plans. *Saturday Night Live*—ever the hecklers of authority—lampooned reporters badgering military men in a sketch of Gulf briefings: "Is there going to be an amphibious invasion of Kuwait? And if so, where?"

In assessing the realism of pictures, it is clear that prejudices, policies, words of description, and interpretation matter. Certainly, the living-room, live-from-ground-zero, instantaneous vision of warfare has technical, aesthetic, and temporal components that mark it as a departure from all previous incarnations of the visions of war. In addition, television images are the main medium through which argumentation about war policy is expressed. Yet pictures are not hypodermic needles of emotion that in and of themselves change opinions and make or break policies in wartime. This was as true in the Stone Age as it is now in the era of the living-room war. America's inaction in a hundred other loci of human tragedy throughout the world—prominently and recently Rwanda, where at least one million people were killed while the world actively did nothing—suggests that there is absolutely no relationship between the transmission of suffering and the reception of compassion.[76] Indeed, during the Rwanda tragedy, the president of the United States, Bill Clinton—a man who is renowned for his ability to exude a sense of empathic compassion—directed his administration to avoid intervention by the most obvious means necessary: denying that a genocide was occurring and thus avoiding triggering the 1948 Genocide Convention. The presence of a camera does not alter the fact that human beings have an infinite capacity to ignore the misery of others.

Economic considerations play an important role in this new visual order. In the wake of the Vietnam War, American leaders—and indeed almost all military commanders throughout the world—have become interested in finding new ways to influence the images that make up the news. This is because such images are valuable commodities of international journalism; news organizations compete to procure and display them first. That is why pictures of war from news cameras (or provided by military sources) will continue to be contested objects. The battle to control pictures of war will not be separate from warfare; it will be part of warfare. The vision of war in the age of satellites and video is circular, reflecting upon itself. The crucial factor, often lost in the instantaneousness of the arrival of the images and their lifelike (or documentarylike) attributes, is that they are creations, no more and no less than a cave painting or a bas-relief. They are not unfiltered reality that shows us all the truth; their representativeness should always be questioned, probed, and explored, if possible through contrasting angles and alternative voices.

Such reactions are, however, unlikely. A skeptical audience will not emerge in this age of multimedia, living-room wars. However false, misleading, or irrelevant to the greater events and context of the war the Persian Gulf images were, they were riveting, kinetic—entertaining. It seems inappropriate to apply such a word to images of war today, but battle pictures have always partly served that function. The cave painters, the Assyrian kings, the bishop of Bayeux, no doubt, all enjoyed looking at the images that decorated their institutions. War makes interesting rock art; it also makes good music videos. In a culture that increasingly draws less distinction between news and entertainment, it follows that images of war could bridge the gap between the two realms of mass media.

President Eisenhower's farewell prophecy about the growing power of a military-industrial complex has relevance here. Modern mass media are owned by giant corporations with worldwide, diversified holdings. These demand maximum profitability from both news and entertainment divisions: where once TV news was an area of lower profit and greater prestige, now it is expected to contribute high returns on investment at minimum cost. The media giants' connection to the traditional military is tenuous; rather, they constitute an *entertainment-industrial complex*. Their profit pressure demands that all pictures win audiences. Images of war are perfect fodder to be processed in such a fashion. The Gulf War, therefore, may be logged as a variety program cast and shot for our benefit.

The latest development in the evolution of the vision of war may be to serve as part of the great tide of entertainment that enters our homes through television. "The future," wrote Erik Erikson, "always belongs to those who combine a universal enough new meaning with the mastery of a new technology."[77] In this onslaught of live, real-time battles, distinctions between real wars and fantasy ones become negligible; military commanders will need to play the role of emcee as well as strategist.

## THE EFFECTS OF WAR IMAGES

The final temptation of the visual age is to conclude that when images of war do appear in the medium to which they have largely been consigned, they can be powerful; and in defining "power," we must include the changing of public opinion and the driving of national policy. Yet, quixotically, the power of pictures to change real-world events has been vastly overrated; or rather, it has become part of the lexicon of describing the relationship between images and history to say that a picture or pictures had a "powerful impact," with little material evidence to back the claim. In books about paintings of war and compilations of war photography, it seems to be a commonplace that pictures of war are not just cultural windows but also play a role in war itself. This book is premised on that idea.

Assessing the effects of images, however, requires caution and an admission of the complexity of that role. Consider one of the exemplars of the American war in Vietnam. [**Fig. 40**] In the spring of 1968, throughout the major cities in the South, National Liberation Front (Viet Cong) insurgents attacked government posts, and in many cases executed officials and their families. Begun on the eve of the Vietnamese Lunar New Year, Tet Mau Mau, the events of the weeks have come to be known as the Tet Offensive.

On February 1, a day into the fighting, Brigadier General Nguyen Ngoc Loan of the South Vietnamese National Police fired a single bullet into the head of a Viet Cong suspect on a street in Saigon. Several journalists were present, including Eddie Adams, an Associated Press photographer, who raised his camera and pressed the shutter at what turned out to be the very instant that the .38-caliber bullet penetrated the man's skull. An NBC film crew recorded a sequence of the execution. The actual moment of the shot was lost when someone walked in front of the television camera, but a day later twenty million NBC viewers saw the spectacle of the man falling backwards, a fountain of blood popping from his head. Loan, by all description, remained impassive, turned to the on-lookers, and said—the exact words are debated—"Many Americans have been killed these last few days and many of my best Vietnamese friends. Now do you understand? Buddha will understand."[78] Then he walked away. "Rough justice on a Saigon street as the charmed life of the city of Saigon comes to a bloody end," observed NBC's John Chancellor on the *Huntley-Brinkley Report*, which aired the film. It was one of thousands of brutal acts on both sides that day. An American news bureau chief in Saigon even recalled that his Vietnamese re-porter, who was present at the scene, did not bother to tell him about the incident because "General Loan does that all the time. That's not news."[79]

The film and the photo composed a "shot seen 'round the world" in news-papers, magazines, and television. Adams won the Pulitzer Prize for the photo, which was thrust into the pantheon of photojournalism. The picture is still a sine qua non of any book about the Tet Offensive. Moreover, at the time and

40. South Vietnamese National Police Chief Brigadier General Nguyen Ngoc Loan executes a Viet Cong officer with a single pistol shot in the head in Saigon, February 1, 1968.
*Photo: Eddie Adams © AP/World Wide Photos*

still today, the image elicited commentary about its power and effects.[80] The statements are in the following vein:

*[it] shocked the world*

*[its] impact was arguably the turning point of the war, for it coincided with a dramatic shift in American public opinion, and may well have helped to cause it*

*Of all the images of terror, none was more brutal than the day viewers watched an execution of a suspected Vietcong...*

*[The Saigon execution] was an act of cruelty which did not help the world image of the South Vietnamese at a critically important time for them*

*A world-wide furor was created*

*The brutality of the South Vietnamese against captured Vietcong shocked the American consciousness as nothing in the war had done before*

*[T]he Loan shooting seemed to many people to confirm the suspicion that this was a "wrong war" on the "wrong side"*

*[T]he immediate reaction to such scenes was a gut revulsion to the barbarity of the war which tended to supersede more rational, long-term considerations*

*No film footage did as much damage as AP photographer Eddie Adams's 35-mm shot taken on a Saigon street on February 1*

*Images [of Tet] proved indelible. They scarred the American psyche*

*Americans viewing Eddie Adams' picture said to themselves, "That's enough, we've had it, we're not going to support a dictatorship, that's no democracy as we know it"*

*People were just sickened by this, and I think this added to the feeling that the war was the wrong war at the wrong place. . . .*

And so on. These utterances were made by journalists, generals, statesmen, historians, a former South Vietnamese ambassador, and war protesters—people of all political stripes and sympathies. What they have in common is a *first-person assumption of effects*. No one is simply appreciating the image—the ballet of the moment of death—on an aesthetic level. They speak and write, based upon their own personal reactions, or what they assume a socially desirable reaction *should* be. Then they project onto the world a similar reaction.

The problem is that effects must be measured, and not just assumed—this is as true of a news image studied by an art historian as an antibiotic submitted to the FDA. Obviously, the tools available to the latter (clinical trials and minute analysis of chemical composition) can be much more reliable and valid. Assumptions about the effect of an image, in contrast, must often be inferred. In fact, there was no evidence of any public fury in reaction to the Saigon shooting image. Support for the war effort actually temporarily *increased* during Tet. It did not begin to wane until after President Johnson announced a pullback in operations in South Vietnam in late March. It was this move that convinced many that the war would never be won by conventional means. More revealing, of the twenty million Americans who watched the *Huntley-Brinkley Report*, only ninety people sent in letters about the film.[81] Of these a third were from parents of young children complaining about such violence during the dinner hour. Indeed, almost none of the writers were irate about the death of the man; after all, there was little sympathy for the Viet Cong in the United States. Only a few letters in any way expressed political views. In short, by one traditional measure at least, if Americans were "shocked," "upset," or "amazed" by the images, they did not reveal it. It is much more likely that viewers were impressed by the scene as an episode of war than pondered its political implications.

First-person assumptions result from confusing three different powers or qualities of images of war or any other subject. First, images can have *aesthetic* power. They can be interesting, attractive, captivating, fascinating. War images, despite their subject matter, are no exception. Sculptures, paintings, and photographs of war's glories and horrors have often won places of honor in museums and praise from those who appreciate striking imagery. The wall paintings at the Mayan site of Bonampak, for example, display human beings slaughtered, degraded, tortured, imprisoned, debased, stripped. When looking at the images, however, Mayan scholar Michael Coe comments, appreciatively, "No verbal description could do justice to the beautiful colors and to the skill of the hand (or hands) which executed these paintings."[82] Of course, on such aesthetic grounds, he is correct. They are also spectacles to power—but to what end? In fact, the dynasty that commissioned the Bonampak murals apparently collapsed at about the time they were being finished: so what power besides the beauty and cultural expression did the art really have?

Indeed, for many "great" works of art, the line between political effect and aesthetic appreciation seems thin—for both artist and audience. For example, in 1937, Pablo Picasso painted the largest canvas of his life (26 x 11½ feet) to express his horror, as he put it, "at the military caste which has plunged Spain into a sea of suffering and death." *Guernica* was a sensation when it was shown at an international exhibition in Paris. The appreciation of the painting was largely for aesthetic reasons and political motivations. Partisans on the left who sympathized with the Spanish Republic deemed it a masterpiece of illustration of the cause; those on the right either ignored it or challenged the story of the massacre. Herschel B. Chipp, in his study of the history of the image, suggests that it was more powerful after the war was over; it became so famous that the

Fascists themselves, Franco most of all, tried to lay claim over it. The painting, Chipp maintains, acted to bring together many sides in post-Franco Spain, and "was now a significant force both in the reconciliation of the old hatreds and in the final healing of the wounds from that war."[83]

We should, however, consider such pronouncements carefully: would Spain not have become a democracy without *Guernica*? Or as Jean-Paul Sartre put it more bluntly, "Et *Le Massacre de Guernica*, ce chef-d'oeuvre, croit-on qu'il ait gagné un seul coeur à la cause espagnole?" ("Did the masterpiece *Guernica* win a single heart to the cause of [Loyalist] Spain?")[84] Certainly, during the first years of the picture's existence, its greatness as art was appreciated. But the insurgent legions of General Franco, assisted by Germans and Italians, won the war. America, France, and Britain did little to help the Basques or the Spanish government forces. After the war, Franco was a trusted NATO ally until his death of extreme old age. It is evident then that the "power" of the image is its status as "great art"; those who write about it thus feel some compulsion to exaggerate its power over men's personal and political destiny. In general, there is little evidence that any antiwar image has ever stopped a war. Aesthetic power is independent, and may have no influence on political power.

A second power of images draws from their celebrity: a picture can also be an icon. These are the celebrated, famous, "indelible" images, the ones that are featured in the writings of art historians. They reappear in texts (including this one) and treatises; Joe Rosenthal's picture of the flag-raising by U.S. Marines and other soldiers at Iwo Jima [see **Fig. 25**] has been the subject of several books. And, of course, when people talk or write about Tet, at least a sentence is devoted (often with an illustration) to the Eddie Adams picture. It is unclear whether icons endure forever in the public mind; new generations may be unfamiliar with the icons of their parents. In any case, their fame is a kind of power. Attention is paid to such fame, and these images are most likely to be employed as metonyms of a war.

The third power of pictures (which may or may not coincide with the other two) is political power, that of driving policy and publics. On balance, there are certainly instances where pictures of conflict affected the conflict itself. One prominent case where visualized press coverage may have directly influenced events in another country was the fall of Philippine leader Ferdinand Marcos in 1986 in what amounted to a brief and largely bloodless civil war. Marcos and his family were undermined by a foreign press that not only highlighted the poverty, corruption, and violence within his country, but also headlined lurid stories about his family's wealth and the implausibility of his war hero status. Marcos's stashed lucre and brutal tactics were exposed, his opponents lauded, and election irregularities uncovered. Commentaries by public officials and journalists suggested strongly that this was an instance when mass media were influential. Tom Brokaw boasted of "the role of the press, print and electronic.

Through television cameras and newspapers, the whole world was watching. President Marcos could lie and cheat, but in the end he could not hide." Senator Richard G. Lugar (R-Ind.) commented, "I think the concentration by media on the election—the opportunity the American people had to see it on TV and read about it in the papers—stirred up interest throughout the country in what happened there." Ron Powers, the *CBS News Sunday Morning* media critic, exclaimed, "Let's hear it for saturation television."

But it would be disingenuous to say that the press exposed Marcos out of altruistic motives. The context of the events was important to set the stage for the images to come. The press acted when they sensed elite disagreement on policy (support for Marcos in the United States ranged from tepid to weak); when many events that presented good visual material for cameras (riots, uprisings, demonstrations) were occurring quickly; and when a simple narrative was available complete with typecast actors (evil dictator, greedy wife, and the crusading widow of a martyred human rights leader). Crucially, Marcos was not powerful enough to crush his opposition or break his country's dependence on the United States, or simply to expel foreign journalists, as the Chinese government eventually accomplished during the 1989 Tiananmen protests. Also, the reckoning in the Philippines did not pose any great danger to American soldiers. To the further benefit of saturation television, the events did not drag out forever. Act followed act to dramatic conclusion, and the wicked leader was driven from power. Finally, the "good guys"—the rebel soldiers, the common people, the housewives, the students—were framing themselves (with assistance from press coverage) with slogans bearing the code words of American values: freedom and democracy.

Likewise, whatever the actual power of pictures, the first-person effect can drive the way we make war if political and military leaders base policy on it. "Public opinion wins wars," maintained General Eisenhower,[85] and if leaders believe that opinion is driven by images, they will act accordingly to encourage or forestall the opinion. This may have been the case in the Gulf War in 1991. The fear that "bad" pictures might overturn the supportive public mood resulted in the conflict's termination; in retrospect, considering Saddam Hussein's survival, this was premature at least in terms of American policy objectives. In his autobiography, Colin Powell admits explicitly that he suffered a form of *iconophobia*:

> Saddam had ordered his forces to withdraw from Kuwait. The last major escape route, a four-lane highway leading out of Kuwait City toward the Iraqi city of Basrah, had turned into a shooting gallery for our fliers. The road was choked with fleeing soldiers and littered with the charred hulks of nearly fifteen hundred military and civilian vehicles. Reporters began referring to this road as the "Highway of Death."

I would have to give the President and the Secretary [of Defense Dick Cheney] a recommendation soon as to when to stop, I told Norm [Schwarzkopf]. The television coverage, I added, was starting to make it look as if we were engaged in slaughter for slaughter's sake.[86]

"Look" is the key verb; the Basra "Road of Death" was, in retrospect, a misnomer. Two giant Iraqi convoys streamed north from Kuwait on February 25. Land- and sea-based Coalition planes encountered no resistance as they raided the long lines of vehicles day and night; pilots likened it to strafing "Daytona Beach on spring break." Yet subsequent estimates put the Iraqi casualty figures as very low in proportion to the amount of visible material destruction— some hundred to a thousand soldiers killed, much fewer than in previous operations of the air war, or indeed of most air wars. As journalist Michael Kelly points out, the awesome American firepower scared off the drivers and riders; most of the vehicles bombed were probably abandoned.

But from the air, even from a close distance, any body count was obscured by a several-mile-long column of burned-out trucks and cars. That it looked like a slaughter was more important than whether it really was, from the point of view of public relations. The gutted machinery was taken as a metonym of human carnage, though in fact it turned out to be simply abandoned military vehicles, and stolen civilian cars and loot.

Some images of the Basra road, of charred bodies and vehicles, did make it into the media. It is unclear, however, whether such a visualized slaughter would really have upset a U.S. public primed and inclined to hate Saddam Hussein, be disdainful of Arabs, supportive of "our troops," and happy for a relatively quick and bloodless (for the United States) victory. As in the case of the Saigon execution and, as we have seen, all the horrors of war, prejudice drives the way we appreciate images. Colin Powell was worrying unnecessarily about the power of pictures, but that is the point, and that is the power of the picture. The perception of the threat of "bad" pictures can be a check on modern political and military thought and behavior, especially in an age where governments have less than absolute control over the images that appear in the international news stream. The line between the policy and the picture is uncertain; both are part of the process of starting, fighting, and ending war.

# 8

---

# FUTURES

## SEEK

Clausewitz wrote of the battlefield, "All action must, to a certain extent, be planned in a mere twilight, which in addition not infrequently—like the effect of a fog or moonshine—gives to things exaggerated dimensions and an unnatural appearance."[1] To pierce this veil, to see the enemy in his dispositions, weigh his strength, and catch his maneuvers as they are executed—and at the same time throw up dark clouds around one's own forces and movements—these are the goals of every war commander. Each age offers its own limitations to this quest. In the ancient and later the Napoleonic battles, nearly all combatants would gather within a few square miles. Commanders however, had only their own eyes and the reports of scouts and spies upon which to base intelligence. As the numbers of soldiers in armed forces grew with revolutions in agriculture and industry, so did the dispersion of men in the battle. In World War II, 100,000 men covered 2,400 kilometers of land. The area for Allied Coalition forces in the Persian Gulf War was a hundred times greater than this. To dispel the modern fog of war, then, new technologies are required to encompass the view of the more widely scattered armies, and to pinpoint individual units and installations across the entire globe.

Accordingly, lack of access to visual data—at least for a regular army, as opposed to a guerrilla force—is fatal. In the Gulf War, the Iraqi army was practically blind compared to the U.S. and Coalition forces.[2] SPOT, the French remote-sensing satellite system, and other civilian satellite systems, such as the European EOSAT, followed the UN embargo and provided no images during the war to Saddam Hussein's regime.[3] Coalition bombing and jamming degraded the enemy's radar and aircraft warning system and destroyed communications networks and many command facilities. The sky and space eyes spying for Coalition forces, in contrast, were untouched. American planes could raid almost with impunity, giving their enemy no warning.[4] When Iraqis fired missiles such as the Scud (which was only designed to be accurate within two to three kilometers) toward allied positions, that they hit anything at all was only because of their knowledge of general target locations, such as cities, before the war.[5] On the ground, U.S. M1A1 Abrams tanks destroyed their opponents with a single shot, from beyond 4,000 meters, a rate of accuracy and distance unexcelled in the history of land warfare.[6] Only seven American tanks were damaged by Iraqi gunfire, none seriously. Coalition forces saw almost everything, while the enemy's entire knowledge of the war came from spies or sympathizers in Arab countries and from watching CNN.

The Iraqi situation also reveals that the battlefields of modern war are scanned by many viewers (from drone planes to up-front observers) and from numerous locations (in the sky and on the ground) attempting to construct a three-dimensional diorama of war. Many satellite images are available free to anyone, in lower resolution, through the Internet. The most powerful viewing device is the spy satellite. From 250 kilometers above the earth's surface, American KH-11 (KEYHOLE) satellites can focus objects 15 to 20 centimeters long.[7] Another major innovation, begun in 1977, is the capturing and transmission of digital, real-time images taken by KH-11.[8] Satellites can also provide information to help warriors see where they are in unfamiliar locations in relation to the enemy. Cueing into the Navstar GPS (global positioning system), a field soldier can gauge his or her location on a schematic screen map within a few feet anywhere on the planet; a commander can map out units instantly. During the Gulf War, American troops employed as many as 10,000 GPSs. The system was especially useful for U.S. Navy special forces SEAL teams and other reconnaissance units that penetrated deep into Iraq. They were so popular that some soldiers even purchased their own from mail-order catalogues.[9] Commercial software linked to GPS, such as *Skymap*, can position the owner in real time onto colorful terrain maps.

The integrated information weapons system in which man and machine are linked through computer, digital, and visual displays is incorporated by the latest version of America's main battle tank, the M1A2 Abrams, a more advanced version of the M1A1 deployed during the Gulf War. The tank is fully computerized; indeed, it is variously known as an "armored computer" or a "Jedi tank" (referring to the Jedi knights in the *Star Wars* films).[10] It reaches speeds of 40 to 50 mph, but crews typically slow to the machine's "stabe speed" (optimum speed) of 20 mph to fire and maneuver. Using a CITV (commander's independent thermal viewer), the tank's commander can target one enemy while the gunner fires at another. With a skilled crew, up to six targets can be sequentially selected, engaged, and destroyed within a minute. Using a modem/radio link and GPS system, the commander can also keep track of and in contact with other vehicles, plot his position on the battlefield, and receive information about the enemy.

New communication and visualization technologies will also be available to the ordinary foot soldier. It is here, perhaps, where science fiction and reality will most notably merge. Through an integration of robotics, computers, and flesh, the "cyborg" of science fiction is now virtually achievable.[11] The U.S. Army is presently testing a prototype infantryman weapons system called the "Land Warrior," also known as the "Robocop in the army." The system includes a lightweight helmet with a face shield that offers protection against particle and beam weapons; a computer display, to be dropped over one eye, with infrared and normal target-sensing capability; or a fully encompassing head-mounted display helmet. The soldier will also carry a backpack containing a computer, a battery, a GPS system, a digital camera processor, and other communications gear. His weapon will be a modification of the M4 carbine and M16 rifle, including a laser rangefinder and aiming light, digital compass, video camera, thermal sight, and special close-combat optics.[12] To complete the Robo look, the soldier will also wear modular body armor and garments that protect against chemical or biological weapons.

Already, Land Warrior–type experiments have been deployed in the field. American soldiers involved in Operation Uphold Democracy in Haiti in March 1995 used commercial video and single-shot cameras as well as micro-cameras installed in their helmets. The captured images were digitized, sent by radio to the command post, and then transmitted to Fort Monmouth, New Jersey, the headquarters of the Land Warrior research team. Eleven minutes after the pictures had been taken, the color-digitized images arrived at the Pentagon in Washington, D.C. Further developments include a computer-guided targeting system not unlike that in battle tanks. A soldier would be able to acquire a target at a distance beyond the range of his gun and lock it in; he would track it until it came within range, and in the meantime be able to focus his attention elsewhere. A thermal-imaging system would also allow him to detect mines, which information he would pass on to other soldiers and commanders.

Another tool with which soldiers will gather visual data about the battlefield for transmission to superiors and team members (as well as potential political leaders, the press, and the public) is the Technology Advanced Mini Eye-Safe Raser, or TAMER, developed by the Space and Systems Technology group of Motorola Corporation. TAMER resembles a pair of bulky binoculars on a small tripod. It is the integration of many devices, including a computer, a laser rangefinder, a digital compass, and a GPS receiver. It also contains a cellular phone interface, a digital micro display in its eyepiece, and a digital camera. Soldiers can carry the seven- to eight-pound device into forward positions or to spy behind enemy lines. TAMER can then take digital pictures—at this time they are black and white, still images—which in turn can be transmitted via cellular phone to intelligence operations in the home country or command headquarters in theater. Aggressive deployment possibilities include a picket line of TAMERS that survey a front, perhaps linked to auto-firing weapons or remote-controlled mines. As technology progresses, color and motion video will be added to TAMER's visualizing arsenal. Future platoon leaders and generals will have the ability to see live from the front the soldier's point of view and even observe areas where there are no men.

The goal of such technologies is threefold. First, the army of the future should be versatile, with technology assisting in all types of conflicts in any environment. Land Warrior, for example, is meant to be equally efficacious in a Third World urban battlefield such as Somalia during a house-to-house sweep, or defending a ridge in Korea from a massed infantry assault. As Colonel Henry L. Kinnison, one of the directors of the project, points out, "The problem is, the battlefield of the future is not only the open plain, which certainly can happen, but it's [also] a building . . . room, or hallway."[13]

The second objective is integration, to make the Land Warrior literally an on-line extension of the war commander. In turn, the soldier at the front will have available all the resources of information necessary for the mission. Visualization techniques will allow human soldiers to see an object in the environment and register it with a backpack computer or send data to a mainframe or central computer elsewhere, which would then check a database to match the object with possible map coordinates, known topographical and structural features in the area, or identification profiles of enemy vehicles and personnel. These data would be instantly available on-line to the soldier and to his or her commander. What would appear would be similar to the pop-up menus in a Macintosh or advanced Windows-style icon display. A moving object in the plane of vision would be identified as an enemy tank, for example; all its relevant features, powers, and vulnerabilities would be available for scrolling through, as well as tactical advice on incapacitating or avoiding it.

Defense strategist Martin Libicki foresees a "mesh"—an information platform that is the convergence of many tens of thousands of sensing devices, ranging from nanotech technology-designed "fire-ants" (tiny, roving bombs) to space satellites, from drone airplanes to seismic detection equipment.[14] All the sensors of this mesh report to central computers that sort and sift the data. In essence, the result would be a type of organization completely new in warfare: a "digitized division" or "information corps," in which each unit and vehicle is part of a web of "seamless communications" with every other. Computers in airplanes would contact those in tanks and infantry platoons and command headquarters, all instantly sharing and coordinating information to deploy an attack or respond to enemy threats.

The final goal of the new visualization technology is a variation on one of the oldest rules of war: If you can, choose the ground to fight upon which is most favorable to the characteristics of your forces. In the battlefield of the future, visualization technology may be most attractive to commanders who will be able to get a "god's-eye view" of the battlefield using sensors, cameras, and probes on the ground, in the air, and in orbit from both manned and unmanned vehicles.[15]

It is precisely in that digital frontier that the United States has a preponderance of research (and funding) to "out-tech" an enemy. Policy analyst Eliot Cohen has written, "If the key to future warfare would be the rapid processing of electronically acquired information, how could a society that was virtually incapable of manufacturing a simple personal computer keep up in the technological race?"[16] His assessment was directed toward the Soviet Union in its waning days, but could equally be made about possible future enemies of American armed forces, including Iraq, Libya, Cuba, and North Korea. General Gordon R. Sullivan, as chief of staff of the U.S. Army, claimed that this was part of the inception of "information-age warfare," in which "we know where you are. We know where we are and we know where you are not. We're coming after you day and night until we win."[17] Sullivan sees the digital battlefield not as "some kind of George Lucas Hollywood fantasy—it is reality. We have seen the future of war and we are dealing with it."[18] Another military analyst claims, "I hesitate to call the soldier of the future 'Starship Trooper.' But we *are* creating that character."[19] By continually racing to make visualization technology more sophisticated, the U.S. military hopes it can wage war cheaply in terms of the lives of American soldiers.[20]

These are the prototypes and the plans for an all-seeing soldier and army. The caveats, however, are considerable, no less so because of the complexity of the technology, used and foreseen, to pierce the fog of war. Besides the difficulties of data overload, there is the alternative problem of using technology as a crutch, for those with either a god's or ant's-eye view of the battlefield. Soldiers trained in such warfare might rely on centralized decision making (and pop-up information) to the detriment of their own responsiveness and initiative. For example, as David Shukman suggests, "members of the armed forces may well become dependent on GPS and begin to abandon their skills in other forms of navigation."[21]

More problematic in the battlefield of a thousand cameras is the temptation for commanders, often at senior level, to mistake para-proximity with understanding. This has led to disaster in the past. In Vietnam, the American military initiated a strategy of "vertical envelopment": troops were deployed by fleets of helicopters, and once on the ground, were directed by commanders cruising above the battlefield.[22] The advantages of the maneuver were obvious: the war leader could, it was hoped, see all of the battle at every point. Helicopters, however, were unfortunately not suited to stealthy approach; constant lift-and-land traffic revealed unit strengths and planned actions; smoke signals and incessant radio chatter between units in the air and on the ground pinpointed American positions.[23] As a result, as one army officer admitted after the war, "The enemy knew everything there was to know about us. They knew when we were going to strike, where we were going to strike, under what conditions. . . ."[24] Even more crucially, the enemy had a better perspective on events than did the American commanders. The distances on the ground, and the density and irregularity of terrain, were not accurately judged by the hovering colonels and generals; despite their proximity to the action, they "lost touch with realities faced by ground troops."[25] While new visualization machines thus can clear some of the fog of war, overuse of the technology can add to war's clouds of confusion and chaos.

## HIDE

The fourth-century Roman Vegetius wrote of the maneuvers before battle: "Of all precautions, the most important is to keep entirely secret which way or by what route the army is to march."[26] Today, the greatest innovations in hiding from those seeking are electrodigital: stealth technology. The F-117A (Stealth) fighter-bomber, with its sloped, almost featureless omni-wing and black, non-reflective radar-dampening and -minimizing surfaces, is one example. Stealth technologies are planned for all components of the battlefield, from tanks to individual soldiers. The military victory of the Coalition forces in the 1991 Gulf War, however, was due less to stealth than to the enemy's inhibited vision. As Martin Libicki points out, against a more technologically sophisticated opponent, "Virtually everything we used on the battlefield would have been vulnerable had it been visible."[27] All advances in seeking out an enemy breed countermeasures, improvements in the art and science of hiding—if, but only if, the enemy has the funds to pay for them or bothers to acquire them. Super technologies of seeking and hiding compete—none will ever definitively and permanently defeat the other. Each side in a future war will try to cloud the other's diorama while clarifying its own. In combat between nations with advanced abilities to seek and hide, war itself, in its extreme, may become pop-up: machines of battle in air and on land remain in hiding, attempting to avoid detection until the instant when they are required for fire engagement.[28] The real arms race will be between stealth and antistealth, between trying to hide and trying to see, using sensors while disrupting the enemy's sensing equipment, gathering data and attempting to confuse the opposition.

The army that develops sophisticated means of seeking out the enemy will encounter four major obstacles to building an accurate diorama:

1. *The enemy will use traditional cover* (that hides and protects, like a bunker) *and concealment* (which may not offer protection, like trees)

Naturally available camouflage and cover have always been employed in hiding from an opponent. The earliest hunters learned to approach game downwind and under cover of trees or behind rocks and bushes. In the Napoleonic era, the British under Wellington pioneered the tactic of "reverse-slope" deployment.

The duke would, as was the case at Waterloo, keep the main body of his force behind cover, typically a hill. This positioning accomplished three goals. First, the French enemy would not see Wellington's full dispositions; second, the British units would avoid suffering direct artillery fire; finally, when the French charged, the covered defenders could quickly rise up to meet them, often with the element of surprise. In the modern era, guerrilla armies have always attempted to use terrain to hide, or to construct fortifications in caves and tunnels; people themselves, the urban and rural masses, provided cover for revolutionary armies in Indochina and elsewhere. Today, advanced countermeasures against remote viewing include artificial fog—metallic confetti that blocks radar.

Yet simple concealment will still impede satellite viewing. During the hostage crisis in Iran in 1979–80, for example, American spy satellites were directed continuously to observe the embassy compound in Tehran. But the data, however clear, were limited. A CIA officer recalled:

> We had a zillion shots of the roof of the embassy and they were each magnified a hundred times. We could tell you about the tiles; we could tell you about the grass and how many cars were parked there. Anything you wanted to know about the external aspects of the embassy we could tell you in infinite detail. We couldn't tell you shit about what was going on inside that building.[29]

Intelligence about the movement and placement of hostages within the embassy had to come from a deep-cover human spy. The satellite photos, however, did provide some enlightenment. Charles Beckwith, one of the commanders of the failed rescue mission, asserted that analysts were able to infer how many outsiders there were in the embassy compound by how many cars were in the parking lot, and could deduce the level of fortification and preparedness in the outside walls and open areas.[30]

New ways of seeing, then, are not all-powerful. In fact, it would be dangerous for us to believe that the visual data that satellites and other sensing techniques provide is either all that exists or all that is relevant to wartime decision making. As in earlier eras, what we cannot see may surprise and kill us.

2. *Sensing technology is dependent on the maintenance of a stable use environment, including access to electrical power*

The survival or failure of information war machines may be fundamentally challenged. What if the "plug" is pulled? One of the hazards for information warriors is operating in "no infrastructure environments," that is, in areas that have no electrical power or phone lines to send a fax, or where weather or terrain blocks sighting of satellite transmission equipment. Barren Third World cities would especially offer sparse technological opportunities. For sensing stations behind the lines—perhaps those processing data sent from aerial, satellite, or land-based sources—the key protection will be to maintain access to a dependable power supply. In the field, often-repeated tourist's advice is the best: bring plenty of extra batteries (and heavy generators).

3. *The enemy will employ technological counterweapons such as stealth or sabotage*

A further vulnerability is inherent in the very nature of the goal of "digital divisions" whose communications networks are fully integrated. The Department of Defense has defined command and control warfare (C2W) as "the military strategy that implements information warfare. . . . On the battlefield it integrates physical destruction. Its objective is to decapitate the enemy's command structure from its body of command forces."[31] As Martin Libicki graphically words it, the decapitation can occur by a "blow to the head or by severing the neck." Integrating a combat soldier into a mesh of information about his unit, the plans of his commanders, and the positions of all relevant friendly combatants can, in theory, be the source of military disaster. Capturing such a soldier's PC would be the equivalent of downloading the battle plans of an army.[32] The response might be to equip front-line computers with a self-destruct or self-erase device. The pantheon of war heroes may soon include men who died saving their laptop.

The next potential obstacle in identifying an enemy is at a greater level of sophistication: sabotage of the hardware or software that allows the new visions of war to be collected and the diorama to be fleshed out in all dimensions. A nuclear blast, for example, will erase magnetic media and fry the circuitry of most silicon-based processing equipment. Phones would go dead, vehicles halt, computers crash. The more technologically advanced a society, the more vulnerable it is to such attacks. Ninety-five percent of U.S. military communications traffic travels over civilian channels. Satellites too are vulnerable to sabotage from the ground, through electronic warfare, direct attack by missiles or energy beams, and indirect incapacitating of their ground control station.[33]

Sabotage of computers building the diorama can also occur more subtly, not by unplugging or destroying the hardware, but by damaging or reprogramming the software.[34] Hackers, whether anarchist loners or employed by terrorists or enemy governments, could severely disrupt an information war machine. During the Gulf War, a group of Dutch computer hackers allegedly offered their services for a million dollars to undermine U.S. military communications. More recently, viruses were found on half the client computers used by American forces in the Bosnia peacekeeping mission. As viruses grow more sophisticated, the precision of an Internet attack may resemble the mass lethality of nuclear war, a "digital Pearl Harbor," the difference being that at Pearl Harbor the Japanese did not find and hit what they were seeking: the American aircraft carriers. Another opportunity for anti-information warfare is the creation of false data: bogus orders, unit positions, or SOS calls. These would clog up a system or add a measure of chaos.

Even more intriguingly, visual disinformation might become part of the propaganda of modern war. It would be difficult to prove, for example, that a digitally created atrocity picture, distributed via the World Wide Web, was a fantasy construction, since by their nature digital images have no original. How would "news" from the front be confused by, for instance, a master Iraqi CGI (computer-generated imagery) technician creating lifelike photos of U.S. Marines bayoneting babies?

4. *We will fail to interpret the data efficaciously and correctly*

The foremost challenge to new sensing technologies has less to do with attempts by opponents to hide than in the nature of the diorama-building process. This is the problem of *data overload*.[35] As George and Meredith Friedman explain in *The Future of War*, "Data is the material gathered by sensors. Interpreting that data, transforming it into useful, real-time information is a more difficult task. . . . The fog of war . . . has been multiplied exponentially."[36] They outline five steps in the conversion process: acquiring the raw data; transmitting it to a computer or a human who transforms it into information; "fusing" the data, collating and gathering information from multiple sources into a single, relevant package; interpreting the information for use in battle; and finally, deploying the information in command and battle arenas.[37] Most of the developments of information war contribute to one or all of these steps. The computer itself enables the machines, their operators, and their interpreters to gain mastery over the most crucial element in the process: time.[38] Therefore, "The problem is no longer gathering sufficient intelligence, it has become screening and distributing what has become an unmanageable amount of data."[39] The ability to control all these data, to convert them into useful information, and to act upon that information decisively, a perennial requisite of warfare, is the challenge. Seeing more does not necessarily mean seeing more clearly. A comprehensive view of the battlefield is fundamentally confusing; more data are not better if minds cannot process them.

The massive flow of visual data will tax the processing capabilities of master computers and the technicians and commanders who employ them. In 1992, Army chief of staff Gordon R. Sullivan noted that the past century of war has depended on the strength of a nation's heavy industry, but modern warfare "is dependent more on the microprocessor than the steel mill."[40] He also argued, "The battlefield has expanded across the dimensions of speed, space and time. Today's fights are likely to be at a faster tempo, to cover more ground, and to be more continuous—day and night in all weather."[41] Bogged down in too much detail, then, commanders may be slow to respond to changing situations, or to avail themselves of random or contingent opportunities. This suggests that a variation of the "hide" imperative may be, in counter-information war, to flood the enemy mesh with information, to clog up his processing capacities. Possibilities range from the traditional dummy tanks to sophisticated false images of nonexistent battles uploaded into enemy computers.

Another problem is the basic characteristic of all human beings to seek out "feedback that fits," to scan through the data we view in the world and seize upon those bits that support our prejudices.[42] Complementary to our focusing on that which confirms our suspicions, human beings also tend to ignore what contradicts them. A historian of aerial photography notes that "Probably the greatest disappointment in the entire photo-reconnaissance history of the war in Europe was the inability to predict the final death surge of the German army in the Ardennes. Later study, however, showed that the camera had obtained the evidence, but faulty photo-intelligence had not pieced the entire picture together."[43] Thus, the cornucopia of data provided by modern visual-sensing technology may equally be a Pandora's box.[44] Even when the lessons of war seem simple and clear, the prejudices of the analysts can redirect the data to fulfill varying interpretations. These temptations are compounded as the complexity and comprehensiveness of data increases. In the cycle of trying to find more innovative and technologically superior ways both to seek out an enemy and to hide from him, it is worth recalling that even satellites and computers will not help a fool see his own folly.

## VIRTUAL WARRIORS

At the start of the Third (and final) Punic War (149–146 B.C.E.) between Republican Rome and its great enemy, the North African city-state of Carthage, the Romans demanded that the Carthaginians turn over all weapons to guarantee peace. Feeling both hopeful and terrified, the cowed citizens delivered some 200,000 spears, swords, shields, and panoplies of armor. The concession won them nothing, for the Romans continued the war. In response, as described by the historian Appian:

> All the sacred places [in Carthage], the temples, and every other wide and open space, were turned into workshops, where men and women worked together day and night, on a fixed schedule, without pause, taking their food by turns. Each day they made 100 shields, 300 swords, 1,000 missiles for catapults, 500 darts and spears, and as many catapults as they could. For strings to bend them the women cut off their hair for want of other fibers.[45]

The effort only postponed the holocaust. After hard fighting and a difficult siege, the Roman legions conquered the city, and under orders of the Senate, tore

down its walls and buildings, mixing salt into its earth so that no one would
dare settle Carthage again.

Such a feat of national will, however stirring or foolish, would be inconceivable in today's era of technowar. Modern weapons cannot be thrown together at the last minute and handcrafted from household odds and ends. Nor can volunteerism pay the bills of decades of cumulative research and development, as well as technical training. Any nation making the pretension to fight a large-scale modern war must invest in the long term. Hence the adoption of the doctrine of Land Warrior, Stealth, and the Digital Division by the U.S. armed forces. Advanced technologies of hunt, sense, kill, and hide are sustainable only by First World economies.[46] In addition, elite, high-tech armies do not require huge pools of manpower; this saves money in the short term in salaries and benefits, and in the long term in veterans' pensions and health care. Other fiscal savings may result from reduction in the amounts and scale of weapons procurement. The age of mass warfare in the traditional sense will give way to the pinpoint, pop-up, precision-guided, customized army.

A Digital Division is also a necessity, according to military planners, because of new budgetary and geopolitical realities. Simply put, the army is scaling back; it is getting smaller, and funds for the most basic requirements of training and fuel are decreasing. The U.S. Army's "active component" shrank by 40 percent from the mid-1980s to the mid-1990s.[47] During the Gulf War, the United States committed seventeen of its twenty-one armored brigades to the conflict; since the war, five of these have stood down or demobilized. The nation, in contradiction to thirty years of previous doctrine, no longer seems capable of fighting two major conflicts simultaneously.[48] It is precisely because of these trends that military planners are finding new vision technologies most attractive. On the battlefield, these advances make the few and the well trained much more valuable and lethal than the mass force.

Hence the utility of the most innovative aspect of vision technology, virtual simulations. The American military is like a formerly sprawling giant corporation, downsizing and investing its future in modernization. That virtual war gaming will be useful, and indeed will to some extent replace live-fire training, is now taken for granted in the military. New recruits learning to operate "armored computers" train in battle simulators, which are essentially rooms fitted out like the individual compartment that one of the four crew members will inhabit in a real tank.[49] The men simultaneously engage in war games, seeing on video screens enemy tanks, troops, and planes, as well as friendly troops and vehicles. Movement and firing is fully coordinated with the images on the screen; digitally exploding enemy tanks blast apart and flames appear.

This is the essence of the future of the vision of war: convergence between imagery and reality, what planners in the Pentagon intend for the military beyond the millennium. Evidence for this convergence comes from the simulation with which civilians—especially the young—are most familiar. The modern video or computer game is now at an extremely advanced level of realism. Among the most developed of the genre is the air war simulator, one gaming example of which is *if22*, created by Interactive Magic, Inc. [**Fig. 41**] The screen view consists of a heads-up display, in which a cockpit instrument panel gives the player vital readings such as fuel, altitude, distance to target, radar information, weapons capacity, and expenditures. The main part of the screen is devoted to the world beyond the glass of the cockpit. From both sides and from the front, the virtual pilot can gaze upon 250,000 square miles of photo-realistic terrain. Different CD modules allow the player to be part of a peacekeeping force in a Bosnian war in 2004, fighting to defend Ukraine against a Russian attack in 2003, or reprising missions on a Persian Gulf campaign.

The game's realism is enhanced by various methods. For example, it can

41. Screen shot of *if22* video game. View from airplane cockpit.
*Image: Interactive Magic, Inc.*

proceed at real time, the plane flying at its normal relative speed to the Earth. However, the player may simply press the tab button to accelerate the progression of time. No two missions, even within the same campaign, are identical. New enemies appear in different places, and the orders given to the player by his or her central ground station change with each maneuver. The war itself can be affected over the course of a campaign by the success or failure of individual missions. The game features a 3D acceleration card, allowing the player to look up or to the side and never see a blank area. *if22* is also highly maneuverable. Real-time speed allows the "pilot" to dive, spiral, and bank without encountering the jerky movement of older video games. The soundtrack enhances the simulation. The engines thunder, the cabin shakes, explosions burst; audio traffic from other planes and headquarters barks continuously. *if22* can also be played through modems with others in "an on-line community of games with gamers ready for action." Another recent step toward realism in such games is the introduction of sensory joysticks—such as the Sidewinder Force Feedback Pro from Microsoft—that vibrate when the plane dives on a strafing run or experiences heavy G-forces, during the shake and shimmer of dogfighting, and when firing off missiles.

Games like *if22* are essentially slightly simpler versions of the flight simulators utilized by military pilots in training. Military personnel are adapting game systems from private industry, but the trend is developing in both directions: games designed for the military will also be marketed to the public, allowing research and development costs to be "borne by trigger-happy teenagers rather than taxpayers."[50] An example is MARINE DOOM. *Doom* is the most popular of the combat games. Players have a first-person view of various battle arenas—fields, caves, or buildings—where they fight with monsters or enemy soldiers, or in the case of one of the most recent versions, demons in hell. The U.S. Marine Corps uses its version as part of its Modeling and Simulation Program, in its Training and Education Division. MARINE DOOM can be played by up to four people and it simulates, as advertised, "The fog of war, friendly fire, principal direction of fire, importance of communication and immediate action."

New commercial devices being developed will provide an increasingly realistic experience to home games as well. For example, electrical responses would give special gloves a tactile feel, also creating sensations of boundaries, walls, and surfaces in cyberspace. A "response" chair will encase the player in the blast and shake of the game's special effects. A data glove would eventually merge into a data suit. Also, larger-capacity storage technologies like digital video disk (DVD) and more efficient compression algorithms for compact disks allow photorealistic pictures to be used in games. The photos will become more detailed; the speed with which the game processes them will increase. Improvements in holographic and computer-generated imagery (CGI) technology will no doubt continue. Computer games of the decades to come may be indistinguishable from, for instance, an interactive film in which the player is a seamless cast member of a Roman legion, German Panzer crew, or Land Warrior squad. Digitally generated, moving, interactive characters from history or film and television may "play" in the simulation along with the at-home gamer or his or her avatar. The dream of gamers and of military planners will merge.

At the same time, real weapons of war look increasingly like their blocky and angular cyber images. This is for reasons of stealth. The more free of projections—such as guns or antennae—a vehicle is, the better it can avoid being detected by radar and other electronic sensing devices. An example is the experimental vessel *Sea Shadow*, a SWATH (small waterplane area twin-hull) design that employs a water-propulsion jet.[51] The 560-ton, 164-feet-long, all-black *Sea Shadow* is streamlined both above and below the water. The angle of the hull is specially designed to avoid significant registering on enemy radar. The ship is a weapons carrier and platform; its defensive and offensive weapons would, like those on the future battlefield, pop up when needed. Other nations are also experimenting with the possibility of a stealth navy. *Sea Shadow* and its cousins are an initial foray into a future where all vehicles are designed with stealth in mind; they literally look like a low-resolution computer image of themselves.

These are the new conceptions and possible future of virtual war and its imagery. "Virtual reality's time has come," writes retired naval officer and policy analyst James Hazlett. "A virtual picture (supported by holographic displays and large color screens) of the battle space may now be more accurate and usable than the real one."[52] Virtual war, however—the likely form of future combat—is presented with several challenges to being fully realistic, and thus an effective training instrument.

*1. Will virtual war allow the testing and training of unit cohesion—the bonding of men under fire?*

The technology of visualization may make the *sensory-extended* soldier, the Land Warrior on foot, wired to a GPS, monitoring through a palm-top computer or a helmet visor visual display, psychologically return to the ranks of the hoplites. In his visor he will see the other men of the platoon, no matter how distant they may be from him physically. He will also view the flow of orders from commanders, and receive information about upcoming support or warnings of danger. These may be palliatives, para-proxemic reminders that he is not alone. He may be part of a virtual community of a real war, in the same way that computer users virtually interact in bulletin board services and chat rooms or through Web-connected video conferencing. The chatter, and above all the visions of friendly faces, may assist in keeping the soldier from freezing up in shock or despair. This virtually provided comfort, however, may dissipate when, through the same sensing technology, the soldier "sees" friendly faces ripped by machine-gun fire, and comforting icons blip off the computer screen. The shock of seeing buddies in the virtual platoon being killed may be as great as that experienced in person.

Alternatively, and this may depend not only on training but on the psychology of the individual, the lack of physical contact in the flood of digital information, visual and verbal, may undermine morale. A soldier will undergo a form of sensory deprivation of his greatest support—physical contact with his fellows— and conversely receive sensory overload of information that seems extraneous to the immediate concern of survival. This is the primary question for war managers in the future. Just as in World War II and Korea where it proved difficult to identify the true warriors—those who would take up the duties of their many stunned fellows and fight the battle in close combat—it may be equally difficult to identify the super virtual warriors of the future. It is clear, however, from the style of Pentagon recruiting, that the modern generation, raised on computers and video games, perhaps inured to the dangers of sensory overload and quite accustomed to the deprivation of human contact when immersed in a virtual reality, is well poised to feel comfortable in virtual wars.

2. *How well will virtual war simulate the conditions and uncertainties of the real battlefield?*

The question is, how real will be the reality of the future vision of war? It is likely that the *Star Trek* representation of a holodeck, where the image also has substance and actuality, will be forever physically impossible. However, technological devices can give the *sensation* of objects being real, present, and live. For example, a sensory suit might stimulate the wearer's nerve endings to approximate a cold wind on a snowy battlefield, the pain of a bullet to an arm, the recoil of a pistol. Yet, as of now, such constants of war as mud, fear, bad food, and the fatigue of a hundred days in the field are difficult to insert into a simulation, at least as we know it today. In addition, Land Warriors, tank (armored computer) operators, monitors of roaming sensors and missiles, and pilots of stealth planes will all face battles of much greater complexity than ever before in human history. Typically, sensors react to only one or two signals in the environment; for example, infrared sensors respond to heat and movement. They can be "fooled" by brush fires and even waved torches. This is also why, in most science fiction films, CGI battles tend to occur against matte or flat backgrounds. The skirmishes with giant alien insects in *Starship Troopers* take place on a completely barren planet. The incorporation of extensive scenery, of plant life, would be too complex and too costly for present-day CGI technology. The human brain and its visual system is still the best way of sorting through the complexity, context, and texture of real life. It follows that hiding strategy and tactics will try to maximize the clutter to confuse enemy sensing.

Can virtual simulations create such a degree of clutter? To do so would be to anticipate what exactly those new data will look like, when they will appear, and the extent to which they pose a threat. Yet, in the seek and stealth future war, deception and trickery will be mainstays of the dance of maneuver and combat. Innovations—unanticipated events—are precisely those that are most difficult to incorporate into a simulation, since by definition computers are programmed to do what programmers expect. Again, the answer to this problem is not definitive. Improved software will program error, irrationality, and unforeseen circumstances into war games; computer logic may be altered to be as fuzzy as that of the battlefield. In reaction, counterprogrammers will try to confuse and overload the enemy's data processors. The paradox, then, is that computers themselves, or soldiers playing the enemy side in games, can probably realistically mimic the chances, complexities, and contingencies of war; but only if they are allowed to cheat, that is, break the rules of the game.

3. *Will soldiers be able to train as if virtual war was real, and not "just a game"?*
The essence of the computer game is that the player is important; his or her abilities will save the princess, destroy the legions of evil, or sink the enemy fleet. The Greek term "hero" referred to such a being, like Achilles or Hercules, who was somewhere between man and god. His emotions, ideas, and actions were beyond the conception or the emulation of ordinary men. So, will the Land Warrior be an Achilles or just a cog in a machine? Almost all video games allow the user to "save" the campaign in progress and start over at another time. Death has little impact, because resurrection is a button click away. Could training in virtual war simulations, no matter how realistic in the other elements of war—including noise, jolting movement, and variations in temperature—fail to teach nascent warriors to fear death? The entire thrust of the digitized division, wielding precision-guided munitions, is to turn the ordinary soldier into a lethal technician, seeing with little chance of being seen, killing with little danger of being killed. As a result, will those raised and trained in virtual war be too gung-ho, too eagerly heroic, and thus a danger to themselves and to the units of which they are a component? Will our young men and women, fresh from triumphs at *if22* and *Doom*, fear no evil?

## INREALITY AND DISENGAGEMENT

The question of whether virtual wars can better prepare soldiers for real battles may not be fully answerable for another generation. But what can be said is this: it would be easy for a technocrat-dominated army to forego the rigors, expenses, and dangers of live-fire for virtual-fire exercises. Past examples show, however, that this would be a mistake, especially in the training of elite units. Although computer gamers may suffer from eyestrain or inflamed carpal tunnels, the hazards of actual battle—trench foot, blisters, hunger, and the tedium of days of waiting—are as difficult to program into any computer simulation as they are to recreate in any vision of war. This is precisely because of the instantaneousness of the modern war-viewing experience. The essential attribute of the video computer game is its speed. No video game, no war film, recreates the lingering aspects of war. Even real-time missions, such those in *if22*, are never completed without some action occurring. There has never been, nor will there ever be, a war movie that consists of two hours of potato peeling; nor conceivably could there be a video game in which this is the sole objective.

That the propagators of war and those who witness it in living rooms (on a monitor that receives transmissions via phonelines, cables, broadcasts, or satellite signals) will seek out kinetic images is almost certain; it is, in fact, a product of an innate biological imperative. The best argument to be made for transforming the way warriors fight and the way war is seen is that such an integration co-incides with the generation of soldiers born in the last twenty years (what the U.S. Army prophetically and hopefully calls the "Net" generation). One of the radical new developments in the vision of war is that policy formulators—states-men and generals—are largely making decisions about war and assessing how the public views war by watching television news. The eagerness to absorb data through multimedia sources is not simply one of cultural affection. Children raised viewing kinetic and colorful imagery do not appreciate it only for aesthetic reasons; rather, their brains have, through the development process, come to prefer data presented in these forms. In the baby boom generation we had the first crop of viewers who were raised on comic books and television. In the twenty-year-olds of today, we have the first generation raised on MTV, video games, and the superkinetic imagery of the contemporary action film. The gen-eration born now, and coming of age in the decade of the next century—the "Netters" or millennial generation—will be even more eager for the fast pace of a digitized environment.

It is a circular process of conditioning. The human brain is wired to retrieve and deploy the data that it is familiar with during its physical and mental mat-uration. Modern children and teenagers are seekers of "inreality"—intensified, speeded-up reality.[53] They want kinetic, rapid movement in their images; more vital, they need such images and delivery style to remain interested in the data presented. This makes the modern generation most receptive to the visions of future war that the age of cyber communications will provide. Unlike past gen-erations, imprinted with deliberate learning methods inculcated by long lectures and reading, Gen Xers and Netters prefer the staccato sound, visbytes, and fast scan and shift.[54] Traditional forms of data acquisition like reading a book do not provide the ceaseless variable stimulations of sight and sound demanded by those raised on TV and computer games. Or, to paraphrase a famous line from *Rambo*, "what you [the older person] call a headache, they call home."

This represents a revolution in human cognition, a rewiring of the brain, perhaps the first since the invention of writing, to complement and even replace oral communication. Virtual war thus will probably become an integrated part of warfare not because human beings at age eighteen are so trained, but because in the modern world the training for virtual war actually begins almost at birth. Of course, there will always be paintings and sculptures (and still photographs) of war; but the future of the vision of war will in one sense bring ordinary people, the home-front audience, closer to the battle, faster, more vividly than ever before. The visions will no longer amaze; instead, it will be an ordinary occurrence to look through a warhead as it impacts, a bomb as it lands, a bullet as it strikes. We will see through the pilot's goggles and the video array helmet of a Land Warrior. The video game is the prototype of future war visions.

This does not mean that real-life explosions will not occur, villages will not be burned, and men will not die when hit with a self-guided bullet rather than a dumb one. It does portend that increasingly, at least in virtual war, those who fire the bullets, who cause the deaths, will be disengaged from the shock of a real combat situation. Their most stressful encounter will be with the many flickering lights, words, and shapes on their video screen. The American pacifist James Douglass argues that the more war becomes technologically sophisticated in this way, the lesser will be its degree of humanity: "In modern war, however, it is by no means certain that the warrior will ever experience that moment of truth when war reveals its killing nature through a sudden insight into the enemy's humanity. . . . [W]hat is becoming more and more common with the perfection of military technology, is the warrior's failure to have any confrontation whatsoever with the enemy."[55] Or, to recall the fatal moment in the bomb crater in *All Quiet on the Western Front*, no *Landser* will meet and kill a *poilu* and realize that the blood on his hands is that of a real human being. That this makes it all the easier to press the button that destroys a tank or a city is both the brightest hope for the future warrior and the worst nightmare of the species.

On the other hand, total digitalization may make war less hellish for all involved. Information technology, says Admiral William Owens, vice chairman of the Joint Chiefs of Staff, "is America's gift to warfare." Lieutenant General Jay Garner, head of the army's Space and Strategic Defense Command, claims, "One day national leaders will fight out virtual wars before they decide to go to war at all."[56] Virtual war fighting would be conventional, in bits and blips, big and small wars in air, land, sea, and space. Such exercises may prevent war; battles may be fought wholly in cyberspace, and the victors and vanquished agree to abide by terms of treaties as if the skirmishes and casualties had been real. Perhaps this is the glowing digital screen at the end of the long tunnel of the history of human organized conflict. Will virtual war replace war? Is this the ultimate evolution of the vision of war: to supersede, make obsolete, the real thing?

Both prophecies of the results of virtual warring strain the bounds of reason and the weight of history. Human beings have shown themselves quite able to kill each other by the trenchful even though they confront the enemy face to face. Nor is it the case that the sense of disengagement comes only from the sterility of the images. Many modern attack or combat video games are hardly immaculate visions of violence. In games like *Doom*, enemy creatures explode, heads burst open, internal organs ooze out, blood splatters with each strike. Some of these games even have mirror boxes that show one's own body in deteriorating health after taking hits. Video games thus show some realities of war much more graphically than many films or news broadcasts or even live-fire training exercises. Neither do hard-core gamers reject blood and body counts; they are advertised features of many combat games. A recent ad for a tactile joystick to be used with first-person shoot-'em-ups reminds the consumer that "Psychologists say it's good to feel something when you kill." Indeed, " 'gorier is better' . . . you need blood and guts to sell games," notes designer Sid Meier.[57]

Moreover, using low-tech weapons and reckless guile, future enemies are unlikely, to borrow H. G. Wells's insight, to be "too stupid to do anything more than play their [our] game." Nations not as technologically advanced in warfare, from Somali militias to Serb insurgents to Saddam Hussein–style megalomaniacs, would likely feel less political restraint in sacrificing tens of thousands of their countrymen's lives to demoralize American opinion by killing a few hundred of our own virtually trained and lavishly equipped soldiers. As well, any nation that might agree to abide by the results of a virtual war would presumably prefer to find solutions to conflicts through diplomacy. Even if wars are fought on the Web, there is no guarantee that the losers will not try again on real fields of battle. It is unlikely that virtual war will make war itself—including real killing and seizing of territory—obsolete or unthinkable. Despite what computer projections might warn, leaders will still be tempted to throw young men and women into the cauldron of battle.

What we cannot know is how the new methods of obtaining images will affect audience reaction. Will it be especially disheartening or enraging for television or Web viewers to look through the helmet camera of one of "its boys" as a Fifth World gunman, grinning into the lens like an antagonist from some video game, fires his low-technology rifle into the soldier's face? As the $20,000 camera and the priceless life of one American are extinguished and the screen turns to static, what will be our response? At that moment will the demand for the continual flow of data of inreality stop, if only for an instant? Will this method of visualizing war accomplish something that no vision of war has truly done before: will we, the distant spectator, die a little with the warrior? And will "Game Over" really mean something for military strategy, national policy, public opinion, and the judgment of history?

In creating the myth that modern war is quick and precise, with few casualties, future war commanders also feed prejudices about the vision of war. That many wars to come will be quick and precise may confirm the myth; but there is no guarantee that new weapons, new strategies, new enemies might not upset the electro-optical cyber routine. Again, superweapons of any kind, including those of seek and stealth, will always beget superweapons of counterprogramming and attack; these may frustrate optimistic predictions as much as new weapons and tactics did in the past.

So, how will the desire for instant gratification in battle affect the warriors and their audience? It is doubtful that the post-Vietnam American public could ever endure a stalemated war lasting three, four, or five years again, unless it was perceived to be a war of national survival or liberation. (Of course, such prophecies have been made often before.) A public bombarded by video game–like imagery may, ironically, tire much earlier than one whose only exposure to war was the delayed news photograph or the art exhibition. Virtual war thus may not only reflect what modern brains are tuned for, but also our expectations of what war *should be like*. The vision of war may not replace war; but it may determine how it is fought, for how long, with what cost in lives and material, and, more important, how it is presented to the home audience for their sanction.

These questions will not be answered before another generation grows to maturity; and, with the fractionalization of audiences brought about by cable and satellite television, the Internet, and the myriad channel and content choices that the modern middle-class viewer is offered, no one future vision of war will be dominant. But that, perhaps, is a hint of things to come. In the era of broadcast network monopoly (during Vietnam), or when the technology of new warfare was truly new (during the Persian Gulf War), war had little competition or could well compete with other sources of entertainment. But now, and in the future, the situation may be different. In early 1999, after another series of Cruise missile attacks on Iraq, the comedian Jon Stewart wryly noted, "Hey, isn't that a rerun, bombing Baghdad? Been there, done that!" And, in pure marketing terms, ratings for the new military action were quite low.

Whatever the evolution of the vision of war, it will now find itself hustling for attention on 500-channel bandwidths and millions of Web sites. We have the potential to see more of the world's conflicts faster than ever before, yet we may grow weary of the repetitiveness of the narrative and the familiarity of the special effects. If future wars are interchangeable with video or interactive online games or TV programs or even living-room-based holo-simulations, then their popularity will be threatened by viewer fatigue and fickleness as much as any other entertainment product.

And how routine that future will be! As this book was going to press, a new vision of war pioneered in Vietnam and tested in the Persian Gulf War became the industrial standard in Operation Allied Force in Yugoslavia. Images and narration that would have seemed impossible (and treasonous) a generation ago are now the norm: Enemy ministers of state appear live on television talk shows to answer call-ins; American commanders give in-studio interviews in which they explain and justify hour-by-hour tactical decisions; reporters stand outside air bases observing that: "The planes came back today with all their bombs still under the wings—obviously not a successful mission"; 'round the clock commentary by the punditocracy makes twenty-four hours of war *seem* like a year's campaign: "Three days into the air war and victory is still not in sight." This is typical saturation fare on most news channels; the future does not seem shocking when it's a rerun. The adaptable human being is capable of altering the vision of war to fit any new technology and new mindset of war. Ending war itself, however, may be permanently beyond our grasp.

# NOTES

## INTRODUCTION

1. Wood, 1997: 57. See also Cohen, 1997.
2. I use a standardized dating system. "B.C.E." refers to dates before common era, or before the traditional date of the birth of Jesus of Galilee. This is a slightly unwieldy but typical concession to secularism employed by historians and archeologists. Any dates after this era are usually noted by number, e.g., 452 will mean A.D. 452 and "first century" will refer to the first hundred years of the common era. "Before present" refers to the span before our time, c. 2000.
3. Plutarch notes that in a later battle Alexander could make out Darius "from a distance over the foremost ranks, conspicuous in the midst of his life-guard, a tall and fine-looking man, drawn in a lofty chariot." It was a case of a commander making himself central and noticeable with disastrous results. Plutarch, 1864: 826.
4. Arrian, 1971: 120.
5. Glezer, 1995: vii.
6. Gucwa & Ehmann, 1985.
7. Gilliard, 1969. See also Sebeok, 1981.
8. This statement is controversial. Until recently, many anthropologists—and some philosophers—assumed that visual representation is as conventional a form of representation as any other, such as words (see Segall, Campbell, & Herskovits, 1966). The most extreme Culturalist view, held by the philosopher Nelson Goodman (1976), asserts that the term "convention" is itself not useful, because it falsely implies that some forms of representation are more or less iconic than others. Other researchers—so-called Neo-realists—argue that many aspects of visual imagery are perceived precognitively and thus constitute a perceptual system very different from that of symbolic language. First, as visual researcher Paul Messaris (1994) argues, "recognition of objects in pictures seems unproblematic under a broad range of circumstances. Furthermore, many pictorial conventions that might at first blush seem quite 'unrealistic' appear in fact to be interpretable on the basis of any viewer's real-world visual skills" (13–14). For example, naive

viewers from cultures that have no tradition of creating, employing, or encountering visual images are able to recognize the contents of line drawings (Brimble, 1963; Guma, 1982); black and white photographs (Cook, 1981; Cook, Fussell, & Haaland, 1978); and even the negative of a color photograph (Collier & Collier, 1986). Basically, once naive viewers "got it," they were able to read photographs as accurately as a sophisticated viewer, and in a much shorter time than would be required to learn a new language. Research with young children, both Western and African, also supports the Neo-realist hypothesis (Barrera & Maurer, 1981; Dirks & Gibson, 1977; Maurer, 1985; Liddicoat & Koza, 1963). In addition, in a famous experiment, two psychologists raised their son to the age of three without exposing him to any kind of constructed visual images (Hochberg & Brooks, 1962). Nevertheless, when tested, the child had no difficulty seeing form and shape in human-made visual images or in partly recognizing objects within them. It is clear, then, that the skills which viewers need in order to understand many pictorial media develop quickly and do not appear to differ from those learned by previous experience in the act of seeing. In sum, recognition of familiar objects in realistic pictures is an "unlearned ability," that is, a precognitive skill. We can only conclude that there is a distinction between seeing and interpreting what we see.

9. Messaris, 1992. See also Kraft, 1987; Meyers-Levy & Peracchio, 1992; Zettl, 1990.
10. Arrian, 1971: 123.
11. Brecht, quoted in Benjamin, 1980: 213.
12. Gombrich, 1969[1960]: 67–68.
13. Perlmutter, 1992; 1997c.
14. Murrow & Friendly, 1955: 1.
15. The coffee table compendium is the dominant mode of showing war images in book form. A study of war imagery could be an encyclopedia, organized by subjects (pictures of victory in battle), cultures (the war imagery of India), or events (portrayals of Gettysburg in painting, sculpture, film, and television). Another option is to concentrate on a single famous image—e.g., *Guernica*, the Alexander Mosaic, or the U.S. Marines raising the flag at Iwo Jima. See Perlmutter, 1998.
16. Marshall, 1947: 27.
17. Arendt, 1979: 305, f1.
18. The earnestness of the portrayal of war in the film was undermined by the exigencies of Hollywood showmanship. In one scene, members of the squad sent to find Private Ryan sort through dog tags of GIs killed during the D-Day invasion. Tension is released in humor, and the soldiers callously joke about the names of the dead until they realize they are being watched accusingly by the comrades of the men killed. It is an effective moment; but how deeply it influenced the filmmakers is unclear. Among the "wrap" gifts given by the DreamWorks studio to the cast and crew of the film were sets of custom-made silver dog tags ensconced in tiny Tiffany blue boxes.
19. Gould, 1994: 85.

# 1: ORIGINS

1. "War is the father and king of all, and some he shows as Gods, others as men; some he makes slaves and others free" (fr. 53). The fragment, attributed by several ancient writers to Heraclitus of Ephesus, has been variously translated and interpreted; Kirk (1970) suggests "War controls all human destiny" for the first clause.
2. De Bloch, 1972: lxv.
3. Sorokin, 1937: 351–52.
4. Sluka, 1992: 19.
5. Wilson, 1975.
6. Goodall, 1986, 1990. See also Nishida, et al., 1985.
7. Dart, 1957; Roper, 1969. The problem with such data is that the wounds suffered by the dead are not connected to weapons—for example, embedded arrow points—found *in situ*. Rather, homicide as the cause of a wound was inferred by the kind of perforation. Also, natural traumas, such as animal bites or accidents, can be confused with wounding by primitive weapons. For discussion of this subject in the Australopithicines, see Brain, 1981. For the question about Neanderthals, see Trinkaus, 1993; Vencl, 1991.
8. Kunter, 1981.
9. Stiner, 1993: 70.
10. See reviews in Bahn, 1991, 1994.
11. Leroi-Gourhan, 1971; Roper, 1969. There are many problems in interpreting the art of the Stone Age. First and foremost is that we have no reference point. The artists and their culture are long dead. While it is tempting to compare modern hunter-gatherer societies and their ideas and behaviors, this is only of limited value because the peoples of the Stone Age were not influenced by civilization. Most modern hunter-gatherers are fringe dwellers, driven into the barren lands they occupy—deep jungle, desert, tundra—by agriculturists. There is no place on earth, with the exception of the modern zoo, which recreates exactly the lush bioenvironment of the Upper Paleolithic in the Franco-Cantabrian region. Another problem is one of representation: any new finds skew the sample. For example, one of the most recently found caves, named Chauvet after its discoverer, displays many pictures of large carnivores like lions formerly under-represented in pictures (Chauvet, Deschamps, & Hillaire, 1996). Much may lie buried in the sea, in what used to be the outward coast of the Franco-Cantabria. Just recently (Clottes & Courtin, 1996) a cave was found half submerged, with many drawings and stenciled outlines (including those of humans hands). So what we may think is a plan or pattern may be an accident of discovery. Also, and this almost effectively cripples our ability to make any conclusions about Stone Age art, it is unclear what is the position of cave art in the prehistoric world. The cave paintings have survived because, after the age of their artists passed, they were forgotten and isolated; they were thus the most likely art to

survive. This does not mean that they were quantitatively the most prevalent form of art or even of painting, nor does it mean that they were the most important to the artists or the most revealing of their thought and culture. For example, entire outdoor galleries of animal paintings have been found on rock outcroppings in Portugal; it may very well be that cave painting was a relatively minor subgenre in the prehistoric corpus.

Most of the art existed outdoors, from where it has of course disappeared. For these reasons as well as others, conclusions about the peoples of the time and the reasons they created their imagery must always be speculative. Finally, it is unclear if the art of the Upper Paleolithic was actually a complete revolution in human history. There is evidence of artistic activity before anatomically modern humans arose, but a simple distinction is one of degree or extent. Before 40,000 years ago, artistic activity was rare and difficult to identify. Afterwards, it became widespread, frequent, and obviously an important part of human culture.

12. It is difficult to appreciate cave art that is converted into other media. The twists and crags of the rocks contribute to the shape, dimensionality, and vitality of the figures. The humped chest of the bison or the swollen belly of the horse is accentuated by the choice of a protuberance of stone on a cave wall. At the Altamira cave in Spain, for example, the outward curve of the wall ceiling mimics the plump haunch of a painted bison. Some researchers even find patterns in the use of convex and concave surfaces; these cannot be replicated in photography. Rock images, as one writer reminds us, were "never intended to be seen through a camera" (Godden, 1982: 27). Different types of stone, with various grains and colorings, may alter the contour, texture, and tone of the pictures (Maggs, 1979: 9). Gustaf Hallström (1960), who examined the Ice Age imagery of northern Sweden, argued that every attempt to correctly transfer a rock painting into other media loses some of its original communicative intent. Indeed, it is common for one researcher to accuse previous scholars of too imaginatively sketching or outlining the art to support a favored view of its contents.

13. Breuil, 1952: 10.

14. Binford, 1972: 119.

15. White, 1986.

16. Pfeiffer, 1982; cf. Halverson, 1992.

17. Bahn, 1994: 122.

18. Bahn, 1983; Clark & Straus, 1983; Mellars, 1985; White, 1982.

19. Sahlins, 1972.

20. Delpech, 1983.

21. See literature reviewed briefly in Cordain, Miller, & Mann, 1999; Cassidy, 1980; Cohen, 1987.

22. Bachechi, Fabbri, & Mallegni, 1997.

23. Divale & Harris, 1976: 521; Vencl, 1991.

24. Dastugue & de Lumley, 1976.

25. Bachechi, Fabbri, & Mallegni, 1997.

26. See also Svoboda & Vlcek, 1991; Wendorf & Schild, 1986; Wendorf, 1968.

27. Vencl, 1991.

28. Ferrill, 1985: 17.

29. See Chapter 5 for discussion of why the Spartans, one of history's most milita- ristic societies, had an impoverished visual culture on all subjects, including war.

30. Even when we are confronted with an image of "peace"—for example, a tranquil scene of farmers harvesting their rice crop—this may actually display the *results* of war. A case in point is much of the art of the Yüan Dynasty (1260–1368) of China. The emperors of this line were of Mongol stock, invaders who swarmed in from the barren northern plains to wipe out the native Chinese Sung Empire. The conquest was one of the bloodiest in history. As many as a hundred million Chinese were killed. Once in power, however, the newcomers quickly tried to take on the mantle of the conquered, setting up a court in imitation of previous emperors and gathering to it native Chinese Mandarin bureaucrats and scholars. Also, to pass themselves off as the heirs of Chinese civilization, they adopted the forms, arts, and rituals of the previous dynasties (Weidner, 1982, 1989; Lee & Ho, 1968).

    A school of painting of the time was the *keng-chih t'u*, or pictures of ploughing and weaving, which one Yüan emperor ordered copied by the thousands and distributed "to persuade the Chinese that *they* [the Mongols] were the rightful rulers of China, supportive of agriculture and other traditional Chinese occu- pations" (Cahill 1988: 20). The Mongols employed rustic subjects and traditional styles of art—deliberately archaic—to make themselves seem part of a great continuum where they were inheritors, not interlopers. Such images did show some semblance of reality; under the Mongols, China was at peace, the peace of the victorious enemy. The minds of the observers—the scholar-bureaucrats whom the Mongols were trying to entice to rejoin the state in their service— would fill in appropriate details. Whatever the origin of the new rulers, peace was preferable to renewed war. In one sense, then, the image of peace was honest: obedience to Mongol rule brought normalcy. In another sense, it was a sinister conceit; the "peace" was built on near genocidal war.

31. Leroi-Gourhan, 1967. See also Rice & Paterson, 1985, 1986.

32. Altuna & Apellaniz, 1978: 106–07. Associations between bone records and cave paintings are difficult to assess, however, because the dates ascribed to the art are continually being revised.

33. Delluc & Delluc, 1981, 1984.

34. Delporte, 1984: 132.

35. Delpech, 1983: 226–27.

36. Rice & Paterson 1985, 1986.

37. Rice & Paterson, 1986: 658.

38. Ibid.: 665.

39. The basic divisions are: monsters (0.4%), birds (0.2%), and fish (0.3%). Leroi- Gourhan, 1982: 49.

40. Hawkes, Hill, & O'Connell, 1982; Redford & Robinson, 1987.
41. The dependence of the Upper Paleolithic economy on salmon versus reindeer is hotly debated. Compare Jochim (1983) to Hayden, Chisholm, & Schwarcz (1987).
42. Ucko & Rosenfeld, 1967; Guthrie, 1984.
43. Leason, 1939; Ucko & Rosenfeld, 1967: 185–86; Bahn, 1997.
44. Hadingham, 1980.
45. Orwell, 1954: 187–88. Cf. Freeman, 1981.
46. Cf. Leroi-Gourhan, 1982, fig. 42.
47. Survival techniques of the circumpolar hunters of the north are detailed in Binford, 1978; Grønnow, 1986.
48. *Food & Nutrition News*, 1998: 1.
49. Smith, 1992: 14.
50. Yesner, 1980: 95. On average, humans eat more meat than any other primate (Hayden, 1981b: 394). Our rates of meat consumption fall between those of carnivores like big cats and nonhuman primates (Hill, 1982: 527–28).
51. Speth, 1983.
52. Speth & Spielmann, 1983.
53. Mowat, 1975[1951].
54. Hawkes, 1993; Kent, 1993. The same claim is made about foragers (Peterson, 1993).
55. Hill & Kaplan, 1988; Kaplan & Hill, 1985a, 1985b.
56. For example, the Kung (San) of South Africa. See Shostak, 1983.
57. Kaplan & Hill, 1985a, 1985b.
58. Hill, 1982: 527.
59. Women may have been and are involved in butchering and food preparation. It is the males, however, who kill animals—including other primates—for food, vengeance, and territory. The ethnographic evidence too seems overwhelming, and in this case it is a useful measure of the past.
60. Hayden, 1981b; see also Hayden, 1981a, 1992.
61. Murdock & Provost, 1973.
62. Katz & Konner, 1981.
63. Brown, 1970; Burton, Brudner, & White, 1977; Murdock & Provost, 1973; Testart, 1986.
64. For definition and discussion of women's work, see Brown, 1970; Brudner & White, 1977.
65. Pontius, 1986; Rice, 1981.
66. See Morbeck, Galloway, & Zihlman, 1997; Tanner, 1981.
67. This does not mean that women are demeaned. The same author argues, "Women seem to have been privileged, perhaps owing to the importance of their physiological role, since they combined the functions of mothers, sexual partners and social partners." Duhard, 1993: 89. See also Duhard, 1991; Testart, 1986. But cf. Fisher, 1979.

68. Himmelheber stated, "Women do not carve. Nearly all African handicrafts are exercised by either men or women, but carving is men's trade. Women could show their talent in plastic art in pottery. Pottery is women's trade all over Africa" (1963: 84).

69. Marshack, 1972: 272.

70. Marshack, 1976.

71. Wagner, 1981.

72. Valladas, et al., 1992.

73. Knecht, 1994: 84.

74. Ruspoli, 1987: 35.

75. Kehoe, 1987: 46.

76. Chittenden & Richardson, 1905; Fletcher & La Flesche, 1906; Gilmore, 1924: 209; Grinnell, 1962; Mandelbaum, 1940: 190–91.

77. Frison, 1970, 1971.

78. Stanford, 1979.

79. The Indians of the Plains, as most likely did the paleohunters, dried strips of meat and removed and boiled down fats. Frison, 1967.

80. Frison, 1987: 209.

81. Kehoe, 1987: 46.

82. Leaders also act as agents to help suppress intragroup conflict. Even among chimps, Jane Goodall notes, "Under the rule of a powerful male the conflicts between the other members of the community are kept to a minimum, for he uses his position to prevent too much fighting among his subordinates. What motivates him is not always clear. Sometimes there may be a genuine desire to help the underdog. At other times it may be that the alpha feels his position is challenged if another male initiates a fight" (1990: 57).

83. Livingstone, 1857; Stow, 1905.

84. DeGroot, 1980; Greene, 1987.

85. Cant & Temerin, 1984.

86. Guthrie, 1984.

87. Bahn & Vertut, 1988.

88. Riddle, 1940: 158–59.

89. See Mithen, 1988.

90. The beginnings of agriculture will never be determined, but the dates, as so many others in human advancement, have continually been pushed back. Claims are made of evidence of rye cultivation as early as 13,000 years ago in the Near East. Domestication of animals certainly occurred as early as 10,500 years ago. The beginnings of urbanism—people gathering together, building permanent housing, staying in the same place over seasons—are also variable. Recent excavations have found overgrown villages dating back to 9,000 years ago in Anatolia. But it is unclear why the population accumulation took place. Was it due to agricultural innovations or something more ominous? One of the oldest sites, Asikli in central Anatolia, dating to perhaps about 10,000 years ago, has strong

evidence for mutual protection against neighbors being an early incentive to "civilize." Like Crow Creek, the town of several hundred is partly surrounded by a wall.

91. Wallace, 1962[1876]: 150; cf. Martin, 1967.

92. Martin, 1958, 1966, 1967; Mosimann & Martin, 1975.

93. Raup, 1991: 91–92.

94. Diamond, 1992; Wilson, 1992. For discussion of the New Zealand cases, see Martin & Kline, 1984; Anderson, 1989a, 1989b; Caughly, 1988. Anderson is less committed to the moa-hunters as the proximity cause of the die-offs.

95. Climate change has been suggested as a culprit, but it is quite possible that the moas died out due to a combination of factors. With man the hunter came to New Zealand his silent partners in predation, dogs and rats that had a fondness for moa chicks and eggs (Fleming, 1969).

96. Mowat, 1975[1951]. Mowat also wrote a follow-up on the fate of the people of the deer appropriately titled *The Desperate People*. For more academic ethnographic accounts of the arctic hunters, see Binford, 1978; Grønnow, 1986; Nelson, 1969.

97. MacArthur & Wilson, 1967; Simberloff, 1986.

98. Stuart, 1991; Soffer, 1991.

99. Vartanyan, Garutt, & Scher, 1993.

100. Dan Fisher, cited in Ward, 1997: 218.

101. Kelly & Todd, 1988.

102. Miller, 1998. Personal communication.

103. Kirch, 1984; Flenley, 1979; Flenley & King, 1984.

104. Quoted in Pringle, 1996: 49.

105. Wilson, 1992: 253.

106. McAllister, 1993. To proclaim that an area devoid of human dwellings or crops is natural is misleading. Even the uninhabited areas of the Amazon rain forest have still been subdivided into smaller and smaller blocks, by roads and river traffic. Many of the species in natural parks such as Yellowstone are refugees from civilization, animals driven there to cede land to ranchers, farmers, and shopping malls. Even seemingly pristine stands of woodland are in fact leftovers of a green holocaust. The forests of northern Minnesota, for example, contain no trees older than a hundred years. We are approaching both the end of nature and the end of any reasonable definition of something being natural.

107. MacArthur, 1972.

108. Mann, 1981: 10.

109. Mann, 1981.

110. Wilson, 1992: 230.

111. Obviously, nature can resist such efforts. Rain, contrary to the beliefs of early agronomists in dust-bowl America, does not "follow the plow." Desert, of course, will result from destruction of tree cover and overplanting of soil.

## 2: Primitive War

1. Taçon & Chippindale, 1994: 222.
2. Dates cited for the first evidence of farming in Europe continue to grow earlier (Rowley-Conwy, 1995).
3. Keeley's work (1996) systematically destroys the view that tribal peoples were unwarlike, or were spurred into warfare largely through contact with expanding centralized states.
4. Vencl, 1991.
5. Ibid.
6. Other studies of tribal societies have found ratios of male-to-female war-caused mortality ranging from 2.4: 1 to 20.8: 1. See Glasse, 1968: 98; Heider, 1970: 231; Chagnon, 1974: 160; Meggitt, 1977, 110–12; Werner, 1983: 241; Beckerman & Lizarralde, 1995.
7. Lowie, 1983[1935]: 228. See also Bamforth, 1994.
8. Tyrrell, 1968[1916]: 329. See also Bamforth, 1994.
9. Almagor, 1977.
10. Sandars, 1985[1968]: 159. See also Piggott, 1965.
11. Blick, 1988; Ferguson, 1992; Ferguson & Whitehead, 1992; Ross, 1984.
12. Blick, 1988.
13. An example of the effects of living in the tribal zone is the Yanomamö people of the Amazon. Napoleon Chagnon spent years living with the Yanomamö in the 1950s and 1960s, and his observations and reports on the "fierce people" became famous. The subjects that he encountered were a combative lot, always fighting among themselves and in a state of perpetual war with their neighbors. Yet tribal zone anthropologists like Ferguson and his colleagues have argued that the warlike behavior exhibited was not a natural part of folkways from time immemorial, but was directly produced because of contact with encroaching Portuguese, Spanish, and Dutch conquerors and colonialists and their indigenous allies, beginning in the seventeenth century. The Yanomamö were driven from their ancestral homes, where they had established a relatively complex, settled existence as river traders, and were forced to inhabit the fringes of the colonial empires in the jungle highlands. Ferguson (1990a, 1995) argues that almost always what was at stake in a Yanomamö conflict was access to trade goods derived from the central state-level societies. Essentially, he claims that contact with Europeans made the Yanomamö fierce.
14. Ferguson, 1990a, 1990b, 1992; Ferguson & Whitehead, 1992.
15. Ferguson earlier admits that "even in the absence of any state, archaeology provides unmistakable evidence of war among sedentary village peoples" (1992: 113).
16. Ibid.
17. Otterbein, 1994: 163.
18. See reviews in Bamforth, 1994; Keeley, 1996.

19. In the Oneota cemetery in Illinois, reseachers uncovered 264 burials; 43 skeletons belonged to people who were killed through violent trauma. See Milner, Anderson, & Smith, 1991: 583.

20. Milner, Anderson, & Smith, 1991.

21. Blainey, 1976: 108–09.

22. Harris, 1984; Shankman, 1991; Vayda, 1976.

23. Willey, 1990. See also Lehmer, 1971; Kivett & Jensen, 1976; Zimmerman & Whitten, 1980.

24. Raphael Lemkin first defined genocide as "the destruction of a nation or of an ethnic group." He divided genocide into three types. The first, which he saw originating in the Middle Ages, was the annihilation of victim groups and nations. The second type, originating in the modern era, was the destruction of a people's culture without necessarily effecting the abolition of the people. The third type, of which he saw the Nazis as the prime example, combined the other two, annihilating the people and extinguishing any remains of their culture as well (1973: 79–82). As Crow Creek suggests and ancient history attests, however, all forms of genocide reach back thousands of years.

25. Keyser, 1987: 47, fig. 3a. See also Keyser, 1977, 1979; Mulloy, 1958; Conner & Conner, 1971.

26. Roper, 1969.

27. Beckerman & Lizarralde, 1995.

28. Kottak, 1991: 108.

29. Beckerman & Lizarralde, 1995: 500.

30. Keegan, 1976: 173; cf. Eliade, 1960.

31. The men are less uniform in step, equipment, and appearance. See Brooks & Wakankar, 1976: 80; Mazonowicz, 1974: 149, 188.

32. McNeill, 1995: 2.

33. Rappaport, 1967b: 26–27. See also Schieffelin, 1976.

34. Marshall, 1969; Katz, 1982.

35. Cf. Beaumont, 1974: 16.

36. Quoted in Essame, 1974: 28.

37. Richard Mollica, quoted in Gourevitch, 1995: 84.

38. Maringer & Bandi, 1953: 124, fig. 158. See also Ferrill, 1985: 22; Keeley, 1996: 44–45.

39. The key to the maneuver is cooperation and coordination in the center; it must hold—even nearly to the point of being sacrificed—and not rashly counterattack. In World War I, the center of the German line was placed under the command of the crown prince. In his vainglory, he pressed the French into their central lines; when the trap door began to close, the French were able to swing up to meet the threat from the north. See Wallbank, 1957; Keppie, 1984; Ritter, 1958; Turner, 1985.

40. Powell, 1995: 495. Indeed, the Allied Coalition's reconquest of Kuwait and southern Iraq was simply a variation on Hannibal's strategy. Less mobile Arab and

American infantry advanced frontally in Kuwait while the American, French, and British armor and light units sped around the Iraqi western flank.
41. Mazonowicz, 1974: 158. See also Lajoux, 1963: 159, 164–66. The image is a confused one, but the figures, motions, and basic physiognomy seem almost identical to those found throughout Southern Europe, Africa, and Asia in the Neolithic. Unquestionably, we are witnessing a battle.
42. Mooney, 1907; Grinnell, 1892. See more recent commentary and discussion in Moore, 1990.
43. Caesar, 1982: 199.
44. Chandler, 1973: 325-326.
45. Selby, 1968: 22.
46. Quoted in Essame, 1974: 28, 208
47. Storr, 1988[1965]: 49–50.
48. Milgram, 1974.
49. Ibid.: 8.
50. Ibid.
51. Lewis-Williams, 1981a: 19, 1981b. See also Vinnicombe, 1976: 363.
52. Keeley, 1996: 174.
53. Frobenius & Fox, 1937: 60, fig. 79.
54. The "big man" leadership cultures of the South Pacific, especially Melanesia and New Guinea, are well studied. There the big men primarily achieve status by doling out wealth through feasts and gifts; but in pre-colonial days they sought out wealth through endless warfare. Getting goods to keep and to distribute to loyal henchmen (warriors and other elites) may be the genesis of the perpetuation of both war and complex societies. See reviews and research in Harris, 1978; Sahlins, 1972; Whitehouse, 1992; Oliver, 1955.
55. Woodburn, 1980, 1982.
56. Sahlins, 1972: 134, 139. See Betzig, 1988, for reviews and an exception.
57. Knauft, 1987. It was done so for both symbolic and practical reasons. Mutual defense alliances between small groups can be the response to an external threat. Withdrawal to more defensible locations is one step in this grouping. See Brookfield & Brown, 1963; Heider, 1970: 99–133, 1979: 88–112; Meggitt, 1977; Morren, 1984; Netting, 1974; Rappaport, 1967a: 109–52. Even small-scale warfare produces its own causes. Food stocks and growing areas are destroyed or devastated by raiding; increasing numbers of healthy male individuals are diverted from food growing or hunting to defense and raiding. The cycle of violence causes increased desperation and reliance on violence as the solution to intergroup conflict. Chagnon, 1983: 73, 179; Heider, 1970, 1979; Meggitt, 1977: 99; Trigger, 1969: 30.
58. Frank, 1952: 237 (entry for May 3, 1944).

## 3: COMMANDERS

1. Finegan, 1959: 215.
2. See Cassidy, 1991.
3 Diaz, 1963: 91.
4. Quoted in Pagden, 1986: 100.
5. Gray, 1990: 288.
6. Whiting, 1960.
7. Cohen & Gooch, 1991: 192; Perlmutter, 1997c.
8. This is not to value live seeing over pictorial reporting. Military leaders can be just as blind about what they witness in person. A telling example is provided by Jack Snyder in his study of the ideology of the offensive in the early battles of World War I. Most armies marched to that war firmly rooted in the notion that only by all-out offensive action could victory be achieved. Each nation created its own set of maxims and doctrines to support this ideology. The French especially, embarrassed at their defeats in the War of 1870, declared fortifications and entrenchment useless in war. They believed that *élan*, the ardent quality of bravery and audacity, could overcome modern artillery and machine guns.

   This doctrine was not based upon fanciful abstractions. Many military experts drew the lesson of the offensive from their own observations in previous wars. The Boer War of 1899–1902 and the Russo-Japanese War of 1905 demonstrated the exponential growth in the firepower of entrenched defensive units, wielding modern rifles and supported by massed artillery. Frenchmen in the latter war particularly noted the killing potential of the machine gun. One described vividly, "Machines without nerves and without a soul, the machine guns in these circumstances literally mow down the attackers" (Snyder, 1984: 79). But supporters of the doctrine of the *offensive à l'outrance* looked past the losses on the field to what they saw as the more important datum: in such battles, the more mobile Japanese forces which attacked the stationary Russian armies suffered losses of up to twice as many in proportion, yet the Japanese eventually won the battle and the war. To the French, this showed that "morale was the decisive factor" (Ibid: 80).

   Indeed, the French observers contradicted themselves to support their beliefs. When British attacks failed against the concentrated rifle fire of the Boers, the French asserted this was due to "British ineptitude." But the failure of the Russian defense to hold back the Japanese was assumed to be an inevitability of battle, not due to "Russian ineptitude." When World War I arived, the lessons of massed artillery and machine gun were not learned because seeing was believing, but only when what was seen was reconfigured to fit into belief. It is doubtful whether we have improved on this fundamental human tendency, which can ultimately lead to victory or defeat.
9. Desroches Noblecourt, 1996; Yadin, 1963: 104–05; Robins, 1997: 179.
10. Goedicke, 1985.

11. Wilson, 1956: 246.
12. Goedicke, 1985: 93. It is the rhetorical opposite of Henry V's Agincourt speech: I, the war commander, am the unhappy few who had to do the real fighting.
13. Jamieson, 1992.
14. Ryan, 1959: 170
15. Berdan & Anawalt, 1997.
16. Tuchman, 1962: 61.
17. Kracauer, 1974[1947]: 94.
18. See overview in Harrington, 1993: 33–35.
19. Galt, 1960: 46; see also Staley, 1980.
20. Galt, 1960: 48; Mitchell, 1944.
21. Galt, 1960: 50.
22. Von Erffa & Staley, 1986: 58.
23. Montagna, 1981: 84.
24. Abrams, 1985: 164.
25. Ibid.
26. Crombie, 1959: 57.
27. Quoted in Freeman, 1941: 109.
28. Abrams, 1985: 173.
29. In West's case, membership under the proscenium arch of the attendants was not without immediate benefit. West apparently charged people a fee to be painted as models in the picture.
30. Reade, 1976; Barnett, 1976.
31. Luckenbill, 1927: 310–11.
32. Curtis & Reade, 1995: 80.
33 Clausewitz, 1991: 119, 104.
34. Hughes, 1988: 445.
35. Priestley, 1972: 148
36. McNeill, 1976: 251.
37. Mathews, 1957; Knightley, 1975.
38. Royle, 1987: 26.
39. The culmination of this important phenomenon is that it has become politically almost impossible to publicly criticize the fighting ability of ordinary troops. For example, in the American operation in Grenada in 1983, military sources agree that regular U.S. Army forces, as opposed to the marines, performed poorly. This assessment was never released to the public or proclaimed by political leaders. Moreover, the U.S. Army distributed over 2,000 medals to the 700–plus soldiers who landed; this was one of the most generous ratios in military history.
40. Freund, 1980: 106–07.
41. Gernsheim & Gernsheim, 1954: 20.
42. Lalumia, 1983: 32.
43. Mauldin, 1991[1944]: 131.

44. Ibid.: 184.

45. Carmichael, 1989: 87.

46. Barker, 1967: 15. He continues: "The army in Mesopotamia was the Forgotten Army of World War I, or so it seemed to those who were there. All it got was anything that was too old, too worn or too inadequate for use elsewhere" (p. 17).

47. Ibid., 285.

## 4: COMRADES

1. Modern recruiting ads are action-packed, and stress camaraderie and self-development, but they only show mock combat (if at all) or training exercises. They never show scenes from actual combat or its results.

2. Quoted in Woodman, 1988: 89, f79.

3. Dio Cassius, 68.7.5.

4. Pliny, *Panegyricus*, 13.

5. Ibid., 13, 15. Napoleon, too, was able to cite the battle accomplishments of men he met in the line.

6. Dio Cassius, 68.8.2.

7. Dio Chrysostom in Jones, 1978: 121.

8. Dio Cassius, 68.8.2; Fronto, Vol. II: 204; Pliny, *Panegyricus*, 15.5.

9. Shils, 1950: 32.

10. Ibid.: 33.

11. Plutarch, 1864: 497.

12. Pliny, *Panegyricus*, 13

13. Hale, 1988.

14. Goscinny & Uderzo, 1976: 6.

15. Gibbon, n.d.: 10.

16. Josephus, 1981: 3.86.

17. Shirer, 1969: 438–39.

18. Macqueen, 1975.

19. May, Stadler, & Votaw, 1984: 3–5.

20. In Xenophon's accounts of the battles fought by the "Ten Thousand" hoplites (and some pelasts or lighter troops) against archers and cavalry in their march through the Persian Empire (c. 401 B.C.E.), it was a rare thing for a hoplite to be killed, but more common to suffer a wound (Xenophon, 1972).

21. In many battles, the breaking of the enemy line was a signal of his defeat, because loose, divided, or scattered hoplites would be crushed under the weight of a unified mass.

22. Plutarch, 1864: 454.

23. Eisenstein, 1988: 67.

24. Gammage, 1975: 115.

25. Homer, 1961, 18.22–27.
26. Shilts, 1993.
27. The French philosopher Gustave Le Bon commented in the last days of the nineteenth century that groups of people in contact—crowds—were an entity where "the conscious personality has entirely vanished; will and discernment are lost" (1896: 35).
28. Quoted in Shils, 1950: 18.
29. Remarque, 1975[1929]: 181–82.
30. Mendelssohn Bartholdy, 1937: 286.
31. Mosse, 1990: 5.
32. Ibn Khaldun, 1950: 109.
33. Marshall, 1947: 42, 43.
34. Thrasher, 1936[1927]: 33–46; Whyte, Jr., 1956: 330–61.
35. Cooley, 1929: 20.
36. Richthofen, 1995: 58.
37. Charles Moskos (1970) argues that the primary group attachment, while important, is interrelated with other factors such as the survival instinct and beliefs like pro-Americanism and anti-communism. Obviously men do not go to war only to be with their buddies; reducing everything to the group and the dyad ignores many motivations to join up, endure, fight, and sacrifice life and limb in war.
38. Hale, 1988.
39. Gernsheim & Gernsheim, 1954.
40. Thomey, 1996. See also Marling & Wetenhall, 1991; Albee & Freeman, 1995.
41. Stein, 1966: 287.
42. Hitler, 1973: 403.
43. De La Maziere, 1974: 36.
44. Hallahan, 1994: 126–27.
45. Marshall, 1947: 54, 57.
46. Ibid.: 60, 61.
47. Grossman, 1995: 251.
48. Thomas, 1993: 9.
49. These studies have been expanded upon recently by Robert Scales (1990).
50. Scales, 1990: 231.
51. Ibid.: 232.
52. Ibid.: 230.
53. Dornbusch, 1955.
54. Quoted in Rieber & Kelly, 1991.

## 5: ENEMIES

1. Welté, 1989: 215–35; Leroi-Gourhan, 1967: 57, fig. 31.
2. Harrington, 1993: 63; Buddle, 1990.

3. Pal & Dehejia, 1986: 52.

4. Tipu himself cooperated to some extent in his own exoticization; for example, he identified himself with the tiger and employed that image as a family crest (Tillotson, 1990; Archer, 1979).

5. Weller, 1972: 80.

6. Cited in Weller, 1972: 80.

7. Division of the Chief of Staff Intelligence Branch, 1908: 23.

8. Bayly, 1989: 113–14; Colley, 1984: 113, 1986.

9. Simmel, 1955; cf. Coser, 1956. Psychologist Sam Keen, in his book *Faces of the Enemy* (1986), chose examples—largely from various wars—most of which are images that seem unambiguously designed for propaganda: posters and editorial cartoons. To explain the "enemy" phenomenon, he posits an "adversarial symbiosis." Enemies serve the function to project internal "accumulated, disowned, psychological toxins."

10. Secord & Backman, 1964; Thrasher, 1936[1927]; Festinger, Schachter, & Back, 1963; Whyte, 1956; Dornbusch, 1955; Lofland, 1969; Clark, 1972.

11. Freud, 1940: 53.

12. Erikson, 1966: 606.

13. Roberts, 1989: 137–38; cf. Chandler, 1966: 155; Dowd, 1948; Dadrian, 1995: 159.

14. Political scientists have identified a "rally 'round the flag" effect whereby in times of a foreign affairs crisis, if the president is seen to act decisively, he receives a temporary boost of public support (Brody, 1984; Kernell, 1978; Mueller, 1973).

15. Dadrian, 1995: 193.

16. Popovich, 1991.

17. Davis, 1992; Emery, 1961; Saleh & Sourouzian, 1987; Williams, 1988; Millet, 1990; Fairservis, 1991.

18. Davis, 1992: 160, 173.

19. Fairservis, 1991: 11.

20. The mourning of a soldier for a fallen comrade is thus established very early as a genre scene in the war story or picture. As noted, the range of emotion expressed by the survivor is extremely varied. In some cultures, such as the audience for *Le Chanson de Roland*, a virile hero could shed bitter tears. Conversely, although John Wayne is often offered up by his critics as improbably stoic in grieving situations, in many films, like *The Sands of Iwo Jima* or *The Horse Soldiers*, his tone of voice, moist eyes, and taut face express pathos and empathy that in their subtle way are equally wrenching.

21. Powell, 1988. In many of the Northern cultures, from the Celts to the Goths and Germans, and later the Vikings, the nude (but often elaborately tattooed) warriors commonly displayed their splendid anatomy to an enemy. In ancient Greece the nude warrior fighting in battle was a heroic symbol.

22. Livy (1929), XXII, VI.11–12.

23. These pictures could be found in almost all media. For example, on a cylinder

seal from the city of Uruk in northern Syria, victorious soldiers march forward as women beg for mercy and a prisoner is executed (Collon, 1987: 162).

24. Saggs, 1984: 261.
25. Kubler, 1984: 277–78; Coe, 1993: 104–08; Miller, 1986.
26. Marcus & Flannery, 1996.
27. Ibid.: 1996: 152.
28. Ibid.: 153; Marcus, 1974.
29. Marcus & Flannery, 1996: 153.
30. Xenophon, 1972: 162.
31. The weapons deployed in the film are less advanced than those in Heinlein's novel, where each "Cap" Trooper wears his own 2,000-pound armored fighting suit. The computers and the electrical machinery of the suit are designed to create a symbiosis with the body and mind of the soldier. He can literally leap over tall buildings and crush steel girders while firing missiles. Much to the disappointment of the book's fans, the filmmakers found that recreating such scenes and suits was prohibitively expensive, so they returned to a more archaic, hoplite-GI look. Interestingly, the film does deal with human arrogance directly as well. The first landing on an enemy planet is defeated and we are clearly told it is because, as in *Aliens*, the humans had no interest in learning about their enemy.
32. Mass-market science fiction films (e.g., *Terminator I* and *II*, *Star Trek*, *Star Wars*, *Stargate*, *E.T.*, *Independence Day*, etc.) are fifty years behind the genre of science fiction prose. Most of their plots would be rejected as old chestnuts if submitted to a genre publication. Gardner Dozois, the influential editor of *Isaac Asimov's Science Fiction Magazine*, commented that most sci-fi fans were "grumpy" about *Independence Day*, "considering it an insulting farrago of the dumbest sci-fi cliches" (1997: xxxviii).
33. This is ridiculous. Their fifteen-mile-long ships cross between stars, hover in defiance of Earth's gravity, raise defense shields that absorb nuclear blasts, and fire lasers that incinerate a city. The engines and weapons are powered by mysterious technology beyond human imitation, though not beyond our theft. Any civilization so advanced could extract all their material needs (even water) from uninhabited planets, asteroids, and moons, and energy from the stars.
34. Hine, 1980: 111.
35. Jaubert, 1989[1986]: 177.
36. Scherman, 1977: 151.
37. Dadrian, 1995: 159.
38. Quoted in Fest, 1972: 177.
39. Höhne, 1970: 502.
40. Quoted in Conquest, 1986: 129.
41. Quoted in Lemarchand, 1996: 104.
42. Arendt, 1977 [1965].
43. Read, 1941: 210–11.

44. Ibid.: 215.
45. Ibid.
46. Lasswell, 1972: 33. See also Roetter, 1974; Bruntz, 1938; Sanders & Taylor, 1982.
47. Tuchman, 1962: 82.
48. Hitler, 1971[1927]: 182.
49. Ibid.: 470.
50. Ibid.: 118.
51. Rhodes, 1987: 107–08.
52. Jowett & O'Donnell, 1992: 169.
53. Rhodes, 1987: 139.
54. But the most significant side effect of the distaste for propaganda of World War I was disbelief (fueled by latent anti-Semitism) of stories about German atrocities against the Jews during World War II. See Lipstadt, 1986, 1993; Wyman, 1984; Zalampas, 1989.
55. Paret, Lewis, & Paret, 1992: 198.
56. Dower, 1986.
57. Truman, 1955: 421.
58. Prange, 1981: 559.
59. Ibid.: 558.
60. Carter, 1900: 3.
61. Herzstein, 1987: 64.
62. Hinz, 1979: iii.
63. Hitler, 1973: 445.
64. Grosshans, 1983: 87.
65. Mayer, 1978: 1. See also Perlmutter, 1991, 1994, 1997b.
66. Hoffner & Cantor, 1991: 65. See also Babrow, et al., 1988; Perse & Rubin, 1989; Reeves, 1979.
67. Commisky & Bryant, 1982; Zillman, 1980. The oldest and largely unbroken rule of entertainment media is that an audience must have someone for whom to cheer, to identify with.
68. Viewers develop para-social interaction with media figures and stars (Horton & Wohl, 1956).
69. Ferro, 1976.
70. Allison, 1918: 46–47.
71. Mauldin, 1991[1944]: 21.
72. Fussell, 1991.

6: HORRORS

1. Trueheart, 1994; Farnsworth, 1994.
2. Daniel, 1948; Ternois, 1962; Schröder, 1982, I, II.
3. Tippett, 1984: 81.

4. Viereck, 1931: 277.
5. Tippett, 1984: 86.
6. Carter, 1900: 30.
7. Stearn, 1986: 61.
8. Hogan, 1994: 52.
9. Orwell, 1980[1952].
10. See the discussion in Trachtenberg, 1989: 90–92.
11. Fussell, 1989: 267–68. His argument is an important one: we undermine the honor of the troops if we make their sacrifice seem more pristine, less sordid.
12. But see *Capitaine Conan* (1996), directed by Bertrand Tavernier. In one scene, a general, sheltered from pouring rain and mushy snow by an umbrella, reads notes of commendation to the soldiers granted by General Foch, announcing the end of World War I. The words speak of glorious victories, undying honor, "sublime endurance and enduring heroism." Meanwhile, men sporadically slink out of the line and rush behind a wall to drop their pants, succumbing to a widespread bout of diarrhea. The general continues to read his uplifting message: "... The greatest battle in history. Take pride in it. It is with immortal glory that you have bedecked the flag. Posterity shall remember you with gratitude." ["C'est la gloire immortelle que vous avez paré vos drapeaux. La posterité vous gardera la reconnaissance."]
13. Quoted in Corliss, 1987: 56.
14. Karnow, 1983: 15.
15. Mead, 1968: 215.
16. Tolstoy, 1894: 323.
17. Orwell, 1962: 63.
18. Scherer, 1963: 123.
19. Collon, 1987.
20. Hankinson, 1982: 126.
21. Gibbon, n.d.: 69.
22. Hannestad, 1986: 240; Ryberg, 1967; Birley, 1987[1966]; Marcus Aurelius, 1930 ed.
23. Safer, 1990: 91.
24. Hammond, 1988: 189. Safer narrated: "Today's operation shows the frustration of Vietnam in miniature. There is little doubt that American fire power can win a military victory here. But to a Vietnamese peasant whose home means a lifetime of backbreaking labor, it will take more than presidential promises to convince him that we are on his side" (quoted in Hammond, 1988: 188; see also pp. 186–91). Most important, there was no noticeable shift in public support for the war.
25. Noakes & Pridham, 1988: 1069.
26. Klee, Dressen, & Riess, 1988: 158–59.
27. Noakes & Pridham, 1988: 1069.
28. Vogel, 1974: 180.

29. Arnett, 1994: 412.

30. Significantly, though, a process of self-editing occurred on CNN and other American news outlets. The unedited footage, according to one reporter who obtained it, "showed scenes of incredible carnage. . . . Among the corpses were those of at least six babies and ten children, most of them so severely burned that their gender could not be determined." Garrett, 1991.

31. Rosensteil, 1994: A14.

32. Gailey, 1991: 3A.

33. Goldhagen, 1996: 381.

34. Solzhenitsyn, 1973: 168.

## 7: Living-Room Wars

1. Arlen, 1969.

2. Despite its status as event, it is still likely a tall tale or a confusion of Phidippides with another man. (Frost, 1979).

3. Ivins, 1969[1953]: 15.

4. Because the coins were hand-stamped, oddities and irregularities of depth and spacing could mar execution of even the most aesthetically pleasing designs. Also, because of the coins' small size, subtleties were lost; only easily recognizable shapes could be used. These could be captioned by few, often abbreviated, words. Of course, the messages could be pointed as well, making a connection between the emperor, a divinity, or a specific event (a victorious battle, even when technically won by a general far away) and the value of money. In coins' favor too was their ubiquity in daily life. The medium was a message; the war leader's image was precious. Even those who lived unwillingly in the Roman world, like Jesus the Galilean, well understood that the coin belonged "unto Caesar."

5. A. H. M. Jones (1956: 16) thought that coins, like postage stamps today, "mainly reflect the mentality of the post-office officials." On the other hand, Michael Grant (1950: 8) asserted that Roman coins "served a propagandist purpose far greater than has any national coinage before or since. . . . [otherwise], the hard-headed Roman government would not have been so foolish as to continue, for centuries, this lavish outlay of energy and ingenuity." Indeed, Brutus followed suit with his own coins after the assassination of Caesar.

6. Sutherland, 1974: 95.

7. Cited in Vermeule, 1968: 200.

8. Epstein, 1973; Mosettig & Griggs, 1980; Larson, 1992.

9. Fenton, 1980: 36–38; Mosettig & Griggs, 1980; Larson, 1992.

10. Wiemer, 1992.

11. Girardet, 1993: 51.

12. Lederman, 1992: 132.

13. Shaw, 1992: A16.

14. Westmoreland, 1976: 419.

15. Douglas Kinnard writes, "Westmoreland's generals shared his negative view of the performance of the news media in Vietnam . . . 89 percent negative toward the press, and 91 percent negative toward television. On only one other matter in the survey, the quality of ARVN [South Vietnamese army], was a consensus so nearly approached. It should be noted that the different wording of the two negative questions on each medium indicates a far deeper negative orientation toward television than toward the press." Indeed, 59 percent of his respondents felt that print media were "Generally responsible" or "uneven," but 91 percent thought that television coverage was "Probably not a good thing" or "Not a good thing" (1977: 132–33).

16. Walt, 1970: 200.

17. Pine, 1992: A13.

18. Kurtz, 1992: A33.

19. Ibid.

20. Gordon, 1992: A18.

21. Lee, 1992: 1A.

22. Bowker, 1992; Ed Turner, quoted on CNN News, December 9, 1992.

23. Gombrich, 1974: 241.

24. Cairncross, 1997: 7.

25. Greek civilians sat and stood on the slopes of Mount Agrieliki to watch the battle between their soldiers and the Persians on the Plains of Marathon.

26. al-Khalil, 1991: 10.

27. Kelly, 1993: 5.

28. al-Khalil, 1991: 151.

29. An exception was erected by the French government to honor the dead of World War I. The Ossuary of Douaumont contains the remains of some 130,000 men killed in the battles around Verdun. It is marked by a white tower, but at ground level the onlooker can gaze through glass walls at bones and artifacts still in the earth as they were interred in battle. In the cemetery nearby, there is another visual testament to the dead. A rank of rifles extends their bayonets from the soil. Now sheltered by a concrete canopy, it marks a wartime trench in which the wake of an artillery blast buried alive a troop of French soldiers. It was at this site, in the dedication ceremonies in 1932, that German and French veterans pledged to each other never to fight another war.

30. Vietnam Veterans Memorial Fund, 1980: 5. The controversy is described in Scruggs & Swerdlow, 1985.

31. Haines, 1986: 7. See also Blair, Jeppeson, & Pucci, 1991.

32. deBlaye, 1989: 263.

33. Of course, here is an important role for the vision of war: a stirring representation, a new movie, perhaps—*Gallipoli, Saving Private Ryan*—can rekindle memories in the old and spark interest for the young.

34. Coombs, 1983.

35. Diodorus Siculus, 1946[1933]: I, 2.5.
36. Thucydides, 1988[1920]: 283.
37. Boone, 1996: 181.
38. Naquin & Rawski, 1987: 70; Cheng, 1983.
39. Manheim, 1991: 130.
40. Robbin, 1995: A22.
41. Quoted in King, 1993: 18.
42. Devroy, 1991: A26.
43. Beschloss, 1993: C1.
44. Gutstadt, 1993: 399.
45. Gans, 1979; Galtung & Ruge, 1965.
46. Schwartz, 1992; Becker, 1982; Gans, 1979; Fishman, 1980; Turow, 1992; Tuchman, 1978.
47. Sawyer, 1994: 1B.
48. Fenton, 1980: 37.
49. Fischhoff, Slovic, & Lichtenstein, 1978; Sloman, 1994.
50. O'Kane, 1995: T12.
51. See Newhall, 1982: 19–23.
52. Quoted in Gernsheim, 1982: 199.
53. Quoted in Goldberg, 1981: 64.
54. Carlebach, 1992: 165. As Carlebach points out, "With few exceptions photographers from 1839 to 1880 spent their careers making studio portraits and scenic views" (p. 2).
55. Cobb, 1962; cf. Frassanito, 1983: 28.
56. Ivins, 1969[1953]: 177.
57. Ezickson, 1938: 48.
58. Pliny, *Natural History*, Vol. IX: XXXV. 65.
59. Messaris, 1994: 149. See also Custen, 1980; Gross, 1985; Messaris & Gross, 1977; Liebes & Katz, 1985.
60. Parry, 1992: A26.
61. Ritchin, 1990: 9; Harris, 1991.
62. Rosenblum, 1978a, 1978b; Schwartz, 1992.
63. Codrescu, 1991.
64. Ibid.: 205.
65. Viorst, 1991: 58.
66. Ibid., 61.
67. Quoted in Allen, et al., 1991: 141.
68. Hilterman, 1991: 46.
69. Hallion, 1992: 200.
70. Despite thousands of sorties over the course of the war, as one reviewer put it, "all of these efforts did little more than hit decoys and fuel trucks" (Cohen, 1993, Part II: 331–32).
71. Ibid.: 330–31.

72. For his pains, Ritter was denied promotion; he quit the armed forces to become a UN arms inspector in Iraq, only to resign again in protest because of careless enforcement of the inspections.
73. Cordesman & Wagner, 1996: 873–74.
74. Reed, 1985.
75. Dunnigan & Bay, 1992: 415.
76. Destexhe, 1995: 48–51; Prunier, 1995: 336–45.
77. Erikson, 1958: 225.
78. Bailey & Lichty, 1972: 223.
79. Speaking on *Vietnam, The Camera at War*, History Channel, 1997.
80. Perlmutter, 1998.
81. Carolyn Page, an English researcher, claims that the reaction in the U.K. was stronger (1996: 223–24).
82. Coe, 1993: 108.
83. Chipp, 1988: 198.
84. Sartre, 1948: 17.
85. Quoted in Ryan, 1974: 67.
86. Powell, 1995: 505.

## 8: FUTURES

1. Clausewitz, 1991: 189.
2. Libicki, 1994.
3. SPOT is known to have sold earth images to Saddam Hussein during the Iranian war, and just prior to the invasion of Kuwait (Trux, 1991: 32).
4. "Communication links [were] running at peak capacity and saturated specialists, who were sifting and analysing it in both the U.S. and Saudi Arabia" (Ibid.: 33).
5. The effectiveness of any weapon depends on the response of the enemy. As an example, the Bradley Fighting Vehicle was much lambasted as being poorly armored, a "death trap," a boondoggle (cf. the HBO TV movie *Pentagon Wars*). Yet in the Gulf War, it acquitted itself well.
6. Shukman, 1995: 171, f3.
7. Trux, 1991: 30.
8. Burrows, 1986: 227.
9. Shukman, 1995: 163.
10. The main tank of American forces in the Gulf War was the M1A1 "HA," or Heavy Armor, designating the shield of depleted uranium armor attached to their sides. Army slang had adapted to the new era in describing tank personnel as well; formerly known as DATs, or "Dumb Ass Tankers," they are now dubbed "Computerized Dumb Ass Tankers." The M1A2 has of this writing only been employed in one U.S. battalion, though others have been sold to Saudi Arabia and Egypt.

11. It is unlikely that robots will, within the foreseeable future, have enough intelligence, especially humanlike cunning, to replace soldiers on the battlefield, à la *Terminator*. Independent robots such as smart cameras or tripwires controlling auto-firing guns, however, do play a role.

12. His kit will include the OICW, Objective Individual Combat Weapon (Hasenauer, 1995).

13. Quoted in Gilmore, 1997.

14. Libicki, 1994.

15. Stix, 1995: 92.

16. Quoted in ibid., 93.

17. Quoted in Shukman, 1995: 169.

18. Quoted in ibid., 170.

19. Charles Sutton, quoted in Hasenauer, 1992: 49.

20. As George and Meredith Friedman point out, "In Desert Storm, we saw the Model-Ts of precision-guided munitions . . . what will fully mature systems achieve? The forest is far more important than an accountant's trees" (1996: xii). The mainstays of the Gulf—the laser-guided bombs, the Patriot antimissile, and the cruise missile—are all undergoing continued refinements. Only another war will prove, under battlefield conditions, whether these constitute improvements.

21. Shukman, 1995: 164. Moreover, since GPS is already and will increasingly become a civil, industrial, and consumer service, it can also be employed by enemies, from lone terrorists to military establishments. In an extreme case, a technologically impoverished enemy could piggy-back onto the GPS to create a "poor-man's cruise missile."

22. Gibson, 1986: 104–08.

23. Commanders would routinely break radio silence to give orders and demand updates (Cincinnatus, 1981: 70; Gibson, 1986: 106).

24. See Thompson & Frizzell, 1977: 143.

25. Gibson, 1986: 107.

26. Vegetius, 1993: 69–93.

27. Libicki, 1994.

28. Ibid.

29. See Emerson, 1988: 20.

30. Beckwith & Knox, 1983: 220.

31. Libicki, 1994.

32. Ibid. One unconfirmed story is that, during the Desert Shield operation, U.S. operatives secretly placed "cooked" electronic microchips into a computer printer of French make that the Iraqis had ferreted into their country. The chips contained a virus that crippled any computers it was connected to.

33. Friedman & Friedman, 1996: 364.

34. Libicki, 1997, 1994; Johnson & Libicki, 1995.

35. Burrows, 1986: 251.

36. Friedman & Friedman, 1996: 150, 37.

37. Ibid.: 150–51.

38. Ibid.: 151.

39. Ibid.

40. Sullivan, 1992: 6.

41. Ibid.: 6–7; see also Sullivan & Dubik, 1993.

42. Swann & Read, 1981a, 1981b.

43. Heiman, 1972: 105.

44. Ian Hamilton, a British observer of the 1904–05 Russo-Japanese War, noted: "on the actual day of battle naked truths may be picked up for the asking; by the following morning they have already begun to get into their uniforms" (1908: v).

45. Appian, 1912: VIII, 93.

46. Modern warfare demands not only that the soldier be trained adequately to use the technology, but that he or she come from a society that supports both financially and educationally the high levels of technical sophistication.

47. National Defense University, 1996.

48. Vuono says that because of the smaller U.S. force structure, there will be "increased pressure for urgent decision making" (1991: 57).

49. At present, such programs are still embryonic, and the 19K AIT trainees (new recruits learning how to be tankers) may only spend an hour in the UCOFT gunnery simulation and the SIMNET, which trains commanders, from section leaders to higher echelons.

50. Bray, 1997.

51. Brown, 1993; Starr, 1993: 5.

52. Hazlett, 1995.

53. Perlmutter, 1995, 1997a.

54. Cf. Jensen, et al., 1997.

55. Douglass, 1968: 245.

56. Both quoted in Washington, 1995.

57. Sid Meier [interview], 1998: 35.

# BIBLIOGRAPHY

Abrams, A. U. (1985). *The valiant hero: Benjamin West and grand-style painting*. Washington, DC: Smithsonian.

Albee, P. B., Jr., & K. C. Freeman (1995). *Shadow of Suribachi*. Westport, CT: Praeger.

al-Khalil, S. (1991). *The monument: Art, vulgarity and responsibility in Iraq*. Berkeley: University of California Press.

Allen, T. B., et al. (1991). *War in the Gulf*. Atlanta: Turner Publishing.

Allison, J. M. (1918). *Raemaekers' cartoon history of the war*. Vol. I. New York: Century Co.

Almagor, U. (1977). Raiders and elders: A confrontation of generations among the Dassanetch. In K. Fukui & D. Turton, eds., *Warfare among East African herders*. Osaka: Museum of Ethnology.

Altuna, J., & J. M. Apellaniz (1978). Las figuras rupestres de la cueva de Ekain (Deva). *Munibe*, 30: 1–151.

Anderson, A. (1989a). Mechanics of overkill in the extinction of New Zealand moas. *Journal of Archaeological Science*, 16, 137–151.

———— (1989b). *Prodigious birds*. Cambridge: Cambridge University Press.

Appian (1912). *Appian's Roman history*. Vol. I [H. White, trans.]. London: William Heinemann.

Archer, M. (1979). *India and British portraiture, 1770–1825*. London: Sotheby Parke Bernet.

Arendt, H. (1977[1965]). *Eichmann in Jerusalem: A report on the banality of evil*. Rev. ed. New York: Penguin.

———— (1979). *The origins of totalitarianism*. New York: Harcourt Brace Jovanovich.

Arlen, M. J. (1969). *Living-room war*. New York: Viking.

Arnett, P. (1994). *Live from the battlefield*. New York: Simon & Schuster.

Arrian (1971). *The campaigns of Alexander* [A. de Sélincourt, trans.; rev. J. R. Hamilton]. New York: Penguin.

Babrow, A. S., et al. (1988). Person perception and children's impressions of television and real peers. *Communication Research*, 15, 6, 680–698.

Bachechi, L., P.-F. Fabbri, & F. Mallegni (1997). An arrow-caused lesion in a late Upper Palaeolithic human pelvis. *Current Anthropology*, 38, 1, 135–140.

Bahn, P. G. (1983). Late Pleistocene economies of the French Pyrenees. In G. Bailey, ed., *Hunter-gatherer economy in prehistory: A European perspective*. Cambridge: Cambridge University Press.

———— (1991). Pleistocene images outside of Europe. *Proceedings of the Prehistoric Society*, 57 (i), 99–102.

———— (1994). New advances in the field of Ice Age art. In M. H. Nitecki & D. V. Nitecki, eds., *Origins of anatomically modern humans*. New York: Plenum.

———— (1997). *Journey through the Ice Age*. Berkeley: University of California Press.

————, & J. Vertut (1988). *Images of the Ice Age*. New York: Facts on File.

Bailey, G. A., & L. W. Lichty, (1972). Rough justice on a Saigon street: A gatekeeper study of NBC's Tet execution film. *Journalism Quarterly*, Summer, 221–229, 238.

Bamforth, D. B. (1994). Indigenous people, indigenous violence: Precontact warfare on the North American Great Plains. *Man* (n.s.), 29, 95–115.

Barker, A. J. (1967). *The neglected war: Mesopotamia 1914–1918*. London: Faber & Faber.

Barnett, R. D. (1976). *Sculptures from the North Palace of Ashurbanipal at Nineveh*. London: British Museum Publications.

Barrera, M. E., & D. Maurer (1981). Recognition of mother's photographed face by the three-month-old infant. *Child Development*, 52, 2, 714–716.

Bayly, C. A. (1989). *Imperial meridian: The British Empire and the world, 1780–1830*. London: Longman.

Beaumont, R. A. (1974). *Military elites*. Indianapolis: Bobbs-Merrill.

Becker, H. S. (1982). *Art worlds*. Berkeley: University of California Press.

Beckerman, S., & R. Lizarralde (1995). State-tribal warfare and male-biased casualties among the Barí. *Current Anthropology*, 36, 3, 497–500.

Beckwith, C. A., & D. Knox (1983). *Delta Force*. New York: Harcourt Brace Jovanovich.

Benjamin, W. (1980). A short history of photography. In A. Trachtenberg, ed., *Classic essays on photography*. New Haven, CT: Leete's Island.

Berdan, F. F., & P. R. Anawalt (1997). *The Essential Codex Mendoza*. Berkeley: University of California Press.

Beschloss, M. R. (1993). The video vise. *Washington Post*, May 2, C1.

Betzig, L. (1988). Redistribution: Equity or exploitation. In L. Betzig, M. Borgerhoff Mulder, & P. Turke, eds., *Human reproductive behavior: A Darwinian perspective*. Cambridge: Cambridge University Press.

Binford, L. R. (1972). Contemporary model building: Paradigms and the current state of Palaeolithic research. In D. L. Clarke, ed., *Models in archaeology*. London: Methuen.

———— (1978). *Nunamiut ethnoarchaeology*. New York: Academic Press.

Birley, A. (1987[1966]). *Marcus Aurelius: A biography*. Rev. ed. New Haven, CT: Yale University Press.

Blainey, G. (1976). *Triumph of the nomads: A history of aboriginal Australia*. Woodstock, NY: Overlook.

Blair, C., M. S. Jeppeson, & E. Pucci, Jr., (1991). Public memorializing in postmodernity: The Vietnam Veterans Memorial as prototype. *Quarterly Journal of Speech*, August, 263–288.

Blick, J. (1988). Genocidal warfare in tribal societies as a result of European-induced culture conflict. *Man* (n.s.), 23, 654–670.

Boone, E. H. (1996). Manuscript painting in service of imperial ideology. In F. F. Berdan, et al., *Aztec imperial strategies*. Washington, DC: Dumbarton Oaks.

Bowker, H. (1992). "Involve the community," Increase security in Somalia. [Live report], CNN, August 21.

Brain, C. (1981). *The hunters or the hunted*. Chicago: University of Chicago Press.

Bray, H. (1997). Wargame software finds military and civilian uses. *Boston Globe*, April 17.

Breuil, H. (1952). *Four hundred centuries of cave art* [M. E. Boyle, trans.]. Dordogne: Centre d'Etudes et de documentation Préhistoriques.

Brimble, A. R. (1963). The construction of a non-verbal intelligence test in Northern Rhodesia. *Rhodes-Livingston Journal*, 34, 23–35.

Brody, R. A. (1984). International crisis: Rallying point for the president? *Public Opinion*, 6, 41–43.

Brookfield, H. C., & P. Brown (1963). *Struggle for land*. Melbourne: Oxford University Press.

Brooks, R. R. R., & V. S. Wakankar (1976). *Stone Age painting in India*. New Haven, CT: Yale University Press.

Brown, J. K. (1970). A note on the division of labour by sex. *American Anthropologist*, 72, 1073–1078.

Brown, S. F. (1993). The secret ship. *Popular Science*, October, 93–96.

Bruntz, G. G. (1938). *Allied propaganda and the collapse of the German empire in 1918*. Stanford: Stanford University Press.

Buddle, A. (1990). The Tipu Mania: Narrative sketches of the conquest of Mysore. *Marg*, XL, 4, 53–70.

Burrows, W. E. (1986). *Deep black: Space espionage and national security*. New York: Random House.

Burton, M. L., L. A. Brudner, & D. R. White (1977). A model of the sexual division of labor. *American Ethnologist*, 4, 2, 227–251.

Caesar, Gaius Julius. (1982 ed.). *The conquest of Gaul* [S.A. Handford, trans.]. [Rev. By Jane F. Gardener.] New York: Penguin.

Cahill, J. (1988). *Three alternative histories of Chinese painting*. Lawrence, KS: University of Kansas.

Cairncross, F. (1997). *The death of distance: How the communications revolution will change our lives*. Boston: Harvard Business School Press.

Cant, J. G. H., & L. A. Temerin (1984). A conceptual approach to foraging adaptations in primates. In P. Rodman & J. Cant, eds., *Adaptations for foraging in nonhuman primates.* New York: Columbia University Press.

Carlebach, M. L. (1992). *The origins of photojournalism in America.* Washington, DC: Smithsonian Institution Press.

Carmichael, J. (1989). *First World War photographers.* London: Routledge.

Carter, A. C. R. (1900). *The work of war artists in South Africa.* London: Art Journal Office.

Cassidy, C. M. (1991). The good body: When big is better. *Medical Anthropology,* 13, 3, 181–213.

———— (1980). Nutrition and health in agriculturalists and hunter-gatherers. In N. W. Jerome, R. F. Kendal, & G. H. Pelto, Eds., *Nutritional anthropology: Contemporary approaches to diet and culture.* Bedford Hills, NY: Redgrave.

Caughly, G. (1988). The colonization of New Zealand by the Polynesians. *Journal of the Royal Society of New Zealand,* 18, 245–270.

Chagnon, N. A. (1974). *Studying the Yanomamö.* New York: Holt, Rinehart & Winston.

———— (1983). *Yanomamö: The fierce people.* 3rd ed. New York: Holt, Rinehart & Winston.

Chandler, D. (1973). *Marlborough as military commander.* New York: Charles Scribner's Sons.

Chandler, D. G. (1966). *The campaigns of Napoleon.* New York: Macmillan.

Chauvet, J.-M., E. B. Deschamps, & C. Hillaire (1996). *Dawn of art: The Chauvet cave, the oldest known paintings in the world.* New York: Harry N. Abrams.

Ch'ên, J. (1965). *Mao and the Chinese revolution.* London: Oxford University Press.

Cheng, T. (1983). *Studies in Chinese art.* Hong Kong: Chinese University Press.

Chipp, H. B. (1988). *Picasso's Guernica: History, transformations, meanings.* Berkeley: University of California Press.

Chittenden, H. M., & A. T. Richardson (1905). *Life, letters and travels of Father Pierre Jean DeSmet, S.J. 1801–1873.* Vol. 3. Francis P. Harper.

Cincinnatus. (1981). *Self-destruction: The disintegration and decay of the United States Army during the Vietnam era.* New York: W. W. Norton.

Clark, G. A., & L. G. Straus (1983). Late Pleistocene hunter-gatherer adaptations in Cantabrian Spain. In G. Bailey, ed., *Hunter-gatherer economy in prehistory: A European perspective.* Cambridge: Cambridge University Press.

Clark, R. E. (1972). *Reference group theory and delinquency.* New York: Behavioral Publications.

Clausewitz, C. von. (1991). *On war* (A. Rapoport, ed. J. J. Graham, trans.). New York: Dorset.

Clottes, J., & J. Courtin (1996). *The cave beneath the sea: Paleolithic images at Cosquer* [M. Garner, trans.]. New York: Harry N. Abrams.

Cobb, J. (1962). Photographers of the Civil War era. *Military Affairs,* 26, 127–135.

Codrescu, A. (1991). *The hole in the flag: A Romanian exile's story of return and revolution*. New York: William Morrow.

Coe, M. D. (1993). *The Maya*. 5th ed. London: Thames & Hudson.

Cohen, A. (1997). *The Alexander Mosaic: Stories of victory and defeat*. Cambridge: Cambridge University Press.

Cohen, E. A., ed. 1993. *United States Air Force Gulf War power survey*. Vol. II Washington, DC: U.S. Air Force/Government Printing Office.

———, & J. Gooch (1991). *Military misfortunes: The anatomy of failure in war*. New York: Vintage.

Cohen, M. N. (1987). The significance of long-term changes in human diet and food economy. In M. Harris & E. B. Ross, eds., *Food and evolution: Toward a theory of human food habits*. Philadelphia: Temple University Press.

Colley, L. (1984). The apotheosis of George III: Loyalty, royalty and the British nation, 1760–1820. *Past and Present*, February, no. 102, 94–129.

——— (1986). Whose nation? Class and national consciousness in Britain, 1750–1830. *Past and Present*, November, no. 113, 97–117.

Collier, J. Jr., & M. Collier (1986). *Visual anthropology: Photography as a research method*. Rev. ed. Albuquerque: University of New Mexico Press.

Collon, D. (1987). *First impressions: Cylinder seals in the ancient Near East*. Chicago: University of Chicago Press.

Commisky, P., & J. Bryant (1982). Factors involved in generating suspense. *Human Communication Research*, 9, 49–58.

Conner, S. W., & B. L. Conner (1971). *Rock art of the Montana High Plains*. Santa Barbara: University of California Press.

Conquest, R. (1986). *The harvest of sorrow: Soviet collectivization and the terror-famine*. New York: Oxford University Press.

Cook, B. L. (1981). *Understanding pictures in Papua New Guinea*. Elgin, IL: David C. Cook.

———, D. Fussell, & A. Haaland, (1978). Communicating with pictures in Nepal. *Educational Broadcasting International*, 11, 25–32.

Cooley, C. H. (1929). *Social organization: A study of the larger mind*. New York: Charles Scribner's Sons.

Coombs, R. B. (1983). *Before endeavors fade*. London: Battle of Britain International.

Cordain, L., J. B. Miller and N. Mann. (1999) Scant evidence of periodic starvation among hunter-gatherers. *Diabetologia* [42, 383–384].

Cordesman, A. H., & A. R. Wagner (1996). *The lessons of modern war. Vol. IV: The Gulf War*. Boulder, CO: Westview Press.

Corliss, R. (1987). Platoon: Vietnam, the way it really was, on film. *Time*, 26.

Coser, L. (1956). *The functions of social conflict*. New York: Free Press.

Crombie, T. (1959). The death of Wolfe in paintings. A bicentenary review. *The Connoisseur*, CXLIV, 579, 56–57.

Curtis, J. E., & J. E. Reade, eds. (1995). *Art and empire: Treasures from Assyria in the British Museum*. New York: Metropolitan Museum of Art.

Custen, G. (1980). "Film talk: Viewers' responses to a film as a socially situated event." Ph.D. dissertation, University of Pennsylvania.

Dadrian, V. N. (1995). *The history of the Armenian Genocide: Ethnic conflict from the Balkans to Anatolia to the Caucasus.* 3rd ed. Providence, RI: Berghahn.

Daniel, H. (1948). *The world of Jacques Callot.* New York: Lear.

Dart, R. (1957). The Ostoedontokeratic culture of the *Australopithecus Africanus. Memoirs of the Transvaal Museum,* 10, 1–105.

Dastugue, J., & M. A. de Lumley (1976). Les maladies des hommes préhistoriques du Paléolithique et du Mésolithique. In *La préhistorique Française.* Vol. 1(2). Paris: Centre National de la Recherche Scientifique.

Davis, W. (1992). *Masking the blow: The scene of representation in late prehistoric Egyptian art.* Berkeley: University of California Press.

De Bloch, J. (1972). *The future of war in its technical, economic and political relations* [R. C. Long, trans.]. New York: Garland.

De La Maziere, C. (1974). *The captive dreamer* [F. Stuart, trans.]. New York: Saturday Review Press/E.P. Dutton.

deBlaye, E. (1989). *Dollarwise USA, 1989–1990* [Susan Poole, ed; Maxwell R. D. Vos, trans.]. New York: Simon & Schuster.

DeGroot, P. (1980). Information transfer in a socially roosting weaver bird (*Quelea quelea*; Ploceinae): An experimental study. *Animal Behavior,* 28, 1249–1254.

Delluc, B., & G. Delluc (1981). La Grotte ornée de Comarque à Sireuil (Dordogne). *Gallia Préhistoire,* 24, 1–97.

———— (1984). Faune figurée et faune consommée: Une magie de la chasse? *Histoire et Archaeologie,* 87, 28–29.

Delpech, F. (1983). *Les faunes du Paléolithique Supérieur dans le sud-ouest de la France.* Paris: Centre National de la Recherche Scientifique.

Delporte, H. (1984). L'art mobilier et ses rapports avec la faune paléolithique. In H.-G. Bandi, et al., eds., *La contribution de la zoologie et de l'éthologie à l'interprétation de l'art des peuples chasseurs préhistoriques.* Fribourg, Switzerland: Editions Universitaires.

Desroches Noblecourt, C. (1996). *Ramsès II: La véritable histoire.* Paris: Pygmalion.

Destexhe, A. (1995). *Rwanda and genocide in the twentieth century* [A. Marscher, trans.]. New York: New York University Press.

Devroy, A. (1991). Commander-in-Chief leaves military details to Pentagon. *Washington Post,* January 19, A26.

Diamond, J. (1992). *The third chimpanzee: The evolution and future of the human animal.* New York: Harper Perennial.

Diaz, B. (1963). *The conquest of New Spain* [J. M. Cohen, trans.]. Harmondsworth, UK: Penguin Classics.

Dio Cassius. (1970). *Dio's Roman history.* Vol. 8. [E. Cary, trans.]. Cambridge, MA: Harvard University Press.

Diodorus Siculus. (1946[1933]). Vol. I [C. H. Oldfather, trans.]. Cambridge, MA: Harvard University Press.

Dirks, J. A. & E. Gibson (1977). Infants' perception of similarity between live people and their photographs. *Child Development*, 48, 124–130.

Divale, W. T., & M. Harris (1976). Population, warfare, and the male supremacist complex. *American Anthropologist*, 78, 3, 521–538.

Division of the Chief of Staff, Intelligence Branch. (1908). *Wellington's campaigns in India*. Calcutta: Superintendent Government Printing.

Dornbusch, S. (1955). The military academy as an assimilating institution. *Social Forces*, 33, 316–321.

Douglass, J. W. (1968). *The non-violent cross: A theology of revolution and peace*. London: Geoffrey Chapman.

Dowd, D. L. (1948). *Pageant master of the republic: Jacques-Louis David and the French Revolution*. Lincoln: University of Nebraska Press.

Dower, J. W. (1986). *War without mercy: Race and power in the Pacific War*. New York: Pantheon.

Dozois, G. (1997). Summation: 1996. In G. Dozois, ed., *The year's best science fiction: Fourteenth annual collection*. New York: St. Martin's Press.

Duhard, J-P. (1991). The shape of Pleistocene women. *Antiquity*, 65, 552–561.

——— (1993). Upper Palaeolithic figures as a reflection of human morphology and social organization. *Antiquity*, 67, 254, 83–91.

Dunnigan, J. F., & A. Bay (1992). *From shield to storm*. New York: William Morrow.

Eisenstein, S. M. (1988). *Eisenstein: Writings, 1922–1934* [R. Taylor, ed. and trans.]. Bloomington: Indiana University Press.

Eliade, M. (1960). *Myths, dreams and mysteries* [P. Mairet, trans.]. New York: Harper & Brothers.

Emerson, S. (1998). *Secret warriors: Inside the covert military operations of the Reagan era*. New York: Putnam.

Emery, W. B. (1961). *Archaic Egypt*. Harmondsworth, UK: Penguin.

Epstein, E. J. (1973). *News from nowhere*. New York: Random House.

Erikson, E. H. (1958). *Young man Luther: A study in psychoanalysis and history*. New York: W. W. Norton.

——— (1966). Ontogeny of ritualization. In R. M. Loewenstein, et al., eds., *Psychoanalysis—A general psychology*. New York: International Universities Press.

Essame, H. (1974). *Patton: A study in command*. New York: Charles Scribner's Sons.

Ezickson, A. J. (1938). *Get that picture! The story of the news cameraman*. New York: National Library Press.

Fairservis, W. A., Jr. (1991). A revised view of the Na'rmr palette. *Journal of the American Research Center in Egypt*, 28, 1–20.

Farnsworth, C. H. (1994). Torture by army peacekeepers in Somalia shocks Canada. *New York Times*, November 27.

Fenton, T. (1980). Bringing you today's war—Today. *TV Guide*, November 15, 36–38.

Ferguson, R. B. (1990a). Blood of the Leviathan: Western contact and warfare in Amazonia. *American Ethnologist*, 17, 237–257.

————— (1990b). Explaining war. In J. Haas, ed., *Explaining war*. New York: Cambridge University Press.

————— (1992). Tribal warfare. *Scientific American*, January, 108–113.

————— (1995). *Yanomami warfare: A political history*. Santa Fe, NM: School of American Research Press.

—————, & N. L. Whitehead, eds. (1992). *War in the tribal zone*. Santa Fe, NM: School of American Research Press.

Ferrill, A. (1985). *The origins of war: From the Stone Age to Alexander the Great*. New York: Thames & Hudson.

Ferro, M. (1976). The fiction film and historical analysis. In P. Smith, ed., *The historian and film*. Cambridge, England: Cambridge University Press.

Fest, J. C. (1972). *The face of the Third Reich* [M. Bullock, trans.]. London: Penguin.

Festinger, L., S. Schachter, & K. Back (1963). *Social pressures in informal groups: A study of human factors in housing*. Stanford: Stanford University Press.

Finegan, J. (1959). *Light from the ancient past*. 2nd ed. Princeton: Princeton University Press.

Fischhoff, B., P. Slovic, & S. Lichtenstein (1978). Fault trees: Sensitivity of estimated failure probablities to problem representation. *Journal of Experimental Psychology: Human Perception and Performance*, 4, 2, 330–344.

Fisher, E. (1979). *Women's creation*. New York: McGraw-Hill.

Fishman, M. (1980). *Manufacturing the news*. Austin: University of Texas Press.

Fleming, C. (1969). Rats and moa extinction. *Notornis*, 16, 210–211.

Flenley, J. (1979). Stratigraphic evidence of environmental change on Easter Island. *Asian Perspectives*, 22, 33–40.

—————, & S. King (1984). Late Quaternary pollen records from Easter Island. *Nature*, 307, 47–50.

Fletcher, A. C., & F. La Flesche (1906). The Omaha tribe. *Bureau of American Ethnology, Annual Report*, 27, 281.

*Food & Nutrition News* (Summer 1998).

Frank, A. (1952). *The diary of a young girl* [B. M. Mooyaart-Doubleday, trans.]. New York: Modern Library.

Frassanito, W. (1983). *Grant and Lee: The Virginia campaign, 1864–1865*. New York: Charles Scribner's Sons.

Freeman, J., ed. (1941). *The Englishman at war*. London: Allen & Unwin.

Freeman, L. G. (1981). The fat of the land: Notes on Paleolithic diet in Iberia. In R. Harding & G. Teleki, eds., *Omnivorous primates*. New York: Columbia University Press.

Freud, S. (1940). *Group psychology and the analysis of the ego*. 2nd ed. [J. Strachey, trans.]. London: Hogarth Press.

Freund, G. (1980). *Photography and society*. Boston: David R. Godine.

Friedman, G., & M. Friedman (1996). *The future of war: Power, technology, and American world dominance in the 21st century*. New York: Crown.

Frison, G. C. (1967). The Piney Creek sites, Wyoming. *University of Wyoming Publications*, 3, 1–92.

—— (1970). The Glenrock buffalo jump, 48CO304: Late prehistoric period buffalo procurement and butchering. *Plains Anthropologist Memoir*, 7, 4–5.

—— (1971). The buffalo pound in Northwestern Plains prehistory: Site 48CA302, Wyoming. *American Antiquity*, 36, 77–91.

—— (1987). Prehistoric, plains-mountain, large-mammal, communal hunting strategies. In M. H. Nitecki, & D. V. Nitecki, eds., *The evolution of human hunting*. New York: Plenum.

Frobenius, L., & D. C. Fox (1937). *Prehistoric rock pictures in Europe and Africa*. New York: Museum of Modern Art.

Fronto. (1920) *Correspondence*. [C.R. Haines, trans.]. London: Heinemann.

Frost, F. J. (1979). The dubious origin of the marathon. *American Journal of Archeological History*, 4, 159–163.

Fussell, P. (1989). *Wartime*. New York: Oxford University Press.

—— (1991). *Bad, or, The dumbing of America*. New York: Summit.

Gailey, P. (1991). Deaths of Iraqi civilians throw U.S. on defensive. *St. Petersburg Times*, February 14, 3A.

Galt, J. (1960). *The life of Benjamin West*. Part II. Gainesville, FL: Scholars' Facsimiles & Reprints.

Galtung, J., & M. H. Ruge (1965). The structure of foreign news. *Journal of International Peace Research*, 1, 64–90.

Gammage, B. (1975). *The broken years: Australian soldiers in the Great War*. New York: Penguin.

Gans, H. J. (1979). *Deciding what's news*. New York: Vintage.

Garrett, L. (1991). The dead. *Columbia Journalism Review*, May–June, 32.

Gernsheim, H. (1982). *The origins of photography*. London: Thames & Hudson.

——, & A. Gernsheim (1954). *Roger Fenton, photographer of the Crimean War*. London: Secker & Warburg.

Gibbon, E. (n.d). *The decline and fall of the Roman Empire*. Vol. I. New York: Modern Library.

Gibson, J. W. (1986). *The perfect war: Technowar in Vietnam*. Boston: Atlantic Monthly Press.

Gilliard, E. T. (1969). *Birds of paradise and bower birds*. Garden City, NY: Natural History Press.

Gilmore, G. J. (1997). Soldier system transforms infantrymen. *Army News Service*, March 7 [on-line ed.].

Gilmore, M. R. (1924). Old Assiniboine buffalo-drive in North Dakota. *Indian Notes*, 1, 204–211.

Girardet, E. (1993). Public opinion, the media, and humanitarianism. In T. G. Weiss and L. Minear, eds., *Humanitarianism across borders: Sustaining civilians in times of war*. Boulder, CO: Lynne Rienner.

Glasse, R. (1968). *Huli of Papua*. Paris: Mouton.

Glezer, V. (1995). *Vision and mind: Modeling mental functions.* Mahwah, NJ: Lawrence Erlbaum.

Godden, E. (1982). *Rock paintings of aboriginal Australia.* Wellington, Australia: Reed.

Goedicke, H. (Ed). (1985). *Perspectives on the battle of Kadesh.* Baltimore: Halgo.

Goldberg, V. (Ed.). (1981). *Photography in print.* New York: Simon & Schuster.

Goldhagen, D. J. (1996). *Hitler's willing executioners: Ordinary Germans and the Holocaust.* New York: Alfred A. Knopf.

Gombrich, E. H. (1974). The visual image. In D. R. Olson, ed., *Media and symbols: The forms of expression, communication, and education.* Chicago: National Society for the Study of Education.

———— (1969[1960]). *Art and illusion: A study in the psychology of pictorial representation.* Rev. ed. Princeton: Princeton University Press.

Goodall, J. (1986). *The chimpanzees of Gombe: Patterns of behavior.* Cambridge, MA: Belknap.

———— (1990). *Through a window: My thirty years with the chimpanzees of Gombe.* Boston: Houghton Mifflin.

Goodman, N. (1976). *Languages of art: An approach to a theory of symbols.* Indianapolis: Hackett.

Gordon, M. R. (1992). TV army on the beach took U.S. by surprise. *New York Times,* December 10, A18.

Goscinny & Uderzo. (1976). *Obélix et compagnie: Une aventure d'Astérix.* Paris: Dargaud.

Gould, S. (1994). The evolution of life on Earth. *Scientific American,* October, 85–91.

Gourevitch, P. (1995). Letter from Rwanda: After the genocide. *The New Yorker,* December 18, 78–95.

Grant, M. (1950). *Roman anniversary issues.* Cambridge: Cambridge University Press.

Gray, J. (1990). *Rebellions and revolutions: China from the 1800s to the 1980s.* Oxford: Oxford University Press.

Greene, E. (1987). Individuals in an osprey colony descriminate between high and low quality information. *Nature,* 329, 239–241.

Grinnell, G. B. (1892). *The Cheyenne Indians.* Vol. 2. New Haven, CT: Yale University Press.

———— (1962). Blackfoot lodge tales. Lincoln: University of Nebraska Press.

Grønnow, B. (1986). Recent archaeological investigations of West Greenland caribou hunting. *Arctic Anthropology,* 23, 57–80.

Gross, L. (1985). Life vs. art: The interpretation of visual narratives. *Studies in Visual Communication,* 11, 4, 2–11.

Grosshans, H. (1983). *Hitler and the artists.* New York: Holmes & Meier.

Grossman, D. (1995). *On killing: The psychological cost of learning to kill in war and society.* Boston: Little, Brown.

Gucwa, D., & J. Ehmann (1985). *To whom it may concern: An investigation of the art of elephants.* New York: W. W. Norton.

Guma, T. A. (1982). "A comparison of the effects of black and white photographs vs. black and white line drawings on comprehension of a written or an oral text in English by Zulu children." Unpublished doctoral dissertation. University of Pittsburgh.

Guthrie, R. D. (1984). Ethological observations from Palaeolithic art. In H.-G. Bandi, et al. eds., *La contribution de la zoologie et de l'éthologie à l'interprétation de l'art des peuples chasseurs préhistoriques.* Troisième Colloque de la Société Suisse des Sciences Humaines. Fribourg, Switzerland: Editions Universitaires.

Gutstadt, L. E. (1993). Taking the pulse of the CNN audience: A case study of the Gulf War. *Political Communication,* 10, 389–399.

Hadingham, E. (1980). *Secrets of the Ice Age: The world of the cave artists.* London: William Heinemann.

Haines, H. W. (1986). "What kind of war?": An analysis of the Vietnam Veterans Memorial. *Critical Studies in Mass Communication,* 3, 1–20.

Hale, J. R. (1988). The soldier in Germanic graphic art of the Renaissance. In R. I. Rotberg & T. K. Rabb, eds., *Art and history: Images and their meaning.* Cambridge: Cambridge University Press.

Hallahan, W. H. (1994). *Misfire: The history of how America's small arms have failed our military.* New York: Charles Scribner's Sons.

Hallion, R. P. (1992). *Storm over Iraq: Air power and the Gulf War.* Washington, DC: Smithsonian Institution Press.

Hallström, G. (1960). *Monumental art of northern Sweden from the Stone Age.* Stockholm: Almquist & Wiksell.

Halverson, J. (1992). Paleolithic art and cognition. *Journal of Psychology,* 126, 3, 221–236.

Hamilton, I. (1908). *A staff officer's scrap book during the Russo-Japanese War,* Vol. I. London: Arnold.

Hammond, W. M. (1988). *Public affairs: The military and the media, 1962–1968.* Washington, DC: Center of Military History.

Hankinson, A. (1982). *Man of wars: William Howard Russell of "The Times."* London: William Heinemann.

Hannestad, N. (1986). *Roman art and imperial policy.* Aarhus, Denmark: Aarhus University Press.

Harrington, P. (1993). *British artists and war: The face of battle in paintings and prints, 1700–1914.* London: Greenhill Books.

Harris, C. R. (1991). Digitalization and manipulation of news photographs. *Journal of Mass Media Ethics,* 6, 164–74.

Harris, M. (1978). Cannibals and kings: The origins of culture. New York: Vintage.

———— (1984). A cultural materialist theory of band and village warfare: The Yanomamo test. In R. B. Ferguson, ed., *Warfare, culture, and environment.* Orlando, FL: Academic Press.

Hasenauer, H. (1992). Glimpsing the future soldier. *Soldiers*, November, 49–50.

———— (1995). The 21st century soldier. *Soldiers*, August, 37–39.

Hawkes, K. (1993). Why hunter-gatherers work. *Current Anthropology*, 34, 341–361.

———— K., Hill, & J. O'Connell (1982). Why hunters gather: Optimal foraging and the Aché of eastern Paraguay. *American Ethnologist*, 9, 379–398.

Hayden, B. (1981a). Research and development in the Stone Age: Technological transitions among hunter-gatherers. *Current Anthropology*, 22, 5, 519–548.

———— (1981b). Subsistence and ecological adaptations of modern hunter/gatherers. In R. Harding & G. Teleki, eds., *Omnivorous primates*. New York: Columbia University Press.

———— (1992). Observing prehistoric women. In C. Claassen, ed., *Exploring gender through archaeology. Monographs in World Archaeology*. Madison: Prehistory Press.

————, B. Chisholm, & H. P. Schwarcz (1987). Fishing and foraging: Marine resources in the Upper Paleolithic of France. In O. Soffer, Ed., *The Pleistocene old world: Regional perspectives*. New York: Plenum.

Hazlett, J. (1995). Just-in-time warfare. In S. Johnson and M. Libicki, eds., *Dominant battlespace knowledge*. Washington, DC: National Defense University Press [online].

Heider, K. G. (1970). *The Dugum Dani*. Viking fund publications in anthropology, no. 49. New York: Wenner-Gren Foundation for Anthropological Research.

———— (1979). *Grand Valley Dani: Peaceful warriors*. New York: Holt, Rinehart & Winston.

Heiman, G. (1972). *Aerial photography: The story of aerial mapping and reconnaissance*. New York: Macmillan.

Herzstein, R. E. (1987). *The war that Hitler won: Goebbels and the Nazi media campaign*. New York: Paragon House.

Hill, K. (1982). Hunting and human evolution. *Journal of Human Evolution*, 11, 521–544.

————, & H. Kaplan (1988). Tradeoffs in male and female reproductive strategies among the Ache: Parts 1 & 2. In L. Betzig, M. Borgerhoff Mulder, & P. Turke, eds., *Human reproductive behavior: A Darwinian perspective*. New York: Cambridge University Press.

Hilterman, J. R. (1991). Bomb now, die later. *Mother Jones*, 16, 4, July–August, 46.

Himmelheber, H. (1963). Personality and technique of African sculptors. In M. Mead, J. B. Bird, & H. Himmelheber, eds., *Technique and personality*. New York: Museum of Primitive Art.

Hine, L. (1980). Social photography. In A. Trachtenberg, ed., *Classic essays on photography*. New Haven, CT: Leete's Island.

Hinz, B. (1979). *Art in the Third Reich*. New York: Pantheon.

Hitler, A. (1973). *Hitler's table-talk, 1941–1944: His private conversations* [N. Cameron & R. H. Stevens, trans.]. London: Weidenfeld & Nicolson.

———— (1971[1927]). *Mein Kampf* [R. Manheim, trans.]. Boston: Houghton Mifflin.

Hochberg, J., & V. Brooks (1962). Pictorial recognition as an unlearned ability: A study of one child's performance. *American Journal of Psychology*, 75, 624–628.

Hoffner, C., & J. Cantor, (1991). Perceiving and responding to mass media characters. In J. Bryant & D. Zillman, eds., *Responding to the screen: Reception and reaction processes*. Hillsdale, NJ: Lawrence Erlbaum.

Hogan, J. M. (1994). *The nuclear freeze campaign: Rhetoric and foreign policy in the telepolitical age*. East Lansing: Michigan State University Press.

Höhne, H. (1970). *The order of the death's head* [R. Barry, trans.]. New York: Coward-McCann.

Homer. (1961). *The Iliad of Homer* [R. Lattimore, trans.]. Chicago: University of Chicago Press. Copyright 1951 by The University of Chicago.

Horton, D., & R. R. Wohl (1956). Mass communication and para-social interaction. *Psychiatry*, 19, 215–229.

Hughes, R. (1988). *The fatal shore: The epic of Australia's founding*. New York: Vintage.

Ibn Khaldun (1950). *An Arab philosophy of history* [C. Issawi, trans.]. London: John Murray.

Ivins, W. M., Jr. (1969[1953]). *Prints and visual communication*. Cambridge: M.I.T. Press.

Jamieson, K. H. (1992). *Dirty politics: Deception, distraction, and democracy*. New York: Oxford University Press.

Jaubert, A. (1989[1986]). *Making people disappear*. Washington, DC: Pergamon-Brassey's.

Jensen, P. S., et al. (1997). Evolution and revolution in child psychiatry: ADHD as a disorder of adaptation. *Journal of the American Academy, Child and Adolescent Psychiatry*, 36, 12, 1672–1679.

Jochim, M. A. (1983). Paleolithic art in ecological perspective. In G. Bailey, ed., *Hunter-gatherer economy in prehistory*. Cambridge: Cambridge University Press.

Johnson, S., & M. Libicki, eds. (1995). *Dominant battlespace knowledge*. Washington, DC: National Defense University Press [on-line].

Jones, A.H.M. (1956). Numismatics and history. In R. A. G. Carson & C. H. V. Sutherland, eds., *Essays in Roman coinage presented to Harold Mattingly*. Oxford: Oxford University Press.

Jones, C. P. (1978). *The Roman world of Dio Chrysostom*. Cambridge, MA: Harvard University Press.

Josephus. (1981). *The Jewish war* [G. A. Williamson, trans.; E. M. Smallwood, ed.]. New York: Penguin.

Jowett, G. S., & V. O'Donnell (1992). *Propaganda and persuasion*. 2nd ed. Newbury Park, CA: Sage.

Kaplan, H., & K. Hill (1985a). Food sharing among Ache foragers: Tests of explanatory hypotheses. *Current Anthropology*, 26, 223–246.

——— (1985b). Hunting ability and reproductive success among male Ache foragers. *Current Anthropology*, 26, 131–133.

Karnow, S. (1983). *Vietnam: A history.* New York: Penguin.

Katz, M. M., & M. J. Konner (1981). The role of the father: An anthropological perspective. In M. E. Lamb, ed., *The role of the father in childhood development.* New York: John Wiley & Sons.

Katz, R. (1982). *Boiling energy.* Cambridge, MA: Harvard University Press.

Keegan, J. (1976). *The face of battle.* New York: Dorset.

Keeley, L. H. (1996). *War before civilization: The myth of the peaceful savage.* New York: Oxford University Press.

Keen, S. (1986). *Faces of the enemy: Reflections of the hostile imagination.* San Francisco: Harper & Row.

Kehoe, T. F. (1987). Corralling life. *Wisconsin Academy Review,* March, 45–48.

Kelly, M. (1993). *Martyr's day: Chronicle of a small war.* New York: Random House.

Kelly, R. L., & L. C. Todd (1988). Coming into the country: Early Paleoindian hunting and mobility. *American Antiquity,* 53, 231–244.

Kent, S. (1993). Variability in faunal assemblages. *Journal of Anthropological Archaeology,* 12, 232–285.

Keppie, L. (1984). *The making of the Roman Army: From republic to empire.* Totowa, NJ: Barnes & Noble.

Kernell, S. (1978). Explaining presidential popularity. *American Political Science Review,* 72, 506–522.

Keyser, J. D. (1977). Writing-on-Stone: Rock art on the northwestern plains. *Canadian Journal of Archaeology,* 1, 15–80.

——— (1979). The Plains Indian war complex and the rock art of Writing-on-Stone, Alberta, Canada. *Journal of Field Archaeology,* 6, 1, 41–48.

——— (1987). A lexicon for historic Plains Indian rock art: Increasing interpretive potential. *Plains Anthropologist,* 32, 43–71.

King, L., with M. Stencel. (1993). *On the line: The new road to the White House.* New York: Harcourt Brace.

Kinnard, D. (1977). *The war managers.* Hanover, NH: University Press of New England.

Kirch, P. V. (1984). *The evolution of the Polynesian chiefdoms.* Cambridge: Cambridge University Press.

Kirk, G. S., ed. (1970). Heraclitus (of Ephesus).*The cosmic fragments.* Cambridge: Cambridge University Press.

Kivett, M. F., & R. E. Jensen (1976). Archeological investigations at the Crow Creek Site (39BF11). *Nebraska State Historical Society Publications in Anthropology,* no. 7. Lincoln, NE: Nebraska State Historical Society.

Klee, E., W. Dressen, & V. Riess, eds. (1988*). "The good old days": The Holocaust as seen by its perpetrators and bystanders.* New York: Konecky & Konecky.

Knauft, B. (1987). Reconsidering violence in human societies: Homicide among the Gebusi of New Guinea. *Current Anthropology,* 28, 457–500.

Knecht, H. (1994). Late Ice Age hunting technology. *Scientific American,* 271, 1, 82–87.

Knightley, P. (1975). *The first casualty, from the Crimea to Vietnam: The war correspondent as hero, propagandist, and myth maker*. New York: Harcourt Brace Jovanovich.

Kottak, C. (1991). *Cultural anthropology*. New York: McGraw-Hill.

Kracauer, S. (1974[1947]). *From Caligari to Hitler: A psychological history of the German film*. Princeton, NJ: Princeton University Press.

Kraft, R. N. (1987). The influence of camera angle on comprehension of pictorial events. *Memory and Cognition*, 15, 291–307.

Kubler, G. (1984). *The art and architecture of ancient America: The Mexican, Maya and Andean peoples*. 3rd ed. New York: Penguin.

Kunter, M. (1981). Frakturen und Verletzungen des vor- und frühgeschichtlichen Menschen. *Archäologie und Naturwissenschaft*, tome 2, 221–246.

Kurtz, H. (1992). TV viewers join military critics of media spectacle on beach, *Washington Post*, December 10, A33.

Lajoux, J.-D. (1963). *The rock paintings of Tassili*. London: Thames & Hudson.

Lalumia, M. (1983). Realism and anti-aristocratic sentiment in Victorian depictions of the Crimean War. *Victorian Studies*, XXVII, 4, 25–52.

Larson, J. F. (1992). *Television's window on the world*. Norwood, NJ: Ablex.

Lasswell, H. D. (1972). *Propaganda technique in the World War*. New York: Garland.

Le Bon, G. (1896). *The crowd: A study of the popular mind*. London: Ernest Benn.

Leason, P. A. (1939). A new view of the western European group of the Quaternary cave art. *Proceedings of the Prehistoric Society*, 5, 51–56.

Lederman, J. (1992). *Battle lines: The American media and the intifada*. New York: Henry Holt.

Lee, J. (1992). Somalia landing hours away. *USA Today*, December 8, 1A.

Lee, S., & W-K Ho. (1968). *Chinese art under the Mongols: The Yüan Dynasty*. Cleveland: University of Cleveland Press.

Lehmer, D. J. (1971). Introduction to Middle Missouri Archeology. Anthropological Papers 1. Washington, DC: National Park Service.

Lemarchand, R. (1996). *Burundi: Ethnic conflict and genocide*. New Yok: Cambridge University Press.

Lemkin, R. (1973). *Axis rule in occupied Europe*. New York: Howard Fertig.

Leroi-Gourhan, A. (1967). *Treasures of Prehistoric art*. New York: Harry N. Abrams.

——— (1971). *Préhistoire de l'art occidental*. Paris: Mazenod.

——— (1982). *The dawn of European art: An introduction to Palaeolithic cave painting* [S. Champion, trans.]. Cambridge: Cambridge University Press.

Lewis-Williams, J. D. (1981a). *Believing and seeing: Symbolic meanings in southern San rock paintings*. New York: Academic Press.

——— (1981b). The thin red line: Southern San notions and rock paintings of supernatural potency. *South African Archaeological Bulletin*, 36, 133, 5–13.

Libicki, M. (1994). The mesh and the net: Speculations on armed conflict in an age of free silicon. *McNair Paper*, March, 28.

———— (1997). *Defending cyberspace and other metaphors*. Washington, DC: National Defense University.

Liddicoat, R., & C. Koza (1963). Language development in African infants. *Psychologia Africana*, 10, 108–116.

Liebes, T., & E. Katz (1985). Dallas and Genesis: Primordiality and seriality in popular culture. In J. W. Carey, ed., *Media, myths, and narratives*. Beverly Hills: Sage.

Lipstadt, D. E. (1986). *Beyond belief: The American press and the coming of the Holocaust, 1933–1945*. New York: Free Press.

———— (1993). *Denying the Holocaust: The growing assault on truth and memory*. New York: Free Press.

Livingstone, S. (1857). *Missionary travels and researches in South Africa*. London: James Murray.

Livy (1929). *History of Rome from 29 B.C.*. Vol. VI [B. O. Foster, trans.]. London: William Heinemann.

Lofland, J. (1969). *Deviance and identity*. Englewood Cliffs, NJ: Prentice-Hall.

Lowie, R. H. (1983[1935]). *The Crow Indians*. Lincoln: University of Nebraska Press.

Luckenbill, D. D. (1927). *Ancient records of Assyria and Babylonia*. Vol. II. Chicago: University of Chicago Press.

MacArthur, R. H. (1972). *Geographic ecology*. New York: Harper & Row.

————, & E. O. Wilson (1967). *The theory of island biogeography*. Princeton: Princeton University Press.

Macqueen, J. G. (1975). *The Hittites and their contemporaries in Asia Minor*. Boulder, CO: Westview Press.

Maggs, T., ed. (1979). *Major rock paintings of southern Africa*. Bloomington: Indiana University Press.

Mandelbaum, D. G. (1940). The Plains Cree. *Anthropological Papers of the American Museum of Natural History*, 37, 155–316.

Manheim, J. B. (1991). *All of the people, all the time: Strategic communication and American politics*. New York: M. E. Sharpe.

Mann, A. E. (1981). Diet and human evolution. In R. Harding & G. Teleki, eds., *Omnivorous primates*. New York: Columbia University Press.

Marcus Aurelius (1930). *The communings with himself of Marcus Aurelius Antoninus* [C. R. Haines, trans.] Cambridge, MA: Harvard University Press.

Marcus, J. (1974). The iconography of power among the classic Maya. *World Archaeology*, 6, 83–94.

————, & K. V. Flannery (1996). *Zapotec civilization: How urban society evolved in Mexico's Oaxaca Valley*. New York: Thames & Hudson.

Maringer, J., & H.-G. Bandi (1953). *Art in the Ice Age: Spanish Levant art, Arctic art*. New York: Frederick A. Praeger.

Marling, K. A., & J. Wetenhall (1991). *Iwo Jima: Monuments, memories, and the American hero*. Cambridge, MA: Harvard University Press.

Marshack, A. (1972). *The roots of civilization: The cognitive beginnings of man's first art, symbol and notation*. New York: McGraw-Hill.

———— (1976). Implications of the Palaeolithic symbolic evidence for the origin of language. *American Scientist*, 64, 136–145.

Marshall, L. (1969). The medicine dance of the !Kung Bushmen. *Africa*, 39, 347–381.

Marshall, S. L. A. (1947). *Men against fire: The problem of battle command in future war*. New York: William Morrow.

Martin, P., & R. Kline (1984). *Quaternary extinctions*. Tucson: University of Arizona Press.

Martin, P. S. (1958). Pleistocene ecology and biogeography of North America. In C. L. Hubbs, ed., *Zoogeography: Publ. 51*. American Association for the Advancement of Science.

———— (1966). Africa and Pleistocene overkill. *Nature*, 212, 339–342.

———— (1967). Prehistoric overkill. In P. S. Martin & H. E. Wright, Jr., eds., *Pleistocene extinctions: The search for a cause*. New Haven, CT: Yale University Press.

Mathews, J. J. (1957). *Reporting the wars*. Minneapolis: University of Minnesota Press.

Mauldin, B. (1991[1944]). *Up front*. New York: W. W. Norton.

Maurer, D. (1985). Infants' perception of facedness. In T. M. Field & N. A. Fox, eds., *Social perception in infants*. Norwood, NJ: J. Erlbaum.

May, E. C., G. P. Stadler, & J. F. Votaw (1984). *Ancient and medieval warfare*. Wayne, NJ: Avery.

Mayer, S. L., ed. (1978). *The best of* Signal: *Hitler's wartime picture magazine*. Wigston, Leicester, UK: Magna.

Mazonowicz, D. (1974). *Voices from the Stone Age: A search for cave and canyon art*. New York: Thomas Crowell.

McAllister, D. E. (1993). How much land is there on Earth? For people? For nature. *Global Biodiversity*, 3, 6–7.

McNeill, W. H. (1976). *Plagues and peoples*. Garden City, NY: Anchor.

———— (1995). *Keeping together in time: Dance and drill in human history*. Cambridge, MA: Harvard University Press.

Mead, M. (1968). Alternatives to war. In M. Fried, M. Harris, & R. Murphy, eds., *War: The anthropology of armed conflict and aggression*. Garden City, NY: Natural History Press.

Meggitt, M. (1977). *Blood is their argument*. Palo Alto, CA: Mayfield.

Meier, S. [interview]. (1998). *NewMedia*, June 2, 35.

Mellars, P. (1985). The ecological basis of social complexity in the Upper Paleolithic of Southwestern France. In T. D. Price & J. A. Brown, eds., *Prehistoric hunter-gatherers: The emergence of cultural complexity*. New York: Academic Press.

Mendelssohn Bartholdy, A. (1937). *The war and German society: The testament of a liberal*. New Haven, CT: Yale University Press.

Messaris, P. (1992). "Visual 'manipulation' ": Visual means of affecting responses to images. *Communication*, 13, 181–195.

————— (1994). *Visual "literacy": Image, mind, and reality.* Boulder, CO: Westview Press.

—————, & L. Gross (1977). Interpretations of a photographic narrative by viewers in four age groups. *Studies in the Anthropology of Visual Communication,* 4, 2, 99–111.

Meyers-Levy, J., & L. Peracchio (1992). Getting an angle on advertising: The effect of camera angle on product evaluations. *Journal of Marketing Research,* 29, 454–461.

Milgram, S. (1974). *Obedience to authority.* New York: Harper & Row.

Miller, G. (1998). Personal communication.

Miller, M. E. (1986). *The murals of Bonampak.* Princeton: Princeton University Press.

Millet, N. B. (1990). The Narmer macehead and related objects. *Journal of the American Research Center in Egypt,* 27, 53–59.

Milner, G. R., E., Anderson, & V. G. Smith (1991). Warfare in late prehistoric west-central Illinois. *American Antiquity,* 56, 4, 581–603.

Mitchell, C. (1944). Benjamin West's "Death of Wolfe" and the popular history piece. *Journal of the Warburg and Courtauld Institutes,* 7, 20–33.

Mithen, S. (1988). Looking and learning: Upper Paleolithic art and information gathering. *World Archaeology* 19, 297–327.

Montagna, D. (1981). Benjamin West's *The Death of General Wolfe*: A nationalist narrative. *American Art Journal,* XIII, 2, 72–88.

Mooney, J. (1907). The Cheyenne Indians. *American Anthropological Association,* Memoir I, 412–414.

Moore, J. H. (1990). The reproductive success of Cheyenne war chiefs: A contrary case to Chagnon's Yanomamö. *Current Anthropology,* 31, 3, 322–330.

Morbeck, M. E., A. Galloway, & A. L. Zihlman, eds. (1997). *The evolving female: A life-history perspective.* Princeton University Press.

Morren, G.E.B., Jr. (1984). Warfare on the Highland Fringe of New Guinea: The case of the Mountain Ok. In R. B. Ferguson, ed., *Warfare, culture, and environment.* Orlando, FL: Academic Press.

Mosettig, M., & H. Griggs, Jr. (1980). TV at the front. *Foreign Policy,* 38, 67–79.

Mosimann, J., & P. S. Martin (1975). Simulating overkill by Paleoindians. *American Scientist,* 63, 304–313.

Moskos, C. C., Jr. (1970). *The American enlisted man.* New York: Russell Sage Foundation.

Mosse, G. L. (1990). *Fallen soldiers: Reshaping the memory of the World Wars.* New York: Oxford University Press.

Mowat, F. (1975[1951]). *People of the Deer.* Toronto: Seal.

Mueller, J. (1973). *War, presidents and public opinion.* New York: John Wiley & Sons.

Mulloy, W. (1958). A preliminary historical outline for the Northwestern Plains. *University of Wyoming Publications,* 22, 1, 118–134.

Murdock, G. P., & C. Provost (1973). Factors in the division of labour by sex: A cross cultural analysis. *Ethnology*, 12, 2, 203–225.

Murrow, E. R., & F. W. Friendly, eds. (1955). *See it now*. New York: Simon & Schuster.

Naquin, S., & E. S. Rawski (1987). *Chinese society in the eighteenth century*. New Haven, CT: Yale University Press.

Nelson, G. (1969). *Hunters of the northern ice*. Chicago: University of Chicago Press.

Netting, R. McC. (1974). Kofyar armed conflict: Social causes and consequences. *Journal of Anthropological Research*, 30, 139–163.

Newhall, B. (1982). *The history of photography*. New York: Museum of Modern Art.

Nietzsche, F. (1954). *The twilight of the idols* [A. Ludovici, trans.]. New York: Russell & Russell.

Nishida, T., et al. (1985). Group extinction and female transfer in wild chimpanzees in the Mahale National Park, Tanzania. *Zeitschrift für Tierpsychologie*, 67, 284–381.

Noakes, J., & G. Pridham, eds. (1988). *Nazism: A history in documents and eyewitness accounts, 1919–1945*. Vol. II: *Foreign policy, war and racial extermination*. New York: Schocken.

O'Kane, M. (1995). Bloodless words, bloody war. *The Guardian* (London), December 16, T12.

Oliver, D. (1955). *A Solomon Island society: Kinship and leadership among the Siuai of Bougainville*. Cambridge, MA: Harvard University Press.

Orwell, G. (1954). Marrakech. In *A collection of essays by George Orwell*. New York: Doubleday.

——— (1962). *Inside the whale and other essays*. London: Penguin.

——— (1980[1952]). *Homage to Catalonia*. San Diego: Harcourt Brace Jovanonich.

Otterbein, K. F. (1994). The anthropology of war. In K. F. Otterbein, ed., *Feuding and warfare: Selected works of Keith F. Otterbein*. New York: Gordon & Breach.

Pagden, A., ed. & trans. (1986). *Hernán Cortés: Letters from Mexico*. New Haven, CT: Yale University Press.

Page, C. (1996). *U.S. official propaganda during the Vietnam War, 1965–1973: The limits of persuasion*. New York: Leicester University Press.

Pal, P., & V. Dehejia (1986). *From merchants to emperors: British artists and India, 1757–1930*. Ithaca, NY: Cornell University Press.

Paret, P., B. I. Lewis, & P. Paret (1992). *Persuasive images: Posters of war and revolution from the Hoover Institution Archives*. Princeton: Princeton University Press.

Parry, J. (1992). Senior U.S. official, Serb diplomat get in heated argument at U.N. meeting. *Washington Post*, August 14, A26.

Perlmutter, D. D. (1991). Face-lifting the Death's Head: The calculated pictorial legacy of the Waffen-SS and its modern audience. *Visual Anthropology*, 4, 2, 217–245.

——— (1992). The vision of war in high school social science textbooks. *Communication*, 13, 143–160.

———— (1994). Visual historical methods: Problems, prospects, applications. *Historical Methods*, 27, 4, 167–184.

———— (1995). Opening up photojournalism. *Visual Communication Quarterly*, 2, 2, 9–11.

———— (1997a). Manufacturing visions of society and history in social science textbooks. *Journal of Communication*, 47, 3, 1–14.

———— (1997b). Re-visions of the Holocaust: Textbook images and historical myth-making. *Howard Journal of Communication*, 8, 2, 151–159.

———— (1997c). A picture's worth 8,500,000 people: American news photos as symbols of China. *Visual Communication Quarterly*, 4, 2, 4–7.

———— (1998). *Photojournalism and foreign policy: Framing icons of outrage in international crises.* Westport, CT: Greenwood/Praeger.

Perse, E. M., & R. B. Rubin (1989). Attribution in social and parasocial relationships. *Communication Research*, 16, 59–77.

Peterson, N. (1993). Demand sharing: Reciprocity and the pressure for generosity among foragers. *American Anthropologist*, 95, 860–874.

Pfeiffer, J. E. (1982). *The creative explosion: An inquiry into the origins of art and religion.* New York: Cornell University Press.

Piggott, S. (1965). *Ancient Europe: From the beginnings of agriculture to classical antiquity.* Chicago: Aldine.

Pine, A. (1992). TV's bright lights turn off Pentagon chiefs. *Los Angeles Times*, December 10, A13.

Pliny the Elder (1938). *Natural history.* Vol. IX, Books XXXIII–XXXV. Cambridge, MA: Harvard University Press.

Pliny the Younger (1969) *Letters and Panegyricus.* Vol. II [B. Radice, trans.]. Cambridge, MA: Harvard University Press.

Plutarch (1864). *The lives of the noble Grecians and Romans* [J. Dryden, trans.]. New York: Modern Library.

Pontius, A. A. (1986). Stone-age art "Venuses" as heuristic clues for types of obesity: Contribution to "Iconodiagnosis." *Perceptual and Motor Skills*, 63, 2, 544–546.

Popovich, L. D. (1991). The battle of Kosovo (1389) and battle themes in Serbian art. In W. S. Vucinich & T. A. Emmert, eds., *Kosovo: Legacy of a medieval battle.* Vol. 1. Minneapolis: University of Minnesota Press.

Powell, A. (1988). *Athens and Sparta: Constructing Greek political and social history from 478 BC.* New York: Routledge.

Powell, C. L., with J. E. Persico. (1995). *My American Journey.* New York: Ballantine.

Prange, G. W. (1981). *At dawn we slept: The untold story of Pearl Harbor.* New York: Penguin.

Priestley, J. B. (1972). *Victoria's heyday.* London: William Heinemann.

Pringle, H. (1996). *In search of ancient North America: An archaeological journey to forgotten cultures.* New York: John Wiley & Sons.

Prunier, G. (1995). *The Rwanda crisis: History of a genocide.* New York: Columbia University Press.

Rappaport, R. A. (1967a). *Pigs for the ancestors.* New Haven, CT: Yale University Press.

—————— (1967b). Ritual regulation of environmental relations among a New Guinea people. *Ethnology,* 6, 17–30.

Raup, D. M. (1991). *Extinction. Bad genes or bad luck?* New York: W. W. Norton.

Read, J. M. (1941). *Atrocity propaganda, 1914–1919.* New Haven, CT: Yale University Press.

Reade, J. E. (1976). Elam and Elamites in Assyrian sculpture. *Archäologische Mitteilungen aus Iran,* 9, 97–106.

Redford, K. H., & J. G. Robinson (1987). The game of choice: Patterns of Indian and colonist hunting in the Neotropics. *American Anthropologist,* 89, 650–667.

Reed, F. (1985). Why the media's military coverage misses the mark. *National Review,* December 13, 32.

Reeves, B. (1979). Children's understanding of television people. In E. Wartella, ed., *Children communicating: Media and development of thought, speech, understanding.* Beverly Hills: Sage.

Remarque, E. M. (1975[1929]). *All quiet on the western front* [A. W. Wheen, trans.]. Boston: Little, Brown.

Renfrew, C., & P. Bahn. (1996). *Archaeology: Theories, methods and practice.* 2nd ed. London: Thames and Hudson.

Rhodes, A. (1987). *Propaganda: The art of persuasion. World War II* [V. Margolin, ed.]. Secaucus, NJ: Wellfleet.

Rice, P. C. (1981). Prehistoric Venuses: Symbols of motherhood or womanhood? *Journal of Anthropological Research,* 37, 402–414.

——————, & A. L. Paterson (1985). Cave art and bones: Exploring the interrelationships. *American Anthropologist,* 87, 1, 94–100.

——————, & A. L. Paterson (1986). Validating the cave art—Archeofaunal relationship in Cantabrian Spain. *American Anthropologist,* 88, 3, 658–667.

Richthofen, M. von (1995). *The Red Baron: The autobiography of Manfred von Richthofen* [S. M. Ulanoff, ed.; P. Kilduff, trans.]. New York: Barnes & Noble.

Riddle, W. H. (1940). Dead or alive? *Antiquity,* 14, 151–162.

Rieber, R. W., & R. J. Kelly (1991). Substance and shadow: Images of the enemy. In R. Rieber, ed., *The psychology of war and peace: Images of the enemy.* New York: Plenum.

Ritchin, F. (1990). *In our own image: The coming revolution in photography.* New York: Aperture.

Ritter, G. (1958). *The Schlieffen Plan: Critique of a myth.* New York: Frederick A. Praeger.

Robbin, C. (1995). CIA's Guatemala scandal turns up pressure for quick, broad reform of intelligence services. *Wall Street Journal,* April 11, A22.

Roberts, W. E. (1989). *Jacques-Louis David, revolutionary artist: Art, politics, and the French Revolution.* Chapel Hill: University of North Carolina Press.

Robins, G. (1997). *The art of ancient Egypt.* Cambridge, MA: Harvard University Press.

Roetter, C. (1974). *The art of psychological warfare, 1914–1945.* New York: Stein & Day.

Roper, M. (1969). A survey of the evidence for intrahuman killing in the Pleistocene. *Current Anthropology,* 10, 427–459.

Rosenblum, B. (1978a). *Photographers at work.* New York: Holmes & Meier.

———— (1978b). Style as social process. *American Sociological Review,* 43, 422–438.

Rosensteil, T. B. (1994). Role of TV news in shaping foreign policy under increasing scrutiny. *Los Angeles Times,* July 25, A14.

Ross, J. B. (1984). Effects of contact on revenge hostilities among the Achuarä Jívaro. In R. B. Ferguson, ed., *Warfare, culture, and environment.* Orlando, FL: Academic Press.

Rowley-Conwy, P. (1995). Making first farmers younger: The West European evidence. *Current Anthropology,* 36, 2, 346–353.

Royle, T. (1987). *War report: The war correspondent's view of battle from the Crimea to the Falklands.* London: Mainstream.

Ruspoli, M. (1987). *The cave of Lascaux: The final photographic record.* London: Thames & Hudson.

Ryan, C. (1959). *The longest day: June 6, 1944.* New York: Simon and Schuster.

———— (1974). *A bridge too far.* New York: Simon & Schuster.

Ryberg, I. S. (1967). *Panel reliefs of Marcus Aurelius.* New York: Archeological Institute of America.

Safer, M. (1990). *Flashbacks: On returning to Vietnam.* New York: Random House.

Saggs, H. W. F. (1984). *The might that was Assyria.* London: Sidgwick & Jackson.

Sahlins, M. (1972). *Stone age economics.* Chicago: Aldine-Atherton.

Saleh, M., & H. Sourouzian (1987). *Official catalogue: The Egyptian Museum, Cairo.* Mainz, Germany: Philipp von Zabern.

Sandars, N. K. (1985 [1968]). *Prehistoric art in Europe.* 2nd ed. New York: Penguin.

Sanders, M., & P. M. Taylor (1982). *British propaganda during World War I, 1914–18.* London: Macmillan.

Sartre, J.-P. (1948). *Qu'est-ce que la littérature?* Paris: Gallimard.

Sawyer, J. (1994). Managing chaos. *St. Louis Post-Dispatch,* December 4, 1B.

Scales, R. H., Jr. (1990). *Firepower in limited war.* Washington, DC: National Defense University Press.

Scherer, M. R. (1963). *The legends of Troy in art and literature.* New York: Phaidon Press for the Metropolitan Museum of Art.

Scherman, D. E., ed. (1977). *Life goes to war: A picture history of World War II.* New York: Simon & Schuster.

Schieffelin, E. L. (1976). *The sorrow of the lonely and the burning of the dancers.* New York: St. Martin's Press.

Schröder, T. (1982). *Jacques Callot: Das gesamte Werk.* Vol. I: *Handzeichnungen.* Vol. II: *Druckgraphik.* Munich: Manfred Pawlak.

Schwartz, D. (1992). To tell the truth: Codes of objectivity in photojournalism. *Communication*, 13, 2, 95–109.

Scruggs, J. C., & J. L Swerdlow (1985). *To heal a nation: The Vietnam Veterans Memorial*. New York: Harper.

Sebeok, T. A. (1981). *The play of musement*. Bloomington: Indiana University Press.

Secord, P. F., & C. W. Backman (1964). *Social psychology*. New York: McGraw-Hill.

Segall, M. H., D. T. Campbell, & M. J. Herskovits (1966). *The influence of culture on visual perception*. Indianapolis: Bobbs-Merrill.

Selby, J. (1968). *Stonewall Jackson as military commander*. London: B. T. Batsford, Ltd.

Shankman, P. (1991). Culture contact, cultural ecology, and Dani Warfare. *Man* (n.s.), 26, 299–321.

Shaw, D. (1992). News often has to be seen before it is heard. *Los Angeles Times*, October 26, A16.

Shils, E. A. (1950). Primary groups in the American Army. In R. K. Merton & P. F. Lazarsfeld, eds., *Continuities in social research: Studies in the scope and method of "The American Soldier."* Glencoe, IL: Free Press.

Shilts, R. (1993). *Conduct unbecoming: Lesbians and gays in the U.S. military, Vietnam to the Persian Gulf*. New York: St. Martin's Press.

Shirer, W. L. (1969). *The collapse of the Third Republic: An inquiry into the fall of France in 1940*. New York: Simon & Schuster.

Shostak, M. (1983). *Nisa*. New York: Academic Press.

Shukman, D. (1995). *Tomorrow's war: The threat of high-technology weapons*. New York: Harcourt Brace.

Simberloff, D. (1986). Are we on the verge of mass extinction in the tropical rain forest? In D. K. Elliott, ed., *Dynamics of extinction*. New York: Wiley-Interscience.

Simmel, G. (1955). *Conflict* (K. H. Wolff, trans.). New York: Free Press.

Sloman, S. A. (1994). When explanations compete: The role of explanatory coherence on judgements of likelihood. *Cognition*, 52, 1, 1–21.

Sluka, J. A. (1992). The anthropology of conflict. In C. Nordstrom & J. Martin, eds., *The paths to domination, resistance, and terror*. Berkeley: University of California Press.

Smith, C. (1992). *Late Stone Age hunters of the British Isles*. London: Routledge.

Snyder, J. (1984). *The ideology of the offensive: Military decision making and the disasters of 1914*. Ithaca, NY: Cornell University Press.

Soffer, O. (1991). Upper Paleolithic adaptations in central and eastern Europe and man/mammoth interaction. In O. Soffer & N. D. Praslov, eds., *From Kostenki to Clovis: Upper Paleolithic-Paleoindian adaptations*. New York: Plenum.

Solzhenitsyn, A. (1973). *The Gulag Archipelago*. Vols. I–II [T. P. Whitney, trans.]. New York: Harper & Row.

Sorokin, P. A. (1937). *Social and cultural dynamics*. Vol. III. New York: American Book Co.

Speth, J. D. (1983). *Bison kills and bone counts: Decision making by ancient hunters.* Chicago: University of Chicago Press.

———, & K. A. Spielmann (1983). Energy source, protein metabolism, and hunter-gatherer subsistence strategies. *Journal of Anthropological Archaeology*, 2, 1–31.

Staley, A. (1980). West's Death on the Pale Horse. *Bulletin of the Detroit Institute of Arts*, LVIII, 137–149.

Stanford, D. (1979). Bison kill by Ice Age hunters. *National Geographic*, 155, 1, 114–121.

Starr, B. (1993). Sea shadow emerges into the daylight. *Jane's Defense Weekly*, April 24, 5.

Stearn, R. T. (1986). War and the media in the 19th century: Victorian military artists and the image of war, 1870–1914. *Journal of the Royal United Services Institute for Defence Studies*, September, 55–62.

Stein, G. H. (1966). *The Waffen-SS: Hitler's elite guard at war, 1939–1945.* Ithaca, NY: Cornell University Press.

Stiner, M. C. (1993). Modern human origins: Faunal perspectives. *Annual Review of Anthropology*, 22: 35–82.

Stix, G. (1995). Fighting future wars. *Scientific American*, December, 92–98.

Storr, A. (1988[1965]). *Churchill's black dog, Kafka's mice, and other phenomena of the human mind.* New York: Grove Press.

Stow, G. W. (1905). *The native races of South Africa.* London: Swan Sonnenschein.

Stuart, A. J. (1991). Mammalian extinctions in the late Pleistocene of northern Eurasia and North America. *Biological Reviews*, 66, 453–562.

Sullivan, G. R. (1992). Doctrine: A guide to the future. *Military Review*, February, 2–9.

———, & J. M. Dubik (1993). *Land war in the 21st century.* Carlisle, PA: Strategic Studies Institute, Army War College.

Sutherland, C. H. V. (1974). *Roman coins.* New York: G. P. Putnam's Sons.

Svoboda, J., & E. Vlcek (1991). La nouvelle sépulture de Dolni Vestonice (DV SVI), Tchecoslovaquie. *L'Anthropologie*, 95, 323–28.

Swann, W. B., Jr., & S. J. Read (1981a). Acquiring self-knowledge: The search for feedback that fits. *Journal of Personality and Social Psychology*, 41, 6, 1119–1128.

——— (1981b). Self-verification processes: How we sustain our self-conceptions. *Journal of Experimental Social Psychology*, 17, 351–372.

Taçon, P., & C. Chippindale (1994). Australia's ancient warriors: Changing depictions of fighting in the rock art of Arnhem Land, N.T. *Cambridge Archaeological Journal*, 4, 2, 211–248.

Tanner, N. M. (1981). *On becoming human.* Cambridge: Cambridge University Press.

Ternois, D. (1962). *L'art de Jacques Callot.* Paris: F. de Nobele.

Testart, A. (1986). Essai sur les fondements de la division sexuelle du travail chez les chasseurs-cueilleurs. *Cahiers de l'Homme* (n.s.), 25. Paris: Editions de l'Ecole des Hautes Etudes en Sciences Sociales.

Thomas, H. (1993). *Conquest: Montezuma, Cortés, and the fall of Old Mexico.* New York: Simon & Schuster.

Thomey, T. (1996). *Immortal images: A personal history of two photographers and the flag raising on Iwo Jima.* Annapolis, MD: Naval Institute Press.

Thompson, W. S., & D. D. Frizzell, eds. (1977). *The lessons of Vietnam.* New York: Crane, Russak.

Thrasher, F. M. (1936[1927]). *The gang: A study of 1,313 gangs in Chicago.* Chicago: University of Chicago Press.

Thucycides (1988[1920]). *History of the Peloponnesian war.* Vol. II [C. Forster Smith, trans.]. Cambridge, MA: Harvard University Press.

Tillotson, G. H. R. (1990). The Indian picturesque: Images of India in British landscape painting, 1780–1880. In C. A. Bayly, ed., *The Raj: India and the British 1600–1947.* London: National Portrait Gallery Publications.

Tippett, M. (1984). *Art at the service of war: Canada, art, and the Great War.* Toronto: University of Toronto Press.

Tolstoy, L. (1894). *The kingdom of God is within you.* London: Walter Scott.

Trachtenberg, A. (1989). *Reading American photographs: Images as history, Mathew Brady to Walker Evans.* New York: Hill & Wang.

Trinkaus, E. (1993). *The Neandertals: Changing the image of mankind.* New York: Knopf.

Trigger, B. G. (1969). *The Huron.* New York: Holt, Rinehart & Winston.

Trueheart, C. (1994). Canadian guilty of killing Somali. *Washington Post,* March 18, A24.

Truman, H. S. (1955). *Memoirs by Harry S. Truman.* Vol. I: Year of decisions. Garden City, NY: Doubleday.

Trux, J. (1991). Desert Storm: A space-age war. *New Scientist,* July 27, 30–34.

Tuchman, B. W. (1962). *The guns of August.* New York: Macmillan.

Tuchman, G. (1978). *Making news: A study in the construction of reality.* New York: Free Press.

Turner, L. C. F. (1985). The significance of the Schlieffen Plan. In Paul M. Kennedy, ed., *The War Plans of the Great Powers 1880–1914.* Boston: Allen & Unwin.

Turow, J. (1992). *Media systems in society: Understanding industries, strategies, and power.* New York: Longman.

Tyrrell, J. B., ed. (1968[1916]). David Thompson's narrative of his explorations in western America, 1784–1812. Toronto: Champlain Society.

Ucko, P. J., & A. Rosenfeld (1967). *Paleolithic cave art.* London: Weidenfeld & Nicolson.

Valladas, H., et al. (1992). Direct radiocarbon dates for prehistoric paintings at the Altamira, El Castillo and Niaux caves. *Nature,* 357, 68–70.

Vartanyan, S. L., V. E. Garutt, & A. V. Scher (1993). Holocene dwarf mammoths from Wrangl Island in the Siberian Arctic. *Nature,* 362, 337–340.

Vayda, A. P. (1976). *War in ecological perspective: Persistence, change, and adaptive processes in three oceanian societies.* New York: Plenum.

Vegetius. (1993). *Epitome of military science.* [N. P. Milner, trans.]. Liverpool: Liverpool University Press.

Vencl, S. (1991). Interprétation des blessures causées par les armes au Mésolithique. *L'Anthropologie,* 95, 1, 219–228.

Vermeule, C. C. (1968). *Roman imperial art in Greece and Asia Minor.* Cambridge, MA: Harvard University Press.

Viereck, G. S. (1931). *Spreading germs of hate.* London: Duckworth.

Vietnam Veterans Memorial Fund. (1980). *The Vietnam Veterans Memorial Design Competition.* Washington, DC.

Vinnicombe, P. (1976). *People of the Eland.* Pietermaritzburg: Natal University Press.

Viorst, M. (1991). Report from Baghdad. *The New Yorker,* June 24, 55–73.

Vogel, A. (1974). *Film as a subversive art.* New York: Random House.

von Erffa, H., & A. Staley (1986). *The paintings of Benjamin West.* New Haven, CT: Yale University Press.

Vuono, C. E. (1991). Desert Storm and the future of conventional forces. *Foreign Affairs,* 70, 2, 49–68.

Wagner, E. (1981). Eine Lowenkopfplastik aus Elfenbein von der Vogelherdhohle. *Fundberichte Baden-Württemberg,* 6, 29–58.

Wallace, A. R. (1962[1876]). *The geographical distribution of animals.* Vol. 1. New York: Hafner.

Wallbank, F. W. (1957). *A historical commentary on Polybius.* Oxford: Clarendon.

Walt, L. W. (1970). *Strange war, strange strategy: A general's report on Vietnam.* New York: Funk & Wagnalls.

Ward, P. D. (1997). *The call of distant mammoths: Why the Ice Age mammals disappeared.* New York: Copernicus.

Washington, D. W. (1995). Onward cyber soldiers. *Time,* August 21, 8 [on-line].

Weidner, M. S. (1982). *Painting and Patronage at the Mongol Court of China 1260-1338.* Berkeley: University of California.

—— (1989). Aspects of painting and patronage at the Mongol court, 1260-1368. In Kress Foundation Dept. of Art History, eds., *Artists and Patrons: some social and economic aspects of Chinese painting.* Lawrence, KS: University of Kansas Press.

Weller, J. (1972). *Wellington in India.* London: Longman.

Welté, A.-C. (1989). An approach to the theme of confronted animals in French Palaeolithic art. In H. Morphy, ed., *Animals into art.* London: Unwin Hyman.

Wendorf, F. (1968). Site 117: A Nubian final Paleolithic graveyard near Jebel Sahaba, Sudan. In F. Wendorf, ed., *The Prehistory of Nubia.* Vol. 2. Dallas: Southern Methodist University Press.

——, & R. Schild (1986). *The Wadi Kubbaniya skeleton: A late Paleolithic burial from southern Egypt.* Dallas: Southern Methodist University Press.

Werner, D. (1983). Fertility and pacification among the Mekranoti of central Brazil. *Human Ecology,* 11, 227–245.

Westmoreland, W. C. (1976). *A soldier reports.* Garden City, NY: Doubleday.

White, R. A. (1982). Rethinking the Middle/Upper Paleolithic transition. *Current Anthropology*, 23, 2, 169–192.

White, R. K. (1986). *Dark caves, bright visions: Life in Ice Age Europe*. New York: American Museum of Natural History in association with W. W. Norton.

Whitehouse, H. (1992). Leaders and logics, persons and polities. *History and Anthropology*, 6, 1, 103–124.

Whiting, A. S. (1960). *China crosses the Yalu: The decision to enter the Korean War*. New York: Macmillan.

Whyte, W. H., Jr. (1956). *The organization man*. New York: Simon & Schuster.

Wiemer, R. (1992). *Live from ground zero*. New York: Doubleday.

Willey, P. (1990). *Prehistoric warfare on the Great Plains: Skeletal analysis of the Crow Creek massacre victims*. New York: Garland.

Williams, B. (1988). Narmer and the Coptos Colossi. *Journal of the American Research Center in Egypt*, 25, 93–101.

Wilson, E. O. (1975). *Sociobiology*. Cambridge, MA: Harvard University Press.

—————— (1992). *The diversity of life*. Cambridge, MA: Harvard University Press.

Wilson, J. A. (1956) *The culture of ancient Egypt*. Chicago: University of Chicago Press.

Wood, M. (1997). *In the footsteps of Alexander the Great*. Berkeley: University of California Press.

Woodburn, J. (1980). Hunters and gatherers today and reconstruction of the past. In E. Gellner, ed., *Soviet and western anthropology*. New York: Columbia University Press.

—————— (1982). Egalitarian societies. *Man*, 17, 431–451.

Woodman, A. J. (1988). *Rhetoric in classical historiography*. London: Croom Helm.

Wyman, D. S. (1984). *The abandonment of the Jews: America and the Holocaust, 1941–1945*. New York: Pantheon.

Xenophon. (1972). *The Persian expedition* [R. Warner, trans.]. London: Penguin.

Yadin, Y. (1963). *The art of warfare in biblical lands in the light of archaeological study*. [M. Pearlman, trans.]. New York: McGraw-Hill.

Yesner, D. R. (1980). Nutrition and cultural evolution: Patterns in prehistory. In N. W. Jerome, R. F. Kandel, & G. H. Pelto, eds., *Nutritional anthropology*. Pleasantville, NY: Redgrave.

Zalampas, M. (1989). *Adolf Hitler and the Third Reich in American magazines, 1923–1939*. Bowling Green, OH: Bowling Green State University Popular Press.

Zettl, H. (1990). *Sight, sound, motion: Applied media aesthetics*. 2nd ed. Belmont, CA: Wadsworth.

Zillman, D. (1980). Anatomy of suspense. In P. H. Tannenbaum, ed., *The entertainment functions of television*. Hillsdale, NJ: Lawrence Erlbaum.

Zimmerman, L. J., & R. G. Whitten (1980). Mass grave at Crow Creek in South Dakota reveals how Indians massacred Indians in 14th century attack. *Smithsonian*, 11, 6, 100–109.

# INDEX

BC Evening News, 189
chilles, 105–6, **106**
dams, Eddie, 203–4, **204**, 207
eneid (Virgil), 165
fghanistan War, 159
gamemnon, 96, 103
gesilaos, 128
hab, 161
lamo, Battle of, 126
lbert, Prince consort of England, 82
lexander Mosaic (Pompeii), 2–3, **4– 5**
lexander the Great, 2–3, 3, **4–5**
li, Haidar, 122
liens (film), 133
ll Quiet on the Western Front (film), 146–47, 148, 228
ll Quiet on the Western Front (Remarque novel), 107, 145
merican Civil War
  Battle of Gettysburg, 104, 182–83, **183**
  coverage and depictions of, 109, 161, **162**, 178
  devastation of, 175
  Fort Wagner, 54th Massachusetts Colored Infantry assault on, 104–5
  gleaners, 116
merican Indians. See Native Americans
natolia, extermination of Armenians, 135
ntigonos, 2
ppian, 220
rab-Israeli Wars, 159, 178
rendt, Hannah, 9
rens, Moshe, 200
rmenians, Turkish extermination of, 135
rnett, Peter, 171, 179, 199
rnhem Land rock paintings (Australia), 12, 41, **42–43**, 52–53, 57, 121, 153
rthur, King of England, 65
shurbanipal, King of Assyria, 79
shur-nasir-pal, King of Assyria, 129
ssad, Hafez al-, 179
ssyrian wall reliefs , 73–74, **74–75**, 79, **81**, 96, 128–29
styanax, 164

Athenian cup (Achilles), 105–6, **106**
Atlantic Monthly, 161
"Audience watching a moving picture" (Albert sketch), 175, **176**
Australia
  aboriginal effect on environment, 37–38
  rock paintings (Arnhem Land), 12, 41, **42–43**, 52–53, 57, 121, 153
Austro-Prussian War, 104
Ayres, Lew, 146–47
Aztec codices, 187
Aztec empire
  appearance of warriors, 72
  conquest of, 66–67

Babi Yar massacre, 49, 172
Babochkin, Boris, 145
Baird, Sir David, 121, **122**, 123
Barí (Brazilian aborigines), murder of, 52
Barker, A. J., 87
Bataan (film), 112
Battle of Britain, The (film), 146
Battleship Potemkin (Eisenstein film), 101–2, **102**, 146
Bay, Austin, 201
Bayeux Tapestry, 188
Beckwith, Charles, 217
Begazcoy (Anatolia) mural, 96
Berliner Zeitung, 102
Blenheim, Battle of, 92
Block, Harlon H., 115
"Boer Treachery" (Woodville drawing), 142–43, **143**
Boer War, 142–43, **143**, 157
Bogart, Humphrey, 112
Bolton, John R., 194
Bonampak murals (Mayan civilization), 130–31, **130, 131**, 206
Bonaparte, Napoleon, 60, 65, 124, 125
  army of, 53, 59, 159
  Waterloo, Battle of, 103–4, 216– 17
Borodino, Battle of, 60
Bosnia-Herzegovina
  Muslims, persecution of, 49, 190, 191
Bradley, John H., 115

Brady, Mathew, 109, 117, 175
Breakthrough (film), 160
Brecht, Berthold, 5–6
Breuil, Henri, 13–14
Broderick, Matthew, 104
Brokaw, Tom, 180, 207–8
Burns, Ken, 8
Bush, George, 188, 189
Butler, Lady, 157

Caesar, Julius, 60, 65, 78, 177
Cagney, James, 118
Callot, Jacques, 154–55
Cambodian killing fields, 49
Canada's Golgotha (Wood sculpture), 155, **156**, 164
Cannae, Battle of, 55–56
Capra, Frank, 101
Carlebach, Michael, 193
Carter, A. C. R., 157
Carthage, Roman sack of, 175
Cassius, Dio, 91
cave paintings and graphics
  abandonment, 41
  big-game hunting as a masculine pursuit, 25–27
  big-game imagery, scorings on, 27– 29
  Cougnac Cave art, 15–16, **16**
  Franco-Cantabria Region, 14–17, 17–20
  Lascaux cave paintings, 12–14, **13**, 21, **23–24**, 24–25, 153
  Niaux cave painting, 28, **30–31**
Cavell, Edith, 137–38, 149
CBS Evening News, 167–68
Ceaucescu, Nikolai, 195
Central America and tribal warfare, 48
Chancellor, John, 204
Chapayev (Vasiliev brothers film), 145–46
Chaplin, Charlie, 78–79
Charge of the Light Brigade (Crimean War), 81, 82, 104
Cheney, Richard, 180, 209
Cheyenne dog soldiers, choosing chiefs, 60
Chicago Tribune, 139–40
Chin emperor, terra-cotta army of, 98
Chipp, Herschel B., 206–7

Churchill, John, First Duke of Marlborough, 60, 92
Churchill, Winston, 60–61, 140–41
Cid, El, 161
CITV (commander's independent thermal viewer), 212
*Civil War* (Burns televison series), 8
Civil War. *See* American Civil War; Spanish Civil War
Clausewitz, Carl von, 80, 120
Clinton, Bill, 166, 188
Clovis people, 35, 36–37
CNN and the Persian Gulf War, 178, 188
Codrescu, Andrei, 195–96
Coe, Michael, 206
Cohen, Eliot, 215
*Collier's* magazine, 113
*Commander-in-Chief of the British Forces in the Crimea* (Paton caricature), 83–84, **83**, 88
commanders, 65–88
  appearance and image of, 57–62, 65–71
  racial minorities as, 112
  subverting the war commander, 78–84
  visualizing dominance, 71–78
  voluntary inversions, 84–88
communication technology, 175
  *See also* new technology (communications and visualization)
computer and video games
  *Doom*, 229
  holographic and computer-generated imagery (CGI), 223
  *if22* (air war simulator), 222–23, **223**, 227
  MARINE DOOM, 223
  sensory joysticks, 223
computer-generated imagery (CGI), 223
computer sabotage, 218–19
comrades (soldiers), 89–120
  buddyhood and buddy posing, 105–9
  equipment and armament, 99
  fear and unification, 116–20
  marching and parading, 93–105
  multicultural/multiracial platoons, 110–16
  recruitment, 89–93
Constantine XI Palaeologus, 125–26
Cooley, Charles H., 108
Coombs, Rose, 185
Cooper, Gary, 112
Cordesman, Anthony, 200
Cortés, Hernán, 67
Coser, Lewis, 124
Cougnac Cave art (man pierced with arrows), 15–16, **16**
Courtenay, Tom, 78
Coward, Noël, 111
Cree Indians and tribal warfare, 46
Crimean War, 80–84, 88, 104
  coverage of, 192
  dysentery and, 153
Crombie, Theodore, 77

Crow Creek massacre (South Dakota), 49–50, **50**, 63, 172
Crow Indians and tribal warfare, 46
Cuban Missle Crisis, 188

Daguerre, Louis Jacques Mandé, 193
dance as ritual of primitive war, 52–55
*Dances With Wolves* (Costner film), 44
Darius II, King of Persia, 2–3, 186
David, Jacques-Louis, 124, 125
Davis, Whitney, 126
*Day After, The* (TV movie), 158–59
De La Mazière, Christian, 116
*Dead at Antietam, The* (Gardner photo), 61, **162**
*Death of General Wolfe, The* (West painting), **6**, 6–7, 75–78, 123, 160, 188
Delaroche, Paul, 193
Delbrück, Hans, 56
*Dersu Uzala (Dersu the Hunter)* (Kurosawa film), 7
Diamond, Jared, 35
Digital Division, 221
disease and warfare, 153
Disney, Walt, 162
"Don't mention it, lootenant" (Mauldin cartoon), 84–86, **85**, 142
Dornbusch, Sanford, 120
Douglas, James, 228
Dowding, Sir Hugh, 146
*Dr. Zhivago* (Lean film), 78
Dukakis, Michael S., 69, **70**, 71, 74, 79
Dunnigan, James, 201

East Timor, persecution in, 191
Easter Island, deforestation of, 38
Eastwood, Clint, 105
Eisenhower, Dwight D., 71–72, 202, 208
Eisenstein, Sergei, 101–2, **102**
El Mozote (El Salvador), massacres in, 49, 172
enemies, 121–51
  ambiguous enemy, 149–51
  animalization, 135–37
  the defeated enemy, 124–33
  enemy corpses, stripping, 127–28
  the hated enemy, 133–41
  off-camera (absent) enemy, 141–46
  prisoners, mutilation of, **132**, 132–33
  the useful enemy, 121–24
EOSAT (European satellite system), 211
Erikson, Erik, 124, 203
Esarhaddon, King of Assyria, 65
Essame, H., 55
*Eternal Jew, The* (Nazi documentary), 170

Falklands War, 119–20
  media coverage of, 178
Fenton, Roger, 82–83, 109, **110**

Fenton, Tom, 191
Ferguson, R. Brian, 48
Ferrill, Arthur, 17
*Fighting 69th, The* (film), 118
firearms, introduction of, 154–55
*Forrest Gump* (film), 86
*Fort Apache* (film), 95, 134
Fort Wagner (South Carolina), 54th Massachusetts Colored Infantry assault on, 104–5
*Four Hundred Centuries of Cave Art* (Breuil), 13–14
Franco, Francisco, 207
Franco-Prussian War, 104
"Fresh, Spirited Troops" (Mauldin cartoon), 150, **151**
Freund, Gisèle, 82
Friedman, George and Meredith, 219
Fussell, Paul, 150, 161–62
*Future of War, The* (Friedman/Friedman), 219

Gagnon, Rene A., 115
*Gallipoli* (Weir film), 103
Gallipoli, Battle of, 103
Gammage, Bill, 103
Garner, Jay, 228
Gasulla Gorge (Spain) rock paintings (archers or dancers marching), 46–47, **47**, 53–54, 57, 96
Genaust, Bill, 113
genocide
  Armenians, Turkish extermination of, 135
  genocidal warfare, 48
  Genocide Convention, 202
  *See also* holocaust, 135–36
George III, King of England, 75–76
*Gettysburg* (film), 117
Gettysburg, Battle of, 104
  historical reenactments of, 182–83, **183**
Gibbon, Edward, 94, 166
Girardet, Edward, 178
gleaners, 116–17
*Glory* (film), 104, 112–13
Goebbels, Joseph, 144
Goering, Hermann, 144
Goettge, Frank, 196
Goldhagen, Daniel, 172
Gombrich, Ernst, 7
Gordon, Michael, 180
Goscinny (cartoonist), 93–94, **93**
Gould, Stephen Jay, 10
Goya, Francisco, 155
Grant, Cary, 111
*Great Dictator, The* (Chaplin film), 78–79
*Green Berets, The* (film), 134
Grenada invasion
  media coverage of, 178–79
*Guernica* (Picasso painting), 157, 206–7
*Gulag Archipelago, The* (Solzhenitsyn), 173
Gulf War. *See* Persian Gulf War
*Gulf War Air Power Survey*, 200

Gunga Din (film), 111
"Gunga Din" (Kipling poem), 111

Hallion, Richard P., 199
Hama (Syria), massacres in, 49
Hanks, Tom, 112
Hannibal, 55–56, 128
Harmsworth, Alfred, Lord
    Northcliffe, 139
Hazlett, James, 224
Hephaestion, 2, 3
Heraclitus, 11
Hermogenes, 90
Herodotus, 125
Hiltermann, Joost R., 199
Himmler, Heinrich, 100–101
historical reenactments of warfare,
    182–83, **183**
Hitler, Adolf, 78–79, 126, 129–30,
    138–39
    and anti-Semitism, 144–45
Hittites, 12
    mural of warrior procession, 96
Hobbes, Thomas, 48
Hobsbawm, Eric, 11
Hogan, J. Michael, 159
Holmes, Oliver Wendell, 161
holocaust
    anti-Semitism and, 135–36, 144–
        45
    Auschwitz, 63
    Babi Yar massacre, 49, 172
    Jews of the Warsaw Ghetto, 168–
        70, **169**
    See also genocide; massacres
Holmes, Richard, 119–20
holographic imagery, 223
Horace, 78
horrors of war, 153–73
    horror and sympathy, 153–59
    "just" horrors, 164–73
    noble deaths, 159–64
    prisoners, castration and
        mutilation of, **132**, 132–33, 154
Horrors of War, The (Goya
    sketches), 155
Housman, Alfred, 103
Hughes, Robert, 80
humans as omnivores, 39
Huntley-Brinkley Report, 204, 206
Hussein, Saddam, 57, 154, 171, 186,
    208–9
    See also Iraq

If It's Tuesday, This Must Be Belgium
    (film), 149–50
if22 (air war simulator), 222–23,
    **223**, 227
Ihalmiut people, 24, 36
Iliad, 105, 106, 127, 160, 181
Illustrated London News, 82, 142–43,
    **143**
images of warfare
    accessibility of, 187–88
    and "news-worthiness," 178–79,
        190–91
In Which We Serve (Coward film),
    111
Independence Day (film), 133, 134

Indians. See Native Americans
inreality and disengagement, 226–31
integrated information weapons
    systems, 212–13
Internet
    and real-time access to events,
        187
Iran
    satellite technology and the
        hostage crisis, 217
Iraq, 190
    the Victory Arch (Baghdad), 183–
        84
    See also Hussein, Saddam; Persian
        Gulf War
"Is it you, Mother?" (Raemaekers
    cartoon), 147–48, **148**
Ivins, William, 193
Iwo Jima, photo of flag rasing on,
    111–12, 113–15, **114**, 207

Jackson, Andrew, 103
Jackson, Thomas J., 60
Jacob, Fritz, 169
Jamieson, Kathleen Hall, 71
Jericho, stone walls of, 44
Jews of the Warsaw Ghetto
    (photograph), 168–70, **169**
Johnson, Lyndon B., 206
Johnson, Samuel, 6
Jomini, Antoine-Henri, 9
Josephus, 94

Kadesh, Battle of, 12, **69,** 69–71
Keegan, John, 53
Keeley, Lawrence, 62
Kehoe, Thomas, 29
Kelly, Michael, 184
Kelly, Walt, 151
Khaldun, Ibn, 107
Khargurtahl (Libya) rack painting
    (battle for bull), **62,** 62–63
Kinnison, Henry L., 214
Kipling, Rudyard, 111
Kitchener, Horatio Herbert, 90
Knox, Frank, 141
Knox, John, 77
Königgrätz, Battle of, 104
Koppel, Ted, 180, 190
Korean War, 67–68, 118, 119
Kosovo, Battle of, 126
Kracauer, Siegfried, 73
Kurds, persecution of, 190
Kurosawa, Akira, 7, 186
Kut (Iraq), siege of, 87

La Grande Illusion (Renoir film),
    111
Lagash (Mesopotamia) mural of
    warrior procession, 96
Lalumia, Matthew, 84
Lancken, Baron von der, 138
Land Warrior, 213–14
Landor, Walter Savage, 81
Larry King Show, 188
Lascaux cave paintings
    Chinese horse, 21, **23–24,** 24–25
    Man with bird head and bison, 12–
        14, **13,** 153

Lasswell, Harold, 138
Last of the Mohicans, The (film), 44–
    45
Lawson, Howard, 112
leadership. See commanders
Lean, David, 78
Lederman, Jim, 178
L'Entente Cordiale (Fenton
    photograph), 109, **110**
Leonidas, 124–25
Leonidas at Thermopylae (David
    painting), 124, 125
Libicki, Martin, 214, 216
Life Goes to War: A Picture History
    of World War II, 135
Life magazine, 135, 161
Lin, Maya Ying, 184
living-room wars, 175–209
    communal viewing (satellite/
        television/ Internet), 187–92
    real-time war (media coverage),
        175–81
    realism, 192–203
    war in everyday life (public
        militarism and
        monumentalism), 181–87
Livingstone, Stanley, 32
Livy, 128
Loan, Nguyen Ngoc, 203–4, **204**
London Daily Mail, 155
London Times, 81, 82, 102
Long Range Recon Commandos,
    appearance of, 59
Lugar, Richard G., 208
Lusitania, sinking of, 137

MacArthur, Douglas, 67–68
McCormick, Tom, 139–40
Machiavelli, Niccolò, 95
McLuhan, Marshall, 179
McNamara, Robert S., 188
McNeill, William H., 54
Magay tribe (East Africa) and tribal
    warfare, 46
mammoth and mastodon
    extinctions, 37
Manheim, Jarol, 188
Marathon, Battle of, 176–77
Marcos, Ferdinand, 207–8
Marcus Aurelius, 166
Marcus Aurelius' column, 166, 188
    destruction of a Gothic village,
        166–67, **167**
MARINE DOOM, 223
Maring people (New Guinea),
    dances of, 54
Marlborough Tapestries, 92
Marshall, S. L. A., 9, 107, 117–18
Martin, Paul, 34–35
massacres, 49, 172
    Crow Creek massacre (South
        Dakota), 49–50, **50,** 51, 63, 172
    as policy and/or ideological
        policy, 63–64
    Rwandan massacres, 49, 63, 136,
        153, 190, 202
    See also holocaust
Mathew Brady Company, 109, 175

Mauldin, Bill, 84–86, **85**, 142, 150, **151**
Mayan civilization
   appearance of military leaders, 59
   Bonampak murals, 130–31, **130**, **131**, 206
   Monte Albán carvings (castrated and mutilated prisoners), **132**, 132–33, 154
Mayer, S. L., 145
Mead, Margaret, 164
media
   military-industrial complex and, 202–3
   misrepresentation and manipulation, 198–201, 208–9
   *See also* Internet; photography; televison
Médicins Sans Frontières, 190
*Meditations* (Marcus Aurelius), 166
*Mein Kampf* (Hitler), 138–39
*Men Against Fire* (Marshall), 117–18
Mendelssohn Bartholdy, Albrecht, 107
Mesolithic era (Middle Stone Age)
   and the onset of urbanism, 44
   systematic tribal warfare, 15, 45, 121
   *See also* Neolithic era; Upper Paleolithic era
Meyer, Nicholas, 158
Milgram, Stanley, 61
Miller, Gifford, 37
moas, extinction of, 35
Monte Albán carvings (Mayan civilization), **132**, 132–33, 154
Montezuma, 66–67
Montgomery, Bernard, 198
*Monty Python and the Holy Grail* (film), 65
monumentalism. *See* public militarism and monumentalism
Morella la Vella (Spain) rock painting, 55, **56**, 153
Mosse, George L., 107
Mowat, Farley, 24
Murrow, Edward R., 8

Narmer, Pharaoh of Egypt, 126–27, **127**
Native Americans
   and bison drives, 29, 32
   Crow Creek massacre (South Dakota), 49–50, **50**, 51, 63, 172
   homicide rate prior to European contact, 49
   tribal warfare, 44–45, 46, 121
   Writing-On-Stone site (Alberta, Canada), 50–51, **51**, 121
Navstar GPS (global positioning system), 212–13
Nazis
   anti-Semitism and, 135–36, 144–45, 168–70, **169**
   coverage of, 178
   propaganda of, 170–71, 178
Neanderthals and violence, 12
Nelson, Horatio, 78
Neolithic era (New Stone Age)

art of, 53, 66
dance as ritual of primitive war, 52–55
Morella la Vella (Spain) rock painting, 55, **56**, 153
and the onset of urbanism, 44
Sefar site (Sahara) rock paintings (archer battle scene), 58, **58**
systematic tribal warfare, 15, 46–47, **47**, 121
   *See also* Mesolithic era; Upper Paleolithic era
Neoptolemus, 164–65
New Orleans, Battle of, 103
new technology (communications and visualization), 211–31
   CITV (commander's independent thermal viewer), 212
   integrated information weapons systems, 212–13
   Land Warrior, 213–14
   Navstar GPS (global positioning system), 212–13
   satellite technology, 175, 211–16
   stealth technology, 216–20
   TAMER (Technology Advanced Mini Eye-Safe Raser), 213–14
   virtual warriors, 220–26
   *See also* communication technology; Internet; satellite technology
*New York Times*, 175
*New York Times Magazine*, 194
*New York World*, 102
New Zealand aboriginals
   and the extinction of moas, 35
Newman, Aubrey "Red," 90
*Newsweek* magazine, 189
Niaux cave painting (wounded bison), 28, **30–31**
Nicholas II, Tsar of Russia, 73
Niépce, Joseph-Nicéphore, 193
Nightingale, Florence, 81
*Nightline*, 190
North America and tribal warfare, 48
   *See also* Native Americans
nuclear warfare, depiction of, 158–59

*Obélix et Campagnie* (Goscinny-Uderzo cartoon), 93–94, **93**
Oedipus, 160
O'Kane, Maggie, 192
Operation Allied Force
   military action in Yugoslavia, 230–31
Operation Uphold Democracy
   military action in Haiti, 213
origins of warfare, 11–40
   big game, focus on, 17–20
   big-game hunting as a masculine pursuit, 25–27
   big-game imagery, scorings on, 27–29
   caloric consumption and, 21–25
   communal cooperation, 29, 32–34
   the first images and instances of, 11–17

overkill and the genesis of war, 34, 40
Orwell, George, 21, 159
Otterbein, Keith, 48
Owen, Wilfred, 146
Owens, William, 228
"Ozymandias" (Shelley), 69

Palette of Narmer, 126–27, **127**
Panama invasion, media coverage of, 179
*Panegyric* (Pliny), 91
*Paris Soir*, 102
Paterson, Ann L., 18–19, 20
Patroclus, 105, 106
Patton, George S., Jr., 55, 60, 78
Patton, Joseph Noel, 83–84, **83**
Pauley, Jane, 189
Pearl Harbor, attack on, 126, 141
Peck, Gregory, 112
*Pencil of Nature, The* (Talbot), 192
Pentagon. *See* U.S. military
Perry, Oliver Hazard, 150–51
Persian Gulf War, 53, 57, 124
   Al-Firdus air-raid shelter, attack on, 171–72
   Basra "Road of Death," 208–9
   F-117A (Stealth) fighter and, 216
   *Gulf War Air Power Survey*, 200
   media coverage and censorship, 178, 179, 188–89, 192, 208–9
   media misrepresentation and manipulation, 198–201, 203
   satellite reconnaissance, 211, 212–13
Petty-Fitzmaurice, Henry, Marquis of Lansdowne, 137–38
phalanx formation (Macedonian/Greek army), 53, 98–99
Phidippides, 176–77
photography
   and depictions of warfare, 109, **110**, 178
   photojournalism and authenticity, 194–97
   realism of, 192–203
   technological advancements, 192–93
   war images, effects of, 203–5, **204**
Picasso, Pablo, 157, 206–7
Pickett, George Edward, 104
*Platoon* (Stone film), 112, 163, 168
Pliny, 91
Plutarch, 92, 99
*Pocahontas* (Disney film), 44, 45
"Pogo" (comic strip), 151
Powell, Colin, 57, 180, 208–9
Powers, Ron, 208
Prange, Gordon, 141
Priam, 164, 165
Priestley, J. B., 81
primitive war, 41–56
   dance as ritual of, 52–55
   early images of interhuman combat, 41–45
   and gender preference, 45–46
   leadership and appearance, 57–62
   tribal warfare, 45–52

rinting (development of)
  and depictions of warfare, 177–78
risoners
  castration and mutilation of, **132**,
    132–33, 154
ublic militarism and
    monumentalism, 181–87
  historical reenactments of
    warfare, 182–83, **183**
  Victory Arch (Iraq), 183–84
  Vietnam Veterans Memorial
    (Washington, D.C.), 184–85
  World War I memorials, 185

aemaekers, Louis, 147–48, **148**
ambo (film), 227
ameses II, 12, **69**, 69–71, 72
appaport, Roy, 54
ead, James Morgan, 138
eagan, Ronald, 159
econnaissance (problems of)
  computer sabotage, 218–19
  failure to interpret data correctly,
    219–20
  sensing technology and a stable
    use environment, 217–18
  technological counterweapons,
    218–19
  traditional cover, 216–17
eed, Fred, 201
emarque, Erich Maria, 107, 145
enoir, Jean, 111
eynolds, Sir Joshua, 76
ice, Patricia C., 18–19, 20
ichthofen, Manfred von (the Red
    Baron), 108
iefenstahl, Leni, 100–101
itchin, Fred, 194
itter, Scott, 200
oarke's Drift, Battle of, 104
obida, Albert
  sketch of an audience watching a
    moving picture, 175, **176**
rock paintings
  Arnhem Land (Australia), 12, 41,
    **42–43**, 52–53, 57, 153
  Gasulla Gorge (Spain) (archers or
    dancers marching), 46–47, **47**,
    53–54, 57, 96
  Khargurtahl (Libya) (battle for
    bull), **62**, 62–63
  Morella la Vella (Spain), 55, **56**,
    153
  Sefar site (Sahara) (archer battle
    scene), 58, **58**
Rockwell, Norman, 162
Rohingya, persecution of, 190
Roman army, 95, 165–66, 220–21
  commilito (fellow soldiership), 90
  enemy corpses, stripping, 128
  and the sack of Carthage, 175
  testudo formation, 53, 90
  Triumphs, 177
  See also Trajan
Romanian revolution, authenticity
  of, 195–96
Roosevelt, Franklin D., 141
Roosevelt, Theodore, 149
Rosenthal, Joe, 113–14, **114**, 207

Rousseau, Jean-Jacques, 39
Rowse, A. L., 11
Russell, William Howard, 81–82
Rwandan massacres, 49, 63, 136,
    153, 190, 202
Ryan, Cornelius, 72

Safer, Morley, 168
Sahara (film), 112–13
Sahlins, Marshall, 24, 64
Samuel, 165
Sands of Iwo Jima, The (film), 112
Sartre, Jean-Paul, 207
satellite technology, 175
  EOSAT (European satellite
    system), 211
  and the Iran hostage crisis, 217
  Navstar GPS (global positioning
    system), 212–13
  and real-time access to events,
    187
  SPOT (French remote-sensing
    satellite system), 211
Saukamapee (Cree Indian), 46
Saul, 165
Saving Private Ryan (Spielberg film),
    9, 10, 112
Sawyer, Forrest, 189
Saxe, Maurice de, 65
Schlieffen, Alfred von, 57
Schliemann, Heinrich, 97, 98
Schwarzkopf, H. Norman, 65, 180,
    198–99
sci-fi movies and fictional enemies,
    133–34
See It Now (CBS TV), 8
Sefar site (Sahara) rock paintings
  (archer battle scene), 58, **58**
Selous Scouts (Rhodesia), motto of,
    55
Seneca, 175
Serbia
  Muslims, persecution of, 190,
    191, 194
  See also Bosnia-Herzegovina
serotonin, repetitive motor activity
  and, 54
Seven Samurai (Kurosawa film), 186
Shakespeare, William, 106
Shaw, David, 178
Shaw, Robert Gould, 104
Sheen, Charlie, 112, 168
Shelley, Percy, 69
Shilts, Randy, 106
Shirer, William, 96
Shoshone Indians and tribal warfare,
    46
Shukman, David, 215
Siculus, Diodorus, 91, 185
Signal magazine, 145
Simmel, George, 124
Sir David Baird Discovering the Body
  of Tipu Sultan (Wilkie
  painting), 121–22, **122**
Smyrna (Anatolia), massacres in, 49
Solzhenitsyn, Aleksandr, 173
Somalia (UN/U.S. intervention)
  invasion, 154

media coverage, 180–81, 189–90,
    190–91
Somerset, Fitzroy, Lord Raglan, 83–
    84, 88
Sorokin, Pitirim, 11
Sousley, Franklin R., 114–15
South America and tribal warfare,
    48
Soviet Russia
  Afghanistan, atrocities and war
    crimes in, 159
  and the animalization of the
    enemy, 135–37
  propaganda of, 145–46
space aliens as fictional enemies, 133–
    34
Spanish Civil War, 157
Spanish Succession, wars of, 154
specialization, 39
Sphere newspaper, 86–87
Spielberg, Steven, 9, 10, 163
SPOT (French remote-sensing
  satellite system), 211
Stalin, Joseph, 171
Stallone, Sylvester, 59
Star Wars (film series), 133
Starship Troopers (film), 133, **134**
stealth technology, 216–20
  computer sabotage, 218–19
  data overload, 219
  F-117A (Stealth) fighter, 216
  failure to interpret data correctly,
    219–20
  Sea Shadow (SWATH), 225
  sensing technology and a stable
    use environment, 217–18
  technological counterweapons,
    218–19
  traditional cover, 216–17
Steiner, George, 11
Stewart, Jon, 230
Stimson, Henry, 141
Stone, Oliver, 163, 168
Storr, Antony, 60–61
Strank, Michael, 115
Sukhomlinov, Vladimir, 73
Sullivan, Gordon R., 215, 219
Sun Tzu, 6

Talbot, Henry Fox, 192, 193
TAMER (Technology Advanced
  Mini Eye-Safe Raser), 213–14
technology. See new technology
television
  authenticity, 194–97
  censorship, 179, 180
  image and "news-worthiness,"
    178–79, 190–91
  misrepresentation and
    manipulation, 198–201, 208–9
  political influence of, 179–80, 188–
    89
  as propaganda, 178
  and real-time access to events,
    187
Teumann (Elamite king), 128
Texas War of Independence, 126
Thermopylae, Battle of, 124–25,
    127

Third Mysore War, 123
Third Punic War, 220–21
Thirty Years' War, 154, 175
Thrasher, Frederick, 108
*300 Spartans, The* (film), 125
Thucydides, 186
Tiananmen Square protests (China), 208
Tiglath-pileser III, King of Assyria, 128
*Time* magazine, 189, 189–90, 194
Tipu Sultan, 121–22, **122**, 123–24, 160, 165
Titus, 165
torture
  Canadian paratroopers in Somalia, 154
  Mayan wall paintings, 206
Trajan, 90–92, 165
Trajan's column, 90–91, 165–66, 188
Trasimeno, Battle of, 128
Treaty of Versailles, 126
tribal zone theory, 48–49
*Triumph of the Will* (Riefenstahl film), 100–101
*Troilus and Cressida* (Shakespeare), 106
Trojan War, 96, 97–98, 105–6, **106**, 164–65
Truman, Harry, 67–68, 140
Tuaregs of the Sahara, persecution of, 190
Tuchman, Barbara, 73, 138
Turner, Ed, 181

Uderzo (cartoonist), 93–94, **93**
Ulundi, Battle of, 104
Ummanaldash (Elamite king), 79, **81**
Ummanigash (Elamite king), 73–74, **74–75**
*Unknown Soldier, The* (documentary)
  authenticity of, 196–98
Upper Paleolithic era (Old Stone Age), 12–17
  art of, 53, 121
  big-game hunting as a masculine pursuit, 25–27
  interhuman violence, 15–17, 121
  overkill and the genesis of war, 34–40
  women's role in, 26–27
  *See also* Mesolithic era; Neolithic era
U.S. military
  budgetary and geopolitical realities and, 221
  Digital Division, 221
  homosexuality in, 106–7
  marching and parades, 93–105

propaganda of, 154
recruitment, 89–90
*USA Today,* 180–81
Utley, Garrick, 189

Varo, Consul, 56
Vegetius, 216
Venus figurines (Upper Paleolithic), 26
Venus Genetrix, 177
Verus, Lucius, 177
Victory Arch (Iraq), 183–84
video games. *See* computer and video games
Vietnam Veterans Memorial (Washington, D.C.), 184–85
Vietnam War
  atrocities and war crimes, 159
  horror of warfare, depictions of, 161, 163–64, 167–68
  media coverage of, 178, 179–80, 203–6
  war images, effects of, 203–5, **204**
Viorst, Milton, 199
Virgil, 165
virtual warfare, 220–26, 229–30
  DVD (digital video disk), 223
  *if22* (air war simulator), 222–23, **223**, 227
  inreality and disengagement, 226–31
  real battlefield, simulating, 225–26
  reality vs. game playing, 226
  sensory joysticks, 223
  the testing and training of unit cohesion, 224–25
  *See also* computer and video games
visual images, first artificially created, 12
Vlad the Impaler (Dracula), 133
Vogel, Amos, 170
Vukovar (Bosnia), massacres in, 49

Wagner, Abraham, 200
*Walk in the Sun, A* (film), 112
Wallace, Alfred, 34
Walt, Lewis W., 180
*War of the Worlds* (film), 134
"Warrior vase" (Mycenae), 96–98, **97**
*Washington Post,* 188
Waterloo, Battle of, 103–4, 216–17
Watt, James, 184
Wayne, John, 95, 105, 112, 162
Weir, Peter, 103
Wellington, Arthur, First Duke of, 80, 216–17
Wells, H. G., 229
West, Benjamin, **6**, 6–7, 75–78, 160, 162
Westmoreland, William, 179

*Why We Fight* (Capra film series), 101
Whyte, William F., 108
Wilhelm, Kaiser of Germany, 137, 138
Wilson, Edward, 35, 38
Wolfe, James, **6**, 6–7, 75–78, 160, 161
Wood, Derwent, 155, **156**, 164
Wood, Sir Evelyn, 82
Wood, Michael, 2
Woodville, R. Caton, 142–43, **143**
World War I (the Great War), 87, 118
  buddyhood and, 107–8
  memorials, 185
  propaganda of, 136–38, 139–40, 146–50, 155, **156**
  recruitment, 89–90
  Treaty of Versailles, 126
World War II, 104
  anti-Semitism and, 135–36, 144–45, 168–70, **169**
  Bastille Day parade (1939), 95–96
  *Blitzkrieg,* 57, 96
  devastation of, 175
  flag rasing on Iwo Jima, 111–12, 113–15, **114**, 207
  horror of warfare, depictions of, 157, 160, 161–62
  nuclear weapons use, 140, 157
  Pearl Harbor, attack on, 126, 141
  propaganda of, 140–41, 150–51, 196–98
  reconnaissance, 211
  soldiers, fighting behavior of, 117–18
  SS (*Schutzstaffel,* or Black Shirts), 100–101, 135–36
  Third Reich and anti-Semitism, 135–36, 144–45
  *Unknown Soldier, The* (documentary), authenticity of, 196–98
  Waffen SS, cultural/racial makeup of, 115–16
  *See also* genocide; holocaust
Writing-On-Stone petroglyphs (Alberta, Canada), 50–51, **51**, 121

Xenophon, 128, 133
Xerxes, King of Persia, 125, 127

Yugoslavia
  Operation Allied Force in, 230–31

Zeuxis, 194
Zulus
  appearance of, 59
  self-defeating tactics of, 104